International Relations of Asia

ASIA IN WORLD POLITICS
Series Editor: Samuel S. Kim

International Relations of Asia

Edited by
David Shambaugh and Michael Yahuda

ROWMAN & LITTLEFIELD PUBLISHERS, INC.
Lanham • Boulder • New York • Toronto • Plymouth, UK

ROWMAN & LITTLEFIELD PUBLISHERS, INC.

Published in the United States of America
by Rowman & Littlefield Publishers, Inc.
A wholly owned subsidiary of The Rowman & Littlefield Publishing Group, Inc.
4501 Forbes Boulevard, Suite 200, Lanham, Maryland 20706
www.rowmanlittlefield.com

Estover Road, Plymouth PL6 7PY, United Kingdom

British Library Cataloguing in Publication Information Available

Library of Congress Cataloging-in-Publication Data
International relations of Asia / edited by David Shambaugh and Michael Yahuda.
     p. cm.
  Includes bibliographical references and index.
  ISBN-13: 978-0-7425-5695-9 (cloth : alk. paper)
  ISBN-10: 0-7425-5695-6 (cloth : alk. paper)
  ISBN-13: 978-0-7425-5696-6 (pbk. : alk. paper)
  ISBN-10: 0-7425-5696-4 (pbk. : alk. paper)
  eISBN-13: 978-0-7425-5738-3
  eISBN-10: 0-7425-5738-3
  I.   Asia—Politics and government—21st century. 2.   Asia—Foreign relations.
I. Shambaugh, David L. II. Yahuda, Michael B.
  DS35.2.I56 2008
327.5—dc22

                                                                    2008023461

Printed in the United States of America

♾™ The paper used in this publication meets the minimum requirements of
American National Standard for Information Sciences—Permanence of Paper
for Printed Library Materials, ANSI/NISO Z39.48-1992.

Dedicated to

Michael Leifer and Thomas W. Robinson

Cherished colleagues, friends, and pioneers
in the study of the international relations of Asia

Contents

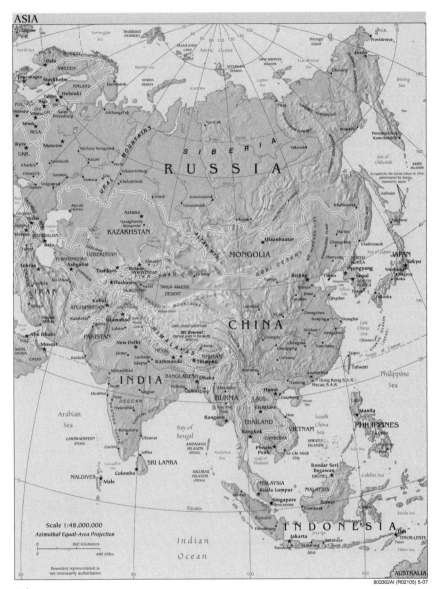

Asia.

Source: CIA.

Figures and Tables

FIGURES

TABLES

Acronyms

ACFTA	ASEAN-China Free Trade Area
AEEAP	ASEAN Environmental Education Action Plan
AFTA	ASEAN Free Trade Area
AMM	Aceh Monitoring Mission
APARC	Walter H. Shorenstein Asia-Pacific Research Center
APEC	Asia-Pacific Economic Cooperation
APT	ASEAN + 3
ARF	ASEAN Regional Forum
ASAT	Anti-Satellite (weapon)
ASEAN	Association of Southeast Asian Nations
ASEAN + 1	ASEAN plus China
ASEAN + 3	ASEAN plus China, Japan, and South Korea
ASEM	Asia-Europe Meeting
ASPI	Australian Strategic Policy Institute
BDA	Banco Delta Asia
BJP	Bharatiya Janata Party
BTE	Baku-Tbilisi-Erzurum
CAREC	Central Asia Regional Economic Cooperation Program
CBM	Confidence-Building Measure
CCP	Chinese Communist Party
CEAC	Council on East Asian Community
CFSP	Common Foreign and Security Policy
CIS	Commonwealth of Independent States
CNOOC	China National Offshore Oil Corporation
CNPC	China National Petroleum Corporation

CPC	Caspian Pipeline Consortium
CPI	Communist Party of India
CPI/M	Communist Party of India/Marxist
CSCAP	Council for Security Cooperation in the Asia Pacific
CSIS	Center for Strategic and International Studies
CSTO	Collective Security Treaty Organization
CTBT	Comprehensive Test Ban Treaty
DPJ	Democratic Party of Japan
DPRK	Democratic People's Republic of Korea
EAFTA	East Asian Free Trade Area
EAI	Enterprise for ASEAN Initiative
EAS	East Asia Summit
EBRD	European Bank for Reconstruction and Development
EC	European Commission
ECO	Economic Cooperation Organization
EIAS	European Institute for Asian Studies
EMEAP	Executives' Meeting of East Asia–Pacific Central Banks
EPG	Eminent Persons Group
ESCAP	United Nations Economic and Social Commission for Asia and the Pacific
ESDP	European Security and Defence Policy
ETIM	East Turkestan Islamic Movement
ETLO	East Turkestan Liberation Organization
EU	European Union
EurAsEC	Eurasian Economic Community
FDI	Foreign Direct Investment
FEALAC	Forum for East Asia–Latin America Cooperation
FPI	Islamic Defenders Front
FPPC	Five Principles of Peaceful Coexistence
FTA	Free Trade Agreement
GATT	General Agreement on Tariffs and Trade
GDP	Gross Domestic Product
GEACPS	Greater East Asian Co-Prosperity Sphere
GONGO	Government-Operated Non-Governmental Organizations
GUUAM	Georgia, Ukraine, Uzbekistan, Azerbaijan, and Moldova Group
HFMD	Hand, Foot, and Mouth Disease
IAEA	International Atomic Energy Agency
IFI	International Financial Institution
IISS	International Institute for Strategic Studies
IMF	International Monetary Fund
INSS	Institute for National Strategic Studies
IPE	International Political Economy

IR	International Relations
IRBM	Intermediate-Range Ballistic Missile
ISG	Inter-Sessional Support Group
ISI	Import-Substituting Industrialization
JI	Jemaah Islamiyah
JMSDF	Japan Maritime Self-Defense Force
KEDO	Korean Peninsula Energy Development Organization
LDP	Liberal Democratic Party
LNG	Liquefied Natural Gas
MITI	Ministry of International Trade and Industry
MRBM	Medium-Range Ballistic Missile
NAM	Non-Aligned Movement
NATO	North Atlantic Treaty Organization
NBR	National Bureau of Asian Research
NEAPSM	Northeast Asia Peace and Security Mechanism
NEAT	Network of East Asian Think-Tanks
NIC	Newly Industrialized Country
NIE	National Intelligence Estimate
NGO	Non-governmental Organization
NPT	Nuclear Nonproliferation Treaty
NSS	*National Security Strategy*
NSSP	Next Steps in Strategic Partnership
NTS	Non-traditional Security
OECD	Organisation for Economic Co-operation and Development
OIC	Organisation of the Islamic Conference
ONA	Office of National Assessments
OPEC	Organization of Petroleum Exporting Countries
OSCE	Organization for Security and Co-operation in Europe
PBEC	Pacific Basin Economic Council
PCA	Partnership and Cooperation Agreement
PD	Preventive Diplomacy
PECC	Pacific Economic Cooperation Council
PIF	Pacific Island Forum
PLA	People's Liberation Army
PLO	Palestine Liberation Organization
PRC	People's Republic of China
PSI	Proliferation Security Initiative
PTA	Preferential Trade Agreement
QDR	Quadrennial Defense Review
R&D	Research and Development
ROK	Republic of Korea
SAARC	South Asia Association for Regional Cooperation

SARS	Severe Acute Respiratory Syndrome
SCO	Shanghai Cooperation Organisation
SEATO	Southeast Asia Treaty Organization
SLMM	Sri Lanka Monitoring Mission
SOM	Senior Officers Meeting
SPT	Six-Party Talks
SWP	German Institute for International and Security Affairs
TAC	Treaty of Amity and Cooperation
TACIS	Technical Assistance for the Commonwealth of Independent States
TCOG	Trilateral Coordination and Oversight Group
TEPSA	Trans European Policy Studies Association
TIFA	Trade and Investment Framework Agreement
TSD	Trilateral Strategic Dialogue
USAID	United States Agency for International Development
WHO	World Health Organization
WMD	Weapons of Mass Destruction
WTO	World Trade Organization

Preface

Given the pace of change in Asia and the increasing complexities of international relations in the region and its importance in the world, we felt there was an urgent need for an up-to-date study on the subject. This volume assembles globally distinguished experts and provides knowledgeable perspectives on key aspects of Asian international relations.

After a year of research and writing, the authors convened at the Sigur Center for Asian Studies of the Elliott School of International Affairs at George Washington University in September 2007 for an in-depth and extended critique of the chapters. The Sigur Center partnered with the Elliott School's China Policy Program to co-sponsor and financially support the meeting and this volume. The contributors benefited enormously from the exchanges and constructive comments on their first drafts from leading Washington, D.C.–based specialists: Muthiah Alagappa, Jeffrey Bader, Richard Bush, Kent Calder, Kurt Campbell, Harry Harding, Paul Heer, Mike Mochizuki, Alan Romberg, and Michael Swaine. Each contributed significantly of their time and expertise in the most collegial "peer-review" tradition, for which the editors and contributors are most grateful. We are especially appreciative of the funding provided by George Washington's Academic Excellence Initiative, the Sigur Center for Asian Studies, and the Elliott School's China Policy Program. Special thanks for his support is also due to distinguished Elliott School alumnus and International Council member Christopher J. Fussner. Our gratitude also goes to the Sigur Center's administrative staff (especially Anita Narayan, Grace Lim, and Ikuko Turner) and director (Shawn McHale) for their important support behind the scenes. Political science Ph.D. student Dawn Murphy served ably as rapporteur.

Participants in the dialogue and contributors to the volume intellectually wrestled with both the component pieces as well as the composite "puzzle," attempting to come to consensus on the principal features that characterize international relations in Asia today and into the future. It is our collective hope that this book adequately captures these complex dynamics, educates students (as it is principally intended as a university-level textbook), and stimulates scholars to break out of traditional paradigmatic ways of thinking about Asia and probe further in their own research to elaborate these trends and their consequences. We also hope that our work will be a useful guide for policymakers and the media. We have done our best to capture the current and complex dynamics of international relations in Asia today, and we believe that this volume will help to inform and educate all those interested in this important aspect of world affairs.

In publishing this book, we have also been most fortunate to work with Rowman & Littlefield Publishers, and particularly commissioning editor Susan McEachern. We are honored to have the book included in Rowman & Littlefield's well-regarded Asia and World Politics series, under the experienced editorship of Samuel Kim.

Finally, we dedicate the volume to the late Michael Leifer and Thomas W. Robinson, two esteemed colleagues and friends who contributed enormously to the study of the international relations of Asia during their lifetimes. Both Michael and Tom were very important in our own professional lives and did much to help shape our understanding of the historical traditions and contemporary complexities of the Asian region. Their intellectual influence is felt both directly and indirectly in the pages of this book.

David Shambaugh and Michael Yahuda
Washington, D.C.

I

INTRODUCTION

1

International Relations in Asia

The Two-Level Game

David Shambaugh

International relations (IR) in Asia are changing in many significant ways and at two principal levels: state-to-state and society-to-society.[1] As a consequence a new regional system is emerging. While the governments in Asia interact and cooperate on many issues, they still evince suspicions and occasional tensions. Major power interactions remain volatile. Yet, at a second level, the societies of the region are interconnected to an unprecedented degree. To some extent, this interdependence acts as a buffer against potential interstate rivalry and conflict. This introductory chapter explicates these two levels for understanding international relations in Asia today.

DEFINING ASIA

The Asian region—stretching from the Pacific Ocean in the east to the Hindu Kush in the west, and from Siberia in the north to the Indian Ocean in the south—is primarily distinguished by its remarkable *diversity* of characteristics in all respects: geographic, cultural, ethnic, religious, social, demographic, political, economic, technological, educational, linguistic, communication and transportation, energy and environment, and military attributes. Asia includes some of the world's most and least developed countries, some of the strongest and some of the weakest. The other principal regions of the world—the European Union, Middle East, or Latin America—all display greater homogeneity in these realms than does Asia.

With such remarkable diversity spanning thirty-seven nation-states, any attempt to identify patterns and overarching processes that define and characterize international relations in Asia must proceed cautiously.

3

Generalizations inevitably do not apply across the region. Indeed, Asian international relations are still an amalgam of interactions occurring in five distinct sub-regions: Australasia, Southeast Asia, Northeast Asia, South Asia, and Central Asia. While the chapters in this volume are testimony to the increased *linkages across* these sub-regions in various ways and at various levels—and to this extent we are witnessing the gradual emergence of a true pan-regional Asian system (at least at the sub-state level)—nonetheless each of these five arenas still tends to operate according to its own dynamics. One consequence of this regional diversity and continuing distinctiveness of the five sub-regions has been the slow development of pan-regional intergovernmental institutions—although each sub-region has its own institutions, the development of a pan-regional multilateral architecture has been slow.

The regional order in Asia today still bears many of the hallmarks that have characterized it for a number of decades: the American presence and alliance system, a "rising" China, an uncertain Japan, a divided Korea and China/Taiwan (and the existence of "security dilemmas" in each instance), an increasingly confident and coherent Association of Southeast Asian Nations (ASEAN), a mixture of political systems amid a general trend toward the growth of democracies, entrenched nationalism, dynamic economic growth, educated societies, and disciplined workforces. These characteristics continue to distinguish Asian international relations.

In addition to the persistence of these traditional features, a variety of new features have also appeared that are reshaping regional dynamics and creating a new regional order. These include the rise of India and its regional role; a reengaged Russia; the rebalancing of major power relations; the growth of intraregional and extraregional multilateral institutions and forums; increased intraregional interdependence in all spheres; the growing impact of "soft power" in intercultural relations; the ascent of political and radical Islam; the advent of terrorism; the rise of various "non-traditional" security threats; the growing danger of a Taiwan independence movement and separatist movements in China, India, Indonesia, and Sri Lanka; an increasingly repressive Myanmar (Burma); and the increased military modernization across the region. Thus, Asian international relations also reflect these relatively new phenomena—all of which have added to their complexity and diversity.

The subsequent chapters in this volume are all testimony to these old and new dynamics. These contributions address the traditional and changing roles of external powers (the United States, Europe, and Russia), regional powers (China and Japan), and the emergence of new actors (India, Australia, Central Asia); the role of ASEAN, the Shanghai Cooperation Organisation, and the gradually emerging multilateral regional architecture; the troublesome Korean Peninsula; and three important functional features of the emerging regional order: economics, globalization, and regional security. In the next two chapters, Samuel Kim and Amitav Acharya, respectively, place contemporary international relations in Asia in both historical and theoretical perspective. While the subsequent chapters raise and elaborate different components of the emerging regional system in Asia, the remainder of this introduction provides my own sense of the dominant macro trends in the region today.

ASIA BY THE NUMBERS: KEY INDICATORS OF IMPORTANCE

Asia's importance in world affairs can be measured in a number of ways. Consider the following indicators.[2]

Demographically, 3.5 billion people live in Asia, comprising 58 percent of the world's population. Eight of the world's fifteen most populated nations are in Asia (China, India, Indonesia, Pakistan, Bangladesh, Japan, the Philippines, and Vietnam). The world's three largest Islamic nations are in Asia (Indonesia, Pakistan, Bangladesh), with 640 million Muslims living across the region—more than anywhere in the world and more than all Middle East nations combined. Asia is home to many of the world's major religions, including Buddhism, Catholicism, Christianity, Confucianism, Hinduism, Islam, Shintoism, and Taoism.

Asia has four of the world's eight societies with longest life expectancies (Japan, Singapore, Hong Kong, Australia), while none of the top twenty infant mortality rates are in Asia—testimony to the dramatic economic development and improved standard of living in the region, as well as the success of China and India in reducing absolute poverty over the last two decades. China alone has lifted two hundred million of its citizens out of absolute poverty since 1980. Despite such progress, eight hundred million Asians (66 percent of the world's poor) still live on less than $1 per day.[3] Asian GDP per capita annual incomes range from a low of $260 in Cambodia to a high of $32,000 in Japan.[4]

Socially, while Asia remains poor—in some places desperately so—various indicators indicate the transition that many societies are making from developing to newly industrialized country (NIC) status. China, Japan, and India rank among the top six nations in terms of GDP (on a purchasing power parity basis), while South Korea, Indonesia, Taiwan, and Australia all rank in the top twenty in the world. On a per GDP capita basis, though, only Hong Kong, Australia, and Japan rank in the top twenty-five internationally. China, India, and Japan rank in the top ten of Internet and mobile phone users—with China alone having an estimated 137 million people online (although with multiple users per account, this number could be 2–3 times higher) and 461 million communicating by cell phone every day.[5]

While Asia has modernized, and in so doing has been able to eradicate a number of chronic diseases, other public health problems have arisen— such as SARS (severe acute respiratory syndrome), avian flu, and HIV/AIDS. India and China now rank among the top fifteen (number two and fourteen, respectively) of people living with HIV/AIDS in the world.

Asia has become the source of innovation and technological advances. China, India, Japan, South Korea, Singapore, and Thailand all have invested in large government spending initiatives on science—dwarfing the shrinking budgets in the West. Japan, South Korea, China, and Singapore all rank among the world's top "core innovators" in terms of share of GDP spent on research and development (R&D). China alone invested $13.6 billion in science and technology R&D in 2006 (about 2.1 percent of GDP)—more than any other nation in the world except the United States.[6]

Since the late 1980s, Asian economies have grown at the fastest rate in the world. Asia accounted for 35 percent of the world economy (global GDP) in 2005; growing at current rates it will account for 43 percent by 2020.[7] Of this total 35 percent, China alone accounted for 14 percent of global economic activity, India for 7 percent, and the rest of Asia for 14 percent collectively.

No Asian nation has known either flat or negative growth during the past quarter century. Even Japan, where the growth rate remained the most stagnant in the region during this period, posted a 1.9 percent growth rate from 1990 to 2006. China's GDP growth was the highest in the region, growing at a clip of 9.2 percent, while India's was 6.2 percent, Singapore's 5.9 percent, Malaysia's 5.7 percent, South Korea's 5.4 percent, Thailand's 4.8 percent, Taiwan's 4.4 percent, and so on. Since 1980 the Chinese economy alone has grown by 878 percent and the Indian economy by 319 percent, as contrasted to 121 percent growth in the U.S. economy and 58 percent in Germany.[8] Ten of the thirty most competitive economies are in Asia.[9]

Asia has become the center of world trade—accounting for nearly one-third of global trade volume. If Hong Kong is included, Asian nations count for six of the top twenty trading nations in the world. Most of this trade travels by shipping containers. Hong Kong, Kaohsiung, Osaka, Pusan, and Singapore are among the world's busiest cargo and container ports. A staggering 55,000–60,000 commercial vessels and oil tankers traverse the strategic Strait of Malacca every year, carrying more than a third of the world's shipping trade and half of its crude oil shipments.[10]

As trade has burgeoned, some nations in Asia have grown rich, very rich. Asia held 64 percent of total global currency reserves in 2008. If Hong Kong is included separately from China, eight of the world's ten largest holders of these reserves are in Asia (China, Japan, Taiwan, South Korea, India, Singapore, Hong Kong, Malaysia). China alone holds $1.75 trillion in 2008, while Asia as a whole has amassed a staggering $2.8 trillion (out of a global total of $4 trillion)! In another notable trend, since the late 1990s, Asian nations do more trade with each other than outside the region.

This dramatic domestic economic growth has been stimulated by the strong growth in intraregional trade and investment. Asia accounts for about 60 percent of global capital inflows, approximately $150 billion per year.

Asia's economic growth has also been fueled (literally) by dramatically increased amounts of energy imports to the region. China, Japan, India, and South Korea ranked respectively as second-, third-, fifth-, and eighth-largest oil importers in the world in 2006. Explosive growth has also produced severe environmental degradation. In 2001 Asia accounted for one-third of global CO_2 emissions (7.4 billion tons),[11] but it is nearing half of the world's greenhouse gas emissions in 2008 (over 10 billion tons).

In terms of regional security, Asia accounted for five of the world's ten largest standing armies in 2008 (China, India, North Korea, South Korea, Vietnam) and the world's four largest surface navies (if the U.S. and Russian navies are included, along with China and Japan).[12] In terms of total defense expenditure, Asia ranked equal to European NATO nations in 2005 ($256 billion for Asia versus $259 billion for European NATO countries),[13] but only half of the United States ($495 billion). The International Institute for Strategic Studies (IISS) estimated that China and Japan had the second- and fourth-largest defense budgets in the world in 2005 (the United States ranked first and Russia third). Almost all militaries across the Asian region are modernizing their forces.[14] For most, this involves importing sophisticated weaponry from abroad. Six of the world's top ten arms importers are in Asia (China, India, Japan, Pakistan, South Korea, Taiwan), although in aggregate the Middle East still imports more (led by Saudi Arabia, the United Arab Emirates, Israel, and Egypt).[15]

Taking Stock

Thus, by many measures, Asia ranks in the top tier globally. These trends are only likely to accelerate into the future. Among other consequences, it means that the entire world would be severely and negatively affected if Asia experienced a major economic downturn, social catastrophe, or military conflict.

Understanding capacities in Asia, as illustrated by the indicators above, is an important starting point for understanding the stakes involved in Asian international relations. But how do the nations and societies in Asia actually interact?

We can distinguish two distinct "levels of analysis" to grasp these interactions.[16] The first is at the regional "systemic" level and involves governments. The interaction of these governments, particularly the major powers,
leads to the question of whether a distinct regional *system* is discernible and,
if so, what are its properties? The second level of analysis is at the societal
level. Here one asks, what are the patterns of non-governmental interactions across the region, and what impact do they have on Asian international relations?

THE ASIAN SYSTEM TODAY:
A COMPLEX REGION IN SEARCH OF COHERENCE

At the systemic level, Asian international relations must be viewed both as
a regional subset of the global system, as well as possessing distinct regional
properties. Samuel Kim's and Amitav Acharya's subsequent chapters illustrate different ways of thinking about Asia's systemic properties—both historically and theoretically. Analysts are well advised to use both prisms
when evaluating the regional system today. Even if the historical features
described by Professor Kim (which he identifies as the "three transformations") no longer define Asian IR today, their lingering influence continues
to be present in the minds of many Asians. As in Europe and the Arab
world, the burden of historical experiences (the "international politics of
memory") weighs heavily on the collective consciousness of Asians.

The traditional hierarchical "Sinic" or "Sinocentric" system (also referred
to as the "tribute system"), which characterized Asia for centuries, continues to cast its shadow today as China undergoes its fourth "rise" in history,[17] and many wonder if China is trying to re-create a modern-day version of the ancient hierarchical hegemonic system. What has been
described as the "Indic system," which lasted from the fourth through eighteenth centuries, still weighs on the South Asian subcontinent although the
region is now comprised of six sovereign states.[18] The European colonial
systems, which penetrated into the region during the eighteenth and nineteenth centuries, have had a lasting impact on South and Southeast Asian
states and societies—although more on intrastate than interstate systems. It
was the colonial period that brought the nation-state to Asia—and with it
the concepts of sovereignty, national governments (many republican) and
militaries, defined boundaries, and other key features of the modern international system. Japan's ascendance from the late-nineteenth through the
mid-twentieth century defined the regional (dis)order for half a century,
and its horrific consequences continue to lie not far below the surface of
Asian minds and memories today (particularly in those societies once occupied by Japan). The Cold War in Asia also defined (and polarized) the re-

gional order for at least a quarter century. While it embodied the same global feature of bipolar competition between the United States and former Soviet Union, the Cold War in Asia also had its own unique characteristics owing to nationalist and communist revolutions in Korea, China, Vietnam, and other Southeast Asian societies.

Since the end of the Cold War, the region has experienced a number of complex trends—which do not make for a single integrated regional "system." Rather, multiple properties constitute a multilayered architecture, which gives international relations in Asia their defining quality today. Such complexity and multiple actors may not make for conceptual coherence, but when taken together, the separate elements constitute a regional *order*, although not necessarily a *system* per se.[19]

Amitav Acharya's chapter helps us understand these elements by examining how the three most prevalent theories of international relations today all illustrate, in some way and to some extent, the properties of the regional order. Asian international relations today simultaneously involve *Realist* features of power politics, *Liberal institutionalist* features of intergovernmental multilateralism, and *Constructivist* features of increasingly shared ideational and behavioral norms among policy elites.

Theoretical Alternatives

There is no shortage of theoretical explanations or alternative models attempting to characterize the Asian regional order/system. The contributors to a stimulating book, edited by G. John Ikenberry and Michael Mastanduno, offer a number of alternatives: hegemonic stability theory, balance of power theory, Liberal institutionalism, Constructivist theory, normative socialization theory, identity theory, economic interdependence theory, and hierarchical stability theory.[20] In another major study, Muthiah Alagappa identifies three conceptions of regional order: hegemony with Liberal features, strategic condominium/balance of power, and normative-contractual conceptions.[21] In my earlier book *Power Shift*, I identified seven distinct alternative models (hegemonic system, major power rivalry, "hub and spokes" American-centric alliance system, concert of powers, condominium of powers, normative community, complex interdependence) but concluded that only three (hub and spokes, normative community, and complex interdependence) had sufficient explanatory power to characterize *parts* of the contemporary Asian order—but *none* were sufficient alone to define it.

Other scholars have tended to emphasize one or another theory/model as possessing definitive power. Aaron Friedberg argues that Asia's future is Europe's past, that is, great power rivalry will prevail.[22] In contrast, David Kang challenges the Friedberg thesis and argues that Asia is not going to follow

Europe's past of great power competition but is naturally returning to a twenty-first-century form of the pre-nineteenth-century Sinocentric hierarchical system, with many Asian states accommodating themselves ("bandwagoning" in political science jargon) to China as the emerging preeminent power in the region.[23] I tend to agree with Kang and have similarly argued that China's proactive engagement of its periphery has transformed international relations in Asia—giving Beijing de facto "veto power" over actions by other states, at a minimum, or the role as the preeminent and most respected power in the region, at a maximum.[24]

However, many other scholars wed to the Realist tradition (e.g., Evan Medeiros and Robert Sutter) see Asian states "hedging" or "balancing" against a rising China,[25] and they see the United States as still being the dominant power in the region.[26] Historian and international affairs commentator Robert Kagan argues that it is a dangerous "illusion to [try and] manage China's rise."[27] Another leading Realist, John Mearscheimer, applies his "offensive Realism" theory (or what I would label "hegemonic inevitability theory") to Asia by arguing that China—like all great powers before—will inevitably seek regional hegemonic dominance and that this "structural asymmetry" between the rising power (China) and existing dominant power (United States) will define the Asian order and inevitably cause great power war—unless the United States takes preemptive action. Both Mearscheimer and Kagan argue that the only viable option to forestall conflict with China is to preemptively contain it.[28] In contrast, Amitav Acharya rejects the applicability of Realist paradigms and has alternatively argued that Asia is experiencing the emergence of shared norms about interstate interaction, rooted in the "ASEAN Way," which are beginning to become rooted in regional institutions.[29]

While no single theory explains all, each contributes in part to our understanding of Asian international politics in the early-twenty-first century. For our purposes here, it is the Realist and Liberal features that contribute to understanding the (regional) systemic level of analysis. Let us examine each of these in turn.

THE ROLE OF MAJOR POWERS

Asian international relations certainly continue to exhibit the features of major power politics. Indeed, power politics has been a distinguishing feature of Asian IR over time.[30] Both Northeast and Southeast Asia have traditionally been fulcrums of conflict (notably the Korea Peninsula, Sea of Okhotsk, Strait of Malacca, Manchuria, and Indochina), while Central Asia was the scene of great power maneuvering (the "Great Game").[31]

In the early twenty-first century, Asia remains the only region of the world where all the major powers interact: the United States, Russia, China, India, and Japan. As Sebastian Bersick's chapter in this volume discusses, the European Union also plays its role economically and diplomatically, although not strategically or militarily. The chapters by Sheldon Simon, Martha Brill Olcott, and Scott Snyder further illustrate that Southeast Asia, Central Asia, and Northeast Asia (particularly the Korea Peninsula) are the principal loci of major power interactions. To date, major power competition has not affected the Western Pacific, as it remains dominated by the United States and its allies Japan and Australia (see the chapters by Michael Green and Hugh White).

The chapters by Robert Sutter, Ralph Cossa, and Michael Yahuda in this volume all argue that the United States remains the key "external balancer," maintaining peace and stability in the region. While the United States remains the region's strongest power, as measured by economic and military capabilities, many Asians perceive U.S. diplomatic influence and moral prestige to have declined markedly during the post–Cold War era.[32] The George W. Bush administration was criticized throughout Asia for being distracted by the war in Iraq and generally neglecting the region, not noticing the successes of China's regional "charm offensive," trying to enlist Asian states in a strategic "hedging" policy against China, not pushing Japan to reexamine its World War II war crimes so as to ameliorate strains in Tokyo's relations with its neighbors, neglecting Southeast Asia altogether (except through the "War on Terror" prism), not engaging in presidential diplomacy, and being preoccupied by the North Korean nuclear issue.

Some U.S. Asia specialists agree with the Asian critique,[33] while others robustly deny it.[34] Those who disagree argue that America's position in Asia is stronger than ever, that Asian countries look to Washington for "leadership," and that the United States provides the "public good" of preserving the regional peace through its military presence, has managed its relationship with China well, has strengthened its alliances and partnerships with key allies, has worked hard to roll back the North Korean nuclear program, has provided significant humanitarian assistance to tsunami and earthquake victims, has promoted democracy, and enjoys strong public opinion ratings.[35]

What is clear is that the United States' power and reputation in Asia are no longer uncontested. Even if it still is the strongest power, its strength is no longer as absolute and has declined *relatively* against other regional powers. Nor does America's power translate as easily into influence as it once did. Washington must now compete with Beijing and ASEAN in the "marketplace of ideas" about regional order. As a result, a more diffuse pattern of major power interactions has emerged.

Since the end of the Cold War, the major powers' roles in Asia have been more those of complex interaction and interdependence than competition or classic rivalry. To be sure, there is strategic maneuvering among these major powers—as the United States attempts to maintain its postwar preeminence, China seeks to become the region's leading power (by design or default), Japan and India try to carve out relatively larger regional (and global) roles for themselves, while Russia tries to "get back in the game" and reassert its presence on the Asian stage. But such maneuvering remains fluid, and no two powers are locked in a dyadic struggle for dominance, as during the Cold War. Indeed, a defining characteristic of major power interaction in Asia today is that each of the powers maintains extensive and interdependent ties with the others. While some scholars, such as Robert Ross, perceive the region to be cleaving into two geographic camps, continental and maritime,[36] structural polarity is not (yet) present, as was the case during the Cold War.

Recognizing this fluidity and interdependence, it is nonetheless apparent that an incipient rivalry for preeminence and influence is taking place at two levels: (1) between the region's two biggest powers, the United States and China, and (2) between Japan and China. This rivalry has both bilateral and trilateral dimensions—but to date has not been truly *triangular* per se, as Japan has not been an equal and autonomous actor (given its alliance with and dependence on the United States). For much of the post–Cold War period Tokyo has tilted strongly toward the United States, as bilateral relations with Beijing deteriorated during the Koizumi period and various voices in Japan warned of the looming "China threat." The Sino-Japanese antagonism during the Koizumi period replaced the long-standing triangular (China–Japan–United States) "Grand Bargain" of simultaneously cooperative relations among the three Asian powers, which had defined Northeast Asian international relations since the 1970s.[37] However, post-Koizumi, as prime ministers Abe and Fukuda came to office, the Japanese government reached out to mend its frayed relations with Beijing. And Chinese leaders readily reciprocated during 2006–2008. By so doing, Tokyo has bought itself greater independence and leverage, and what had been "tilted trilateralism" could increasingly take on the character of traditional triangular politics.

Much has been written about the U.S.-China strategic relationship in Asia, with a wide variety of views presented.[38] As noted above, some Realists advocate "containment" (like Mearscheimer and Kagan) or "hard balancing" (like Friedberg) against China, while others advocate "hedging" or "soft balancing" (like Medeiros or Sutter) against China. Other scholars, like David M. Lampton and this author, believe that the United States and China are not intrinsically caught in a "security dilemma" and can cooperate effectively to maintain regional order.[39] Still other analysts distinguish between the tactics of "internal" and "external" balancing: the former being a kind of self-help policy of military modernization, while the latter entails forging external alignments or alliances with stronger powers (United States) against the would-be threatening power (China).

Japan and India are seen to have adopted both internal and external means to balance China. In so doing, both New Delhi and Tokyo have sought to strengthen their own militaries as well as to consolidate military ties to the United States. While consistent with "external balancing," solidifying defense ties (with Australia as well) can be counterproductive, as it can trigger counter-counterbalancing by Beijing (and Moscow). As Thomas Christensen has aptly noted with respect to the strengthening of the U.S.-Japan alliance, it produces a classic "security dilemma," that is, one side's defensive actions are viewed offensively by another, causing counteractions.[40] In other words, strategic "hedging," if too overtly undertaken, can produce the opposite outcome intended—leading to countermeasures, and the increased militarization and structural rigidity in the region.

While some Southeast Asian states have pursued a counter-China hedging strategy,[41] the majority of ASEAN has opted not just for a strong engagement policy toward China, aimed at tying Beijing into a web of intraregional mechanisms, but has further sought to bind other major powers into the regional order. In particular, Oxford scholar Evelyn Goh argues that Southeast Asians want the United States to remain fully engaged as the region's "primary power," at the top of a regional hierarchy of powers. In this hierarchy, she argues, ASEAN places China just beneath the United States. She describes this as ASEAN's "omni-enmeshment" and "complex balance of influence" strategies, although it seems to be a strategy oriented toward forging a de facto concert of powers.[42] This Southeast Asian strategy derives from its internal sense of vulnerability, as well as what Goh describes as its "profoundly ambivalent feelings towards China." In his chapter in this volume, Sheldon Simon shares Goh's sense about ASEAN's "enmeshment strategy."

Beijing has certainly not idly watched these actions around its periphery. As Phillip Saunders's chapter illustrates, China has embarked on a concerted "reassurance campaign" to persuade its neighbors that its rise poses no threat to them or regional stability.[43] Saunders argues that Beijing's power and influence in Asia—economic, diplomatic, military, ideational—has grown significantly in recent years.

Despite the wide variety of views about the nature of the Sino-American strategic relationship, there appears to be implicit agreement among most analysts that this relationship has become the principal one defining the Asian strategic order—replacing the earlier view held by many that the U.S.-Japan relationship was most central.

Beyond recognizing the paramount importance of Sino-American relations, two other widely shared assumptions among experts are that the U.S.-China-Japan triangle is the critical feature of the regional strategic (and certainly the economic) order and that Asia cannot be strategically stable unless the Sino-Japanese relationship is stable. Michael Green's chapter in this volume argues that Japan's position between the United States and China is not fixed and could well change. He argues that a severe diminution of U.S. power and influence in the region would push Tokyo to balance China more actively—but, alternatively, if China continues its ascent toward regional preeminence, Tokyo would be confronted with the awkward choice of accommodation to, or confrontation with, Beijing (though he argues that this scenario is unlikely). Mike Mochizuki, an astute analyst of Japan's China policy, argues elsewhere that Tokyo pursues a mixed "double hedge" strategy of engagement and balancing—promoting security cooperation with the United States while expanding its own defense capabilities to counter the rise of China, but is simultaneously developing commercial and diplomatic links with China.[44] Japan expert Kenneth Pyle also argues that Tokyo is pragmatically adopting a balanced wait-and-see approach to China's rise, which contains dual elements of engagement and balancing of China, but that—above all—Japan's leaders seek autonomy and do not want to become hostage to the China policy of the United States.[45] Pyle's perspective reminds us that while many Japanese policy elites live with the perpetual fear of "abandonment" by the United States, particularly during periods when Washington flirts with strategic cooperation with Beijing, another group worries about being too closely tied to the United States. It is apparent that the strengthening and redefinition of the alliance from 1998 to 2008 was mirrored by Japan's own declining influence in Asia. In other words, as Tokyo banked its future with Washington, its political capital in Asia declined. This is not good for Japan, for Asia, or for the United States. A Japan that is closely integrated and active in Asia on all levels is most conducive to regional stability, while a Japan tethered solely to the United States is not.

While not all specialists would agree, many also recognize the new importance of India's rise in defining the regional order (see Sumit Ganguly's chapter), as New Delhi becomes increasingly involved on the East and Central Asian stages. India's dramatic economic growth, military modernization, nuclear weapons capability, active diplomacy, and integration into regional institutions have all raised New Delhi's profile in Asia. This is only expected to continue.

Finally, Russia is also trying to reassert itself in Asia. While its commercial interaction with the region remains minimal, Moscow is leveraging its considerable energy resources to increase its influence among Northeast Asian countries. Its arms sales to China and India (averaging approximately $3 billion each per year) also allow Moscow to influence the Asian security environment. Diplomatically, the Sino-Russian relationship is stronger than in decades, while Moscow has also sought to build up a triangular axis with India and China.[46] Russia is also one of the members of the Six-Party Talks (SPT) on North Korea, and Moscow chairs the SPT Working Group to study the feasibility of a Northeast Asia Peace and Security Mechanism (NEAPSM). As Martha Brill Olcott's chapter details, Russia's influence in Asia is greatest in Central Asia.[47] While Moscow has sought to reestablish itself as an Asian player during Vladimir Putin's presidency, its longer term influence is weak due to geographical distance, lack of economic competitiveness, and its essentially Eurocentric identity. Going forward, as the experienced Asia hand and U.S. diplomat J. Stapleton Roy has aptly observed, "Russia needs to have a sense of participation. That's the secret to managing Russia as an Asian power, albeit a somewhat diminished power."[48]

Given the character and interactions described above, what is the overall structural character of major power relations in Asia? Is the region "ripe for rivalry," as Aaron Friedberg has suggested?[49] Is Europe's past Asia's future?

It must first be recognized that the principal major power relationship in the region—between the United States and China—*does* contain elements of classic *balance of power* international politics. Beijing and Washington do not trust each other's strategic intentions, are actively hedging against each other and an uncertain future by competing for the loyalty of other Asian states, and continue to share the intractable but potentially explosive Taiwan issue. The opaqueness of China's military modernization program and strategic intentions, on the one hand, and the paranoid anti-China invective often heard in Washington on the other, both fuel the competition.

Yet, I would argue, the Sino-American strategic competition remains a "soft rivalry"—as neither has designated the other an overt adversary, both governments deal extensively with each other, and both societies are deeply enmeshed in a thick web of interdependence. Even if the rivalry hardened, it is unlikely that it would lead to the bifurcation of international politics in the region—as other Asian states are also deeply interdependent with both America and China, and they would resist the false strategic choice of having to choose sides between Beijing and Washington. As Hugh White reminds us in his chapter, other Asian governments work hard to avoid this nightmare scenario and, as such, act as important buffers against the emergence of Sino-American hostilities and the polarization of international politics in the region. Nor are China and the United States powerful enough to establish their unrivaled *hegemonic dominance* over the region. The element of strategic competition in the relationship similarly forecloses the possibility of the two powers establishing a *condominium* over the region—although on some issues they can work effectively together to maintain regional peace and security.

An Asian Concert of Powers?

A few years ago I dismissed the possibility of a *concert of powers* emerging in Asia, but now it seems more plausible and deserving of consideration.[50] Several new features have emerged since 2005 that make a concert of powers more conceivable.

The relative decline in U.S. power and influence combined with the growth in Chinese and Indian power and influence, and the increased coherence of ASEAN coinciding with its fortieth anniversary and adoption of a new ASEAN Charter, have all contributed to rebalancing the distribution of comprehensive power capabilities among these actors. But, perhaps of greatest importance has been the amelioration of tensions and improvement of relations between China and Japan since 2007. No Asian concert can exist or function if the Sino-Japanese relationship is antagonistic or dysfunctional. While there certainly remain deep suspicions on each side, the rapid improvement of ties during the Abe and Fukuda administrations has brought normalcy back into the relationship—and with it the prospect of Japan becoming a more active and trusted actor in the Asian region.

The return to cooperative ties among China, Japan, and the United States would, to some extent, restore the "Grand Bargain" that prevailed from the early 1980s through the late 1990s,[51] but in today's Asia, India and ASEAN would also be partners in co-managing the region. Thus, a five-power concert of China, India, Japan, ASEAN, and the United States may be emerging as a defining element in Asian international relations. The distribution of power among these actors, and the intensity of government and non-governmental interactions among them, contribute to its potential. Russia could become a sixth partner in the concert over time, but it still has far to go to become regularly involved in regional diplomatic, economic, and security affairs.

For such a concert to more fully emerge would likely require both a more explicit sense of shared community and responsibilities and a higher level of institutionalization among the involved powers. The former requires more explicit agreement of shared normative views about regional order—both minimum standards to be respected by all nations as well as maximum aspirations of regional order and cooperation. The growing consensus on norms of interstate relations among ASEAN, China, India, Japan, and Russia could conceivably form the normative basis of such agreed "rules of the road," but it remains doubtful that the United States could accept many of the strictures concerning non-interference in domestic affairs. It is also unclear how such a five-power concert would affect the existing American alliance system in Asia (the two need not be mutually exclusive). A concert of power would also require a new form of institutionalized consultation exclusively limited to the five powers, which could meet annually at head of state as well as ministerial levels. But such an exclusive grouping would likely aggravate other important regional actors, such as Australia or South Korea, which would experience an unwelcome "second-class" status. It is similarly unclear what such an arrangement would mean for many of the existing multilateral forums in the region—particularly Asia-Pacific Economic Cooperation (APEC) and ASEAN + 3 (again, they need not be mutually exclusive).

Thus, even if some conditions seem ripe for the emergence of an East Asian concert, there also remain serious impediments to realizing the vision. To be sure, the underlying strategic suspicions among China and the United States, China and Japan, Russia and the United States, India and China, and Russia and Japan all exercise a restraining influence. It is difficult to cooperate under conditions of strategic distrust. Yet, the Concert of Powers that kept the peace in Europe for a century, following the Congress of Vienna in 1815 until the outbreak of World War I in 1914, did so as Britain, Russia, Austria, Prussia, France, Italy, and the Ottoman Empire all strategically maneuvered against and balanced each other. Strategic trust among these European powers was not high, yet they cooperated effectively to maintain regional peace and order.

Thus, concerts need not be absent of strategic competition to function. There simply needs to be a roughly equal division of material power and a common recognition that unbridled competition can lead to war and catastrophe and that the merits of cooperation work to stabilize the environment for all. The European Concert of Powers also worked because the powers regularly met in a series of diplomatic conferences. The intensity and extensiveness of bilateral interactions between Asian heads of state and government ministers is staggering—and offers ample opportunity for such "concert consultations." These also occur increasingly on a multilateral level.

THE FUTURE OF ASIAN MULTILATERALISM

For a Concert of Asia to function in the twenty-first century, it too would require a degree of institutionalization. As noted above, the exclusivity of a five-power concert would cause real problems with Russia, South Korea, and Australia (perhaps Pakistan and Kazakhstan as well), whose interests would have to be somehow accommodated. Then there is the issue of ASEAN, itself an amalgamation of ten countries, which is not a unitary major power and may well resist the very concept of a major power concert. Nor does the existing multilayered architecture of regional multilateral groupings lend itself to such a concert-type framework.

The proliferation of Asian multilateral intergovernmental groupings has become a distinguishing feature of the regional order, as discussed particularly in the chapters by Sheldon Simon and Ralph Cossa. The Asian multilateral architecture currently consists of

- The Association of Southeast Asian Nations (ASEAN) brings together the ten nations of Southeast Asia.
- The Asia-Pacific Economic Cooperation (APEC) is a Pacific Rim group that brings together East Asian nations with those of the Western Hemisphere (the Pacific Rim countries).
- The Shanghai Cooperation Organisation (SCO) brings together China, Russia, and the six Central Asian states (with Iran, India, and the EU as observers).
- The South Asia Association for Regional Cooperation (SAARC) brings together eight nations in South Asia.
- The Asia-Europe Meeting (ASEM) brings together twenty-three Asian and European nations.
- The Forum for East Asia–Latin America Cooperation (FEALAC) brings together thirty-one nations from these two regions.
- The Pacific Economic Cooperation Council (PECC) brings together twenty-six Pacific Rim countries.
- The Pacific Island Forum (PIF) brings together sixteen independent states in the Western Pacific, with thirteen dialogue partners from East Asia, North America, and Europe.
- ASEAN has fostered a dialogue with China (ASEAN + 1) and another with China, Japan, and South Korea (ASEAN + 3).
- The ASEAN Regional Forum (ARF) is a security dialogue forum that brings together twenty East Asian states with five from outside the region (United States, Canada, EU, Bangladesh, and India).
- The East Asia Summit (EAS) brings together sixteen nations from East Asia (with India and the EU as observers).
- United Nations Economic and Social Commission for Asia and the Pacific (ESCAP) includes sixty-eight member states in East, South, and Central Asia.

There also exists a wide range of regional organizations that address specific issues—from organized crime to telecommunications to public health to energy security and other functional areas—which meet at the ministerial and expert levels. These intergovernmental groupings are supplemented by a wide range of non-governmental or semi-governmental conferences and groupings—such as the Council on East Asian Community (CEAC), Council for Security Cooperation in the Asia Pacific (CSCAP), and the Shangri-La Dialogue on Asian Security.

Since 1967 when ASEAN was established, many Western observers of Asian international relations have argued that Asia would never be "ripe for regionalism," but they have been proven wrong. The proliferation of multilateral organizations and dialogue groupings noted above is strong evidence to the contrary. As these organizations have mushroomed, so has the literature concerning them.[52] While these groupings lack "hard institutionalization," as one finds in the European Union, they are nonetheless gaining strength and influence with every passing year. Indeed, their relative *lack* of institutionalization is one defining feature of the "Asian Way" of multilateralism. Consensual decision making is another.

No single organization brings all of the Asian states together. Even the ARF, which is the most inclusive, excludes Central Asian states. To date, most of these groupings have not practiced "open regionalism." That is, their memberships are limited to subsets of countries. In particular, the United States has been excluded from a number of them, but it must also be said that Washington has demonstrated a distinct ambivalence and dismissiveness about all except APEC.[53] In lieu of a single pan-regional organization, what has emerged is an architecture of overlapping bodies—similar to overlapping tectonic plates beneath the earth's surface—that supplement each other and work together to foster regional cooperation and stability.

SUB-STATE INTERACTIONS: BUILDING INTERDEPENDENCE

While relations among major powers and other governments are the principal defining characteristic of international relations in Asia, they are not the only level of interaction. Different parts of Asian societies are autonomous actors in their own right. In this respect, one might distinguish between *foreign policy* (among governments) and *foreign relations* (among societies). International relations today is certainly comprised as much by the latter as by the former. This is the second level of the two-level game in Asian international relations. To this end, let us consider some examples of how Asian societies are increasingly knit together into a series of thick, interdependent webs.

Perhaps the clearest indication of intraregional interdependence lies in the trade realm. Since the 2001–2002 economic recovery in the region, following the Asian financial crisis of 1997, the percentage of trade *within Asia* has increased dramatically. All Asian nations now trade more with each other, intraregionally, than with Europe or North America. Central Asian economies now trade 39.2 percent within Asia; China, 53.9 percent; India, 28.2 percent; Japan, 48 percent; Russia, 19.8 percent; South Korea, 51.7 percent; and ASEAN, 61.1 percent.[54] Intraregional direct investment also far outstrips foreign direct investment (FDI) originating in Europe or North America. Ed Lincoln's chapter offers multiple examples of these phenomena.

This surge in intraregional trade and investment has been facilitated by, and has also stimulated, an avalanche of bilateral and regional free trade agreements (FTAs) and preferential trade agreements (PTAs). Figure 1.1 offers a visual illustration of the spaghetti-like web of these arrangements. As of 2007, no fewer than thirty-eight FTAs/PTAs are in force in the region, four pending ratification by participants' parliaments, and an additional sixteen actively under negotiation.[55] With the exception of the ASEAN FTA, which links the ten member states together, the balance of these trade agreements is bilateral. Some consideration is being given to a quadrilateral arrangement among ASEAN, China, Japan, and South Korea (ASEAN + 3), which ASEAN believes can become the basis of an East Asian Free Trade Area (EAFTA).[56]

There are other indicators of the interconnectedness sweeping Asia. Consider tourism and higher education.

Asian tourists with disposable income are fanning out across the region in large numbers. In 2006, 167.2 million tourists visited the Asian region (second globally behind the EU). Of this number, 78 percent was intraregional travel among Asians.[57] About half arrived by air, 40 percent crossed

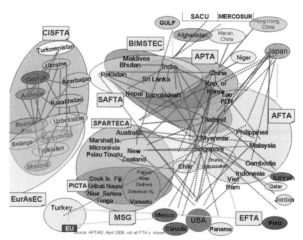

Figure 1.1.   The "Spaghetti-Bowl" of Trade Agreements.

Source: Rajan Sudesh Ratna, "Rules of Origin: Diverse Treatment and Future Development in the Asia and Pacific Region," in *Towards Coherent Policy Frameworks: Understanding Trade and Investment Linkages,* Studies in Trade and Investment 62 (United Nations Economic and Social Commission for Asia and the Pacific, December 2007), 78, www.unescap.org/tid/publication/tipub2469.pdf (accessed January 10, 2007).

land boundaries, and 10 percent traveled by sea. From 2005 to 2006, South Asia showed the fastest growth in tourism (11 percent), followed by Southeast Asia (9.3 percent), and Northeast Asia (7.4 percent). Travel is big business in Asia—generating $152.6 billion in tourist-generated revenue in 2006.[58] Tourism to China continued to dominate the Asian tourist trade, both in volume and rate of growth. A staggering 46.8 million visitors went to China in 2006, an estimated 74 percent of which originated within Asia, with Thailand trailing far behind China at 11.6 million.[59]

As the Asian economies and societies have developed rapidly, opportunities for higher education have expanded around the region. Asia now boasts a number of world-class universities, for example, Tokyo University, Waseda University (Japan), Seoul National University, Beijing University, Tsinghua University (China), Fudan University (China), Hong Kong University of Science and Technology, National University of Singapore, Australian National University, and University of Sydney (Australia). A number of others are close to cracking the top tier, or have already done so in certain subject areas, for example, Hong Kong University, Chinese University of Hong Kong, Nanjing University (China), Zhongshan University (China), Nanyang Technological University (Singapore), Yonsei University (South Korea), National Taiwan University, Malaysian University of Science and Technology, Amity University (India), Jawaharlal Nehru University (India), and the University of Brisbane (Australia).

As a result, Asians are increasingly staying within the region for their university educations, rather than going to the United States or Europe. Chinese and Indian universities now each graduate between three and four million students each year. China alone enrolled twenty-three million students in college-level institutions (including vocational schools) in 2005.[60] China now enrolls 20 percent of the university age cohort, while South Korea and Japan enroll 50 percent. Asian universities are also turning out increasing numbers of graduates in the engineering and hard sciences—another indicator that their economies are transitioning to newly industrialized status. China alone graduates approximately two hundred thousand students with B.A.'s in engineering per year,[61] and in 2005 approximately thirteen thousand Ph.D.'s in science and engineering.[62] Science and engineering account for nearly three in five bachelors now conferred in China, and by 2010 it is projected that doctorates in the natural sciences and engineering will exceed those awarded in the United States. As Chinese universities have revamped and upgraded their curriculums, they are becoming more attractive to foreign students for their undergraduate and graduate training. These students come to China for degrees in subjects other than Chinese studies. In 2006 China was also host to 162,411 foreign university students, 73 percent (118,726) of whom came from other Asian nations.[63] Australian, Japanese, and Singaporean universities are similarly attracting large numbers of Asian students. For example, 64,000 of Australia's 240,000 overseas students come from other Asian countries.

Reflecting the emphasis on education and innovation, Asians have begun to garner an increasing share of Nobel Prizes. If V. S. Naipaul and Gao Xingjian are included, who have emigrated from India and China, respectively, Asians have been awarded ten Nobel Prizes since 1990. This includes Nobel Peace Prize winners and former politicians Aung San Suu Kyi (Myanmar) and Kim Dae Jung (South Korea), four Japanese scientists, one Japanese writer, and one Indian economist.

Asians are also increasingly linked via webs of professional associations, organizations, conventions, conferences, trade shows, and other forums. Some are government sponsored, but most are not. Electronic communications facilitate further collaboration. Through these linkages, Asians are collectively addressing and solving regional problems, and thereby forge lasting partnerships and increasingly regional (rather than national) identities. While "regionalization" may be occurring at the state-to-state multilateral level, "regionalism" is occurring at the societal level.[64]

Some of these processes are the manifestation of globalization, as Nayan Chanda's chapter illustrates, while others result from breaking down barriers among Asian governments—permitting Asian societies to develop their own natural linkages. It would be interesting to have data on cross-national marriages within Asia, but one has the impression that they are rising. Certainly labor migration across national boundaries is accelerating. It is commonplace to find Chinese, Filipino, and Thai laborers and service sector workers throughout the region today (Chanda's chapter cites the figure of eight million Southeast Asians working outside their home countries in 2005). Certainly, much of this labor mobility is illegal, and some is linked to organized crime, the sex trade, and triads.

Non-Traditional Security

Another strong indicator of intraregional linkages is the plethora of "non-traditional security" (NTS) challenges that know no national borders and now span the region.[65] While Ralph Cossa's chapter in this volume appropriately focuses on the "hard security" dimensions, Asian security is increasingly comprised of "soft security" issues.

The NTS menu in Asia is as complex as the region itself. It includes a prolific list of existing and potential threats: proliferation of weapons of mass destruction (WMD) and toxic agents; pandemics and the spread of infectious diseases (e.g., SARS, HIV/AIDS, avian flu); internal and illegal cross-border migration; trafficking in illegal drugs and legal pharmaceuticals; various forms of human security, including kidnapping and trafficking in women (for prostitution and forced marriage) and children; financial contagion and economic insecurity; environmental degradation (including acid rain, air pollution, haze, toxic spills, etc.); terrorism of all kinds; Islamic fundamentalism; natural disasters (earthquakes, tsunamis); arms smuggling; sea piracy; ethnic separatism and communal conflicts; armed militias and insurgencies; religious and millenarian movements (like Falun Gong); poverty and social inequality; energy security; disputes over water resources (e.g., Mekong, Ganges); illegal fishing; organized crime; cyber crime; and so on.

This is a rich menu of potentially serious challenges. What they all have in common is the fact that they ignore national borders and thus require (a) a recognition that state sovereignty is not immutable, and (b) collective action by both national states and local authorities is required to effectively deal with the issues. *Internal issues become external issues.* The following areas have attracted priority attention among NTS specialists in Asia.

Environment

Environmental threats have risen to the top of the NTS regional security agenda in recent years.[66] Acid rain emanating from Chinese factories contaminates the air and threatens lives on the Korea Peninsula, in Japan and Hong Kong, and as far away as British Columbia and California. Despite the 2002 ASEAN Transboundary Haze Pollution Agreement, more than six thousand smoldering fires (2006) in Indonesia continue to spread haze through the air of Indonesia, Singapore, Malaysia, even western Australia, and threaten the lives of people there.[67] Upstream toxic contamination from China (Guangxi and Guangdong) pollutes the downstream Mekong basin in Vietnam and Laos,[68] while heavily polluted rivers and the water table in northern China poison people and make irrigation unusable. Chinese cities are blanketed by air pollution (seven of the world's eleven most air-polluted cities are in China), while cities in India and Southeast Asia also suffer from dangerous levels of air pollution.

While of a different nature, environmental security also includes natural disasters such as tsunamis, typhoons, cyclones, and earthquakes. South and Southeast Asia have suffered more than their share of these recently. The devastating 2004 Christmas tsunami in the Indian Ocean and Andaman Sea, the earthquake that struck northern Pakistan in 2005, and the 2008 earthquake in Sichuan, China were of unprecedented magnitude. China also remains prone to severe flooding every year.

Terrorism and Armed Insurgencies

Islamic terrorists based in Indonesia linked to Jemaah Islamiyah (JI), Islamic Defenders Front (FPI), and al Qaeda have bombed several targets in Bali and central Java—they threaten not only Indonesia but neighboring countries as well. JI operatives have been arrested in Malaysia, Singapore, Thailand, and Australia.[69] Senior al Qaeda operatives have also been arrested in the Philippines and Singapore, prior to executing major attacks. The Philippines has also been the home and victim of the Abu Sayyaf terrorist organization, which has killed about 150 in bombings on ferries and in markets near Manila and has been preempted prior to bombing shopping malls and the U.S. Embassy. Pakistan continues to harbor a variety of terrorist groups within its borders, particularly in the tribal areas along the Afghan frontier. India has also experienced unprecedented attacks (allegedly emanating from Pakistan) in central Delhi, the Punjab, and Kashmir. China has also fallen victim to Islamic terrorists, linked to the East Turkestan Islamic Movement (ETIM) and East Turkestan Liberation Organization (ETLO). There have also been links to al Qaeda, evidenced by the fourteen Uighurs picked up after 9/11 in Afghanistan. The terrorist problem in Xinjiang is linked to pan-regional networks across Central Asia and the Caucasus—which the Shanghai Cooperation Organisation has managed to collectively confront. In this regard (counterterrorism) the SCO seems more effective than its East Asian counterparts.

The Muslim insurgency in southern Thailand has caused six hundred violent incidents and killed two thousand people since 2004.[70] The festering Maoist insurgencies in the southern Philippines and Nepal have resulted in the collapse of local government in the former and national government in the latter. Several ethnic insurgencies fester in northern Myanmar, while Sri Lanka continues to suffer from the prolonged Tamil insurgency.

Public Health and Pandemics

Pandemics in Asia are not a new phenomenon. The region has experienced outbreaks of malaria, tuberculosis, cholera, smallpox, meningitis, encephalitis, influenza, and various air- and waterborne diseases for many years. More recently and of a larger threat, HIV/AIDS, SARS, avian flu (H5N1), and hand, foot, and mouth disease (HFMD) have spread through East and Southeast Asia. Regional governments and ASEAN have worked effectively together to control the spread of these potential pandemics to date.

Transnational Crime

Asia is hardly immune to organized and transnational crime.[71] This takes a variety of forms: money laundering; loan sharking, extortion, racketeering; drug manufacturing, smuggling, and trafficking; small arms smuggling; luxury car theft and smuggling; kidnapping and human smuggling; sex trade networks; gambling; trafficking in ivory and other endangered species; gang violence; pirating and distribution of software, CDs, DVDs, bank robberies; piracy on the high seas; and so on. No country in Asia is immune from these phenomena—although Japan, China, Macao, Taiwan, and Thailand are the worst affected.[72] Chinese triads and tongs and Japanese *yakuza* are legendary and continue to dominate the organized crime scene in Asia, but new transnational networks have also sprung up in Northeast and Southeast Asia.

As a consequence, transnational cooperation among law enforcement is more critical than ever. ASEAN, often working together with American, Japanese, and Chinese law enforcement and intelligence agencies, has spearheaded efforts at regional cooperation.[73] In some cases—particularly piracy on the high seas—regional militaries, coast guards, and navies play an important role.[74]

Many of the region's non-traditional security challenges cluster into these four categories. To be sure, not all are adequately captured. Various forms of human security, for example, are probably best not dealt with as a transnational crime problem. WMD proliferation is a peculiar challenge requiring responses at a combination of levels—national, sub-national, regional, global. The same applies to financial and economic security issues. Energy security policy is really the domain of national governments, although private companies do the exploration, extraction, and delivery. Poverty and inequality are fodder for many other NTS challenges—including human security, migration, and organized crime—and require joint attention of national and sub-national governments, regional institutions like the Asian Development Bank, and global institutions like the World Bank.

THE INTERPLAY OF THE TWO-LEVEL GAME: BUFFERING TENSIONS AND FORGING COOPERATION

From the two levels of analysis discussed in this chapter, it is evident that international relations in Asia today is a two-level phenomenon: intergovernmental and intersocietal. These are not mutually exclusive. They reinforce each other. They may be analytically distinct, but they are interactive phenomena. To be sure, governments play a vitally important role in facilitating intersocietal contact—through signing bilateral agreements as a result of diplomatic relations, which permit sectors of societies to interact with each other. In the absence of such agreements, no students could be exchanged, tourists could not travel, trade would be illicit, and so on. One need only look at isolated nations like North Korea and Myanmar to understand the drawbacks of not enjoying the normal fruits of diplomatic relations. All other nations in Asia are deeply enmeshed in the web of ties that let loose their societies on each other. This bilateral interaction is compounded significantly by the forces of globalization, as Nayan Chanda's chapter amply illustrates.[75]

One sees what they tend to look for (cognitive dissonance). While analysts and scholars traditionally tend to adopt (by design or default) a Realist prism through which to view international relations, including in the Asian region, it is equally important to examine the sub-state level. Those who work in the commercial and financial arenas pay scant attention to state actors—for them, the real "stuff" of international relations occurs electronically and in a millisecond. For intellectuals, what matter are ideas—which know no national boundaries. Other professionals ply their trades directly with each other and care little—if at all—about major power relations, security dilemmas, arms races, diplomatic summits, and so forth. In other words, there exists a huge sphere of intersocietal relations that escapes the purview of most international relations analysts (at least those wed to the Realist and Liberal traditions).

This introductory chapter has sought to "bring society back in" to the analysis of international relations in Asia. In doing so, it only scratched the surface in an illustrative way—but hopefully other scholars will undertake further work at this level of analysis. Research on national identity formation appears particularly promising.

"Bringing society back in" is not to diminish the importance of governments and interstate relations. Particularly in regions such as Asia—where both history and the present are testimony to the potential for interstate conflict—one must be cognizant of the importance of major power relations. Many of the chapters in this book dissect these interstate relationships, and they remain vital to understanding international relations in Asia in the twenty-first century. As in the previous two centuries, the potential for violent conflict still looms on the horizon. But the deep interdependence evident at the societal level can serve as a powerful buffer against potential hostilities being realized. The growth of intra-Asian multilateral groupings and institutions is a further buffer and facilitator of cooperation. While international relations in Asia have known considerable conflict, hopefully the future will be increasingly cooperative and peaceful.

NOTES

I am grateful to Dawn Murphy for her research assistance in preparing this chapter.

1. This is a slightly different use of the concept of "two-level game" from that first introduced by Robert Putnam, which assessed the interaction between domestic politics and foreign policy. See Putnam's "Diplomacy and Domestic Politics: The Logic of Two-Level Games," *International Organization* 42 (1988): 427–461.
2. Unless otherwise noted, these statistics are drawn from CIA, *The World Factbook* (2008), available at www.cia.gov/library/publications/the-world-factbook/rankorder/

(accessed January 4, 2008); and National Bureau of Asian Research (NBR), *Strategic Asia Indicators, 2007–2008,* available at strategicasia.nbr.org/Data/CView/ (accessed January 4, 2008).

3. European Commission, "Communication," in *Europe and Asia: A Strategic Framework for Enhanced Partnerships* (Brussels: Commission of the European Communities, 2001), 6.

4. European Commission, *Europe and Asia,* 6.

5. Also see Nina Hachigian and Lily Wu, *The Information Revolution in Asia* (Santa Monica, Calif.: RAND National Defense Research Institute, 2003).

6. The CDU/CSU Parliamentary Working Group (German Bundestag), *Asia as a Strategic Challenge and Opportunity for Germany and Europe* (2007), available at www.cducsu.de (accessed December 15, 2007), 9.

7. New Zealand Government, *Our Future with Asia* (Wellington: Ministry of Foreign Affairs and Trade, 2007), 15 (calculations based on IMF and Australian Treasury statistics).

8. CDU/CSU Parliamentary Working Group, *Asia as a Strategic Challenge and Opportunity,* 8.

9. IMF, *World Competitiveness Yearbook 2007,* as cited in New Zealand Government, *Our Future with Asia.*

10. Cited in Ellen L. Frost, *Asia's New Regionalism* (Boulder, Colo.: Lynne Rienner, 2008), 5.

11. European Commission, *Europe and Asia,* 6.

12. All figures are from the IISS, *The Military Balance 2007* (London: Routledge, 2007); and NBR, *Strategic Asia, 2007–2008.*

13. SIPRI calculates that in 2006 Asian defense spending amounted to $185 billion while European defense spending totaled $310 billion. See *SIPRI Yearbook* (2007), available at www.sipri.org/contents/milap/milex/mex_wnr_table.html (accessed January 5, 2008).

14. See Ashley J. Tellis and Michael Wills, eds., *Strategic Asia, 2005–2006: Military Modernization in an Era of Uncertainty* (Seattle, Wash.: National Bureau of Asian Research, 2006).

15. See IISS, *The Military Balance 2007,* 412; *SIPRI Yearbook* (2007), available at www.sipri.org/contents/armstrad/output_examples.html (accessed January 5, 2008).

16. The "levels of analysis" schema was first put forward by J. David Singer, "The Levels of Analysis Problem in International Relations," in *The International System: Theoretical Essays,* ed. Klaus Knorr and Sidney Verba (Princeton, N.J.: Princeton University Press, 1961), 77–92.

17. See Wang Gungwu, "The Fourth Rise of China: Cultural Implications," *China: An International Journal* 2, no. 2 (September 2004): 311–322.

18. See the discussion of this system in Muthiah Alagappa, "International Politics in Asia: The Historical Context," in *Asian Security Practice: Material and Ideational Influences,* ed. Muthiah Alagappa (Stanford, Calif.: Stanford University Press, 1998), 71–75.

19. For an illuminating discussion of the concept and typology of "order" in international relations, see Muthiah Alagappa, "The Study of International Order: An Analytic Framework," in *Asian Security Order: Instrumental and Normative Features,* ed. Muthiah Alagappa (Stanford, Calif.: Stanford University Press, 2003), 33–69.

20. See G. John Ikenberry and Michael Mastanduno, eds., *International Relations Theory and the Asia-Pacific* (New York: Columbia University Press, 2003).

21. Muthiah Alagappa, "Constructing Security Order in Asia: Conceptions and Issues," in *Asian Security Order: Instrumental and Normative Features*, ed. Muthiah Alagappa (Stanford, Calif.: Stanford University Press, 2003), 72–78.

22. Aaron Friedberg, "Ripe for Rivalry," *International Security* 18, no. 3 (Winter 1993/1994): 5–33.

23. David Kang, *China Rising: Peace, Power, and Order in East Asia* (New York: Columbia University Press, 2007); David Kang, "Getting Asia Wrong: The Need for New Analytic Frameworks," *International Security* 27, no. 4 (Spring 2003): 57–85.

24. David Shambaugh, "China Engages Asia: Reshaping the Regional Order," *International Security* 29, no. 3 (Winter 2004/2005): 64–99.

25. Evan Medeiros, "Strategic Hedging and the Future of Asia-Pacific Stability," *Washington Quarterly* 29, no. 1 (Winter 2005/2006): 145–167.

26. See Robert Sutter's chapter in this volume, and his *China's Rise: Implications for US Leadership in Asia*, Policy Studies 21 (Washington, D.C.: East-West Center Washington, 2006). Also see Daniel Twining, "America's Grand Design in Asia," *Washington Quarterly* 30, no. 3 (2006): 79–94; Thomas Christensen, "Fostering Stability or Creating a Monster? The Rise of China and US Policy toward East Asia," *International Security* 31, no. 1 (Summer 2006): 81–126.

27. Robert Kagan, "The Illusion of 'Managing' China," *Washington Post*, May 15, 2005.

28. See Kagan, "The Illusion"; and John Mearscheimer, "Clash of the Titans," *Foreign Policy* 146 (January–February 2005); John Mearscheimer, "China's Unpeaceful Rise," *Current History* 105, no. 690 (April 2006): 160–162; John Mearscheimer, *The Tragedy of Great Power Politics* (New York: Norton, 2001), concluding chapter.

29. See Amitav Acharya, "How Ideas Spread: Whose Norms Matter? Norm Localization and Institutional Change in Asian Regionalism," *International Organization* 58 (Spring 2004): 239–275; Amitav Acharya, *Constructing a Security Community in Southeast Asia: ASEAN and the Problem of Regional Order* (London: Routledge, 2001); Amitav Acharya, "Will Asia's Past Be Its Future?" *International Security* 28, no. 3 (Winter 2003/2004): 149–164; Amitav Acharya, "Regional Institutions and Asian Security Order: Norms, Power, and Prospects for Peaceful Change," in *Asian Security Order: Instrumental and Normative Features*, ed. Muthiah Alagappa (Stanford, Calif.: Stanford University Press, 2003), 210–240.

30. Alagappa, "International Politics in Asia: The Historical Context," 111.

31. Peter Hopkirk, *The Great Game: The Struggle for Empire in Central Asia* (London: Kodansha Globe, 1994).

32. See, for example, Jonathan D. Pollack, ed., *Asia Eyes America: Regional Perspectives on U.S. Asia-Pacific Strategy in the Twenty-first Century* (Newport, R.I.: Naval War College Press, 2007); Kishore Mahbubani, "Wake Up Washington: The U.S. Risks Losing Asia," *Global Asia* 2, no. 2 (Fall 2007): 16–23; Yoichi Funabashi, "Power of Ideas: The U.S. Is Losing Its Edge," *Global Asia* 2, no. 2 (Fall 2007): 38–42.

33. See, for example, Morton Abramowitz and Stephen Bosworth, *Chasing the Sun: Rethinking East Asian Policy* (New York: Century Foundation Press, 2006).

34. See Victor Cha, "Winning Asia: Washington's Untold Success Story," *Foreign Affairs* 86, no. 6 (November–December 2007); Robert Sutter, "United States: Leadership Maintained amid Continuing Challenges," in *Strategic Asia: 2004–2005: Confronting Terrorism in the Pursuit of Power*, ed. Ashley Tellis and Michael Wills (Seattle, Wash.: National Bureau of Asian Research, 2004).

35. Cha, "Winning Asia."

36. Robert S. Ross, "The Geography of the Peace: East Asia in the 21st Century," *International Security* 23, no. 4 (Spring 1999): 81–118.

37. On the "Grand Bargain," see Michel Oksenberg and Charles E. Morrison, "East Asian Security and the International System," in *East Asia and the International System*, coordinated by Charles E. Morrison, Trilateral Commission Task Force Report 55 (New York: Trilateral Commission, 2001), particularly 37–40.

38. Aaron Friedberg provides a very useful overview of the debate and "schools" in "The Future of U.S.-China Relations: Is Conflict Inevitable?" *International Security* 30, no. 2 (Fall 2005): 7–45.

39. David M. Lampton, "China's Rise in Asia Need Not Be at America's Expense," in *Power Shift: China and Asia's New Dynamics*, ed. David Shambaugh (Berkeley: University of California Press, 2005), 306–328; David Shambaugh, "Sino-American Relations since September 11th: Can the New Stability Last?" in *China: Contemporary Political, Economic, and International Affairs*, ed. David B. H. Denoon (New York: New York University Press, 2007).

40. Thomas C. Christensen, "China, the U.S.-Japan Alliance, and the Security Dilemma," *International Security* 23, no. 4 (Spring 1999): 49–80.

41. Evelyn Goh, *Meeting the China Challenge: The U.S. in Southeast Asian Regional Security Strategies*, Policy Studies 16 (Washington, D.C.: East-West Center Washington, 2005).

42. Evelyn Goh, "Great Powers and Hierarchical Order in Southeast Asia: Analyzing Regional Security Strategies," *International Security* 32, no. 3 (Winter 2007/2008): 113–157.

43. Also see Bates Gill, *Rising Star: China's New Security Diplomacy* (Washington, D.C.: Brookings Institution Press, 2007); Robert Sutter, *China's Rise in Asia: Promises and Perils* (Lanham, Md.: Rowman & Littlefield, 2005); Joshua Kurlantzick, *Charm Offensive: How China's Soft Power Is Transforming the World* (New Haven, Conn.: Yale University Press, 2007); Shambaugh, "China Engages Asia," 64–99; David Shambaugh, "China's New Diplomacy in Asia," *Foreign Service Journal* 82, no. 5 (May 2005): 30–38; Evan Medeiros and M. Taylor Fravel, "China's New Diplomacy," *Foreign Affairs* 82, no. 6 (2003): 22–35.

44. Mike M. Mochizuki, "China-Japan Relations: Downward Spiral or a New Equilibrium?" in *Power Shift: China and Asia's New Dynamics*, ed. David Shambaugh (Berkeley: University of California Press, 2005), 135–150; Mike M. Mochizuki, "Dealing with a Rising China," in *Japan in International Politics: The Foreign Policies of an Adaptive State*, ed. Thomas U. Berger, Mike M. Mochizuki, and Jitsuo Tsuchiyama (Boulder, Colo.: Lynne Rienner, 2007), 229–255.

45. Kenneth B. Pyle, *Japan Rising: The Resurgence of Japanese Power and Purpose* (New York: Public Affairs, 2007), 339.

46. See "Joint Communiqués on the Results of the Trilateral Meeting of the Foreign Ministers of India, Russia, and China," February 14, 2007, and October 24, 2007, available at meaindia.nic.in/ (accessed January 15, 2008).

47. Also see Richard Weitz, "Averting a New Great Game in Central Asia," *Washington Quarterly* 29, no. 3 (Summer 2006): 155–167.

48. "Top-Level Communications Are Key to Managing Challenges in U.S.-Asia Pacific Ties: U.S. Asia Pacific Council Interview with Ambassador J. Stapleton Roy," *East-West Center Washington Report* 1 (January 2008): 4.

49. Aaron Friedberg, "Ripe for Rivalry: Prospects for Peace in a Multipolar Asia," *International Security* 18, no. 3 (Winter 1993/1994): 5–33.

50. See David Shambaugh, "The Rise of China and Asia's New Dynamics," in *Power Shift: China and Asia's New Dynamics*, ed. David Shambaugh (Berkeley: University of California Press, 2005), 14–15.

51. See Oksenberg and Morrison, "East Asian Security and the International System."

52. See, for example, Frost, *Asia's New Regionalism*; Ralph Cossa and Akihiko Tanaka, eds., *An East Asian Community and the United States* (Washington, D.C.: Center for Strategic and International Studies, 2007); Naoko Munakata, *Transforming East Asia: The Evolution of Regional Economic Integration* (Tokyo and Washington, D.C.: Research Institute of Economy, Trade, and Industry, and Brookings Institution Press, 2006); Gi-Wook Shin and Daniel C. Sneider, eds., *Cross Currents: Regionalism and Nationalism in Northeast Asia* (Stanford, Calif.: Walter H. Shorenstein Asia-Pacific Research Center, 2007); Edward J. Lincoln, *East Asian Economic Regionalism* (New York and Washington, D.C.: Council on Foreign Relations and Brookings Institution Press, 2004).

53. See Cossa and Tanaka, eds., *An East Asian Community and the United States.*

54. Derived from table 1 ("Trade Intensity in Asia") in Ashley Tellis, "Trade, Interdependence, and Security in Asia," in *Strategic Asia, 2006–2007: Trade, Interdependence, and Security*, ed. Ashley Tellis and Michael Wills (Seattle, Wash.: National Bureau on Asian Research, 2007), 13.

55. See Trade and Investment Division, United Nations Economic and Social Commission for Asia and the Pacific (ESCAP), *Toward Coherent Policy Frameworks: Understanding Trade and Investment Linkages*, Studies in Trade and Investment 62 (Bangkok: ESCAP, 2007), table 2.

56. See ASEAN Secretariat, *2004–2005 ASEAN Annual Report*, available at www .aseansec.org/ar05.htm, 67 (accessed January 17, 2008).

57. Trade and Tourism Division, ESCAP, *Study on the Role of Tourism in Socio-Economic Development* (Bangkok: ESCAP, 2007), 12.

58. Trade and Tourism Division, *Study on the Role of Tourism*, 10.

59. Trade and Tourism Division, *Study on the Role of Tourism*, based on UNWTO, *Tourism Highlights 2006*, 15.

60. Kyna Rubin, "Where the Students Are in East Asia," *International Educator* 16, no. 4 (July/August 2007): 28.

61. As cited in Kishore Mahbubani, *The New Asian Hemisphere: The Irresistible Shift of Global Power to the East* (New York: Public Affairs, 2008), 64.

62. Bruce Stokes, "China's High-Tech Challenge," *National Journal*, July 30, 2005, 2454.

63. Department of Policy Planning, Ministry of Foreign Affairs, People's Republic of China, *China's Foreign Affairs 2006* (Beijing: World Affairs, 2007), 749–755.

64. For a good discussion of this distinction, see Frost, *Asia's New Regionalism*, 6–17.

65. This section is adapted from my paper presented at the Second Berlin Conference on Asian Security, German Institute of International and Security Affairs (SWP), 2007. See David Shambaugh, "Internal-External Linkages in Asia Security: The Non-Traditional Security Agenda," available at www.swp-berlin.org/de/common/get_document.php?asset_id=4481.

66. See In-Taek Hyun and Miranda A. Schreurs, eds., *The Environmental Dimension of Asian Security: Conflict and Cooperation over Energy, Resources, and Pollution* (Washington, D.C.: U.S. Institute of Peace Press, 2006).

67. See Sofiah Jamil, "Clearing up ASEAN's Hazy Relations," *NTS-Asia*, no. 2 (November–December 2006): 1–3.

68. See Evelyn Goh, *Developing the Mekong: Regionalism and Regional Security in China–Southeast Asian Relations*, Adelphi Paper 387 (London: IISS, 2007).

69. See Council on Foreign Relations, "Terrorism Havens: Indonesia," www.cfr.org/publication/9361/ (accessed October 3, 2007).

70. Seth Mydans, "Muslim Insurgency Stokes Fear in Southern Thailand," www.iht.com/articles/2007/02/25/news/thailand.php (accessed October 7, 2007).

71. See James O. Finckenauer and Ko-lin Chin, "Asian Transnational Organized Crime and Its Impact on the United States" (final report submitted to the National Institute of Justice, 2004), available at www.ncjrs.gov/pdffiles1/nij/grants/213310.pdf (accessed October 12, 2007).

72. Finckenauer and Chin, "Asian Transnational Organized Crime," 22–24.

73. See Un Sovannasam, *The Association of Southeast Asian Nation's (ASEAN) Efforts in Dealing with Transnational Crime* (Hong Kong: University of Hong Kong Center for Asian Studies, 2005).

74. See Martin Murphy, *Contemporary Piracy and Maritime Security in the Straits of Malacca* (Hong Kong: University of Hong Kong Center for Asian Studies, n.d.).

75. Also see Samuel S. Kim, ed., *East Asia and Globalization* (Lanham, Md.: Rowman & Littlefield, 2000).

II

LEGACIES AND THEORIES

2

The Evolving Asian System

Three Transformations

Samuel S. Kim

Does history repeat itself in Asia? Will the future of Asia resemble the past? Asia's or Europe's past? In the post–Cold War years, this question of both theoretical and real-world significance has been debated among scholars and policy pundits of diverse normative and theoretical orientations, only to generate many competing prognostications. For analytical purposes in this historical chapter, only two "back to the future" images are worth noting as points of departure.

First is a dominant Realist "back to the future of Europe's past" school. The concern for relative power gains at the unit level (i.e., the rise of China) and the destabilizing political dynamics associated with power transitions led Aaron Friedberg and other pessimistic Realists in the 1990s to make dire "back to the future" predictions that Asia was primed for the revival of a classical great-power rivalry as Europe experienced over the past several centuries. In short, Asia's future is considered ready-made to repeat Europe's war-prone past.[1]

Second is a Sinocentric "back to the future of Asia's past" school. Applying the "clash of civilizations" theory—Asia *qua* Asia exceptionalism—to the "rise of China" debates, Samuel Huntington argues that Asian countries will be more likely to bandwagon with China than to balance against it. Both European-type hegemonic wars and a European-style balance-of-power system have been absent from Asia. Instead, for two thousand years before the arrival of the Western powers in the mid-nineteenth century, "East Asian international relations were Sinocentric with other societies arranged in varying degrees of subordination to, cooperation with, or autonomy from Beijing."[2] Asia's Sinocentric past, not Europe's multipolar past, concludes Huntington, "will be Asia's future," even as "China is re-suming its place as regional hegemon."[3]

In a similar exceptionalist vein, David Kang argues that Asian international relations have historically been hierarchic, more peaceful, and more stable than those in the West owing to the region's historical acceptance of a hierar-chical world order with China at its core.[4] Kang makes a sweeping assertion that the Asian international system from 1300 to 1900 was both intensive and extensive as well as stable and hierarchic, thus posing a major challenge to the argument that balance of power is a universal phenomenon across time and region. Indeed, Kang claims that "accommodation of China [bandwago-ning] was the norm in East Asia during the Ming (1368–1644) and Qing (1644–1911) eras."[5] Accordingly, Asia's Sinocentric hierarchical past, not Eu-rope's multipolar past, would guide and ensure its future stability.

Asian history may provide a baseline for a comparative diachronic analy-sis and assessment of the changes and continuities in the evolution of the "Asian" system in modern times. What follows is neither a full history nor an argument in support of historical or cultural determinism, but only a broad synopsis of some salient and system-transforming events in the his-tory of the region.

In pursuit of this line of inquiry, this chapter provides an historical overview of the "Asian" international system as it evolved and mutated through three systemic transformations from the early nineteenth century to the end of the Cold War. The first of four sections critically appraises the main features of the Chinese tribute system as well as its progressive unraveling from the Opium War of 1839–1842 to the Sino-Japanese War of 1894–1895. The second section examines the rise and fall of the Japanese imperial system from the end of the Sino-Japanese War in 1895 to the end of World War II (Pacific War) in 1945. The third section examines the rise and demise of the Cold War system (1947–1989). The fourth and concluding section looks at the impacts and implications of these three systemic transformations for the future of Asian international relations in the post–Cold War world.

The delimited geographical scope of this chapter, defining "Asia" as mainly including East Asia but not South Asia, calls for explanation.[6] Be-cause of its size and central location, China physically dominates Asia, im-pinging on all of Asia's sub-regions with borders adjoining more countries than any other nation-state in the world. Asia is and becomes Sinocentric not only in geographical terms but also in systemic terms. Moreover, the rise of China is often conflated with the rise of East Asia, where China consti-tutes some 70 percent of the region.[7] In terms of the level and intensity of interstate interaction, which is the key marker of an international regional system, the waxing and waning of Chinese power has always been one of the defining characteristics of all "Asian" systems. Although historically there were two distinct interstate systems in Asia—the Sinic system in East

Asia and the Indic system in South Asia[8]—the Indic system is excluded because it withered away with the advent of British rule during the periods of the Chinese tribute system and the Japanese imperial system. Even during the period of the Cold War system, India as a founding father of the Non-Aligned Movement (NAM) remained mostly outside the bifurcated Cold War system. Before World War II "Southeast Asia" had no particularly defined regional identity and had been known by a number of different names (e.g., "further India," "Indochina," "Little China," or "the Far Eastern tropics"). It was Japan's invasion and occupation in the early 1940s that gave rise to the term "Southeast Asia."[9]

TRANSFORMATION I: THE CHINESE TRIBUTE SYSTEM

The image of world order in traditional China seems to bear out the sociological maxim that people and nations react not to the objective reality of the world but to their image of that reality. In theory, if not always in practice, the traditional Chinese image of world order remained tenaciously resistant to change. It was the Chinese officials' image of what the world was like, not what it was actually like, that determined their response to international situations. The strength and persistence of this image were revealed most dramatically during the first half of the nineteenth century, when China was faced with a clear and continuing threat from the imperialist West.

What is so striking about the traditional Chinese image of world order—at least the high Qing scholar-gentry class—is the extent to which it was colored by the assumptions, beliefs, sentiments, and symbols of their self-image.[10] Indeed, world order was no more than a corollary to the Chinese internal order and thus an extended projection of the idealized self-image. As John Fairbank reminds us, even during the golden era of the Sinocentric world order "China's external order was so closely related to her internal order that one could not long survive without the other."[11] In other words, even imperial China with all its pretensions of normative self-sufficiency could not really live in isolation; it needed outside barbarians in order to enact and validate the integrity of its identity/difference.

The chief concern of China's traditional foreign policy centered upon the means of making diplomatic practice conform to that idealized self-image. At times, the desire to preserve the purity of self-image led to a distortion of the official record so as to square deviant practice with idealized theory.[12] The absence of any rival civilization also became a major factor in the development of the Chinese image of world order, and natural geographical barriers exerted considerable influence. China is guarded on the west by almost endless deserts, on the southwest by the Himalayan range, and on the east by vast oceans. Admired but often attacked by the "barbarians" of the semiarid plateau lands on the north and west, and cut off from the other centers of civilization by oceans, deserts, and mountains, China gradually developed a unique sense of its place under heaven.

What is even more striking, if not all that surprising, is the absence of a nationalistic dynamic in the enactment of identity; for judging by the contemporary usage, the Chinese identity as mobilized in specific response to the Western challenge was more civilizational than national. As in days of yore, such civilizational identity was presumed to reproduce itself in expanding concentric circles as the correct cosmic order. Hence we find in traditional China a conspicuous absence of any institution corresponding to a ministry of foreign affairs in the West. Relying on documentary and behavioral referents of Qing diplomacy in the nineteenth century, Immanuel C. Y. Hsü flatly declared, "Doubtless, imperial China was not a nation-state."[13]

What have been the real-world operational consequences of the Sinocentric hierarchical image of world order? Although there is no Chinese term, "tribute system" has been used by Western Sinologists to designate the sum total of complex institutional expressions of the hierarchical Chinese world order. The tribute system served a vital symbolic and political "imperial title-awarding function"—that is, as investiture of a king in each tributary state in order to assure Chinese suzerainty and supremacy—by legitimizing the myth of the Middle Kingdom as the universal state governed by the Son of Heaven. What are conspicuously absent here are the Westphalian principles of state sovereignty and state equality as the foundational principles of modern international law.[14]

The tribute system worked relatively well for centuries, reaching its height of classical refinement in the Ming (1368–1664) and Qing (1644–1911) dynasties. Its longevity may have been due to its ability to foster mutually complementary interests on the part of the tribute receiver and the tribute bearer.[15] Morris Rossabi, among others, has argued that the Chinese institution had a long tradition of interaction with Inner Asian states on equal footing in pre-Qing times, especially when the dynasties were weak or disintegrating, and that at such times China became more flexible and pragmatic, accepting others as equals.[16]

For others, the tribute system proved to be useful in establishing and maintaining their own political legitimacy at home. Korea, which had served as a model tributary state longer than any other, is a case in point. The Sino-Korean tributary relationship was more political than economic. The Confucianized ruling classes in Korea found the tribute system not only congenial ideologically—as expressed in the Korean term *mohwa-sasang* (ideology of emulating things Chinese)—but also proved to be a *sine qua non* for establishing and maintaining political legitimacy at home, explaining its long duration: "To live outside the realm of Chinese culture was, for the Korean elite, to live as a barbarian."[17] As late as the early 1880s, few Koreans regarded their country as equal to or independent of China.[18] Although many Southeast Asian kingdoms sent tribute to China, such "tributary" relations (except in Vietnam) "did not carry the same meaning and obligations as those between China and the states in the Sinic Zone."[19]

For many, however, the tribute system was accepted as an unavoidable price to pay for the privilege of trade, and the China trade was sufficiently lucrative to justify suffering whatever humiliation might be entailed in the ritual requirements, especially the performance of the *kowtow*—nine prostrations and three kneelings—symbolizing acceptance of the hierarchical Chinese world order. In the face of the Russian challenge, the tribute system demonstrated a capacity for adjustment to the power reality. Between 1728 and 1858, the tribute system really worked by avoidance as far as the Sino-Russian relationship was concerned. A special system of communications between court officials of secondary or tertiary rank in both Saint Petersburg and Beijing (Peking) was set up to bypass the sensitive question of the czar's having to address the Son of Heaven as a superior, while Russian trade caravans to Beijing "could be entered in official Manchu court records as tribute caravans, if necessary."[20] Thus, the Chinese image of world order was preserved intact, while the Russians were allowed to pursue their commercial activities in China without direct participation in the tribute system. As these diverse examples show, so long as both parties viewed their respective interests as complementary—or at least mutually acceptable—the tribute system could continue to work.

The (first) Opium War (1839–1842) marked a momentous benchmark event in the reshaping of East Asian international relations in the nineteenth century, the beginning of the end of the tribute system. The crushing defeat of China in its first military confrontation with the West failed to modify the Sinocentric image of outlandish barbarians, but rather the British resort to force reaffirmed it. These conditions became not only the source of contradictory policy for China but also the excuse for arbitrary use of force on the part of the Western powers. Denied any intercourse with the central government and subjected to endless delays by the provincial authorities, the Western powers lost no time in using gunboats at the orders of consular officers to remedy their grievances in the treaty ports. Such was the genesis of the so-called gunboat diplomacy that characterized Western policy in China during much of this transitional or interwar period of 1842–1856.

The conviction gradually grew among Westerners that the source of all troubles was the anomalous mode of conducting diplomatic affairs at the periphery rather than at the center of the Qing government and that direct contact and communication with the court must be established as a prerequisite to normal relations. Demand for such direct contact, whether for the enhancement of trade or for diplomatic prestige, soon became universal among contemporary foreign consuls, merchants, and journalists as well as diplomatic representatives.

The ensuing Sino-Western conflicts in the interwar period of the 1840s and 1850s, which were eventually resolved by the Arrow War of 1856–1860 (the second Opium War), and the allied military expedition to Peking in 1860 highlighted the traditional Chinese image of world order on trial. China once again suffered a humiliating defeat. The reinforced Anglo-French troops launched an all-out military campaign, shooting their way to the capital, burning the Summer Palace, forcing the emperor to flee to Jehol (Chengde), and securing confirmation of all their demands with the ratification of the Tianjin Treaties (constituting the Second Treaty Settlement) and the signing of the Peking Conventions in the fall of 1860. The last fortress of the Chinese world order thus crumbled at the point of Western bayonets. The formal acceptance by China of direct diplomatic intercourse with the Western powers in 1860 marks the end of the long journey China was forced to take, departing from the tribute system at first with resistance and finally with great reluctance. The tribute system continued vestigially until 1894 with Korea but was really destroyed beyond repair in 1860.

Faced with the twin dangers of the internal disorder created by the Taiping Rebellion (1850–1864) and the external menace posed by the West, a recurrence of the traditional *bête noire* (*neiluan waihuan*) of dynastic survival, China began a concerted campaign to put its own house in order under the so-called Self-Strengthening (*ziqiang*) Movement in the 1860s. Protected for the time being by the Cooperative Policy of the Western treaty powers under the sympathetic leadership of the American and British resident ministers, Anson Burlingame and Sir Frederick Bruce,[21] the Qing court was encouraged to initiate a series of self-strengthening reform measures at its own pace and on its own terms. As a result, some important reforms were adopted in the diplomatic, fiscal, educational, and military fields with the help of an increasing number of Western experts.

In the end, however, the Self-Strengthening Movement failed because the requirements for an effective response to Western encroachment ran counter to the requirements of preserving the Confucian internal order.[22] The ideological disruption created by Western imperialism required a revolutionary response, but the self-strengthening reformers were no more than "realistic" conservatives who wanted to borrow Western science and technology—especially "strong warships and efficient guns"—to preserve the Confucian order. All the successive reform measures in economic, administrative, and constitutional matters during the last quarter of the nineteenth century also failed because what China needed was a system transformation not only in institutions but, more importantly, in ideology. Such an ideological transformation did not come about until China was thoroughly humiliated by an Asian neighbor in the Sino-Japanese War of 1894–1895. The vestigial influence of the traditional Chinese image of world order was finally shattered beyond recall.

The net effect of all the concessions extracted by the treaty powers amounted to an "unequal treaty system," which China was unable to change until 1943. It is ironic, then, that China's struggle to preserve its hierarchical system of world order as expressed in the tribute system should have ended with acceptance of the unequal treaty system imposed by the West.

China's response to the West should not be viewed within the framework of the international system. The Sino-Western confrontation was no less than a system-to-system conflict between two diametrically opposed images of world order. The Second Treaty Settlement represented the subordination of the traditional Chinese world order and the tribute system into the Eurocentric system of international relations.

TRANSFORMATION II: THE JAPANESE IMPERIAL SYSTEM

Paradoxically, the rise of Japan in the last quarter of the nineteenth century seems in no small measure due to the Western penetration and dominance of Asia during this century of colonialism and imperialism. Indeed, the nineteenth-century history of Asian international relations can be summed up in terms of three critical geopolitical transformations. First, with the rise of the West, and particularly Great Britain as the dominant hegemonic power, resulting in all the South and Southeast Asian kingdoms and states (except Nepal and Thailand) falling under European colonial rule, the subordination of Asia within the Eurocentric world system was complete by the end of the nineteenth century. Second, China lost its long-standing position as the dominant regional power due to the progressive decaying of the empire, the discrediting and demise of the tribute system, and the gradual disintegration of the state together with the division of coastal Chinese territory into "spheres of influence" among Western and Japanese colonial powers. The nineteenth century began with China still the most dominant regional power—but ended with China as semi-sovereign, or as a "hypo-colony."[23] Third, a rising Japan replaced China as the dominant regional power, starting to expand by fits and starts its own Japancentric imperial domain, the prologue to the "Greater East Asian Co-Prosperity Sphere" as a way of countering Western imperialism.[24]

Symbolically and strategically, the Opium War has come to represent the most significant system-transforming point in the history of Asian international relations. For China it commences a period of transition and marks the transition from the pre-modern to the modern era. For Great Britain it marks the rise as the dominant power in East Asia and in the Indian Ocean.

And for Japan it is the beginning of a momentous ideational change in the Japanese images of China from admiration to contempt, with all the concomitant geostrategic implications for the Meiji Restoration in the second half of the nineteenth century.

In opening Japan to the West, the United States took the initiative in showcasing its version of gunboat diplomacy. By the early 1850s, a combination of interests, power, and ideology had led the United States to expand its presence into the Asia-Pacific. Against this backdrop, Commodore Matthew Perry arrived at Edo Bay with menacing "black ships" in 1853 to carry out his mission to open Japan by diplomacy if possible or with gunboat cannon if necessary. By succumbing to Perry's demands and by signing the Treaty of Kanagawa in 1854 and the United States–Japan Treaty of Amity and Commerce of 1858, Japan's two-hundred-year policy of seclusion came to an end, paving the way for the rise of the Meiji Restoration (1868–1912). The provision of a most-favored-nation clause in Article IX of the Treaty of Kanagawa was most significant for the creation of an unequal system as the Europeans came, one after another, adding extra-territoriality and opening additional ports.[25]

Aided and abetted by the arrival of the Western warships, diplomats, and merchants, the Meiji Restoration served as the chief catalyst and the final blow for the demise of the 265-year feudalistic Tokuga *shogunate*. The success of the Meiji Restoration, unlike China's Self-Strengthening Movement, is evident in the time it took Tokyo to abolish the unequal treaty system: only half as long as Beijing. In 1899 Tokyo had won revision of the unequal treaties, ending the extra-territorial privileges Westerners had enjoyed in Japan.

In the last quarter of the nineteenth century, Meiji Japan's domestic reform and external expansionist policy developed in tandem, following the logic, "If you can't beat them, join them and beat them by their own rules." Japan's immediate challenge was to seek an equal status, with imperialism and domination as later goals that came to be viewed as essential to sustaining its great-power status. Korea provided the most proximate and logical geopolitical point of departure for seeking first equality and then hegemony in greater East Asia. Through the Tokugawa period that preceded the Meiji Restoration, Korea's relations with Japan proceeded with little Chinese involvement. In contrast to the *sadae chui* (serving the great) tributary relationship that traditional (Chosun) Korea had with China, foreign relations with Japan were defined as *kyorin* (neighborly relations). The Korean king and the Japanese shogun treated each other as equals and dealt with each other through the medium of Tsushima, an island between Japan and Korea.[26]

This began to change with the coming of the Meiji Restoration and Japan's opening to the West. Although Japan continued to maintain the same type of relations with Korea, using Tsushima as an intermediary, national opinion regarding Korea became more interested and expansionist, with some intellectuals claiming a traditional tributary role for Korea vis-à-vis Japan. And watching Russian and British interest in Tsushima and various parts of coastal China grow, Japan knew that if it was going to take a dominant role on the Korea Peninsula it would have to hold off Western powers who wanted to stake their own claims there.

In 1871 Japan and China signed the first East Asian treaty based on Western international law. With the door open, Japan also began revising its relations with Korea, first ending the tradition of conducting relations through Tsushima. Following its 1874 expedition in southern Taiwan, a clear challenge to China and a warning to Korea, Japan began taking bold actions in Korea that led quickly to the Treaty of Kanghwa in February 1876.[27] The treaty declared Korea an "autonomous state," terminating traditional relations between Japan and Korea in favor of Westernized relations, and interaction increased markedly.[28] As if to seek equality with the British and American gunboat diplomacy in earlier years, it now became Japan's turn to open the Hermit Kingdom.

These interactions, however, were far from universally positive. A mutiny with an anti-Japanese character led to Japan demanding indemnity, while two years later the Japanese were on the other side of the fence, involved in an attempted coup by Korean progressives. China responded to the coup with military force, and Japan, at the end of the event, again demanded reparations from Korea.[29] The Tonghak Rebellion of 1894 served as the proximate catalyst for the Sino-Japanese War. During the war, the Japanese occupied the royal palace in Seoul, remodeling the Korean government and instituting detailed reform measures that covered almost all aspects of Korean life.[30]

Japan's victory in the first Sino-Japanese War (1894–1895)—the first shot of the Japanese imperial system—resulted not only in China's loss of Korea as the last tributary state but also in the transfer of Taiwan (Formosa), the Pescadores islands, and the Liaodong Peninsula in Manchuria to Japan. And yet it triggered a new round of survival-of-the-fittest competition among Western powers, at the expense of Japan as well as China. Despite its victory in the war, Japan's imperial ambitions and acquisitions were somewhat scaled back when France, Germany, and Russia demanded that Japan return to China both Port Arthur and the Liaodong Peninsula. Japan complied, only to see the Western powers reap the fruits of their victory through the scramble for exclusive spheres of influence over Chinese territory.

Thus the stage was set for another war, this time with a European or Eurasian continental power. Japan's stunning victory in the Russo-Japanese War of 1904–1905, the first military victory by an Asian country over a European power, was a benchmark event for the successful enactment of Japanese national identity as a great power. The Treaty of Portsmouth (1905), brokered by Theodore Roosevelt, gave Japan control over the Liaodong Peninsula, Port Arthur, the southern half of Sakhalin Island, the southern part of the railway built by the Russians in Manchuria, and, most important of all, a free hand in Korea, which Japan formally annexed as a colony five years later. Korea, the "dagger to the heart of Japan," was thus transformed into a springboard to further expansion in China and a major source of cheap food with which to support Japan's rapidly increasing industrial population.[31]

By and large, the twenty-five years after the Russo-Japanese War may be viewed as a consolidation phase. Korea increased in importance to Japan as the essential path to its newly acquired sphere of interest in southern Manchuria. The Russians had conceded Japanese hegemony, and the British posed no challenge. The secret 1905 Taft-Katsura Agreement brought about Washington's acceptance of Tokyo's hegemony over the Korea Peninsula in return for Tokyo's acceptance of American hegemony over the Philippines as well as an expression of support for the Anglo-Japanese alliance. Having obtained support from the United States and Britain, Japan vigorously pursued protectorate status over Korea, achieving in a November 1905 treaty "control and direction of the external relations of Korea" and the stationing of a resident-general in Seoul to manage diplomatic affairs.[32] Within two years, Russia and Japan reached an agreement that would allow for Japan's official annexation of Korea.[33] Opposition to Japanese rule was squelched with brutal efficiency, and the economic and strategic needs of the Japanese home islands, rather than the interests of the Korean population, dictated the course of Korean economic and social development.

These gains were increased further during the First World War. Having joined the war on Britain's side, Japan seized German concessions in China and German possessions in the Northern Pacific. Because of its growing dependence on U.S. and British markets for trade, Japan yielded to U.S. pressure at the 1921–1922 Washington Naval Conference to accept an unfavorable battleship ratio of 5:5:3 for the United States, Britain, and Japan, respectively. With the crash of 1929 unplugging Tokyo from its core overseas financial and commodity markets, imperialist tendencies returned with a vengeance.[34] Fearful that Manchuria was slipping from its grasp, on September 18, 1931, Japan's Kwantung army, after setting off an explosion on the Japanese-owned South Manchuria Railroad in order to allege Chinese provocation, began the military conquest of Manchuria. After consolidating their hold on Manchuria with the puppet government of Manchukuo in 1931–1932, the Japanese gradually edged into a full-scale war with China, triggering the second Sino-Japanese War in 1937. World War II had begun in Asia two years earlier than in Europe.[35]

With the coming of war in Europe in September 1939, the Japanese increasingly looked southward to exploit opportunities created by Hitler's pressures on Britain, France, and the Netherlands. Japan's defeat by Soviet and Mongolian forces near the Soviet/Mongolian border also accelerated Japan's southward expansion. In September 1940 Tokyo forced the French to allow its forces to move into Indochina. And a few days later, September 27, 1940, they concluded the Tripartite Pact—the Axis alliance—with Germany and Italy.

Having, for all practical purposes, already eclipsed Great Britain as the dominant power in East Asia, Tokyo felt confident enough to proclaim the "Greater East Asian Co-Prosperity Sphere" (GEACPS or *Dai-to-a Kyoeiken*). Although official proclamation came only in August 1940 as the policy to create a self-sufficient "bloc of Asian nations led by the Japanese and free of Western powers," its core idea of liberating Asia from Western imperialism was a strong current in Japanese thought from the Meiji period through World War II. Fukuzawa Yukichi's nationalist slogan, "to escape Asia," captured the imagination of a Westernizing Japan. Escaping from Asia meant to abandon Sinocentric Asia, whereas entering Europe was to establish Japan as a European-style great imperial power that could re-enter Asia to establish a new Japancentric world order. As Japan began to feel more secure and confident with its stunning industrial and military accomplishments in the early twentieth century, it flattered itself with the divine right to educate and civilize the rest of Asia still slumbering in the state of "barbarism." The apogee of such thinking came in the form of the GEACPS, "which was presented as a justification for Japanese military expansion in the name of liberating Asia from Western imperialism."[36]

Japan's rise to primacy among the imperial powers in East Asia came with incredible speed and vigor, transforming it from a victim of Western imperialism to a victimizer of its Asian neighbors. Its initial military success in Southeast Asia destroyed the myth of European superiority and paved the way for national independence movements in the region. On December 7, 1941, Japan took a penultimate strategic gamble in attacking the American fleet at Pearl Harbor. In the following six months Japan conquered Southeast Asia, but defeat in the naval Battle of Midway in June 1942 eliminated Japan's capacity to carry the war to the Eastern Pacific. By the summer of 1943, Japanese troubles prompted them to offer more concessions to local nationalists in the vain hope of gaining greater cooperation. In April 1945, the Japanese suffered more than three hundred thousand casualties in Southeast Asia where the British, with American and Chinese assistance, completed the destruction of Japanese forces on the mainland.[37]

World War II, along with the Japanese imperial (interregnum) system, ended in Asia three months later than in Europe, even as it had started in Asia two years earlier than in Europe. The legacies of the Japanese imperial

46   *Samuel S. Kim*

system are legion. Foremost among them for Southeast Asia was a process of decolonization set in motion by imperial Japan that proved unstoppable—an unintended boost to the liberation of Southeast Asian and South Asian countries from Western colonial rule—and the transformation of political units from kingdoms and empires into modern nation-states.[38] For Northeast Asia the historical scars and animosities still resonate strongly in post–Cold War Sino-Japanese and Korea-Japanese relations.

TRANSFORMATION III: THE COLD WAR SYSTEM

In contrast with Europe, where a bipolar Cold War system emerged and morphed into two competing but relatively stable multilateral security institutions with the establishment of NATO in 1949 and the Warsaw Pact in 1955, the Cold War in Asia encountered and developed in tandem with such turbulent transformations as national liberation movements, revolutions, civil wars, and two major international wars. While Europe enjoyed long "cold peace" with no major armed conflict, the Asian Cold War turned into hot war in Korea and Vietnam. With three of the four major Cold War fault lines—divided Germany, divided Korea, divided China, and divided Vietnam—East Asia acquired the dubious distinction of having engendered the largest number of armed conflicts resulting in higher fatalities between 1945 and 1994 than any other region or sub-region. Even in Asia, while Central and South Asia produced a regional total of 2.8 million in human fatalities, East Asia's regional total is 10.4 million including the Chinese Civil War (1 million), the Korean War (3 million), the Vietnam War (2 million), and the Pol Pot genocide in Cambodia (1–2 million).[39]

Studies on the origins of the Cold War have concentrated on the Soviet-American conflict over Europe and the Middle East, as if the Cold War in Asia were but a corollary of its lateral escalation from elsewhere or as if it were the later, unfortunate but inevitable outcome of the Chinese Civil War. Faced with the imminent fall of the Japanese empire in 1945 and with a threat of the Soviet Red Army pushing its way into the Korea Peninsula, the minds of many American policymakers had already shifted to Japan as the possible linchpin of a postwar Pax Americana in Asia.[40] By the end of 1945, a de facto Cold War in Asia had already begun as the United States and the Soviet Union viewed each other as *potential* adversaries, with enormous ramifications for the peoples and countries of Asia, including Southeast Asian states long subject to European colonial powers.[41] Inexorably, the postwar trajectories of almost all the states of East Asia, if not of South Asia, began to be keyed to superpower conflicts and rivalry.

The Cold War was under way in Asia with the declaration of the Truman Doctrine on March 12, 1947, as the ideological turning point for the United

States' global strategy and three of four major Cold War fault lines already drawn or in the process: Korea, China, and Vietnam. The Cold War system reflected three major features: a bipolar order of power, an intense ideological conflict and rivalry, and fear of nuclear war (World War III).[42] This bipolar Asia constituted a break from the two previous attempts at regional integration: the Chinese tribute system over much of the preceding millennium and the ambitious but abortive Japanese imperial system in the first half of the twentieth century.[43] Nonetheless, what really held Washington back from constructing the comprehensive Cold War alliance system in Asia had much to do with a back-to-normalcy domestic politics.

By any reckoning the Korean War (1950–1953) was the single greatest system-transforming event in the early post–World War II era, with the far-reaching catalytic effects of enacting the rules of the Cold War game as well as congealing the patterns of East-West conflict across East Asia and beyond. It was the Korean War that brought about such features of the Cold War as high military budgets (e.g., a quadrupling of U.S. defense expenditures), the proliferation of bilateral defense treaties with Japan, South Korea, Taiwan, South Vietnam, the Philippines, and Thailand—hub and spokes of the San Francisco System—and for an ill-conceived and short-lived multilateral security organization, the South East Asia Treaty Organization (SEATO) and the crystallization of East-West conflict into a rigid strategic culture dependent on a Manichean vision of stark bipolarity.[44]

Particularly significant, but not sufficiently acknowledged, is the role of the Korean War in the creation of Cold War identity for the two Koreas as well as for the Big Four of Asian international relations—the United States, the Soviet Union, China, and Japan. For both Koreas, the war experience triggered a decisive shift in identity politics from the competition of multiple identities to the dominance of the Cold War identity. The United States, too, owes to the Korean War the crystallization of its Cold War identity, which in turn gave birth to an American strategic culture that thrived on the image of global bipolarity and the omnipresent communist threat. Until the latter half of the 1980s, Soviet strategic culture was similarly anchored in and thriving on its own Cold War identity. The simplicity of a stark, bipolarized worldview provided an indispensable counterpoint for the quest for superpower identity and security in a region dominated by American hegemony. Soviet geopolitical conduct seems to make no sense except when viewed as the drive to assume a superpower role and to acquire equal status with the United States in order to compensate for its siege mentality and to legitimize its authoritarian iron hand at home.

The newly established People's Republic of China almost single-handedly rescued Kim Il Sung's regime from extinction, but at inordinate material, human, and political costs. In addition to more than 740,000 casualties[45]— including Mao's son—China missed the opportunity to "liberate" Taiwan, was excluded from the United Nations for more than two decades, and lost twenty years in its modernization drive. However, Beijing succeeded in forcing the strongest nation on earth to compromise in Korea and to accept China's representatives as equals at the bargaining table. No one in the West would ever again dismiss China's power as had General Douglas MacArthur in the fall of 1950. Indeed, the Korean War confirmed for the national self and "significant others" that China could stand up against the world's anti-socialist superpower for the integrity of its new national identity as a revolutionary socialist state.

For Japan, the Korean War turned out to be a godsend because Tokyo reaped maximum economic and political benefits. Thanks to the Korean War, Japan was converted from a defeated enemy to an indispensable regional ally in U.S. Asian strategy. The San Francisco System was designed and constructed in 1951 as the Korean War was raging, in an effort to integrate Japan into the "hub and spokes" of U.S.-led Pacific Cold War alliances through the non-vindictive San Francisco Peace Treaty (1951). The system reflected and effected the Cold War structure of international relations in Asia in general and Northeast Asia in particular.[46]

By the end of the Korean War, Tokyo had regained its sovereignty and had skillfully negotiated a new mutual security treaty that provided for U.S. protection of Japan while allowing Tokyo to escape the burden of joint defense. Without becoming involved in the bloodshed or material deprivation, Japan was able to reap the benefits of a war economy that had been imbued with new potential as a logistical base for the United States and as a key manufacturing center for war supplies.

The Cold War logic and geostrategic situation that emerged after the Korean War also allowed Japan, aided and abetted by Washington, to deflect scrutiny of its domestic politics. This resulted in the quick reintegration into Japanese politics of individuals directly implicated in the expansion of imperial Japan, the war against the United States, and wartime atrocities. Emblematic of this phenomenon was the reemergence of Kishi Nobusuke, who was the former head of the Manchurian railroad as well as minister of munitions in the Tojo government and a signatory of the 1941 declaration of war against the United States. Although he was held briefly as a Class A war criminal after the war, Kishi returned to active politics in the 1950s and became prime minister in 1957, a turn of events that would have been unthinkable in the German context. Japan's conservative leadership, who gathered together under the umbrella of the Liberal Democratic Party (LDP) after 1955, favored a narrative of the origins of the Pacific war that was largely exculpatory in nature, stressing the defensive motives behind the expansion of the empire and neglecting for the most part the issue of Japanese wartime atrocities.

The United States and its Cold War allies were determined to contain communism in Asia as in Europe, and Indochina became the next battle-field in the Cold War. French efforts to restore imperial control by insisting that Indochina was another arena in the Cold War gained credence as the containment of communism became a greater American concern than European colonialism or Asian nationalism. American assistance to the French began as early as May 1950—even before the outbreak of the Korean War on June 25, 1950—and increased substantially over the next few years. As in Korea, the Vietnam War became internationalized with growing U.S. involvement. From the United States' creeping containment in the 1940s and 1950s to the massive enlargement in money and troops in the second half of the 1960s and the final desperate attempts of the early 1970s to seek a diplomatic solution, its policies in Indochina had all ended in ashes, marking the most disastrous chapter in postwar American foreign policy as well as the beginning of the relative decline of U.S. influence in world affairs. Ironically, the United States had fought the Vietnam War ostensibly to prevent the expansion of a monolithic communist bloc, but by early 1975 (even before the North Vietnamese troops marched into Saigon), Washington was already aligning itself with Beijing to oppose the Soviets in the emergent strategic triangle.

One of the many unexpected and paradoxical consequences of the Korean War was that the Sino-Soviet alliance, formally forged on February 14, 1950, was strengthened in the short run and weakened in the long run. The irony is that the Sino-Soviet split became the unavoidable consequence of growing equality in the alliance. The widening gap between Beijing's rising demands and expectations and Moscow's inability and unwillingness to satisfy them undermined an alliance rooted in shared values and shared fears. Still, Sino-Soviet differences in 1956–1958 were confined to esoteric intrabloc communications. From mid-1958 onward, the dispute began to escalate from ideological to national security issues, reaching by early 1964 the point of no return. The Soviet invasion of Czechoslovakia in 1968, the 1969 Sino-Soviet military clashes on Zhenbaodao, and the ensuing Soviet threat to launch a preventive attack on Chinese nuclear installations refocused Beijing's and Washington's minds on strategic considerations. This transformation led China to abandon the dual-adversary policy as it sought to improve U.S.-Chinese relations in order to offset the escalating Soviet threat.

While in Europe the Cold War ended with a bang, in Asia it withered away in installments. Here again China was at the creation as well as at the gradual deconstruction. By the late 1960s, important premises and pillars of the bipolar order in Asia had already begun chipping away. With Sino-Soviet conflict escalating to military clashes and border war in 1969,

Moscow took several measures to isolate China, including the not-so-subtle hint at the possibility of a nuclear strike, the anti-China proposal for an Asian Collective Security System, and the 1971 treaty with India.[47] Meanwhile, China was seeking alignment with the United States to balance against the Soviet Union even as the United States was seeking an exit from the quagmire of the Vietnam War. Thus, the rise and fall of the strategic triangle (tripolarity) was closely keyed to the rise and decline of Soviet power relative to that of the United States.[48]

The Sino-American rapprochement in 1970–1972—also known as the "Nixon in China Shock" in much of Asia, especially in Japan—came to serve as the chief catalyst (and a force multiplier) for China's belated grand entry into the United Nations and UN Security Council as one of the five permanent members in late 1971. By 1978 bipolarity had been not so much destroyed—at least not yet—as shifted and mutated into a U.S.-Soviet-China strategic triangle. Even the Korea Peninsula as the last stronghold of the Cold War could not remain unaffected by the changing geopolitical realities in Northeast Asia: the two Koreas held the first-ever inter-Korean talks, resulting in the North-South Joint Communiqué of July 4, 1972. In addition, the Sino–South Korean rapprochement was well under way even before the end of the Cold War, paving the groundwork for diplomatic normalization in 1992.

The Cold War system worked well in the establishment and maintenance of American hegemony in the region until the beginning of the 1970s. But there were economic ramifications as well. The growing costs of maintaining a far-flung hub-and-spokes system undermined the strength of the dollar and the fiscal foundations of U.S. hegemony.[49] Japan's economic resurgence, followed by that of the newly industrializing countries, also increased American pressures for "burden sharing without power sharing." But in the end the American hegemon, just as the previous ones, could not arrest the cycle of the rise and fall of great power, as the law of imperial overextension turns today's dividends into tomorrow's debts with compound interest. For all practical purposes the Cold War was over by the late 1970s, but it would take the 1989 Sino-Soviet summit and re-normalization to deliver the final blow. "In the end," as Robert Legvold aptly put it, "the demise of the triangle, which had been a profound manifestation of the old order, became one of the profoundest manifestations of its passing."[50]

CONCLUSION

Taken together, these three system transformations lead to one obvious and somewhat paradoxical conclusion: contrary to the Eurocentric and Sinocentric "back to the future" models, there is no past that can serve as a desirable and feasible guide for the future of Asian international relations. Both the Japanese imperial system and the Cold War system reflected a sharp break from their predecessors. The emerging post–Cold War Asian system also represents a discontinuity from the three past systems tracked and analyzed in this study.

The most obvious continuity over the years has been the centrality of the Middle Kingdom, with the waxing and waning of Chinese power as the main reality and critical factor. But the traditional hierarchical Chinese world order—and the tribute system—was neither intensive nor extensive, contrary to Kang's assertion otherwise.[51] The Indic system in South Asia, even during its heyday before British rule, was largely disconnected from the Chinese tribute system, while Southeast Asia, except Vietnam, also remained largely outside of the Sinic zone, fighting its own wars among kingdoms of the region. Despite the cultural and economic interaction among the countries in the Sinic zone, there was no truly Asian international system that enveloped all Asian sub-regions and countries. In terms of interaction intensity, too, the exponential growth of international trade, finance, and investment in the post–World War II era and particularly in the post–Cold War era of globalization, along with the full integration of post-Mao China into the global economic system, has produced a level and intensity of interaction and interdependence such as the world has never known.[52]

There is no disagreement that China is at the center of both competing "back to the future" models. The more popular, Realist, Eurocentric balance-of-power model, in which the rise of China is conflated with the rise of Chinese threat, suffers from several problems. The historically derived correlation between system transition and war causation may no longer hold—Asia has not had a single interstate war in the post–Cold War era. There are many differences between ascendant China and the rise of Wilhelmine Germany. The German case illustrates how national roles can change over time. German nationalism quickly withered away after World War II, whereas previous defeats (1806 and 1918) had only fueled more aggressive nationalism. Harold James offers an explanation in the changing international milieu—the changing international normative cycle—that molded German national role expectations.[53] Indeed, what distinguishes the post–World War II international system, especially the post–Cold War Asian system, is the extent to which regional and global multilateral institutions have become integral parts of complex, increasingly interdependent, regional and global systems. In the post–Cold War era, thanks to globalization dynamics, the games that Asian nation-states play have lost much of the Realist simplicity of the struggle for power and plenty or the choice between anarchy and hierarchy.

The "back to the future" of the Sinocentric past model also fails to meet the desirability and feasibility test. First, thanks to the colonial and post-colonial (decolonization) experience, sovereignty in its full meanings has had a profound impact on the aspirations of all the newly independent Asian states. Consequently hierarchy—whether Sinocentric, Eurocentric, or Americentric—is now more difficult to reconcile with the overwhelming support of Asian states for state sovereignty, state equality, and non-interference, even as solutions that were available for the problems of the early 1800s are now much more difficult to obtain, while others, inconceivable in the heyday of the tribute system, have become more readily available.[54]

Second, China itself has shown no interest in recycling or reproducing the Sinocentric hierarchical world order redux. On the contrary, China's acceptance of state sovereignty and its associated notions in the form of the Five Principles of Peaceful Coexistence (FPPC)—(1) mutual respect for sovereignty and territorial integrity, (2) mutual non-aggression, (3) mutual non-interference of internal affairs, (4) equality and mutual benefit, and (5) peaceful coexistence—has been reaffirmed repeatedly since their official adoption in 1954. The FPPC have become globalized, providing the basic norms governing all types of state-to-state relations, East–West, North–South, South–South, and East–East. With the rise of Deng Xiaoping as the paramount leader in late 1978 came a drastic re-formulation (and relegitimation) of China's future in terms of such hitherto proscribed concepts as the open door, international interdependence, division of labor, and specialization. Even China's backwardness and stunted modernization were attributed not to Western imperialism but to China's own isolationism going back to the Ming dynasty and implicitly to its tribute system.

And third, Asia today has a vastly different set of challenges and threats and a vastly greater range of resources and solutions than those of the Sinocentric tribute system. The forces of globalization have transformed both the context and the conditions under which Asian regional geopolitics and geoeconomics can be played out. Globalization has greatly influenced not only the dynamics of power in the region and on the world stage but also the very meaning of power. The paradox of globalization is, as shown in the post-Mao Chinese case, that a country's integration into the global economy at once strengthens and constrains state power.[55]

All of this said, however, history still matters, not in the sense of recycling any historical system but in the sense of coming clean with historical scars and enmities left by the Japanese imperial system. The 1980s, as the last Cold War decade, were a turning point in bringing the historical issues back into East Asian international relations. As the Cold War world structure began to unravel, issues of national identity construction and enactment became increasingly salient. Most East Asian states, freed of the constraints imposed by the East-West conflict and increasingly wealthy and prosperous in their own right, no longer felt as dependent as they once had on Japanese support. At the same time, the third wave of democratization coming to East Asia in the 1980s created more political space where such sentiments could be voiced without fear of repression. The end of the Cold War was to establish a new world order in Asia by breaking down the extant bipolar hierarchies, but it did so with the revelation of older and deeper historical and national-identity wounds that have now become constant points of contention in Japan's relations with China and the two Koreas. In short, both Japan and its neighboring countries are now faced with the daunting challenge of changing or shifting their national identities from a Cold War to a post–Cold War footing. History does matter after all in Asian international relations.

NOTES

I wish to thank David Shambaugh and Michael Yahuda for their valuable comments and suggestions on an earlier draft of this chapter.

1. For pessimistic Realist analyses along this line with some variations, see Aaron L. Friedberg, "Ripe for Rivalry: Prospects for Peace in a Multipolar Asia," *International Security* 18, no. 3 (Winter 1993/1994): 5–33; Aaron L. Friedberg, *Europe's Past, Asia's Future?* SAIS Policy Forum Series 3 (Washington, D.C.: Paul H. Nitze School of Advanced International Studies, 1998), 1–15; Aaron L. Friedberg, "Will Europe's Past Be Asia's Future?" *Survival* 42, no. 3 (Autumn 2000): 147–159; and Barry Buzan and Gerald Segal, "Rethinking East Asian Security," *Survival* 36, no. 2 (Summer 1994): 3–21.

2. Samuel P. Huntington, *The Clash of Civilizations and the Remaking of World Order* (New York: Simon & Schuster, 1996), 234.

3. Huntington, *The Clash of Civilizations*, 238.

4. See David C. Kang, "Getting Asia Wrong: The Need for New Analytical Frameworks," *International Security* 27, no. 4 (Spring 2003): 57–85; David C. Kang, "Hierarchy in Asian International Relations, 1300–1900," *Asian Security* 1, no. 1 (January 2005): 53–79.

5. Kang, "Hierarchy in Asian International Relations," 174.

6. The idea of "Asia" is not an indigenous invention but a European one, lending itself to highly problematic and often sweeping or misleading generalizations. The notion of Asia—or the Orient (Orientalism)—was constructed by prominent European political philosophers (e.g., Charles de Montesquieu, Adam Smith, Hegel, and Marx) from the eighteenth century onward as a way of sharpening and strengthening European identity (Eurocentrism). In such a teleological image of world history, Europe was depicted as outward looking, dynamic, and progressive in us/them contrast with inward looking, stagnant, and backward Asia. See Edward W. Said, *Orientalism* (New York: Vintage Books, 1994); Wang Hui, "Reclaiming Asia

from the West: Rethinking Global History," *Japan Focus*, February 23, 2005; Gerald Segal, "'Asianism' and Asian Security," *National Interest* 42 (Winter 1995): 59.

7. See Segal, "'Asianism' and Asian Security," 60; see also Warren I. Cohen, *East Asia at the Center: Four Thousand Years of Engagement with the World* (New York: Columbia University Press, 2000); Mark T. Berger and Douglas A. Borer, eds., *The Rise of East Asia: Critical Vision of the Pacific Century* (London: Routledge, 1997); and Giovanni Arrighi, Takeshi Hamashita, and Mark Selden, eds., *The Resurgence of East Asia: 500, 150 and 50 Year Perspectives* (London: Routledge, 2003).

8. For further analysis of the Indic interstate system, see Muthiah Alagappa, "International Politics in Asia: The Historical Context," in *Asian Security Practice: Material and Ideational Influences*, ed. Muthiah Alagappa (Stanford, Calif.: Stanford University Press, 1998), 71–75.

9. Christopher Hemmer and Peter J. Katzenstein, "Why Is There No NATO in Asia? Collective Identity, Regionalism, and the Origins of Multilateralism," *International Organization* 56, no. 3 (Summer 2002): 591.

10. On the traditional Chinese world order, see John K. Fairbank, ed., *The Chinese World Order: Traditional China's Foreign Relations* (Cambridge, Mass.: Harvard University Press, 1968); and Samuel S. Kim, *China, the United Nations, and World Order* (Princeton, N.J.: Princeton University Press, 1979), 19–48.

11. John K. Fairbank, "A Preliminary Framework," in *The Chinese World Order: Traditional China's Foreign Relations*, ed. John K. Fairbank (Cambridge, Mass.: Harvard University Press, 1968), 3.

12. A classical example is the case of Lord Macartney in 1793, who was entered in the Chinese diplomatic record as having performed the *kowtow* before the Chinese emperor. In fact, Lord Macartney refused to perform that ritual. Nor did George III send tributary gifts to the emperor in 1804, contrary to a Chinese documentary assertion.

13. Immanuel C. Y. Hsü, *China's Entrance into the Family of Nations: The Diplomatic Phase, 1858–1880* (Cambridge, Mass.: Harvard University Press, 1960), 13. Lucian Pye is also known for his famous statement, "China is a civilization pretending to be a nation-state." See Lucian W. Pye, "International Relations in Asia: Culture, Nation and State," Sigur Center Asia Papers 1 (Washington, D.C.: The Sigur Center for Asian Studies, 1998), 9.

14. See Michel Oksenberg, "The Issue of Sovereignty in the Asian Historical Context," in *Problematic Sovereignty: Contest Rules and Political Possibilities*, ed. Stephen D. Krasner (New York: Columbia University Press, 2001), 83–104; Samuel S. Kim, "Sovereignty in the Chinese Image of World Order," in *Essays in Honour of Wang Tieya*, ed. Ronald St. John Macdonald (London: Martinus Nijhoff, 1994), 425–445.

15. Curiously and confusingly, the 1818 Collected Statutes of the Qing dynasty (*DaQing hui-tien*) categorized Tibet, Corea (Korea), Liu Ch'iu (Ryukyu), Cambodia, Siam, Sulu, Holland, Burma, Portugal, Italy, and England as tributary states, while Russia, Japan, Sweden, and France were listed merely as states having only commercial relations with China. See Kim, *China, The United Nations and World Order*, 24.

16. See Morris Rossabi, ed., *China among Equals* (Berkeley: University of California Press, 1983); Oksenberg, "The Issue of Sovereignty in the Asian Historical Context," 89–90.

17. Carter Eckert, *Offspring of Empire: The Koch'ang Kims and the Colonial Origins of Korean Capitalism, 1876–1945* (Seattle: University of Washington Press, 1991), 226–227.

18. Key-Huik Kim, *The Last Phase of the East Asian World Order* (Berkeley: University of California Press, 1980), 341. For further analyses of Sino-Korean tributary relations, see Chun Hae-jong, "Sino-Korean Tributary Relations in the Ch'ing Period," in *The Chinese World Order: Traditional China's Foreign Relations*, ed. John K. Fairbank (Cambridge, Mass.: Harvard University Press, 1968), 90–111.

19. Alagappa, "International Politics in Asia," 81.

20. Mark Mancall, "The Persistence of Tradition in Chinese Foreign Policy," *Annals of the American Academy of Political and Social Science* 349 (September 1963): 21.

21. For the inauguration of the Co-operative Policy and the role played by Burlingame, see Samuel S. Kim, "Burlingame and the Inauguration of the Co-operative Policy," *Modern Asian Studies* 5 (October 1971): 337–354.

22. For a comprehensive treatment of this theme, see Mary C. Wright, *The Last Stand of Chinese Conservatism: The T'ung-Chih Restoration, 1862–1874* (Stanford, Calif.: Stanford University Press, 1962).

23. Sun Yat-sen characterized China under the unequal treaty system as a "hypo-colony," which is a grade worse than a semicolony because of the multiple control and exploitation exercised by the imperial powers. Sun Yat-sen, *San Mm Chu I: The Three Principles of the People*, trans. Frank W. Price (Shanghai: Commercial Press, 1932), 39.

24. See Giovanni Arrighi, Takeshi Hamashita, and Mark Selden, "The Rise of East Asia in World Historical Perspective" (Binghamton, N.Y.: Fernand Braudel Center, State University of New York at Binghamton, 1997). Alagappa, "International Politics in Asia," 81–82.

25. Cohen, *East Asia at the Center*, 261–264.

26. On Tsushima, see Kim, *The Last Phase of the East Asian World Order*, 17–20.

27. Kim, *The Last Phase of the East Asian World Order*, 193–194, 200–203.

28. Kim, *The Last Phase of the East Asian World Order*, 253.

29. C. I. Eugene Kim and Han-Kyo Kim, *Korea and the Politics of Imperialism, 1876–1910* (Berkeley: University of California Press, 1967), 34–38, 46–54.

30. Kim and Kim, *Korea and the Politics of Imperialism*, 80–81.

31. Alvin So and Stephen W. K. Chiu, *East Asia and the World-Economy* (Newbury Park, Calif.: Sage, 1995), 91, 94; S. P. S. Ho, "Colonialism and Development: Korea, Taiwan and Kwantung," in *The Japanese Colonial Empire*, ed. R. Myers and M. Peattie (Princeton, N.J.: Princeton University Press, 1984), 340–350.

32. Kim and Kim, *Korea and the Politics of Imperialism*, 125, 131.

33. Kim and Kim, *Korea and the Politics of Imperialism*, 141–143.

34. Peter Duus, "Economic Dimensions of Meiji Imperialism: The Case of Korea, 1895–1910," in *The Japanese Colonial Empire, 1895–1945*, ed. R. H. Myers and M. R. Peattie (Princeton, N.J.: Princeton University Press, 1984), 161–162.

35. So and Chiu, *East Asia and the World-Economy*, 105–108.

36. Masaru Tamamoto, "Japan's Uncertain Role," *World Policy Journal* 8, no. 4 (Fall 1991): 583. For a more detailed analysis of Fukuzawa's influence in Meiji Japan, see Sushila Narsimhan, *Japanese Perceptions of China in the Nineteenth Century: Influence of Fukuzawa Yukichi* (New Delhi: Phoenix, 1999).

37. Cohen, *East Asia at the Center*, 358–359.

38. Alagappa, "International Politics in Asia," 86.

39. See IISS, "Armed Conflicts and Fatalities, 1945–1994" in *The Military Balance 1997/98* (London: International Institute for Strategic Studies, 1997).

40. Cohen, *East Asia at the Center,* 362.

41. See Marc S. Gallichio, *The Cold War Begins in Asia: American East Asian Policy and the Fall of the Japanese Empire* (New York: Columbia University Press, 1988).

42. Barry Buzan, "The Present as a Historic Turning Point," *Journal of Peace Research* 30, no. 4 (1995): 386–387.

43. Mark Selden, "China, Japan and the Regional Political Economy of East Asia, 1945–1995," in *Network Power: Japan and Asia,* ed. Peter J. Katzenstein and Takashi Shiraishi (Ithaca, N.Y.: Cornell University Press, 1997), 306–307.

44. See Robert Jervis, "The Impact of the Korean War on the Cold War," *Journal of Conflict Resolution* 24, no. 4 (December 1980): 563–592.

45. According to one official Chinese estimate, combat casualties were more than 360,000 (including 130,000 wounded) and non-combat casualties were more than 380,000. See Zhang Aiping, *Zhongguo renmin jiefang jun* [China's People's Liberation Army], Vol. 1, Contemporary China Series (Beijing: Dangdai Zhongguo Chubanshe, 1994), 137.

46. See Kent Calder, "U.S. Foreign Policy in Northeast Asia," in *The International Relations of Northeast Asia,* ed. Samuel S. Kim (Lanham, Md.: Rowman & Littlefield, 2004), 225–248.

47. Alagappa, "International Politics in Asia," 93–94.

48. For the rise and fall of tripolarity, see Robert S. Ross, ed., *China, the United States, and the Soviet Union: Tripolarity and Policy Making in the Cold War* (Armonk, N.Y.: M. E. Sharpe, 1993); and Lowell Dittmer, *Sino-Soviet Normalization and Its International Implications, 1945–1990* (Seattle: University of Washington Press, 1992), 147–255.

49. Selden, "China, Japan and the Regional Political Economy of East Asia," 313.

50. Robert Legvold, "Sino-Soviet Relations: The American Factor," in *China, the United States, and the Soviet Union: Tripolarity and Policy Making in the Cold War,* ed. Robert S. Ross (Armonk, N.Y.: M. E. Sharpe, 1993), 87.

51. Kang, "Hierarchy in Asian International Relations," 174.

52. Cohen, *East Asia at the Center,* 480.

53. Harold James, *A German Identity, 1770–1990* (New York: Routledge, 1989).

54. See Oksenberg, "The Issue of Sovereignty in the Asian Historical Context," 87, 91; Amitav Acharya, "Will Asia's Past Be Its Future?" *International Security* 28, no. 3 (Winter 2003/2004): 156.

55. See Samuel S. Kim, "Chinese Foreign Policy Faces Globalization Challenges," in *New Directions in the Study of China's Foreign Policy,* ed. Alastair Iain Johnston and Robert S. Ross (Stanford, Calif.: Stanford University Press, 2006), 276–306; David Shambaugh, ed., *Power Shift: China and Asia's New Dynamics* (Berkeley: University of California Press, 2005).

3

Theoretical Perspectives on International Relations in Asia

Amitav Acharya

Any discussion of theoretical perspectives on the international relations (IR) in Asia confronts the paradox that much of the available literature on the subject remains atheoretical. Whether from within and outside the region, students and analysts of Asia are largely unconvinced that theory is either necessary or useful for studying Asian international relations.[1] Although interest in it is growing in the region, particularly in China,[2] theory is seen as too abstract, or too divorced from the day-to-day concerns of governments and peoples to merit serious and sustained pursuit.

Moreover, theory is criticized by many in Asia as too "Western." Thus, even among those writers on Asian IR who are theoretically oriented, disagreement persists as to whether IR theory is relevant to studying Asia, given its origin in, and close association with, Western historical traditions, intellectual discourses, and foreign policy practices. International relations theory, like the discipline itself, has been, and remains, an "American social science," to quote Stanley Hoffman's much quoted phrase.[3]

The recent advances made by the "English School" and continental European Constructivism have not made IR theory "universal"; it might have entrenched and broadened the Western dominance. The question of how relevant IR theory is to the study of Asian security has evoked strikingly different responses. On the one hand, David Kang has seized upon the nonrealization of Realist warnings of postwar Asia being "ripe for rivalry" to critique not just Realism, but Western IR theory in general for "getting Asia wrong."[4] In analyzing Asian regionalism, Peter Katzenstein comments: "Theories based on Western, and especially West European experience, have been of little use in making sense of Asian regionalism."[5] Although Katzenstein's remarks specifically concern the study of Asian regionalism, they can be applied to Asian IR in general. And it is a view widely shared among Asian scholars. On the other side, John Ikenberry and Michael Mastanduno defend the relevance of Western theoretical frameworks in studying the international relations of Asia. While intra-Asian relationships might have had some distinctive features historically, this distinctiveness had been diluted by the progressive integration of the region into the modern international system. The international relations of Asia have acquired the behavioral norms and attributes associated with the modern interstate system that originated in Europe and still retains much of the features of the Westphalian model. Hence, the core concepts of international relations theory such as hegemony, the distribution of power, international regimes, and political identity are as relevant in the Asian context as anywhere else.[6]

To this observer, this debate is a healthy caveat, rather than a debilitating constraint, on analyzing Asian international relations with the help of an admittedly Western theoretical literature. To be sure, theoretical paradigms developed from the Western experience do not adequately capture the full range of ideas and relationships that drive international relations in Asia. But IR theories—Realism, Liberalism, Constructivism, and critical IR theories—are relevant and useful in analyzing Asian IR provided they do not encourage a selection bias in favor of those phenomena (ideas, events, trends, and relationships) that fit with them and against that which does not. IR scholars should feel free to identify and study phenomena that are either ignored or given scarce attention by these perspectives. They should also develop concepts and insights from the Asian context and experience, not just to study Asian developments and dynamics, but also other parts of the world. In other words, Western IR theory, despite its ethnocentrism, is not to be dismissed or expunged from Asian classrooms or seminars, but universalized with the infusion of Asian histories, personalities, philosophies, trajectories, and practices.

To do so, one must look beyond the contributions of those who write in an overtly theoretical fashion, explicitly employing theoretical jargon and making references to the theoretical literature of IR. A good deal of empirical or policy-relevant work may be regarded as theoretical for analytical purposes because it, like the speeches and writings of policymakers, reflects mental or social constructs that side with different paradigms of international relations.[7] To ignore these in any discussion of theory would be to miss out on a large and important dimension of the debate on, and analysis of, Asian IR. In the sections that follow, I examine three major perspectives on Asian international relations: Realism, Liberalism, and Constructivism.[8]

None of these theories are coherent, singular entities. Each contains a range of perspectives and variations, some of which overlap with those of the others, although this complexity is seldom acknowledged in academic debates. And using even these broad categories is not that simple because a good deal of writings on Asian IR are generated by area specialists, who are unlikely to pigeonhole themselves into Realist, Liberal, and Constructivist slots. So theorizing Asian IR necessarily involves generalizing from a thin conceptual base and making arbitrary judgments about who and what belongs where.

Table 3.1.   Three Perspectives on International Relations

	Realism	*Liberalism*	*Constructivism*
Main Actors	States	States, multinational corporations, international organizations	States, transnational knowledge communities, and moral entrepreneurs
Primary Goals of States	Pursuit of national interest; Power maximization (offensive Realism); Survival and security (defensive Realism)	Cooperation and coordination to achieve collective goals; World peace	Community building through interactions and shared normative frameworks
Preferred International Order	A balance-of-power system underpinned by self-help and alliances to maintain international order	A collective security system underpinned by free trade, liberal democracy, and institutions	Global and regional security communities forged through shared norms and collective identity
Primary Mode of Interaction between Units	Strategic interaction backed by causal ideas and military and economic power	Two-level (domestic and international) bargaining backed by causal ideas; Trade and other forms of functional institutionalization	Socialization through principled ideas and institutions
A Major Variation	Neo-Realism: distribution of power decides outcome	Neo-Liberal Institutionalism: international system anarchic, but institutions created by states in their self-interest do constrain anarchy	Critical Constructivism: challenges the state-centric Constructivism of Wendt

Although theories of IR are built around a set of assumptions and arguments that are broad in scope and supposed to apply to every region, in reality, theoretical debates about the international relations of regions often develop around issues and arguments peculiar to the region. Asia is no exception. Hence in discussing the three theoretical perspectives in the context of Asia, I identify and discuss those arguments and metaphors that have dominated both academic and policy debates (table 3.2).

This chapter looks primarily at international relations and regional order, rather than the foreign policy of Asian states. It is not intended as a survey of the literature on Asian international relations. Furthermore, I am interested in exploring the relationship between theoretical constructs and empirical developments in Asian international relations. Theory does not exist in a vacuum. Both at the global level and in the region, theoretical work responds to major events and changes occurring within and outside (at the global level) the region. In the last section of this chapter I make some general observations about the prospects for developing an Asian universalism in international relations theory, as a counter to both Western dominance and Asian exceptionalism. A final aspect of this chapter is that it is oriented more toward security studies than international political economy. This to some extent reflects the state of the study of Asian international relations, in which the work on security studies exceeds that on international political economy (IPE).

REALISM

Realists take the international system to be in anarchy (no authority above the state), in which states, as the main actors in international relations, are guided mainly by consideration of power and the national interest. International relations is a zero-sum game in which states are more concerned with their relative gains rather than absolute gains (how much one gains vis-à-vis another is more important than the fact that everybody may gain something). The relentless competition for power and influence makes conflict inevitable and cooperation rare and superficial; international institutions operate on the margins of great power whims and caprice. International order, never permanent, is maintained by manipulating the balance of power, with power defined primarily in economic and military terms. A later version of Realism, developed by Kenneth Waltz and called "neo-Realism," stresses the importance of the structural properties of the international system, especially the distribution of power, in shaping conflict and order, thereby downplaying the impact of human nature (emphasized by classical Realists) or domestic politics in international relations. More recently, intra-Realist debates have revealed differences between "offensive

Table 3.2. Theoretical Perspectives on Asia's International Relations

	Classical Realism (Defensive Realism)	Neo-Realism (Offensive Realism)	Liberalism and Neo-Liberal Institutionalism	Constructivism (English School)
What kept order in Asia during the Cold War	U.S. military presence	Bipolarity	Interdependence induced by rapid economic growth	Norms diffused through ASEAN
Likely impact of the end of the Cold War and the rise of China	Multipolar rivalry	Chinese expansionism	Multipolar stability due to expansion of capitalism and commerce	I. Multipolar stability through socialization of Cold War rivals (e.g., Acharya) II. Benign hierarchy (Kang)
The role and impact of regional institutions	Adjuncts to balance of power (effective only if there is a prior balance of power)	Instruments of Chinese sphere of influence	Building economic and security regimes to promote free trade and manage disputes arising from growing interdependence[a]	Norm-setting and community building through habits of dialogue and informal institutions
Asia's future will resemble:	Europe's past (late nineteenth and early twentieth centuries)—Friedberg	America's past (nineteenth century)—Mearsheimer	(no available argument)	Asia's past (pre-colonial benign hierarchy)—Kang[b]

[a] A conflict avoidance regime within a capitalist mode of development.
[b] Not all Constructivists agree with this (see, for example, Amitav Acharya, "Will Asia's Past Be Its Future?" International Security 28, no. 3 [Winter 2003–2004]).

Realists" and "defensive Realists." Offensive Realists such as Mearsheimer argue that states are power maximizers: going for "all they can get" with "hegemony as their ultimate goal." Defensive Realists, such as Robert Jervis or Jack Snyder, maintain that states are generally satisfied with the status quo if their own security is not challenged, and thus they concentrate on maintaining the balance of power.

Whether academic or policy-oriented, Realists view the balance of power as the key force shaping Asia's postwar international relations, with the United States as chief regional balancer.[9] A major proponent of this view is Lee Kuan Yew, Singapore's senior statesman. Lee ascribes not only Asian stability, but also its robust economic growth during the "miracle years," to the U.S. military presence in the region.[10] In his view, the U.S. presence and intervention in Indochina secured the region against Chinese and Soviet expansion and gave the Asian states time to develop their economies.[11] In the wake of the communist takeover of South Vietnam in 1975, Seni Pramoj, the leader of Thailand's Democrat Party, described the U.S. role as the regional balancer in somewhat different terms: "We have cock fights in Thailand, but sometimes we put a sheet of glass between the fighting cocks. They can peck at each other without hurting each other. In the cold war between Moscow and Peking, the glass between the antagonists can be Washington."[12]

Until the end of the Cold War, Realist arguments about Asian IR were closer to classical Realism, rather than the neo-Realism developed by Kenneth Waltz, which stresses the causal impact of the distribution of power. This has changed with the end of the Cold War, which spelled the end of bipolarity. Thus, a new Realist argument about Asian international relations is the view that the end of bipolarity spells disorder and even doom for the region. For neo-Realists, bipolarity is a more stable international system than multipolarity, both in terms of the durability of the system itself and the balance between conflict and order that prevails within the system.[13] The end of the Cold War would witness the "decompression" of conflicts held under check under bipolar management.[14] Hence, Realism paints a dark picture of Asia's post–Cold War order. In policy debates, the favorite Realist cliché in the initial post–Cold War years was the "power vacuum" created by superpower retrenchment, as could be foreseen from the withdrawal of Soviet naval facilities in Cam Ranh Bay, Vietnam, and the dismantling of the U.S. naval and air bases in the Philippines.

Questions about a vacuum of power inevitably beg the question of who is to fill it. Initially, Realist prognosis favored a multipolar contest featuring a rising China, a remilitarized (thanks partly to U.S. retrenchment) Japan, and India (whose potential as an emerging power was yet to be recognized). But with the persistence of China's double-digit economic growth matched by double-digit annual increases in its defense spending, it was the rise of

China that became the focal point of Realist anxieties (delight?) about Asian insecurity.

From a "power transition theory" perspective, Realists foresaw an inevitable confrontation between the status quo power (United States) and its rising power challenger (China). But paving the way for such a confrontation was the logic of offensive Realism, which sees an inevitable tendency in rising powers toward regional expansionism. John Mearsheimer likened the rise of China to that of the United States in the nineteenth century, where the aspiring hegemon went on a spree of acquiring adjacent territories and imposed a sphere of influence (Monroe Doctrine) in the wider neighborhood.[15] Expansionism occurs not because rising powers are hardwired into an expansionist mode, but because anarchy induces a concern for survival even among the most powerful actors. In other words, great powers suffer from survival anxieties no less than weak states, and it is this concern for survival that drives them toward regional hegemony. The result is the paradoxical logic of "expand to survive."

Since a balance of power is likely to be either unstable (if multipolarity emerges) or absent (if Chinese hegemony materializes), is there a role for multilateral institutions as alternative sources of stability? During the Cold War, Realists paid little attention to Asian regional institutions or dialogues, of which there were but a few: an Association of Southeast Asian Nations (ASEAN) preoccupied with the Cambodia conflict, a severely anemic South Asia Association for Regional Cooperation (SAARC), and some loose economic frameworks such as the Pacific Economic Cooperation Council (PECC). But with the end of the Cold War accompanied by a refocusing of ASEAN toward wider regional security issues and the emergence of new regional institutions such as the Asia-Pacific Economic Cooperation (1989) and the ASEAN Regional Forum (ARF, 1994), Realism came under challenge from "institutionalist" perspectives, that is, those who argued that regional norms and institutions, rather than just the balance of power system, have helped to keep the peace in Cold War Asia and would play a more important role in the region's post–Cold War order. Realists responded to this challenge by targeting Asian regional institutions. Their main preoccupation is no longer just to highlight the crucial need for a stable balance of power system, but also to expose the limitations of regional institutions.

Realists dismiss the capacity of regional institutions in Asia to act as a force for peace. For them, regional order rests on bilateralism (especially the U.S. hub-and-spoke system), rather than multilateralism. During the Cold War, Realist scholar Michael Leifer famously described Asian regional security institutions as "adjuncts" to the balance of power.[16] While institutions may be effective where great powers drive them (e.g., NATO), Asian institutions are fatally flawed because they are created and maintained by weak powers. One concession made to Asian institutions by their Realist critics is to accord them a role in smoothing the rough edges of balance of power geopolitics, an argument consistent with the English School perspective. Since weak powers are structurally incapable for maintaining order and achieving security and prosperity on their own terms and within their own means (there can be no such thing as a "regional solution to regional problems"), the best way to manage the security dilemma is to keep all the relevant great powers involved in the regional arena so that they can balance each other's influence.

Such involvement cannot be automatic, however; it has to be contrived, and this is where regional institutions play their useful role as arenas for strategic engagement. Instead of great powers creating institutions and setting their agenda, as would be normal in a Realist world, weak powers may sometimes create and employ institutions with a view to engage those powers that are crucial to equilibrium of power.[17]

But this limited role of regional institutions notwithstanding, Realists generally find Asia's international relations to be fraught with uncertainty and danger of conflict due to the absence of conditions in Asia that ensure a multipolar peace in Europe. In a famous essay, Aaron Friedberg argued that the factors that might mitigate anarchy in Europe resulting from the disappearance of bipolar stability are noticeably absent in Asia, thereby rendering the region "ripe for rivalry."[18] These mitigating factors include not only strong regional institutions like the EU, but also economic interdependence and shared democratic political systems. Some Realists, like Friedberg, have found Asian economic interdependence to be thin relative to what exists in Europe and the interdependence between Asia and the West. Others, like Buzan and Segal and Gilpin, argue that economic interdependence cannot keep peace and may even cause more strife than order.[19] Ironically, Realists have somehow found economic interdependence within Asia to be either scarce or destabilizing, or both at the same time.

In terms of its contributions, Realism can take credit for an analytical and policy consistency in highlighting the role of the balance of power in regional order. This view has been maintained both during the heydays of U.S. hegemony in the 1950s and '60s, through the course of its relative decline in the post-Vietnam years, and in the post–Cold War "unipolar moment." In China, Realism was the one Western theory of IR that broke the monopoly of Marxist-Leninist and Maoist thought. This would later pave the way for other perspectives on international relations, including Liberalism and Constructivism. Realism also gave a certain underlying conceptual coherence to a great deal of atheoretical or policy writings on Asian international relations.

During the Cold War, Realism was arguably the dominant perspective on the international relations of Asia. This was true not just of the academic realm, but also in the policy world. Although it is difficult to find evidence for the cliché that Asians are instinctively wedded to a Realist worldview and approach, Asian policymakers, with the exception of some of those who fought against colonial rule (India's Jawaharlal Nehru in particular), tended to be Realist (even Nehru claimed not to have been a "starry-eyed idealist").[20] Even in communist China, Hans Morgenthau's *Politics among Nations* enjoyed a huge popularity in classrooms, matching or exceeding the appeal of Marx or Mao. The same was true of Nehruvian India, where the indigenous idealism Gandhi and Nehru inspired scarcely formed part of IR teaching and learning.

But, more recently, Realist perspectives on Asian IR have come under attack. The predictions of Realists about Asia's post–Cold War insecurity have yet to materialize.[21] Moreover, Realism's causal emphasis on U.S. military presence as the chief factor behind Asia's stability and prosperity ignores the role of other forces, including Asian regional norms and institutions, economic growth, and domestic politics. In a similar vein, Realism's argument that the Cold War bipolarity generated regional stability can be questioned. China's preeminent Realist scholar of international relations, Yan Xuetong of Tsinghua University, argues that while Cold War bipolarity might have prevented war between the superpowers, it permitted numerous regional conflicts causing massive death and destruction:

> The history of East Asia does not support the argument that the balanced strengths between China and the United States can prevent limited conventional wars in East Asia. During the Cold War, the balance of power between the United States and the Soviet Union did prevent them from attacking each other directly in this region, but it failed to prevent wars between their allies or wars between one of them and the allies of the other, such as the Korean War in the 1950s. Hence, even if a balance of power existed between China and the United States after the Cold War, we would still not be sure it had the function of preventing limited conventional wars in this region.[22]

The Realist explanation of Asia's Cold War stability, while having the virtue of consistency, actually contradicts a key element of its foundational logic, which sees power balancing as a universal and unexceptionable law of international politics (even if Realists disagree whether it is an automatic law of nature, or has to be contrived). The notion of balance of power in Asia as understood from a Realist perspective is actually a fig leaf for U.S. primacy, or even preponderance. Hence, what should be anathema for a classical Realist[23]—the discernable absence of balancing against a hegemonic power—has acquired the status of an almost normative argument about Asian regional order in Realist writings on Asia. This contradiction cannot be explained by simply viewing the United States as a benign power, which can escape the logic of balancing. If Realism is true to one of its foundational logics, then any power (benign or otherwise) seeking hegemony should have invited a countervailing coalition. The fact that the United States has not triggered such a coalition is a puzzle that has not been adequately explained. Adding a qualifier to their causal logic (benign powers are less likely to be balanced against than malign ones) only lends itself to the charge, raised powerfully by John Vasquez, of Realism as a "degenerative" theoretical paradigm.[24]

LIBERALISM

Classical Liberalism rests on three pillars:

1. Commercial Liberalism, or the view that economic interdependence, especially free trade, reduces prospect of war by increasing its costs to the parties;
2. Republican Liberalism, or the "democratic peace" argument which assumes that Liberal democracies are more peaceful than autocracies, or at least seldom fight one another;
3. Liberal institutionalism, which focuses on the contribution of international organizations in fostering collective security, managing conflict, and promoting cooperation.

A modern variant of Liberal institutionalism is neo-Liberal institutionalism. Unlike classical Liberalism, which took a benign view of human nature, neo-Liberal institutionalism accepts the Realist premise that the international system is anarchic and that states are the primary, if not the only, actors in international relations. But it disagrees with neo-Realism's dismissal of international institutions. Neo-Liberals maintain that international institutions, broadly defined—including regimes and formal organizations—can regulate state behavior and promote cooperation by reducing transaction costs, facilitating information-sharing, preventing cheating, and providing avenues for peaceful resolution of conflicts.

While Realism as a theory of international relations is preoccupied with issues of security and order, Liberalism is more concerned with the nature and dynamics of the international political economy. Liberal perspectives on Asia's international relations are no exception. For Liberals, the foundations of the postwar international relations of Asia were laid not by the region's distinctive geography or culture, or by security threats facing the region, but rather by the post–World War II international economic system under American hegemony. The United States was central to the creation of international institutions such as the International Monetary Fund (IMF), the World Bank, and the General Agreement on Tariffs and Trade (GATT), which played a crucial role in diffusing the norms of economic Liberalism.

In Asia, the United States served as a benign hegemon providing the collective goods of security against communist expansion and free access to its vast market to Asia's early industrializers, even at a cost to itself (in terms of incurring huge deficits). The outcome was rapid economic growth in a number of Asian economies, which created a "performance legitimacy" for the region's autocratic rulers, thereby stabilizing their domestic politics. At the same time, the region witnessed a growing interdependence resulting from the pursuit of market-driven and market-friendly economic growth strategies, which furthered the prospects for regional stability and security.

Liberal conceptions of the international relations of Asia have particularly stressed the role of expanding interdependence as a force for peace.[25] The interdependence argument was advanced with ever more vigor with the end of the Cold War and the rise of Chinese economic power. Liberals, both Western and Asian (including many of them within China itself), came to view it as a crucial factor in making China's rise peaceful. Yet, the argument also invited much criticism, especially, as noted earlier, from Realists, who often take the failure of European economic interdependence to prevent the First World War as a severe indictment of the "if goods do not cross borders, soldiers will" logic. Defending against such charges, Liberals stress differences between nineteenth-century and contemporary patterns of economic interdependence. The former was based on trade and exchange, while the latter is rooted in transnational production, which is more "costly to break" and which has a deeper and more durable impact on national political and security autonomy.

The second strand of Liberalism—democratic peace theory—has found very little expression in writings on Asian IR. This need not be surprising since historically Asia has had few democracies to test the claims of this theory meaningfully. Moreover, Asia's democracies tend to be of the "illiberal variety," making it more plausible for us to speak of an "illiberal peace" in the region (especially in Southeast Asia), whereby a group of authoritarian and semi-authoritarian states avoid conflict by focusing on economic growth, performance legitimacy, and sovereignty-preserving regional institutions. Critics of democratic peace in the West, such as Jack Snyder and Ed Mansfield, have also questioned the normative claims of democratic peace by highlighting the danger of war associated with democratic transitions. In Asia, the Liberal/democratic peace argument has found more critics than adherents, but in general it has not been an important part of the debate over the region's international relations.

The neglect is as unfortunate as the criticism of democratic peace is misplaced. Contrary to a popular perception, democratic transitions in Asia have never led to interstate war and only occasionally to serious domestic instability. The case of Indonesia post-Suharto might be an exception to the latter, but didn't more people die in the transition to authoritarian rule in that country in the 1960s than from it? In South Korea, Taiwan, Cambodia, the Philippines, and Thailand, democratic transitions have not caused serious internal strife or interstate conflict. On the contrary, it might be argued that such transitions have often yielded a "cooperative peace dividend," whereby the new democratic governments have pursued cooperative strategies toward their traditional rivals. Examples include Thailand's "battlefields to marketplaces" policy in the late 1980s that helped to break the stalemate in the Cambodia conflict, Kim Dae Jung's Sunshine Policy, and Indonesia's ASEAN Security Community initiative. Pakistan's democratic breakdown under Musharraf might have led to improved prospects for peace with India, but this was induced by a strong external element, the 9/11 attacks, and the U.S.-led war on terror. Democratization fueled demands for Taiwanese independence, thereby challenging East Asian stability, but democratization has also created populist countervailing pressures on Taiwan's pro-independence governments from going over the brink in inviting a Chinese military response. At the very least, there is not much evidence from Asia to support the critics' view that democratic transitions intensify the danger of war, or even domestic strife.

The impact of the third element of the Liberal paradigm, Liberal institutionalism, on Asian IR discourses is both easier and harder to establish. On the one hand, the growth of regional institutions in Asia allows greater space to Liberal conceptions of order-building through institutions. But the Liberal understanding of how institutions come about and preserve order overlaps considerably with social Constructivist approaches. Indeed, institutionalism (the study of the role of international institutions) is no longer a purely Liberal preserve; in Asia at least, it has been appropriated by Constructivists who have both deepened and broadened the understandings of what institutions are and how they impact on Asia's international relations.

Classical Liberal institutionalism was identified with both collective security and, to a lesser extent, regional integration theory, which was closely derived from early West European integration during the 1950s and '60s. But neither type of Liberal institutionalism has had a regional application in Asia, where there have been no collective security (even if one stretches the term to include collective defense) or supranational institutions. The newest Liberal institutionalism, neo-Liberal institutionalism, narrowed the scope of investigation into institutional dynamics (how institutions affect state behavior) considerably. It shared the Realist conception of anarchy while disagreeing with Realism on the importance of institutions as agents of cooperation and change. But it gave an overly utilitarian slant to the performance of institutions. Institutions may (but not always or necessarily) induce cooperation because they can increase information flows, reduce transaction costs, and prevent cheating. But institutions are not really transformative; their end-product may be an international regime rather than a security community where the prospect of war is unthinkable. In Asia, APEC has been the one regime/institution that neo-Liberals have been most attracted to. But even there, and certainly in the case of the more ASEAN-centric institutions (e.g., ASEAN, ASEAN Regional Forum, ASEAN + 3, and East Asian Summit), Constructivism (with its stress on the culture- and identity-derived notion of the "ASEAN Way") has been a more popular mode of analysis than neo-Liberalism or classical Liberalism (collective security and regional integration).

In general then, Liberal perspectives have made little impact on the study of Asia's international relations. This need not have been, or will remain, the case. Liberalism is more notable as a causal theory of peace, just as Realism focuses on the causes of war. In a traditionally Realist-dominated field of Asian international relations, and with the region's domestic politics landscape marked by a durable (if changing) authoritarian pattern, Liberal conceptions of peace and democracy have found few adherents. But as noted above, the criticisms of Liberal notions of interdependence and democracy on the one hand and peace and stability on the other are often rooted in misplaced historical analogies and selective empirical evidence. Liberalism has a brighter future in the analysis of Asia's international relations as the region's historical (post–World War II) combination of economic nationalism, security bilateralism, and political authoritarianism unravels and gives way to a more complex picture where economic Liberalism, security multilateralism, and democratic politics acquire force as determinants of regional order and form the basis of an "Asian universalism" in IR theory.

CONSTRUCTIVISM

For Constructivists, international relations is shaped not just by material forces such as power and wealth, but also by subjective and inter-subjective factors, including ideas, norms, history, culture, and identity. Constructivism takes a sociological, rather than "strategic interaction," view of international relations. The interests and identities of states are not pre-ordained, or a given, but emerge and change through a process of mutual interactions and socialization. Conditions such as anarchy and power politics are not permanent or "organic" features of international relations, but are socially constructed. State interests and identities are in important part constituted by these social structures rather than given exogenously to the system by human nature or domestic politics. Norms, once established, have a life of their own; they create and redefine state interests and approaches. For Constructivists, international institutions exert a deep impact on the behavior of states; they not only *regulate* state behavior, but also *constitute* state identities. Through interaction and socialization, states may develop a "collective identity" that would enable them to overcome power politics and the security dilemma.

Constructivism is struggling to acquire the status of a "theory" of international relations comparable to Realism or Liberalism. Some critics view it as social theory that has no basis in IR. Constructivists are also accused of lacking middle-range theory and not pursuing serious empirical research (although this criticism would be increasingly hard to sustain as more empirical studies emerge employing a Constructivist framework); some Constructivists themselves acknowledge that like rational choice, it is more of a method than a theory per se.[26]

But Constructivism has helped to answer a number of key puzzles about Asian security order. While Constructivism is essentially a post–Cold War theory, it has been employed to explain key puzzles of Asian international relations during the Cold War period. Constructivists stress the role of collective identities in the foundation of Asia's postwar international relations. In an important contribution, Chris Hemmer and Peter Katzenstein explain the puzzle of "why there is no NATO in Asia" by examining the differing perceptions of collective identity held by U.S. policymakers in relation to Europe and Asia.[27] American policymakers in the early postwar period "saw their potential Asian allies . . . as part of an alien and, in important ways, inferior community."[28] This was in marked contrast to their perception of "their potential European allies [who were seen] as relatively equal members of a shared community." Because the United States recognized a greater sense of a transatlantic community than a transpacific one, Europe rather than Asia was seen as a more desirable arena for multilateral engagement: hence there was no Asian NATO. While this explanation stresses the collective identity of an external actor, another Constructivist perspective highlights the normative concerns of Asian actors themselves, especially Asia's nationalist leaders, who delegitimized collective defense by viewing it as a form of great power intervention through their interactions in the early postwar period, culminating in the Asia-Africa Conference in Bandung in 1955.[29]

Constructivism also explains why a different form of regionalism was possible in Asia, one that was more reflective of the normative and cultural beliefs of the Asian states and their collective identities as newly independent states seeking national and regional autonomy. This explains the origins and evolution of ASEAN, Asia's first viable regional grouping. ASEAN's establishment in 1967, Constructivists argue, cannot be explained from a Realist perspective, in the absence of a common external threat perception, or from a Liberal one, which would assume substantial interdependence among its members. Neither of these conditions marked the relationship among ASEAN's founding members at its birth. Instead, regionalism in

Southeast Asia was a product of ideational forces, such as shared norms, and socialization in search of a common identity. Shared norms, including non-intervention, equality of states, and avoidance of membership in great power military pacts were influential in shaping a deliberately weak and relatively non-institutionalized form of regionalism that came to be known as the "ASEAN Way."

Regional institutions have thus been at the core of Constructivist understanding of Asia's postwar international relations. It is through Asian institutions that Constructivists have attempted to project and test their notions about the role of ideas (for example, common and cooperative security), identity ("Asian Way," "ASEAN Way," "Asia-Pacific Way"), and socialization.[30] The influence of Constructivism is especially visible in attempts to differentiate between European and Asian regionalism, stressing the formal, legalistic, and bureaucratic nature of the former with the informal, consensual, and process-centric conception of the latter. That the European-derived criteria should not be used to judge the performance and effectiveness of Asian institutions has been a key element in Constructivist arguments about Asian regionalism.[31]

Apart from conceptualizing the distinctive nature and performance of Asian regional institutions, which are either dismissed (by Realists) or inadequately captured (by neo-Liberal or rationalist institutionalism), Constructivists have also stepped into the debate over Asia's emerging and future security order by frontally challenging the "ripe for rivalry" scenario proposed famously and controversially by Aaron Friedberg.[32] David Kang, noting that Realist scenarios such as Friedberg's have failed to materialize, calls for examining Asian security from the perspective of Asia's own history and culture. He raises the notion of a hierarchical regional system in Asia at the time of China's imperial dominance and the tributary system. Asia was peaceful when China was powerful; now with the (re-)emergence of China as a regional and global power, Asia could acquire stability through bandwagoning with China (which in his view is occurring).[33] While for Mearsheimer, Europe's "back to the future" means heightened disorder of the type that accompanied the rise of Germany in the late nineteenth century, for Kang, Asia's "back to the future" implies a return to hierarchy and stability under Chinese preeminence.

Kang's thesis presents one of the most powerful Constructivist challenges to the Realist orthodoxy in Asian IR. But his argument has been controversial, even among Constructivists,[34] who have questioned its claim about the peaceful nature of the old tributary system, whether China's neighbors are actually "bandwagoning" with China, and the structural differences between Asian regional systems during the tributary system, especially the absence of other contenders for hegemony that can now be found in the United States, Russia, Japan, and India, and the continuing importance of sovereignty to both China and its neighbors that militate against hierarchy (see Samuel Kim's chapter in this volume).

Constructivism has acquired a substantial following among not only Western but also Asian scholars on Asian IR.[35] A key factor behind this is the growing interest in the study of Asian regionalism, with the proliferation of regional institutions and dialogues in Asia in the post–Cold War period. In China, aside from regional institutions, local discourses about China's "peaceful rise" play an important role behind the emergence of Constructivism as the most popular IR theory among the younger generation academics. Constructivism has given an alternative theoretical platform to Chinese scholars wary of Realist (power transition) perspectives from the West (as well as other parts of Asia), which see the rise of China as a major threat to international stability.

Constructivism has advanced the understanding of Asia's international relations in important ways. Their focus on the role of ideational forces, such as culture, norms, and identity, enriches our understanding of the sources and determinants of Asian regional order not compared to a purely materialistic perspective. Second, Constructivists have challenged the uncritical acceptance of the balance of power system posited by Realist and neo-Realist scholars as the basis of Asian regional order by giving greater play to the possibility of change and transformation driven by socialization. Third, Constructivist writings have introduced greater theoretical diversity and opened the space for debate in the field and helped to link the insights of the traditional area studies approach to Southeast Asia to the larger domain of international relations theory.[36]

But the growing visibility of Constructivism in Asian IR has invited criticisms of the "new Constructivist orthodoxy." Despite having begun as a dissenting view, side by side with other critical perspectives on international relations, Constructivism is now bracketed as a "mainstream" perspective. This is ironic, because Constructivism is also dismissed by some as a fad, a passing fancy of a handful of intellectuals, which will fade into obscurity as the optimism generated by the end of the Cold War dissipates. Equally unconvincing are accusations leveled against Constructivism of uncritically emulating their rationalist foes, of normative determinism (too much emphasis on norms at the expense of material forces), and unreformed state-centrism (ignoring the role of civil society actors). While critics see the degree of Constructivist optimism about Asia's future to be as misconceived as Realist pessimism, in reality, Constructivist optimism has been more guarded that what the critics portray. More serious are the criticisms of Constructivism's tendency to ignore domestic politics (how domestic interactions change identity and interests) and its self-serving moral cosmopolitanism (bias toward "universal" ideas and global norm entrepreneurs at the expense of pre-existing local beliefs and local agents). These criticisms mirror complaints about Constructivism.

It is quite obvious that the line separating the three theoretical perspectives on Asian international relations have never been neat. This brings us to the question of what Katzenstein and associates have called the need for "analytic eclecticism" in the study of international relations.[37] I would add that such eclecticism is needed not just between theoretical paradigms but also within them (intra-paradigm and inter-paradigm). Prospects for Asia's future cannot be ascertained from tightly held paradigmatic frameworks, but synthesis between and within them. This chapter has suggested a considerable overlap between Liberalism and Constructivism (which in turn has significant English School foundations), especially when it comes to the study of Asian regional institutions and in countering Realist pessimism about Asia's future international order. But the Realist-favored notion of balance of power can also be seen as having its basis in normative and social foundations, as evident in notions such as "soft balancing" or "institutional balancing."

While the debate between Realist "pessimism" and Liberal/Constructivist "optimism" about the future of Asia's security order remains far from settled, recent contributions to Asian security discussions have been intra-paradigmatic (such as the Kang-Acharya debate) and even within the Realist camp, between offensive and defensive Realists (e.g., Mearsheimer and Christensen, respectively). Moreover, the debate over Asia's future security order is less about whether it will feature some type of cooperative mechanism (rather than approximating a pure Hobbesian anarchy), than which type of cooperation/accommodation (concert, community, soft balancing, hierarchy) will be feasible. And in this context, while traditional conceptions of regional order in Asia revolved around the relationship of competition and accommodation among the great powers, how the great powers relate to weaker states has become especially crucial for a region in which the weaker states drive regional cooperation and institution-building.

CONCLUSION: FROM EXCEPTIONALISM TO UNIVERSALISM

IR theory is increasingly used in the classrooms and writings on Asian IR in Japan, Korea, China, and Taiwan and to a lesser extent Southeast and South Asia. It should be noted that a good deal of "theory" that might be helpful in broadening the scope of IR remains "hidden" due to language barriers, lack of resources in Asian institutions, and the dominance of Western scholarly and policy outlets. But this is changing with the infusion of new scholarship and the broadening intellectual parameters of theoretical discourses.

As elsewhere and in other points of history, theoretical arguments and claims about Asian IR closely approximate shifts in global and regional international relations. The growing popularity of Liberalism and Constructivism in Asian IR is thus closely related to the end of the Cold War and the emergence of new regional institutions in Asia. While events drive theoretical shifts, to some extent, theories have offered rationalization of event-driven policy perspectives and approaches. Thus, Sino-U.S. tensions over Taiwan and other East Asian security issues have given a fresh impetus for Realist pessimism, while the end of the Cambodia conflict, the South China Sea Code of Conduct, and the emergence of the ARF and East Asia Summit (EAS) have given a fillip to Liberal and Constructivist optimism.

What next in the theoretical evolution of Asian IR studies? Realism retains a dominant, if no longer hegemonic, position. Realist arguments such as "power transition," "back to the future," "ripe for rivalry," and "offensive Realism" have often provided the starting point of debate over Asia's emerging and future international order. But newer approaches, especially Liberal and Constructivist perspectives, are enriching academic and policy debates on Asian IR. Realism, especially empirical Realism (i.e., academic and policy writings that reflect the philosophical assumptions of Realism without being self-consciously framed in theoretical jargon), will remain important, but so will Constructivism. While Constructivism has been criticized as a fad, it is likely to retain a central place in writings on Asian IR, because its focus on issues of culture and identity resonate well with Asian thinkers and writers. And Liberal perspectives, such as democratic peace and institutions, which have been neglected thus far, will assume greater prominence, at least insidiously.

More importantly, with the growing interest in theorizing Asia's international relations, the debate over the relevance of Western theory to analyze Asia has intensified. Perspectives that view IR theory as a fundamentally ethnocentric enterprise that does a poor job of analyzing Asian IR are becoming commonplace in Asian writings on the region's IR. And this view is shared by a number of leading Western scholars. This debate has also led to a search for an "Asian IR theory," akin to the English School or the Copenhagen School. But there is little movement in the direction of an Asian IR theory in the regional sense. This is not surprising, given Asia's subregional and national differences.[38] There is a great scope for national perspectives, even in a highly contested manner.[39] For example, some Chinese scholars are attempting to develop a Chinese School of IR, derived either from Chinese historical practices, such as the warring states period and the tributary system, or from the metaphysical Chinese worldview.[40]

An equally vocal group of Chinese scholars rejects this approach, insisting that IR theory must have a universal frame. According to this group, attempts to develop IR theory should be guided by "scientific" universalism, rather than cultural specificity.[41] Going by this immensely helpful and exciting debate, the challenge, then, is to broaden the horizons of existing IR theory by including the Asian experience, rather than either to reject IR theory or to develop a Chinese or Asian School that will better capture and explain China's or Asia's unique historical experience, but have little relevance elsewhere, even though such universalism would still require deeper investigations into Asian history.

There is thus a growing space for an Asian universalism in IR theory. I use the term "Asian universalism" since it is in direct juxtaposition to the Asian exceptionalism found in the extreme form in the notion of Asian values, Asian conception of human rights, Asian democracy, or in a more moderate strain in claims about an Asian form of capitalism, or an Asian mode of globalization. Asian exceptionalism, especially in its extreme form, refers to the tendency to view Asia as a unique and relatively homogenous entity that rejects ideas, such as human rights and democracy, which lay a claim to universality, but which are in reality constructed and exported by the West. Such ideas are to be contested because of their lack of fit with local cultural, historical, and political realities in Asia. Asian universalism by contrast refers to the fit, often constructed by local idea entrepreneurs, between external and Asian ideas and practices with a view to give a wider dissemination to the latter. This involves the simultaneous reconstruction of outside ideas in accordance with local beliefs and practices and the transmission and diffusion of the preexisting and localized forms of knowledge beyond the region. Whereas Asian exceptionalism is relevant only in analyzing and explaining local patterns of IR, Asian universalism would use local knowledge to understand and explain both local and foreign IR.

The impetus for Asian universalism comes from several sources. The first is a historical shift from economic nationalism, security bilateralism, and authoritarian politics in the postwar period to economic interdependence, security multilateralism, and democratic politics of the post–Cold War era. This shift is far from linear, but it is occurring and having a substantial impact on studies of Asian IR. And this need not be seen as a purely or mainly Liberal trend, as it would be mediated by local historical, cultural, and ideational frameworks that have their roots in local conceptions of power politics, utilitarianism, and normative transformation. This shift challenges the distinction between Asian and universal knowledge claims and expands the scope for grafting outside theoretical concepts onto Asian local discourses.

The region also abounds in historical forms of local knowledge with a universal reach. Examples include the ideas of Asian thinkers such as Rabindranath Tagore's critique of nationalism, Nehru's neutralism and nonalignment, and Gandhi's *satyagraha*.[42] There are many Japanese writings that were developed either in association with, or in reaction against, Western concepts of nationalism, internationalism, and international order.[43] Although some of these Indian and Japanese contributions were either critiques of Western ideas (like nationalism) or were borrowed forms of Western ideas (such as Gandhi's borrowing of passive resistance), they were sufficiently infused with a local content to be deemed a form of local knowledge. Moreover, the outcome of this interaction between Western and Asian ideas was "constitutive" in the sense that it redefined both the Western ideas and the local identities. And while the localization of Western ideas might have been originally intended for domestic or regional audiences, the resulting concepts and practices did possess a wider conceptual frame to have relevance beyond Asia. Such ideas deserve a place alongside existing theories of IR. Historical patterns of interstate and intercivilizational relations in Asia, including the tributary system, also have their place, if they can be conceptualized in a manner that would extend their analytical utility and normative purpose (present in any theory) beyond China or East Asia.[44]

Asian practices of international relations are another rich source of Asian universalism in IR theory.[45] Asian regionalism, which manages the balance of power and expands the potential for a regional community, also provides a good potential avenue for such universalism. Instead of drawing a sharp distinction between what is European and what is Asian, theoretical perspectives on Asian regionalism should explore commonalities that are quite substantial and would constitute the core of a universal corpus of knowledge about regionalism in world politics.[46]

While the *distinctive* aspects of Asia's history, ideas, and approaches will condition the way Western theoretical ideas are understood and make their impact, elements of the former will find their way into a wider arena influencing global discourses about international order in the twenty-first century. The challenge for theoretical writings on Asian IR is to reflect on and conceptualize this dynamic, whereby scholars do not stop at *testing* Western concepts and theories in the Asian context, but *generalize from the latter* in order to enrich an hitherto Western-centric IR theory.[47]

NOTES

I wish to thank Muthiah Alagappa, David Shambaugh, and Michael Yahuda for their helpful suggestions for this chapter.

1. In this chapter, I use the term "theory" broadly, focusing on grand theories that have paradigmatic status, such as Realism, Liberalism, and Constructivism. The term "theory" has many different meanings. The American understanding of theory tends

to have a social-scientific bias, whereby the general assumptions of a theory must be translated into causal propositions that can be rigorously tested and yield some measure of prediction. Europeans view theory more loosely as any attempt to systematically organize data, structure questions, and establish a coherent and rigorous set of interrelated concepts and categories. Writings on Asian IR remain atheoretical in either sense, but more so in terms of the American understanding than the European one. For further discussion, see Amitav Acharya and Barry Buzan, "Why Is There No Non-Western IR Theory: An Introduction," *International Relations of the Asia-Pacific* 7 (October 2007): 287–312. The special issue also explores the reasons for the lack of interest in theory in the Asian IR literature, one of the main factors being the dominance of area specialists in the field.

2. In a recent visit to China, the author found widespread evidence of the major growth of interest in theory among Chinese scholars of international relations. This is true not only of universities such as Beijing, Tsinghua, and Fudan, but also think tanks such as the Institute of World Economics and Politics of the Chinese Academy of Social Sciences, which publishes the leading IR journal of China: *World Economics and Politics*. It is published in Chinese. Tsinghua University's Institute of International Studies has launched an English-language journal published by Oxford University Press, entitled *Chinese Journal of International Relations*.

3. Stanley Hoffmann, "An American Social Science: International Relations," *Daedalus* 106, no. 3 (1977): 41–60; Ole Wæver, "The Sociology of a Not So International Discipline: American and European Developments in International Relations," *International Organization* 52, no. 4 (1998): 687–727; Robert A. Crawford and Darryl S. L. Jarvis, eds., *International Relations—Still an American Social Science? Toward Diversity in International Thought* (Albany: State University of New York Press, 2000).

4. David C. Kang, "Getting Asia Wrong: The Need for New Analytical Frameworks," *International Security* 27, no. 4 (Spring 2003): 57–85.

5. Peter J. Katzenstein, "Introduction: Asian Regionalism in Comparative Perspective," in *Network Power: Japan and Asia*, ed. Peter J. Katzenstein and Takashi Shiraishi (Ithaca, N.Y.: Cornell University Press, 1997), 5.

6. G. John Ikenberry and Michael Mastanduno, "The United States and Stability in East Asia," in *International Relations Theory and the Asia-Pacific*, ed. G. John Ikenberry and Michael Mastanduno (New York: Columbia University Press, 2003), 421–422.

7. Stephen M. Walt, "International Relations: One World, Many Theories," *Foreign Policy* 110 (Spring 1998): 29–46.

8. This leaves out critical IR theories, such as Marxism, post-modern/post-structural, post-colonial, and feminist perspectives. Some argue that critical theories have been concerned mostly with critiquing their "mainstream" rivals, especially Realism and Liberalism, and have made little attempt to offer an alternative conception or trajectory of regional order. But the insights of critical perspectives are especially crucial in understanding and analyzing the impact of globalization on Asian IR, the limitations and abuses of sovereign state-system and the national security paradigm, and Asia's uneven and unjust development trajectory. An important recent book applying critical theories of IR to Asia is Anthony Burke and Mat Macdonald, eds., *Critical Asia-Pacific Security* (Manchester: Manchester University Press, 2007). Critical

IR theory includes, among others, post-modernism, post-structuralism, Marxism/ neo-Marxism, Gramscian approaches, feminism, and post-colonialism, often in some combination (e.g., post-colonial feminism).

9. For two well-known perspectives, see Paul Dibb, *Towards a New Balance of Power in Asia*, Adelphi Paper 295 (London: International Institute for Strategic Studies, 1995); Michael Leifer, *The ASEAN Regional Forum*, Adelphi Paper 302 (London: International Institute for Strategic Studies, 1996).

10. Lee has repeatedly asserted his faith in the balance of power, a typical example being his comments in Canberra in 2007 that "the golden strand [in Australia-Singapore relations] is our common strategic view that the present strategic balance in the Asia-Pacific, with the U.S. as the preeminent power, provides stability and security that enables all to develop and grow in peace." "S'pore and Australia Share Common Strategic View: MM," *Straits Times*, March 29, 2007, app.mfa.gov.sg/pr/read_content .asp?View,6860 (accessed January 25, 2008). "MM" refers to "Minister Mentor."

11. For a theoretical discussion of Lee's views, see Amitav Acharya and See Seng Tan, "Betwixt Balance and Community: America, ASEAN, and the Security of Southeast Asia," *International Relations of the Asia-Pacific* 5, no. 2 (2005). For a recent restatement of Lee's position, see "Excerpts from an Interview with Lee Kuan Yew," *International Herald Tribune*, August 29, 2007, www.iht.com/articles/2007/08/29/asia/ lee-excerpts.php?page=1 (accessed September 23, 2007).

12. "Toward a New Balance of Power," *Time*, September 22, 1975, www.time .com/time/magazine/article/0,9171,917875,00.html (accessed September 23, 2007).

13. Kenneth N. Waltz, "The Stability of the Bipolar World," *Daedalus* 93 (Summer 1964): 907; Kenneth N. Waltz, *Theory of International Politics* (Reading, Mass.: Addison-Wesley, 1979), 171; John Mearsheimer, "Back to the Future: Instability in Europe after the Cold War," *International Security* 15, no. 1 (Summer 1990): 5–55. A contrary view that stresses the stabilizing potential of multipolarity is Karl W. Deutsch and J. David Singer, "Multipolar Power Systems and International Stability," *World Politics* 16, no. 3 (April 1964): 390–406.

14. For a discussion and rebuttal of this view in the context of the Third World, see Amitav Acharya, "Beyond Anarchy: Third World Instability and International Order after the Cold War," in *International Relations Theory and the Third World*, ed. Stephanie Neumann (New York: St. Martin's Press, 1997), 159–211.

15. John J. Mearsheimer, *The Tragedy of Great Power Politics* (New York: W. W. Norton, 2001), 41.

16. Leifer, *The ASEAN Regional Forum*, 53–54. For a critique of Leifer's view, see Amitav Acharya, "Do Norms and Identity Matter? Community and Power in Southeast Asia's Regional Order," *Pacific Review* 18, no. 1 (March 2005): 95–118.

17. This shows that Realism is not a homogenous theory as its critics sometimes portray and that important differences exist among Realists insofar as the nature and purpose of international institutions are concerned. It also shows a disjuncture between disciplinary neo-Realist theory and Realist perspectives on Asian institutions. Mearsheimer, a neo-Realist (but not an Asian specialist), viewed international institutions as pawns in the hands of great powers. John J. Mearsheimer, "The False Promise of International Institutions," *International Security* 19, no. 3 (Winter 1994–1995): 5–49. Michael Leifer took a more nuanced view. While institutions

were not able to take care of the fundamental security of nations, great power intervention in Asia was not inevitable, but only occurred when there was a conjunction between great power interests and disputes between or within ASEAN states. Institutions could play a role in the management of regional order if regional actors purposively used institutions to engage different great powers so that none acquired overriding influence. For example, following the end of the Cold War, Leifer saw the ARF as the means for locking China into a network of constraining multilateral arrangements that would in turn "serve the purpose of the balance of power by means other than alliance." See Michael Leifer, "The Truth about the Balance of Power," in *The Evolving Pacific Power Structure*, ed. Derek DaCunha (Singapore: Institute of Southeast Asian Studies, 1996), 51. I am grateful to Michael Yahuda for pointing to this aspect of Leifer's writings. This acceptance that multilateral arrangements can be "constraining" has much in common with institutionalist scholars like Keohane and Martin. Robert O. Keohane and Lisa Martin, "The Promise of Institutionalist Theory," *International Security* 20, no. 1 (1995): 42; Ralf Emmers, *Cooperative Security and the Balance of Power in ASEAN and ARF* (London and New York: RoutledgeCurzon, 2003).

18. Aaron Friedberg, "Ripe for Rivalry: Prospects for Peace in a Multipolar Asia," *International Security* 18, no. 3 (Winter 1993/1994): 5–33; Aaron L. Friedberg, *Europe's Past, Asia's Future?* SAIS Policy Forum Series 3 (Washington, D.C.: Paul H. Nitze School of Advanced International Studies, 1998).

19. Barry Buzan and Gerald Segal, "Rethinking East Asian Security," *Survival* 36, no. 2 (Summer 1994): 3–21; Robert Gilpin, "Sources of American-Japanese Economic Conflict," in *International Relations Theory and the Asia-Pacific*, ed. G. John Ikenberry and Michael Mastanduno (New York: Columbia University Press, 2003), 299–322.

20. See Amitav Acharya, "Why Is There No NATO in Asia? The Normative Origins of Asian Multilateralism," Working Paper 05-05 (Cambridge, Mass.: Weatherhead Center for International Affairs, Harvard University, 2005).

21. Muthiah Alagappa, "Introduction," in *Asian Security Order: Normative and Instrumental Features*, ed. Muthiah Alagappa (Stanford, Calif.: Stanford University Press, 2003).

22. Xuetong Yan, "Decade of Peace in East Asia," *East Asia: An International Quarterly* 20, no. 4 (Winter 2003): 31. This view sets limits to Realist optimism found in Robert Ross's "The Geography of the Peace: East Asia in the Twenty-First Century," *International Security* 23, no. 4 (Spring 1999): 81–118. Ross argues that a geopolitical balance between the United States as the dominant maritime power and China as the leading continental power would preserve stability in post–Cold War East Asia.

23. Although not for Gilpin and others who would attribute international stability to the role of a hegemonic power and consider the absence of balancing against such a power as an indicator of stability. Robert Gilpin, *War and Change in World Politics* (New York: Cambridge University Press, 1981).

24. John Vasquez, "Realism and the Study of Peace and War," in *Realism and Institutionalism in International Studies*, ed. Michael Breecher and Frank P. Harvey (Ann Arbor: University of Michigan Press, 2002), 79–94; John Vasquez and Collin Elman, eds., *Realism and the Balancing of Power: A New Debate* (Upper Saddle River, N.J.: Prentice Hall, 2003).

25. Ming Wan, "Economic Interdependence and Economic Cooperation," in *Asian Security Order: Normative and Instrumental Features,* ed. Muthiah Alagappa (Stanford, Calif.: Stanford University Press, 2003); Benjamin E. Goldsmith, "A Liberal Peace in Asia?" *Journal of Peace Research* 44, no. 1 (2007): 5–27. Goldsmith finds weak empirical support for the pacific effects of democracy and international institutions, but evidence for the pacific effects of interdependence is "robust." For further Asian case studies, see Ashley J. Tellis and Michael Wills, eds., *Strategic Asia, 2006–07: Trade, Interdependence, and Security* (Seattle, Wash.: National Bureau of Asia Research, 2006).

26. Jeffrey Checkel, "The Constructivist Turn in International Relations Theory," *World Politics* 50, no. 2 (January 1998): 324–348.

27. Christopher Hemmer and Peter J. Katzenstein, "Why Is There No NATO in Asia? Collective Identity, Regionalism, and the Origins of Multilateralism," *International Organization* 56, no. 3 (Summer 2002): 575–607. They reject not only the power disparity explanation, but also neo-Liberal explanations that would see alliance design as a function of differing calculations about what would be the most efficient institutional response to the threat at hand. Europe and Asia differed in this respect: the threat in Europe was a massive cross-border Soviet invasion, while the threat in Asia was insurgency and internal conflict. For other explanations (Realist, Liberal, and mixed) of this puzzle see Donald Crone, "Does Hegemony Matter? The Reorganization of the Pacific Political Economy," *World Politics* 45, no. 4 (July 1993): 501–525; John S. Duffield, "Why Is There No APTO? Why Is There No OSCAP: Asia Pacific Security Institutions in Comparative Perspective," *Contemporary Security Policy* 22, no. 2 (August 2001): 69–95; Galia Press-Barnathan, *Organizing the World: The United States and Regional Cooperation in Asia and Europe* (New York: Routledge, 2003).

28. Hemmer and Katzenstein, "Why Is There No NATO in Asia?" 575.

29. Acharya, "Why Is There No NATO in Asia?"

30. Amitav Acharya, "Ideas, Identity and Institution-Building: From the 'ASEAN Way' to the 'Asia-Pacific Way'?" *Pacific Review* 10, no. 3 (1997): 319–346. Amitav Acharya, "How Ideas Spread: Whose Norms Matter? Norm Localization and Institutional Change in Asian Regionalism," *International Organization* 58, no. 2 (Spring 2004): 239–275; Tobias Ingo Nischalke, "Insights from ASEAN's Foreign Policy Cooperation: The 'ASEAN Way,' a Real Spirit or a Phantom?" *Contemporary Southeast Asia* 22, no. 1 (April 2000): 89–112; Jürgen Haacke, *ASEAN's Diplomatic and Security Culture: Origins, Developments and Prospects* (London: RoutledgeCurzon, 2003); Nikolas Busse, "Constructivism and Southeast Asian Security," *Pacific Review* 12, no. 1 (1999): 39–60; Kamarulzaman Askandar, "ASEAN and Conflict Management: The Formative Years of 1967–1976," *Pacifica Review* (Melbourne) 6, no. 2 (1994): 57–69; Amitav Acharya, "Regional Institutions and Asian Security Order: Norms, Power and Prospects for Peaceful Change," in *Asian Security Order: Instrumental and Normative Features,* ed. Muthiah Alagappa (Stanford, Calif.: Stanford University Press, 2003), 210–240.

31. Katzenstein, "Introduction: Asian Regionalism in Comparative Perspective"; Amitav Acharya and Alastair Iain Johnston, eds., *Crafting Cooperation: Regional International Institutions in Comparative Perspective* (Cambridge: Cambridge University Press, 2007).

32. Thomas C. Berger, "Set for Stability? Prospects for Conflict and Cooperation in East Asia," *Review of International Studies* 26, no. 3 (July 2000): 405–428; Thomas C. Berger, "Power and Purpose in Pacific East Asia: A Constructivist Interpretation," in *International Relations Theory and the Asia-Pacific*, ed. G. John Ikenberry and Michael Mastanduno (New York: Columbia University Press, 2003), 387–420.

33. Kang, "Getting Asia Wrong"; David Kang, *China Rising: Peace, Power and Order in East Asia* (New York: Columbia University Press, 2007).

34. Acharya, "Will Asia's Past Be Its Future?" These criticisms from Constructivist scholars suggest that the latter are not a homogenous orthodoxy as some critics allege.

35. In the words of a Malaysian scholar, "Thinking in the constructivist vein has been about the best gift made available to scholars and leaders in the region." See Azhari Karim, "ASEAN: Association to Community: Constructed in the Image of Malaysia's Global Diplomacy," in *Malaysia's Foreign Policy: Continuity and Change*, ed. Abdul Razak Baginda (Singapore: Marshal Cavendish Editions, 2007), 113.

36. Acharya, "Do Norms and Identity Matter?"; Amitav Acharya and Richard Stubbs,"Theorising Southeast Asian Relations: An Introduction," in "Theorising Southeast Asian Relations: Emerging Debates," ed. Acharya and Stubbs, special issue, *Pacific Review* 19, no. 2 (June 2006): 125–134.

37. Peter J. Katzenstein and Rudra Sil, "Rethinking Asian Security: A Case for Analytical Eclecticism," in *Rethinking Security in East Asia: Identity, Power and Efficiency*, ed. J. J. Suh, Peter J. Katzenstein, and Allen Carlson (Stanford, Calif.: Stanford University Press, 2004), 1–33.

38. Acharya and Buzan, "Why Is There No Non-Western IR Theory: An Introduction."

39. Amitav Acharya and Barry Buzan, "Conclusion: On the Possibility of a Non-Western IR Theory in Asia," in "Why Is There No Non-Western IR Theory: Reflections On and From Asia," 427–428.

40. Qin Yaqing, "Why Is There No Chinese International Relations Theory?" in "Why Is There No Non-Western IR Theory?" 313–340.

41. Interviews with Chinese scholars: Tang Shiping, formerly of the Chinese Academy of Social Sciences, September 8, 2007; Qin Yaqing, vice president of China Foreign Affairs University; Yan Xuetong, director of Institute of International Relations at Tsinghua University; Chu Sulong, director of the Institute of Security Studies at Tsinghua University; and Wang Zhengyi, professor of International Political Economy, Beijing University, all during September 10–13, 2007.

42. For a review of Indian ideas that might be of theoretical significance, see Navnita Chadha Behera, "Re-Imagining IR in India," in "Why Is There No Non-Western IR Theory?" See also, George Modelski, "Foreign Policy and International System in the Ancient Hindu World," *American Political Science Review* 58, no. 3 (September 1964): 549–560.

43. Takashi Inoguchi, "Why Are There No Non-Western Theories of International Relations? The Case of Japan," in "Why Is There No Non-Western IR Theory? Reflections On and From Asia." In this essay, Inoguchi highlights the theoretical work of three pre-1945 Japanese writers: Nishida Kitaro, a "constructivist with Japanese characteristics"; Tabata Shigejiro, a normative international law theorist placing popular sovereignty (as with Samuel von Pufendorf) before Grotian state sovereignty; and Hirano Yoshitaro, a social democratic internationalist.

44. One notable such attempt is Victoria Hui, "Towards a Dynamic Theory of International Politics: Insights from Comparing Ancient China and Early Modern Europe," *International Organization* 58 (Winter 2004): 174–205.

45. Muthiah Alagappa, ed., *Asian Security Practice: Material and Ideational Influences* (Stanford, Calif.: Stanford University Press, 1998).

46. Amitav Acharya, *Whose Ideas Matter: Norms, Power and Institutions in Asian Regionalism* (Ithaca, N.Y.: Cornell University Press, 2008).

47. In his study of cultural globalization, Arjun Appadurai calls this process "repatriation" of knowledge. Arjun Appadurai, *Modernity at Large: Cultural Dimensions of Globalization* (Minneapolis: University of Minnesota Press, 1996).

III

THE ROLE OF EXTERNAL POWERS

4

The United States in Asia

Challenged but Durable Leadership

Robert Sutter

The end of the Cold War and collapse of the Soviet Union in 1991 changed the position of the United States in Asia. For the first time since the start of the Cold War in the late 1940s, the United States appeared to become the region's truly dominant power, seemingly facing few challenges from major competitors. The global war on terrorism begun in 2001 saw U.S. leadership and influence spread to South and Central Asia. The United States now became the leading foreign power in South Asia, having good relations with both India and Pakistan. U.S. military and other relationships with several Central Asian countries grew significantly.[1] On the other hand, challenges to U.S. leadership in Asia also grew. U.S. policies in Iraq and the broader war on terrorism offended and alienated majorities in Asia. U.S. policy appeared inattentive to Asian concerns with development, nation building, and regional cooperation in multilateral organizations. Burgeoning intra-Asia trade and investment networks seemed to diminish the importance of the United States in regional economic matters. Rising powers including India and especially China were portrayed as gaining regional influence and leadership as the United States was seen to decline.[2]

This chapter first examines significant challenges to U.S. interests and influence in Asia at the start of the twenty-first century. It then discerns enduring U.S. strengths, forecasts durable American regional leadership, and considers alternative outcomes.

CHALLENGES TO U.S. INTERESTS AND INFLUENCE IN ASIA

Looked at broadly, current U.S. policy represents the culmination of a long-standing pursuit of three sets of objectives in policy toward Asia. First, the United States remains concerned with maintaining a balance of power in Asia favorable to American interests and opposed to efforts at domination of the region by hostile powers. Second, U.S. economic interests in the region grow through involvement in economic development and expanded U.S. trade and investment. Third, U.S. culture and values prompt efforts to foster in Asia and other parts of the world democracy, human rights, and other trends viewed as progressive by Americans. The priority given to each of these goals changed over time. U.S. leaders varied in their ability to set priorities and organize U.S. objectives as part of a well-integrated national approach to the Asia-Pacific.[3]

Following the terrorist attack on America in 2001, the U.S. administration added two specific objectives: elimination of terrorist organizations and curbing proliferation of weapons of mass destruction that might fall into the hands of terrorists. U.S. officials from time to time also advanced a U.S. goal of implicit if not explicit strategic dominance in Asia and other world regions, premised on unsurpassed U.S. military capabilities. The U.S. Defense Department's *Quadrennial Defense Review* of 2006 said,

> It [the United States] will also seek to ensure that no foreign power can dictate the terms of regional or global security. It [the United States] will attempt to dissuade any military competitor from developing disruptive or other capabilities that could enable regional hegemony or hostile action against the United States or other friendly countries, and it will seek to deter aggression or coercion. Should deterrence fail, the United States would deny any hostile power its strategic and operational objectives.

These stated objectives seem generally consistent with the United States seeking favorable balance of power in Asia, though they also seem more assertive than past U.S. positions. It is unclear if and how this posture will be adjusted in the wake of the reevaluation of the U.S. military occupation of Iraq and the broad expansion of U.S. military commitments in the global war on terrorism.[4]

The U.S. government finds the pursuit of its interests challenged by the wide range of changes under way in Asia since the end of the Cold War.[5] Those changes can be grouped under five headings.

Changes in Regional Major Power Relationships. U.S. policy in Asia has been compelled to take account of China's rising power, India's rising power, Japan's greater international assertiveness following a period of economic and political weakness, Russia's greater activism in Asian affairs, and Indonesia's slow comeback from the collapse of the Suharto regime in 1999.

Economic Globalization. The growing force of economic globalization and related free flow of information have required U.S. policy to adjust to these international trends and to deal with Asian governments focused on seeking advantage in a dynamic and increasingly interdependent world economy.

Asian Multilateralism. U.S. policy has reacted to burgeoning Asian multilateral organizations that reflect the Asian governments' growing interest in and convergence over sub-regional and regional multilateral groups and organizations that address important economic, political, and security concerns of Asian countries. The U.S. government privately debates the actual importance of Asian multilateral organizations, which emphasize process over results, but Asian multilateralism has figured more prominently in U.S. policy and diplomacy in Asia.

War on Terror; Nuclear Weapons Proliferation. These recent U.S. priorities have not been shared to the same degree by many Asian governments, challenging U.S. policy to devise means to build appropriate coalitions and approaches.

Change in U.S. Policy. U.S. policy has been compelled to deal with wariness of many Asian governments concerned over perceived changes in U.S. policy involving excessive U.S. activism, unilateralism, and pressures on the one hand, and U.S. neglect, pullback, and withdrawal regarding Asian affairs on the other.

As U.S. policymakers have adjusted to these changes, they have encountered resistance to U.S. leadership. Thus, for example, Asian governments often oppose U.S. pressure for political rights and democracy in Asia that come at the expense of national sovereignty and regional stability. The Asian governments foster some regional economic groupings that endeavor to deal with issues of economic competition and globalization in a regional context, without the interference of the United States.

The Asian governments also show determination to keep the initiative in their security policies as they pursue "hedging" strategies that avoid falling in line with U.S. guidance. It is hard to avoid the term "hedging" when assessing recent discussion of security relations in Asia. The term is widely used to define patterns of interaction between and among regional states, and yet it remains poorly defined and often imprecise. Evelyn Goh, an academic specialist on Asia-Pacific security dynamics, advised that what is referred to as "hedging" is the norm in international relations. Most states adopt insurance policies, and while they establish military relationships with some states, they avoid committing themselves to potentially antagonistic stances toward other states most of the time, thereby preserving a maximum range of strategic options. During the Cold War, such behavior was severely limited by a need to line up with one side among contending blocs. But that era is now over.[6]

Another way to look at hedging is to see it as contingency planning. Asian governments face a complicated and uncertain security situation with many variables. Even though most Asian nations seek to emphasize the positive in their recent security policy and initiatives with one another, negative historical experience reinforces prudence in supporting preparations for negative developments or contingencies at the same time.[7]

Hedging is defined in this chapter as a broad-ranging practice widely used by Asian governments seeking various domestic and international means at the same time in order to safeguard their security and well-being in the prevailing uncertain but generally not immediately threatening environment in post–Cold War Asia. The post–Cold War Asian order has witnessed a tendency on the part of most Asian governments to emphasize nationalistic ambitions and independence. They eschew tight and binding alignments of the past in favor of diverse arrangements with various powers that support security and other state interests in the newly fluid and somewhat uncertain regional environment.[8] The environment is not so uncertain that countries feel a need to seek close alignment with a major power or with one another to protect themselves. But it prompts a wide variety of hedging, with each government seeking more diverse and varied arrangements in order to shore up security interests.

What this means for the United States is that most Asian governments want generally positive relations with the United States, the region's leading military and economic power, but some are wary of U.S. policy and they seek diversified ties to enhance their security and other options. Meanwhile, they remain wary of one another and work with the United States and others to ensure their interests in the face of possible regional dangers posed by their neighbors.

For example, China's rising prominence and power has prompted an array of recent "hedging" activities as the United States and China's neighbors endeavor to engage with China constructively on the one hand, while they prepare for possible contingencies involving a rising China that would be adverse to their interests on the other hand. Indeed, the United States is an active player and receptive partner among Asian governments hedging in the face of China's rise. It hedges notably in regard to possible negative consequences of China's rising military, economic, and political power and influence for U.S. interests in Asian and world affairs.[9]

SPECIFIC CHALLENGES FOR U.S. LEADERSHIP

Opposition to U.S. Foreign Policies

Asian governments, elites, and public opinion generally give priority to national development and greater prominence for their countries, and they increasingly support regional collaboration and consultation in various multilateral groups. The governments, elites, and public opinion have tended to see George W. Bush administration foreign policies to be at odds with these important regional interests and concerns.[10]

Most Asian governments, elites, and public opinion have opposed the U.S.-led war in Iraq. The U.S. emphasis on military means in the war on terror also has been widely seen as excessive and myopic. The scandals and controversies surrounding U.S. treatment of Iraqi prisoners and international terrorist suspects have severely damaged the U.S. image as a government supporting human rights and due process according to democratic principles. The strong U.S. support for Israel in ongoing disputes with Palestinians has offended in particular regional Muslim populations and their administrations. The hard-line Bush administration posture in negotiations over North Korea's nuclear weapons development that was prevalent until recently was seen as misguided and received little regional support.

Perceived U.S. unilateralism in refusing to be bound by United Nations procedures regarding the war in Iraq and other matters, in refusing commitment to the Kyoto Protocol on climate change, and in pushing U.S. initiatives to promote trade and democracy favored by the United States have offended many constituencies in Asia. The U.S. government has been widely seen in the region as absorbed in the conflicts in Iraq, Afghanistan, and the broader war on terror, and insensitive to Asian regional trends emphasizing cooperation, multilateral consultation, and development.

The contradictions between regional priorities and U.S. foreign policy and behavior have dominated recent public and private discourse about the United States in Asia. They have led to major declines in approval ratings of the U.S. government in opinion polls throughout the region. As a result, the U.S. government's image in Asia and the ability of the U.S. government to lead by example or to otherwise persuade the governments and peoples of the region to follow U.S. policies and initiatives on a variety of international issues have declined. Taken together, this mix of disputes, contradictions, and adverse trends appears to pose the most immediate and prominent challenge to contemporary U.S. relations with and leadership in Asia.

Security Issues and Alliance Management

The military power of the United States and the willingness of the U.S. government to bear major security responsibilities that affect U.S. interests as well as those of Asian countries means that the United States is looked to by those countries to play a major role in dealing with salient regional security issues and hot spots.[11] Although the U.S. government has received positive regional reactions to its handling of some issues, recent publicity has focused on sharp criticism and disapproval on salient security issues.

As noted above, the U.S. handling of the war in Iraq is widely criticized, and there is sometimes strong disagreement by some regional governments with aspects of the broader U.S.-led war on terrorism. The latter include opposition to U.S. initiatives regarding security in the Strait of Malacca, military bases in Central Asia, and the Proliferation Security Initiative focused on North Korea and other potential proliferators of weapons of mass destruction. On the other hand, the Asian governments also continue to rely on U.S. leadership in dealing with the global terrorist threat. They seem to recognize that they are ill-equipped to track and counter international terrorists and that they need to cooperate with the United States militarily and through intelligence, law enforcement, and other means.[12]

The U.S. handling of North Korea's nuclear weapons development has elicited more regional support and less criticism as the U.S. administration has moved recently from a hard-line stance to a more flexible negotiating posture.[13] Meanwhile, U.S. handling of the two other regional security "hot spots," the Taiwan Strait and Kashmir, has appeared broadly accepted in the Asian region as conducive to sustaining regional peace and development.[14]

Alliance Management

The Bush administration has markedly advanced U.S. alliance relations with the governments of Japan and Australia. Japanese elite and popular opinion on the whole seem to welcome the closer ties with the United States, though there are significant issues regarding U.S. bases in Japan, burden sharing, and the willingness of the Japanese government to depart from narrowly restrictive defense policies of the past in order to meet U.S. expectations.[15] The long-serving government of Australian prime minister John Howard faced considerable domestic resistance for his pro-U.S. security policies and actions. The government of Prime Minister Kevin Rudd, elected in September 2007, pledged to sustain a close alliance but also diverged from U.S. leadership on sensitive issues including the war in Iraq and the Kyoto Protocol.[16]

Though U.S. policy continues to give high priority to its formal defense allies as part of the "hub" (United States) and "spokes" (U.S. allies) security framework used by the United States and its Asia-Pacific allies for decades, U.S. policy has built important relations with non-treaty allies. The United States has advanced military relations under the rubric of "strategic partnerships" with Singapore and India. It also has striven diligently and with some success to build webs of military connections with a wide variety of Asian states, devoting special attention to advancing ties with Indonesia and to a degree Vietnam in Southeast Asia and Kazakhstan in Central Asia. In South Asia, crisis-prone Pakistan receives annually billions of dollars of U.S. support, advanced equipment, and other backing designed to shore up this key ally against the insurgents in Afghanistan and the broader war on terrorism.[17]

The Bush administration has advanced its alliance relationships with the Philippines and Thailand through training, provision of military assistance and equipment, security consultations, and high-level diplomacy focused on security issues of mutual concern. The advances have met with some set-backs, notably the Philippine decision to withdraw its modest troop contingent from Iraq because of a terrorist threat against a kidnapped Philippine citizen. Thai and Philippine support for the United States also is evidently tempered by their reluctance to be seen as siding with the United States at the expense of their other important international relationships, notably their growing and close relationships with China.[18]

The biggest alliance problem in recent years has been in U.S. relations with South Korea. Over the past decade major changes in South Korean politics, public opinion, and elite viewpoints prompted a major shift in South Korea's approach to North Korea and South Korea's attitude toward and interest in its alliance relationship with the United States. Under the George W. Bush administration, U.S. policy toward North Korea appeared for many years to move in a direction opposite that of South Korea. Frictions in South Korean–U.S. differences over policy toward North Korea, basing and burden-sharing issues, as well as trade policies and other questions periodically reached crisis proportions. U.S.–South Korean frictions over how to deal with North Korea subsided somewhat with the Bush administration's adoption of a more flexible negotiating posture in 2007. The election of a conservative party president in South Korea in December 2007 forecast less acrimonious U.S.–South Korean relations. However, even though leaders on both sides have tended to see their interests best served by continuing the alliance, persisting frictions and disputes have meant that the formerly close U.S.–South Korean alignment on Korea Peninsula issues and other international affairs was a thing of the past.[19]

Asia-Pacific Multilateralism

There is a widely held perception in Asia and in the United States that the U.S. government has been insufficiently attentive to the remarkable growth in recent years of regional and sub-regional organizations and groups of nations dealing with important economic, political, and security matters. Though this perception is often disputed by U.S. government officials and others, a common view is that the United States is losing out to China and other powers that have been more adept in positioning their governments to take advantage of trends toward greater international cooperation among Asian governments. This commonly held view sees Asian governments as driven by common economic concerns and interests, notably growing trade and investment flows among them, and by common security problems that seem to require going beyond bilateral relations or other existing multilateral means to seek solutions. Some see the emergence of a new regional order in Asia that will rely on ever closer cooperation among regional governments in their various groupings and will be less influenced than in the past by the power and policies of what are seen as non-regional powers, notably the United States. Asian and U.S. observers often see an increasing convergence among regional leaders backed by emerging, sizeable middle classes and elites that increasingly resemble each other, having similar lifestyles and interests, as well as extensive communication networks.[20]

To avoid being left behind in the wake of Chinese, Japanese, Indian, and other Asian regional initiatives designed to advance regional groups in ways advantageous to their respective national interests, the United States is seen to need to work harder in order to "catch up." Too often, however, U.S. leaders are viewed as distracted with the war in Iraq, the broader war on terror, and other more immediate problems. They are said to give insufficient attention to the need to conform more to the requirements and norms of the growing number of Asian organizations. Even close American allies and friends like Japan, Australia, and Singapore strongly urge greater constructive U.S. involvement, but the results thus far are said to be unsatisfactory, according to many regional observers and officials.[21]

Managing U.S. Domestic Pressures

In the post–Cold War period, the tendency of U.S. interest groups, constituents, and other domestic forces to work with the Congress, the media, and other means in order to push U.S. foreign policies in sometimes extreme directions has grown and is unlikely to subside soon. The tendency did decline during the first years of the war on terrorism, but it has revived in recent years. It has seriously challenged the George W. Bush administration's policies on trade and China and has complicated U.S. initiatives toward India and U.S. interaction with countries like North Korea, Indonesia, and Kazakhstan.[22]

Gauging the importance of this challenge to U.S. policy toward Asia is hard because it depends on U.S. reactions to unknowable future regional events and on the hard-to-predict outcomes of U.S. elections. Prevailing circumstances seem to indicate that current and future U.S. governments will continue to face major challenges from U.S. constituents concerned over the massive U.S. trade deficit and what this means for U.S. economic interests and trade policies. It is less clear whether strong divisions in the United States over the war in Iraq will translate into greater pressure to restrict U.S. military deployments elsewhere, including in Asia. Thus far, they have not done so.[23]

Emerging Powers: The Rise of China

In addition to the challenges listed above, U.S. policy and leadership in Asia face challenges posed by newly rising powers in the fluid regional environment. China is in the lead in this category of powers. China's strengths in Asia include a burgeoning economy; China is the leading trader with most advancing regional economies, the largest recipient of foreign investment, and the largest holder of foreign exchange reserves. Attentive and adroit Chinese diplomacy fosters ever closer ties with neighboring countries through bilateral and multilateral relations. China's rapidly advancing military has become the region's leading force.[24]

In the United States, some specialists judge that the Chinese administration is set on a goal to use its rising regional prominence to weaken and marginalize the United States as China seeks territorial and regional goals and prominence now blocked by U.S. power and influence. Others judge that China's administration seeks regional prominence for other reasons but they also advise that the net effect of China's smooth diplomacy and collaborative policies with its Asian neighbors is to show the United States as maladroit and ineffective by comparison. Still others judge that the United States need not feel defensive or threatened in the face of rising China, or they judge that the United States can collaborate with a rising China as a means to secure U.S. interests in the Asian region and elsewhere.[25]

U.S. STRENGTHS IN ASIA

Amid the prevailing negative public discourse in Asia regarding Bush administration policies toward Asia and the perceived decline of the United States relative to China in influence in the region, it sometimes has been hard to discern evidence of U.S. strengths in the region. Several of these strengths have been discussed in media and in specialist and scholarly assessments, and they are duly noted below. This assessment of U.S. strengths also comes from private interviews conducted with 175 Asia-Pacific affairs experts in the governments of nine Asia-Pacific states during three trips to the region in 2004–2007. An assumption behind the focus on interviewing regional officials knowledgeable about the regional order is that, in Asia, governments are seen as the key decision makers in foreign affairs. On the whole, the governments of Asia are strong, the peoples look to the governments to make key foreign policy decisions, and government officials do so based on careful consideration of their national interests.

The findings of these interviews also were reinforced in public speeches, briefings, and other interactions with audiences (amounting in total to two to three thousand) of informed Asian-Pacific elites in these nine countries during the course of two seven-week speaking trips in 2004 and 2006 and a two-week speaking tour in 2007.[26]

The interviews—reinforced by the above-noted public speeches and briefings—underlined this author's assessment of twin pillars of U.S. security and economic strength that provide a firm foundation for continued U.S. leadership in Asia. Of most importance is the fact that the United States continues to undertake major costs, commitments, and risks that are viewed by Asian officials as essential to the stability and well-being of the region. No other power, including rising China, is even remotely able and willing to undertake these responsibilities. America thus remains the indispensable leading power of Asia.

Regarding security concerns, it remains the case, despite all the public bonhomie of Asian regional meetings, that Asian governments generally do not trust each other. The kind of suspicion and wariness one sees today between China and Japan characterizes to various degrees most relationships between and among Asian governments. And yet the Asian governments need stability in order to meet their nation-building priorities. Economic development associated with effective nation building is critically important to the legitimacy of most Asian governments. In this context, the United States looms very large in their calculations. Unlike their Asian neighbors, the United States does not want their territory and does not want to dominate them. It too wants stability, and, in contrast with China's and other powers' inability and reluctance to undertake major risks and commitments, the United States is seen to continue the massive expenditure and major risk in a large U.S. military presence in the Asia-Pacific region. This U.S. role is viewed as essential in stabilizing the often uncertain security relationships among Asian governments.

Not only does the United States continue to occupy the top security position as Asia's "least distrusted power," the United States also plays an essential economic role in the development priorities of Asian governments. Most of these governments are focused on export-oriented growth. The United States provides large-scale investment and aid to Asia and, more importantly, allows massive inflows of Asian imports essential to Asian economic development despite an overall U.S. trade deficit of over $700 billion annually. This costly trade imbalance is essential to the web of intra-Asian trading relations that have emerged recently. No other country is willing or able to bear such a cost.[27]

This view of the United States as the indispensable leading power in Asia contrasts with a widely held perception of decline of U.S. power and influence in world affairs evident since the string of setbacks and failures of the U.S. military occupation of Iraq. However, more detached assessments see the consequences of the Iraq conflict for U.S. security commitments and power in Asia as limited.[28] They appear to support the judgment of this author, as well as the interviewed Asia-Pacific officials, that the overall U.S. military power and the U.S. leading security role in the Asian region have not diminished.

Meanwhile, evidence of U.S. economic difficulties and decline is widely seen in the United States, notably in the massive U.S. trade and large government spending deficits. The argument here is that these problems will cause the United States to move in a decidedly protectionist direction that will significantly curb imports from Asia. Additional evidence was provided with the election of the Democratic Party–led 110th Congress in 2006. Democratic leaders Speaker Nancy Pelosi and Majority Leader Harry Reid seemed to favor tougher and more restrictive trade measures against Asian exporters, especially China, the source of the largest U.S. trade imbalance. Nonetheless, more detached assessments showed Democratic Party divisions and weaknesses that made the adoption of significant protectionist measures unlikely, especially during a period of U.S. economic growth and low unemployment. This suggested that the leading U.S. role as Asia's economic partner of choice would continue.[29]

Other strengths in the U.S. position, in comparison with that of rising China and other Asian powers, have been noted in media and in specialist and scholarly assessments.[30] They included

Role of U.S. Non-Government Actors. Unlike China and other nations, the United States has not depended so heavily on government connections and government-led initiatives to exert influence in Asia. The United States has developed an extensive network of non-government connections established over many decades that undergird U.S. influence in Asia. The connections have involved extensive business, educational, religious, and foundation connections. They also have involved an extensive web of personal connections that followed the U.S. government decision in 1965 to end discrimination against Asians in U.S. immigration policy. This step resulted in the influx of many millions of Asians who settled in the United States and entered the mainstream of U.S. society while sustaining strong connections with their country of origin.[31]

Role of the Pacific Command. The U.S. military, and especially the Pacific Command, has been by far the most active U.S. government component in Asia in recent years. It has followed generally quiet and methodical methods to develop ever closer working relations with most Asian governments, while endeavoring to reinforce the U.S. alliance structure in the region. The ability of the U.S. military to quickly and effectively take the lead in the multilateral effort to bring relief to the millions of Asians afflicted by the tsunami disaster of December 2004 was based on the groundwork of connections and trust developed by the U.S. military leaders among Asian governments in recent years.[32]

Managing "Hot Spots." As discussed earlier, the U.S. government has continued to be seen in Asia as responsible for managing and ensuring that the three major hot spots in the region do not lead to war. The U.S. government showing increased flexibility in dealing with North Korea over the past year generally was welcomed by regional governments and public opinion. The Bush administration's positions on Taiwan and Kashmir were seen broadly as sensible and promoting the kind of stability sought by governments in the region.

Greater U.S. Attention to ASEAN and Asian Multilateralism. The U.S. government also developed a more active and positive stance toward multilateral groups in the Asia-Pacific, especially with ASEAN. The U.S. interest at times appeared to wane when senior U.S. leaders were distracted by higher policy priorities, notably the war in Iraq, and failed to participate in ASEAN-led meetings. In general, however, the United States showed strong support for the ASEAN Regional Forum (ARF), the primary regional forum for security dialogue. The Bush administration also strongly supported Asia-Pacific Economic Cooperation (APEC). President Bush in November 2005 began to use the annual APEC leaders' summit to engage in annual multilateral meetings with attending ASEAN leaders. At that meeting, the leaders launched the ASEAN-U.S. Enhanced Partnership involving a broad range of economic, political, and security cooperation, and in July 2006 a five-year Plan of Action to implement the partnership was signed. In the important area of trade and investment, the U.S. and ASEAN ministers endorsed the Enterprise for ASEAN Initiative (EAI) in 2002 that provided a road map to move from bilateral trade and investment framework agreements (TIFAs), which are consultative, to free trade agreements (FTAs), which are more binding. The United States already had bilateral TIFAs with several ASEAN states, and in August 2006 the United States and ASEAN agreed to work toward concluding an ASEAN-U.S. regional TIFA. Meanwhile, the Bush administration announced in 2006 that it would appoint an ambassador to ASEAN. It also announced in 2006 plans for a future Asia-Pacific FTA.[33]

Improved U.S.–Great Power Relations. The Bush administration's success in improving U.S. relations with the great powers in Asia has added to the strength of U.S. leadership in the region. The United States having good relations with Japan and China at the same time is very rare. The United States being the leading foreign power in South Asia and having good relations with both India and Pakistan is unprecedented, as is the current U.S. maintenance of good U.S. relations with both Beijing and Taipei.

Effective China Policy. Effective U.S. policy toward China, emphasizing positive engagement while continuing to balance against negative implications of China's rise, has helped to reinforce China's emphasis on peace and development and to constrain past Chinese objections and pressure against

Asian governments interacting with the United States in sensitive areas.[34] The prevailing circumstances in U.S.-Chinese relations have allowed the United States and Asian countries very sensitive to Chinese preferences and pressures (e.g., Vietnam, Mongolia) to develop closer relations involving such sensitive areas as military cooperation and related intelligence and information exchanges.

Asian "Hedging" Reinforces U.S. Regional Leadership

China's rise adds to incentives for most Asian governments to maneuver and hedge with other powers, including the United States, in order to preserve their independence and freedom of action. As noted earlier, Asian governments hedge against the United States and other powers as well, but the rise of China has made it a recent focal point of regional hedging. The governments tend to cooperate increasingly with China in areas of common concern, but they work increasingly in other ways, often including efforts to strengthen relations with the United States, to preserve freedom of action and other interests in the face of China's rise.[35] As the most important power in the region, and one with no territorial or few other ambitions at odds with Asian governments interested in nation building and preserving a stable regional status quo, the United States looms large in the hedging calculus of Asian states dealing with rising China.

OUTLOOK FOR THE UNITED STATES IN ASIA

The United States faces many challenges and complications influenced by prevailing trends in Asia and pressures at home. The U.S. image in the region has declined in recent years and U.S. foreign policy continues to be widely criticized. However, U.S. ability and willingness to serve as Asia's security guarantor and its vital economic partner appear strong and provide a solid foundation for continued U.S. leadership in the region. No other power or regional organization is even remotely able, much less willing, to undertake these commitments. The U.S. role also seems to fit well with pervasive hedging by most Asian states.

Of course, the balance of strengths and weaknesses of the United States in Asia could change with changing circumstances including U.S. policy choices. There appear to be four plausible alternative outcomes, which are described below. The first and second are premised on substantial change in existing realities and are deemed less likely. The third and fourth are more in line with existing realities, and thus are seen as more likely.

1. *Decay and Decline in U.S. Leadership.* At one extreme is a marked decline in the U.S. leadership position. This could come as a result of strong

protectionist and/or isolationist sentiment in the United States, resulting in major U.S. barriers for Asian exports and/or large-scale withdrawal from U.S. defense commitments in Asia. U.S. leaders may choose this path, or they may be forced to adopt this approach on account of domestic political, economic, or other pressures.

U.S. decline in Asia also could come as a result of U.S. inability or unwillingness to meet major challenges from an Asian competitor or adversary. The most likely competitor seems to be China. The Chinese administration has taken pains not to challenge overtly U.S. leadership in Asia in the twenty-first century. China had a long record of publicly challenging the U.S. position in Asia in the past, and a revived Chinese stance strongly opposed to U.S. interests regarding Taiwan, alliances with Japan and other Asian partners, or Asian multilateral groupings deciding important security, economic, or other issues might cause the United States to back away from past commitments rather than confront the newly assertive China. Or the United States might judge that rather than risk a confrontation with China, it should use negotiations to accommodate and appease the rising power and accept a declining share of leadership on important security, economic, and other Asian issues, even at the expense of longstanding U.S. commitments in Asia.

An author in this volume, Hugh White, has argued strongly that the United States will need to abandon its leadership position in Asia and "accommodate" and share leadership in Asia with a rising China in the interests of Asian stability. He notes the vague line between accommodation and appeasement and argues that the latter would have obvious negative consequences for Asian stability; but he also forecasts that U.S. efforts to sustain primacy in Asia and avoid accommodation of rising China are likely to be very destabilizing in the longer run.[36]

2. Assertive U.S. Leadership. At the other extreme is an assertive and unilateral U.S. posture on salient trade, human rights, and/or security issues in Asia. This approach could involve strident U.S. advocacy of democracy, strong retaliation against Asian trading practices deemed unfair by the United States, and unilateral military actions to protect U.S. interests in free passage in such sensitive areas as the Strait of Malacca or in opposition to weapons proliferation by U.S. adversaries. Meanwhile, the danger posed by China's military buildup could be met by prominent U.S. countermeasures including an overt American arms race involving the buildup of U.S. forces in Asia and other strong U.S. military preparations designed to meet the Chinese challenge in the Taiwan area or elsewhere.

Alternative outcomes 1 and 2 would result in major and probably disruptive changes in the prevailing order in Asia; they would force many Asian powers that have relied on the security and economic support provided by the United States to seek their interests in a much more uncertain regional environment; and they would undermine U.S. interests in preserving a favorable balance of power and smooth economic access to Asia.

3. *Continued Drift.* This alternative would involve a continuation of the largely reactive U.S. stance in the region seen in recent years. U.S. leadership would be sustained in large measure because of prevailing strengths of the United States in the region and the unwillingness or inability of others to bear the risks, costs, and commitments undertaken by the United States. However, U.S. leadership would remain preoccupied with problems in the Middle East and elsewhere. It would be unwilling or unable to translate the U.S. position of power into a position of authority. The generally passive U.S. approach seen in recent years would continue to miss opportunities to establish organizations and norms supporting U.S. security, economic, and political interests in Asia. Emerging issues like growing Asian multilateralism, energy security, and climate change would see the United States playing catch-up rather than leading toward constructive outcomes.

4. *Consultative Engagement.* This alternative would involve much greater U.S. attention to Asian affairs. U.S. leaders would endeavor to use U.S. power and leadership in close consultation with Asian governments in order to establish behaviors and institutions in line with long-standing U.S. interests.[37] Listening to and accommodating wherever possible the concerns of Asian governments would help to ensure that decisions reached would have ample support in the region. Changing the prevailing U.S. image in Asia from a self-absorbed unilateralist to a thoughtful consensus builder would increase U.S. ability to lead in ways likely to have constructive results for U.S. interests in the region. This change in image probably would require some adjustments in U.S. policy in Iraq, the Middle East, and the broader war on terrorism. A new image and a proactive approach would allow the United States to take the lead on the wide range of existing issues as well as newly emerging concerns of the governments and peoples of Asia.

In sum, an important message of this assessment for policymakers in the new U.S. government who take power in 2009 is that the United States remains in a strong position in Asia. U.S. policymakers should not be swayed by various charges of U.S. decline in Asia and should avoid precipitous action in response. Steady U.S. efforts involving much closer attention to Asian governments and accommodation of their concerns, along with reforms in U.S. policy toward Iraq and the war on terror, will allow the United States to translate its existing power into greater authority and to establish norms and institutions beneficial for U.S. security, economic, and political interests.

NOTES

1. Michael Yahuda, *The International Politics of the Asia-Pacific* (New York: RoutledgeCurzon, 2005); G. John Ikenberry, "America in East Asia: Power, Markets, and Grand Strategy," in *Beyond Bilateralism: U.S.-Japan Relations in the New Asia-Pacific,* ed. Ellis Krauss and T. J. Pempel (Stanford, Calif.: Stanford University Press, 2004), 37–54; National Intelligence Council, *Mapping the Global Future: Report on the National Intelligence Council's 2020 Project,* Report NIC 2004-13 (Washington, D.C.: U.S. National Intelligence Council, 2004), 8–36, 38–61, 74–78, 112–114.

2. See Morton Abramowitz and Stephen Bosworth, *Chasing the Sun: Rethinking East Asian Policy* (New York: Century Foundation, 2006); Jonathan Pollack, ed., *Asia Eyes America: Regional Perspectives on U.S. Asia-Pacific Strategy in the 21st Century* (Newport, R.I.: Naval War College Press, 2007); David Shambaugh, "China Engages Asia: Reshaping the Regional Order," *International Security* 29, no. 3 (Winter 2004/2005): 64–99; David C. Kang, *China Rising: Peace, Power, and Order in East Asia* (New York: Columbia University Press, 2007); Bates Gill, *Rising Star: China's New Security Diplomacy* (Washington, D.C.: Brookings Institution, 2007); Joshua Kurlantzick, "Pax Asia-Pacifica? East Asian Integration and Its Implications for the United States," *Washington Quarterly* 30, no. 3 (Summer 2007): 67–77; David Cook, "Pollster: Major Powers Losing World's Public Support," *Christian Science Monitor,* June 28, 2007, www.csmonitor.com (accessed July 2, 2007); "Come in Number One, Your Time Is Up," *Economist,* April 12, 2007, www.economist.com (accessed April 25, 2007).

3. Earnest May and James Thompson, eds., *American-East Asian Relations, a Survey* (Cambridge, Mass.: Harvard University Press, 1972); Warren I. Cohen, *New Frontiers in American–East Asian Relations* (New York: Columbia University Press, 1983); Robert Sutter, *East Asia and the Pacific: Challenges for U.S. Policy* (Boulder, Colo.: Westview Press, 1992), 15–27; William Pendley, "Bases, Places, and Coalitions: Redefining America's Regional Security Architecture," in *Asia Eyes America: Regional Perspectives on U.S. Asia-Pacific Strategy in the 21st Century,* ed. Jonathan Pollack (Newport, R.I.: Naval War College Press, 2007), 241–242.

4. U.S. Department of Defense, *Quadrennial Defense Review Report,* February 6, 2006, www.defenselink.mil (accessed August 27, 2007), 30; Michael McDevitt, "The 2006 *Quadrennial Defense Review* and National Security Strategy," in *Asia Eyes America: Regional Perspectives on U.S. Asia-Pacific Strategy in the 21st Century,* ed. Jonathan Pollack (Newport, R.I.: Naval War College Press, 2007), 33–50.

5. Lowell Dittmer, "Assessing American Asia Policy," *Asian Survey* 47, no. 4 (July/August 2007): 521–535; Robert Sutter, *The United States and East Asia: Dynamics and Implications* (Lanham, Md.: Rowman & Littlefield, 2003), 89–90.

6. Evelyn Goh, "Understanding 'Hedging' in Asia-Pacific Security," *Pacnet* 43, August 31, 2007, available at www.csis.org/pacfor (accessed September 7, 2007).

7. Evan Medeiros, "Strategic Hedging and the Future of Asia-Pacific Stability," *Washington Quarterly* 29, no. 1 (Winter 2005/2006): 145–167.

8. Yahuda, *The International Politics of the Asia-Pacific,* 237; Evelyn Goh, *Meeting the China Challenge: The U.S. in Southeast Asian Regional Security Strategies,* Policy Studies 16 (Washington, D.C.: East-West Center Washington, 2005).

9. Robert Sutter, *China's Rise: Implications for U.S. Leadership in Asia* (Washington, D.C.: East-West Center Washington, 2006), 24–29.

10. "View of U.S.'s Global Role Worse," *BBC World Service Poll*, January 2007, www.BBC.co.uk/worldservice (accessed January 24, 2007); Cook, "Pollster: Major Powers Losing World's Public Support"; "Come in Number One, Your Time Is Up"; Abramowitz and Bosworth, *Chasing the Sun*; Joshua Kurlantzick, "Pax Asia-Pacifica?" in *America's Role in Asia: Asian Views*, ed. Asia Foundation (San Francisco: Asia Foundation, 2004); Pew Research Center, "U.S. Image up Slightly, but Still Negative," June 24, 2005, www.pewglobal.org (accessed June 30, 2005); Bruce Vaughn and Wayne Morrison, *China-Southeast Asia Relations: Trends, Issues, and Implications for the United States*, Report RL32688 (Washington, D.C.: Congressional Research Service of the Library of Congress, 2006); Pollack, ed., *Asia Eyes America*.

11. Abramowitz and Bosworth, *Chasing the Sun*, 49–92.

12. Evelyn Goh, "Southeast Asian Reactions to America's New Strategic Imperatives," in *Asia Eyes America: Regional Perspectives on U.S. Asia-Pacific Strategy in the 21st Century*, ed. Jonathan Pollack (Newport, R.I.: Naval War College Press, 2007), 201–206.

13. Ralph Cossa and Brad Glosserman, "Regional Overview," *Comparative Connections 9*, no. 2 (July 2007): 1–4.

14. Abramowitz and Bosworth, *Chasing the Sun*, 49–59; John Gill, "India and Pakistan: A Shift in Military Calculus?" in *Strategic Asia, 2005–2006: Military Modernization in an Era of Uncertainty*, ed. Ashley Tellis and Michael Wills (Seattle, Wash.: National Bureau of Asian Research, 2005), 238–253.

15. Michael Mochizuki, "Japan's Long Transition: The Politics of Recalibrating Grand Strategy," in *Strategic Asia, 2007–2008: Domestic Political Change and Grand Strategy*, ed. Ashley Tellis and Michael Wills (Seattle, Wash.: National Bureau of Asian Research, 2007), 69–112; Christopher Hughes, *Japan's Security Agenda: Military, Economic, and Environmental Dimensions* (Boulder, Colo.: Lynne Rienner, 2004).

16. Ralph Cossa, "U.S.-Australia: Still Mates?" *Pacnet* 49, December 19, 2007, www.csis.org/pacfor (accessed December 21, 2007).

17. Daniel Twining, "America's Grand Design in Asia," *Washington Quarterly* 30, no. 3 (Summer 2007): 79–94.

18. Bruce Vaughn, *U.S. Strategic and Defense Relationships in the Asia-Pacific Region*, Report RL 33821 (Washington, D.C.: Congressional Research Service of the Library of Congress, 2007), 22–25.

19. Victor Cha, "South Korea: Anchored or Adrift?" in *Strategic Asia, 2003–2004*, ed. Richard Ellings and Aaron Friedberg (Seattle, Wash.: National Bureau of Asian Research, 2003), 109–130; Samuel Kim, "The Two Koreas: Making Grand Strategy amid Changing Domestic Politics," in *Strategic Asia, 2007–2008: Domestic Political Change and Grand Strategy*, ed. Ashley Tellis and Michael Wills (Seattle, Wash.: National Bureau of Asian Research, 2007), 117–126; International Crisis Group, *South Korea's Election: What to Expect from President Lee*, Asia Briefing 73 (Seoul/Brussels: International Crisis Group, 2007).

20. Kurlantzick, "Pax Asia-Pacifica?" *America's Role in Asia*.

21. Greg Sheridan, "China Wins as 'U.S. Neglects Region,'" *Australian*, September 3, 2007, www.theaustralian.news.com.au/story/0,25197,22351401-16953,00.html (accessed September 7, 2007).

22. Robert Sutter, "The Democratic-Led 110th Congress: Implications for Asia," *Asia Policy* 3 (January 2007): 125–150.

23. Phillip Saunders, "The United States and East Asia after Iraq," *Survival* 49, no. 1 (Spring 2007): 141–152.

24. Kenneth Lieberthal, "China: How Domestic Forces Shape the PRC's Grand Strategy and International Impact," in *Strategic Asia, 2007–2008: Domestic Political Change and Grand Strategy*, ed. Ashley Tellis and Michael Wills (Seattle, Wash.: National Bureau of Asian Research, 2007), 29–68.

25. Robert Sutter and Chin-Hao Huang, "China Southeast Asia Relations," *Comparative Connections* 9, no. 2 (July 2007): 84.

26. These interviews are highlighted in Robert Sutter, *China's Rise in Asia: Promises and Perils* (Lanham, Md.: Rowman & Littlefield, 2005), and *China's Rise and U.S. Influence in Asia: A Report from the Region*, Issue Brief (Washington, D.C.: Atlantic Council of the United States, 2006). The 2004 and 2006 trips involved sometimes repeat visits to a total of twenty-two cities in Australia, China, India, Japan, New Zealand, Singapore, South Korea, and Taiwan. The 2007 trip covered cities in China and Indonesia.

27. In light of continued U.S. abilities to sustain massive and extremely important military and economic commitments to Asian security and economic development, when asked if overall U.S. power and influence in the Asia-Pacific region were in decline, Asia-Pacific officials in private interviews generally said no.

28. Saunders, "The United States and East Asia after Iraq."

29. Sutter, "The Democratic-Led 110th Congress: Implications for Asia."

30. For assessments detailing U.S. strengths in Asia in the face of China's rise and other perceived challenges, see Bronson Percival, *The Dragon Looks South: China and Southeast Asia in the New Century* (Westport, Conn.: Praeger Security International, 2007); Twining, "America's Grand Design in Asia"; Thomas Christensen, "Fostering Stability or Creating a Monster? The Rise of China and U.S. Policy toward East Asia," *International Security* 31, no. 1 (Summer 2006): 81–126; Yahuda, *The International Politics of the Asia-Pacific*, 276–277; Ian Story, *The United States and ASEAN-China Relations: All Quiet on the Southeast Asian Front* (Carlisle Barracks, Penn.: U.S. Army War College Institute for Strategic Studies, 2007); Nick Bisley, "Asian Security Architectures," in *Strategic Asia, 2007–2008: Domestic Political Change and Grand Strategy*, ed. Ashley Tellis and Michael Wills (Seattle, Wash.: National Bureau of Asian Research, 2007), 341–370.

31. Reviewed in Robert Sutter, *The United States in Asia* (Lanham, Md.: Rowman & Littlefield, 2008).

32. Victor Cha, "Winning Asia: Washington's Untold Success Story," *Foreign Affairs* 86, no. 6 (November–December 2007), www.foreignaffairs.org/current/ (accessed November 8, 2007).

33. Donald Weatherbee, "Political Change in Southeast Asia: Challenges for U.S. Strategy," in *Strategic Asia, 2007–2008: Domestic Political Change and Grand Strategy*, ed. Ashley Tellis and Michael Wills (Seattle, Wash.: National Bureau of Asian Research, 2007), 235–266; Donald Weatherbee, "Strategic Dimensions of Economic Interdependence in Southeast Asia," in *Strategic Asia, 2006–2007: Trade, Interdependence, and Security*, ed. Ashley Tellis and Michael Wills (Seattle, Wash.: National Bureau of Asian Research, 2006), 271–302.

35. Sutter, *China's Rise and U.S. Influence in Asia*, 4.

36. Hugh White, "In Support of Accommodation," in *Asia Eyes America: Regional Perspectives on U.S. Asia-Pacific Strategy in the 21st Century*, ed. Jonathan Pollack (Newport, R.I.: Naval War College Press, 2007), 153–168.

37. Thus, for example, Kenneth Lieberthal calls on U.S. policymakers to engage in what he calls "focused engagement" with China. See Lieberthal, "China: How Domestic Forces Shape the PRC's Grand Strategy," 64.

5

Europe in Asia

Sebastian Bersick

The EU is already a major economic player in Asia, and we are now becoming a political actor too.

—Javier Solana[1]

Looking back at fifty years of successful economic and political integration,
the European Union (EU) and its member states are the natural partners of
an Asian region that seeks to develop a regional system that transcends the
perceptions, concepts, and behavior patterns of the Cold War. Since signing
the Treaty of Rome in 1957, which established the European Economic
Community, Europeans are aggregating experience and developing institutions that allow for regional integration and, depending on the policy field,
the transfer of sovereignty to supranational institutions. Because of its success, the EU has become a source of inspiration and a reference for regional
organizations, especially in Asia. The Association of Southeast Asian Nations (ASEAN) exemplifies this development—however not to the same extent as the EU. The ten Southeast Asian member countries emphasize the
importance of their national sovereignty. Yet they simultaneously aim to
deepen their cooperation and integration, for example, by an ASEAN charter that gives the organization a legal personality.

Relations between Europe and Asia date back to the times of the Roman
Empire.[2] The colonial legacy of Europe in Asia became an issue in the middle of the 1990s when Asian and European governments and the EU started
to cooperate interregionally. Asians underlined that a so-called senior-jun-
ior relationship belonged to the past. Against the colonial history in which
European countries like the UK, France, or the Netherlands ruled large parts

of Asia, the interaction between Europe and Asia after the end of the Cold War, and in light of the economic development in large parts of Asia, transformed itself from being "based on 'aid and trade' towards the recognition of the importance of a fast developing Asia for the EU."[3] Europe's new interest in Asia resulted from the economic developments in the region, particularly from China's economic modernization. In terms of hard security the Europeans had no vital interests.

The above-quoted statement by the high representative for the Common Foreign and Security Policy (CFSP) Javier Solana highlights the evolutionary change in the Europeans' approach toward Asia. It raises the question of how far the European interest in Asia corresponds with Europe's actual presence and engagement in the Asian region, which accounts for one-fifth of all EU exports. Asia is the EU's third-largest regional trading partner after the European neighborhood and NAFTA.[4] In order to analyze the relationship between Europe and Asia, this chapter will focus on relations between the EU and Asia nationally, institutionally, and regionally.[5] It will discuss the relations between countries as well as between regional actors and, when appropriate, the role and policies of individual EU member states.

In the 1990s most European observers of Asian affairs agreed on the growing importance of Asia. Europe, however, was looking to the West. The transatlantic relationship mainly defined Europe's view of the world as well as its foreign policy–making priorities. In economic, political, security, and cultural respects, the United States was the primary partner and ally. This is changing. We still do not know to which degree the rise of China and India and the related developments in the Asian regional architecture will impact the global pattern and distribution of power. It is, however, the general understanding of European decision makers at the end of the first decade of the twenty-first century that Europe's future will increasingly depend on competition and cooperation with the newly emerging Asian powers.[6] If one does not perceive international relations as a zero-sum game, the question of how the relationship between Europe, Asia, and the United States can be managed or governed is of paramount importance. What has become clear in recent years is that the EU has become an increasingly active actor in Asia.

THE EU AS AN ACTOR IN ASIA

The EU, EU member states, and even national political parties are developing strategies and policies that deal with the changes in Asia.[7] However, the reactions to date remain incoherent. No real European Asia strategy exists because the EU is, unlike a nation-state, an incomplete and evolving global political actor. Only in the area of trade have the twenty-seven member

states successfully overcome the coherence and consistency problem by establishing a supranational foreign trade policy. The EU's foreign and security policy is still based on intergovernmentalism.

Though member states of the EU agreed to share national sovereignty and
created supranational institutions and political actors like the European
Commission (EC), the Council of the European Union (or the EU Council),
and the European Parliament, the EU's instrumentalism is limited. Because of
prevailing national interests of its twenty-seven member states, the resulting
coherence problem limits the EU's capacity to act internationally.[8] While it is
expected that the EU's external policies will become more coherent once the
Lisbon Treaty is ratified, the EU's relations with Asia need to be differentiated
between the supranational and the national foreign policy levels. The resulting European approach to Asia sets Europe's policies apart from other external actors' policies in Asia. Against this background, several levels of interaction between "Europe" and "Asia" can be differentiated, namely (1) relations
between EU member states and individual Asian countries, for example, between Germany and China; (2) relations between the EU and individual
Asian countries, for example, the EU and India; (3) interregional relations between the EU and a specific group of Asian countries, for example, the
ASEAN-EU dialogue or the Asia-Europe Meeting (ASEM).

FOREIGN POLITICS WITH EU CHARACTERISTICS

The specific institutional structure of the EU is mirrored in its relations with
Asia—the most decisive element being the intrinsic tendency of Europeans
to support region-building and community-building processes in Asia. In
this respect, the EC in Brussels is the most forceful actor of regionalizing the
European engagement in Asia. The EC uses political dialogues, cooperation
programs with developing countries,[9] and humanitarian assistance as instruments in its interaction with Asian actors.

Within this context the EU has chosen a policy path that, by its own account, differs from containment or balance of power strategies. It aims to
strengthen regional cooperation and the promotion of a rules-based international system.[10] According to Javier Solana, the EU's foreign policy vis-à-
vis Asia follows a "vision in which a system of global governance, with regional structures as its cornerstones effectively addresses trans-regional
problems."[11] This approach to international relations and the corresponding policy to support the development of regional structures in Asia differs
from the United States inasmuch as that the EU facilitates the development
of regional institutions in Asia even if the United States is excluded.[12] Germany's chancellor Angela Merkel told a Chinese audience that she believes
that the future will belong to regional cooperation. "In order to be success-

ful," she argued, "Germany needs to play its role in Europe and China needs to play its role in the Asian region."[13]

The EU's policies vis-à-vis Asia are based on the premise that the cooperative experience of Europe can and should become part of Asian region-building processes.[14] The policy of the EU toward Asia is a multilevel engagement policy. It combines bilateral and multilateral approaches. Besides interaction on the bilateral level, the EU and its member states seek to develop their relations in multilateral forums like the ASEAN Regional Forum (ARF) or within the Asia-Europe Meeting (ASEM) process. Since March 2007 the EU is also an observer of the South Asia Association for Regional Cooperation (SAARC) and has started to interregionalize its relations with the five Central Asian republics. The assumption that institution building on the intraregional and interregional level will facilitate shaping the context for future policy choices when interacting with Asian actors is an inherent element of this approach.

EVOLUTION OF EU-ASIA POLICIES

The Europeans rediscovered Asia in the beginning of the 1990s. After the German government had presented its *Asienkonzept* in 1993, the EC produced its first strategy for Asia under the title "Towards a New Asia Strategy" a year later. It was followed in September 2001 by a new document that formulated the following objective as a priority in EU-Asia relations: "We must focus on strengthening the EU's political and economic presence across the region, and raising this to a level commensurate with the growing global weight of an enlarged EU."[15] The EC identified six objectives on which the new strategy was to focus:

1. the contribution to peace and security in the region;
2. to increase trade and investment flows;
3. to support the development of poverty-stricken Asian countries;
4. to facilitate the spread of democracy, good governance, and the rule of law, especially in China;
5. to cooperate with Asian countries in international forums on security and global environmental issues, including terrorism, migration, and climate change;
6. to further the awareness of Europe in Asia.

According to the latest Asia Regional Strategy Paper covering the years 2007–2013, regional cooperation will prioritize three areas: (1) the support to regional integration; (2) policy and know-how based cooperation; and (3) the support to uprooted people.[16]

The EU's interaction with Asia continues to grow and so does the relationship between the EU's internal and external security and its implications for the development of Europe-Asian relations. With regard to the ongoing European participation in the international military and civilian engagement in Afghanistan this is obvious. But Europe's security interests in Asia are geographically not restricted to the Himalayas. In this context the German defense minister argued during the 2007 IISS Shangri-La Dialogue in Singapore that the future lies in the "establishment of a cooperative system of alliances and partnerships . . . for instance also between Europe and Asia."[17] Such a development would add a yet not existing security dimension to the European engagement in Asia. What is more the statement is indicative of the EU's interest to further expand its security focus beyond the EU and its neighborhood as expressed in the European Security Strategy of 2003.

A COMMON EUROPEAN FOREIGN POLICY

The EU started to engage with Asia via its European Security and Defence Policy (ESDP), which is part of the Common Foreign and Security Policy (CFSP). The first ever ESDP operation in Asia has been the Aceh Monitoring Mission (AMM) in Indonesia. A second ESDP operation is the deployment of a small-scale police force in Afghanistan in June 2007. The only security agreement in which solely European and Asian state actors are involved is the Five Power Defence Agreement of 1971, which brings together the UK, Malaysia, Singapore, Australia, and New Zealand. Because of the underdeveloped cooperation between Europe and Asia in the security realm, observers have argued for an increase of security cooperation, for example in the area of maritime security and non-traditional threats.[18] Vis-à-vis important security issues in the Asian theater, the EU and its member states have not yet developed a coherent and consolidated position or policy on Asian security.

A case in point is Taiwan.[19] In this respect Europe's relations with Taiwan mirror the European approach to Asia: economic interaction without a comprehensive and responsible political engagement. In view of this deficit and the need for a "more developed, coherent and focussed foreign and security policy in East Asia," the Council of the European Union in December 2007 approved, for the first time, "Guidelines on the EU's Foreign and Security Policy in East Asia."

Although the institutional effectiveness of the EU is limited, the Europeans are actively supporting conflict resolution in the region. For example, the EC supports the Aceh Peace Process and spends €40 mn. on mediation, the monitoring of the peace agreement, an EU Election Observation Mission, reintegration of ex-combatants, and the implementation of a Memorandum of Understanding.[20] With regard to Sri Lanka, the EU was one of the four co-chairs of the Tokyo Conference on the Reconstruction and Development of Sri Lanka. Furthermore, the EU deployed four Electoral Observation Missions to the South Asian country (2000, 2001, 2004, and 2005) and participated in the Sri Lanka Monitoring Mission (SLMM) to observe the cease-fire of 2002.[21] Timor-Leste is another example as the former colonial power Portugal takes a strong interest in the development and security of the country and offers financial support as well as human capital to the UN mission to the small Southeast Asian state.[22]

As a result of the increasing importance of Asia, the EU has decided to extend its relations with Asia into a new strategic partnership that shall be based on an enhanced political dialogue and trade relationship as well as on a sustainable development cooperation partnership.[23]

EUROPE'S STRATEGIC PARTNERSHIPS IN ASIA

In its security strategy the EU underlines the need to pursue its objectives "through partnerships with key actors." The EU established and is developing strategic partnerships with individual countries—namely, the United States, Canada, Russia, Japan, China, India, Brazil, and South Africa.[24] The establishment of strategic partnerships with India, Japan, and China has already been a strong indicator for the prioritized relations with Asia. Recently also the relations between the two regions Asia and Europe have been, for the first time, officially depicted as a "strategic partnership."[25]

CHINA

Over the course of the last ten years the relations between the EU and the People's Republic of China have changed significantly. Annual summits take place, a strategic partnership has been established, the EU is China's largest export market, and China is Europe's largest source of imports. According to the EU, its relations with China are "increasingly focused on addressing global affairs" as China "plays a key role in response to these issues."[26] Four aims are central to the EU's China policy, which are outlined in the EU's "Country Strategy Paper on China, 2002–2006":

1. The further engagement of China on the world stage through an upgraded political dialogue;
2. "To support China's transition to an open society based upon the rule of law and respect for human rights";

3. The encouragement of China's integration into the world economy and support of the continuing social and economic reform in China;
4. "To raise the EU's profile in China."[27]

In October 2006 the EC released two new documents on EU-China relations. The titles, "Closer Partners, Growing Responsibilities" and "Competition and Partnership," are indicative of a policy change on the European side. It is now the EU's objective that "China meets its WTO obligations and continues to liberalize access to its good, services, investment and public procurement markets." Furthermore, the EU will seek an end of forced technology transfers and a "tougher protection of Intellectual Property Rights (IPR)." It is in this context that the Council of Ministers has stated in its adopted conclusions in December 2006 that the adjustment to the "competitive challenge and driving a fair bargain with China will be the central challenge of EU trade policy." The council's conclusions emphasized that for the comprehensive strategic partnership to "develop to its full potential, it must be balanced, reciprocal and mutually beneficial."[28] The demanding character of the documents,[29] and the underlying potential for conflict, became openly apparent during the 10th EU-China Summit in November 2007, when a Joint Statement could not be agreed on in due time.

The EU and China interact in a dense institutional framework. The current architecture of EU-China relations entails the political dialogue, economic relations and twenty-seven sectoral dialogues, the EC-China development cooperation program, and the sectoral agreements and policy dialogues. Furthermore, the EU and China started to negotiate a new Partnership and Cooperation Agreement (PCA) in January 2007. A key objective for the EU is to acquire better access to the Chinese market for European exporters and investors going beyond WTO commitments. The EU stresses that the PCA will encompass the full scope of the EU-China bilateral relationship, including enhanced cooperation in political matters. In addition the PCA will contain a clause on human rights.[30] The clause is to cover issues related to democratic principles and fundamental human rights.[31] It is an objective of the EU to lay the foundation for so-called enhanced cooperation under the agreement. This shall include enforcement and improvement of environmental (including climate change mitigation), social, labor, and safety standards. On the trade side the agreement shall "cover important issues for both sides such as IPR, investment, non tariff trade barriers, capital movements, sustainable trade and natural resources and competition."[32]

An example of the increasingly conflict-laden relationship is the Chinese trade surplus that creates rising protectionist pressures on the European side. Whereas the EU enjoyed a trade surplus with China at the beginning of the 1980s, trade relations are now characterized by a widening EU deficit with China. This represents the EU's largest bilateral trade deficit. Trade commissioner Peter Mandelson stated that EU-China relations are "at a crossroads" and that the EU could consider the usage of defense instruments to guard against Chinese market access barriers. Against this background, senior Chinese "Europe hands" blame the EU of "egoisms in economic relations."[33]

Another issue area that continues to impact negatively on EU-China relations is the continuing European arms embargo against China. From a Chinese perspective it symbolizes the inability and unwillingness of the EU and its member states to act as a responsible and equal partner. Chinese officials, diplomats, cadres, and military personnel alike underscore that the unsolved issue hampers the development of a strategic partnership. In this context, the new "Guidelines on the EU's Foreign and Security Policy in East Asia" are an important document as they demonstrate the EU's change of position. In a highly defensive manner the document recommends that the EU should "in consultation with all partners, deepen its understanding of the military balance affecting the cross-strait situation . . . and factor that assessment into the way that Member States apply the Code of Conduct in relation to their exports to the region of strategic and military items."[34]

Though the EU-China "strategic partnership" is not strategic in the military sense, the issue of lifting the European arms embargo against China shows that hard security issues have entered EU-Asia affairs. What is more, instead of pushing for an early lifting of the embargo, the EU has taken a much more cautious approach—while reacting to severe criticism of the United States as well as Japan.

India

Europe is India's major trade partner. In 2006 the EU accounted for 19.2 percent of the subcontinent's trade, followed by the United States (10.4 percent) and China (8.3 percent). A total of 1.8 percent of the EU's trade with the world is exchanged with India.[35] Institutional relations between the EU and India are based on the 1994 Cooperation Agreement and the Joint Political Declaration of 1993. In June 2004 the EC suggested establishing an EU-India Strategic Partnership. In October 2007 the EU Council adopted its conclusions on the EU-India Strategic Partnership and supported the elaboration of an EU-India Action Plan and a new Joint EU-India Political Declaration. The Joint EU-India Political Declaration was endorsed at the Sixth EU-India Summit in New Delhi.[36] Both sides commit themselves to a strengthened dialogue as strategic partners. According to the European Commission, the main priority for the EU-India Strategic Partnership must be the promotion of peace, security, and democracy in the world by using the partnership to improve international cooperation, strengthen the economic partnership, reform development cooperation, and deepen mutual understanding. The implementation asks for a strategic and comprehensive approach that can happen on the level of multilateral, bilateral, and regional cooperation. The latter shall facilitate regional cooperation to encourage economic development and trade among development countries and aims at, inter alia, the negotiation of a Cooperation Agreement with SAARC.[37]

The Joint Action Plan of September 2005 spells out the content of the EU-India Strategic Partnership, which aims to strengthen consultation mechanisms, deepen the political dialogue, connect the peoples and cultures, enhance the economic policy dialogue and cooperation, as well as develop trade and investment. The document lists 124 action points that range from the dialogue on human rights, the exchange of instructors between Peacekeeping Training Centres of EU member states and India, the establishment of contacts between EU and Indian Counter Terrorism Coordinators, the establishment of a Working Group on Food Processing Industries, and the launch of an India-EU Initiative on Clean Development and Climate Change to the participation of India in the Galileo satellite navigation systems through the conclusion of a framework agreement.

As India and the EU share common values and a commitment to democracy, the rule of law, human rights, and pluralism, both actors regard themselves as "natural partners" that contribute to global stability.[38]

Japan

As a result of a common normative understanding in terms of shared values (such as freedom, democracy, and the rule of law), the EU regards Japan as its "closest partner" in East Asia.[39] The Japanese government stresses the cooperation in the areas of IPR, energy, climate change, and security in East Asia and Central Asia as examples of the EU-Japan strategic partnership.[40] In terms of the commercial and trade relationship, Japan ranked as the fifth major partner of the EU (4.8 percent) in 2006. The EU is Japan's third trade partner (13.2 percent) after the United States (18.7 percent) and China (18.2 percent).[41]

The main areas of EU-Japan cooperation cover political as well as economic relations and sectoral cooperation.[42] The bilateral relationship is legally based on a Joint Declaration from 1991 and the Action Plan for EU-Japan Cooperation from 2001, which covers a ten-year period. The Action Plan consists of four basic objectives: the promotion of peace and security, the strengthening of economic and trade links, "coping with global and societal challenges," as well as the forging of people-to-people and cultural ties. Besides the annual EU-Japan summits the institutional mechanism includes twice-yearly meetings between the EU Troika at foreign ministers' level and the Japanese minister of foreign affairs, meetings of senior officials, as well as expert-level political dialogue meetings between the EU Troika and Japanese officials on a range of thematic issues (e.g., the Middle East, non-proliferation, UN affairs).

Since September 2005, a Japan-EU Dialogue on the East Asian Security Environment has been institutionalized. Furthermore, a similar dialogue between the EU and Japan on Central Asia was first held in July 2006. Against the background of the EU's intention to lift the EU arms embargo against China, the Japanese government has criticized the EU for a lack of understanding of the "security situation in the region" and for regarding East Asia mainly as an economic market.[43] During the 16th EU-Japan Summit in June 2007, global issues (climate change, energy security, the Doha Development Round, IPR) and international issues (North Korea, China, Russia, Afghanistan, and Iran) were the main topics. While the leaders adopted the EU-Japan Action Plan on IPR Protection and Enforcement and welcomed the initialing of the EC-Japan Agreement on Customs Cooperation and Mutual Assistance, Japan again reiterated its opposition to the lift of the embargo while welcoming the EU's "constructive contributions to the regional political architecture in Asia-Pacific" in the context of the ARF, EU-ASEAN relations, and the ASEM process.[44]

Overall, the quality of the strategic partnerships differs significantly—as the EU, India, and Japan share democratic values. This is not the case with regard to the EU-China strategic partnership. However, as the European Commission demands that the normative foundation of the EU-China partnership has to be "based on our [European] values,"[45] the EU also promotes regional cooperation within Southeast Asia and between China and its regional neighbors.

Multilateral Policies

In addition to the bilateral relations between the EU and its member states and their Asian counterparts, Europeans and Asians also interact in multilateral forums. One important dimension of multilateral interaction takes place on the interregional level. The EU and Asia are connected via two main interregional processes—namely the EU-ASEAN dialogue and the ASEM process. The Europeans have been facilitating ASEAN's intraregional cooperation during the last thirty years of joint official EU-ASEAN relations. This policy is being complemented by the ASEM process in which the European side cooperates with Southeast Asian, Northeast Asian, and South Asian actors. In so doing, the EU and its member states had, in the middle of the 1990s, responded positively to the interest of ASEAN countries to engage China. It was particularly the Singaporean government that promoted this concept. The idea to form a new Asian regional grouping that would cooperate with European counterparts interregionally formed the conceptual framework of this approach. In a recent policy initiative the EU started to also interregionalize its relations with the five Central Asian republics. Apart from these interregional processes the EU is also a member of the ARF and intends to participate in the East Asia Summit (EAS). France and the UK are, so far, the two EU member states who seek to participate in the EAS as well.

The ASEAN-EU Dialogue

During the last three years the EU stepped up its activities in Southeast Asian affairs. Not only have European and ASEAN countries successfully shaped and taken part in the Aceh Monitoring Mission in Indonesia, the growing importance that the EU attaches to the Southeast Asian region is demonstrated by the fact that the Europeans intend to accede to the Treaty of Amity and Cooperation in Southeast Asia (TAC), to negotiate Partnership and Cooperation Agreements with individual ASEAN countries, and to pursue a region-to-region Free Trade Agreement (FTA) with the ASEAN countries.

The 2007 ASEAN-EU Ministerial Meeting in Nuremberg, Germany, also saw the commitment of both sides to further enhance their relationship in the areas of political and security, economic, socio-cultural, and development cooperation as well as in the field of energy security and climate change. EU officials emphasized that it provided the relationship with a new dynamic as it enlarged the EU-ASEAN agenda beyond economic, trade, and development issues by agreeing to intensify political and security cooperation.[46] The conference participants in Nuremberg agreed on more intense cooperation in the spheres of climate policy, energy security, and the fight against terrorism. As a result a Plan of Action was agreed on that shall serve as a "master plan" to enhance EU-ASEAN relations and shall support the integration of ASEAN.[47] This is supposed to transform the EU-ASEAN dialogue into "a cornerstone for the strategic partnership between Asia and Europe."[48] In the light of China's and India's growing integration into the world economy and its implications for the development of a new regional and global order—both in economic and political respects—the EU emphasizes the increasing importance for a continuing and accelerating integration process among ASEAN countries.[49]

Ultimately, however, the successful implementation of the Plan of Action, and thus the quality of the cooperation that was proclaimed in Nuremberg, will depend on the ability of the ASEAN countries to successfully implement their declared community-building goals. ASEAN governments have resolved to establish a community by 2015 that will be based on three pillars—namely, security policy, economic policy, and socio-cultural policy. In their integration efforts the ASEAN countries are increasingly orienting themselves toward the EU.

The ASEM Process

The Asia-Europe Meeting (ASEM) was established in 1996 to offer heads of state and government from Europe and Asia a platform for a free and informal exchange of views and to allow for cooperation on an equal basis and in consensus in order to develop common ground and common interests. Its members now generate 50 percent of the world's GDP, represent 58 percent of the world population, and are responsible for 60 percent of world trade. Since its foundation, ASEM has evolved into the central platform for interregional cooperation between Asia and Europe. In addition to the biannual summits, meetings also take place at minister and civil servant levels. The content of the consultations and projects ranges from the fight against terrorism or the facilitation of trade and investment to the discussion of issues of faith and religion or social policy.[50]

The comparative advantage of the ASEM process lies in the very openness of the rules, principles, and norms that the Asian governments and the EU have developed.[51] ASEM is an institution that generates and manages interdependencies in a globalizing world. The ASEM process demonstrates the demand for governance on the inter- and intraregional level of the international system. This demand has increased across the board in the first decade of ASEM's existence. It is the distinctive feature of the process that ASEM partners meet as part of their respective region. Cooperation within ASEM comprises various levels. Besides multilateral efforts they increasingly engage in bilateral state-to-state cooperation. Consequently, two processes of interregional cooperation can be identified: first, bilateral cooperation, second, cooperation between two collective actors (EU and Asia). In order to facilitate the former function, both regions are represented through coordinators. By applying the region-to-region formula Asian actors can formulate and develop common positions and interests. Therefore, the Asian ASEM region is not only defined by geographical criteria but also by functional criteria.

Central Asia

The five Central Asian republics Kazakhstan, Kyrgyzstan, Tajikistan, Turkmenistan, and Uzbekistan are members of the Organization for Security and Cooperation in Europe (OSCE). Europeans and the five republics thus nominally share the values and norms of an organization that, under the name of the Conference for Security and Cooperation in Europe, played a pivotal role in overcoming the Cold War.

Within the Technical Assistance for the Commonwealth of Independent States (TACIS) program the EU supports the transition process of the five republics toward market economies and democratic societies. After autumn 2001 the Europeans had deepened relations with the countries in view of the increasing awareness of the geopolitical importance of Central Asia.[52] The EU intends to further increase its interaction with the five countries and adopted a first strategy in June 2007.[53] Its core objective is to contribute to peace, democracy, and prosperity in Central Asia. The document names the promotion of security and stability as "strategic interests" of the Europeans in the region because: (1) strategic, economic, and political developments in the region "impact directly or indirectly on EU interests"; (2) the EU and Central Asia are "moving closer" because of, for example, the EU enlargement; and (3) "Significant energy resources in Central Asia and the region's aim to diversify trade partners and supply routes can help meet EU energy security and supply needs."

The strategy document differentiates between bilateral and regional cooperation, and the EU will support the regional cooperation among the five countries and between the Central Asian republics and other regions. Seventy percent of the €750 million that has been earmarked in the period 2007–2013 for development assistance to Central Asia will be used for bilateral support programs of which the fight against poverty remains the highest priority. Thirty percent will be spent to support closer economic cooperation within Central Asia, as well as between Central Asia, Southern Caucasia, and the EU.

The underlying geopolitical considerations of the strategy have been voiced by the then German EU Council presidency. Accordingly, the Europeans "have some catching up to do" as countries like Russia, China, Japan, Turkey, and the United States are "very present" in the region.[54] The EU hopes that the oil and gas reserves in the region will contribute to the diversification of its energy imports. Competition for the energy resources of Central Asia is one important explanation for the political will of the EU to increase its presence in Central Asia.[55] European actors know that especially Russia and China have a strategic advantage in the region that results, inter alia, from the similarities of their political systems and the willingness to support the countries without political conditions. In the light of this structural power deficit, the overall approach of the EU aims at promoting the political as well as economic transformation and modernization of the region in order to overcome the political and institutional differences between the EU and the five republics. For this reason, the EU supports regional cooperation in Central Asia. The approach is based on the belief in the socializing power of cooperative diplomacy and negotiations between Europe and Central Asia—even though the actors involved "do not share a common normative basis."[56]

EUROPE AND THE NEW REGIONAL SYSTEM IN ASIA

While the EU's relationship with Asia is becoming ever more complex, the EU's approach to the region is driven by the understanding that a new balance needs to be found between the Westphalian order in which Asia still lives and the post-Westphalian order that the Europeans have successfully constructed during the last fifty years.

During the last five years the Europeans have sought to strengthen their bilateral relations with China, India, and Japan by establishing strategic partnerships. Though no strategic partnership exists with the Republic of Korea, a Free Trade Agreement (FTA) is currently being negotiated between the EU and ROK. The EU is furthermore deepening its bilateral relations with the two emerging countries by negotiating a PCA with China since January 2007 and an EU-India FTA. In addition, the EU is upgrading its interregional relations with ASEAN and its involvement in the ARF. Furthermore, the EU is reaching out to old and new regional cooperation mechanisms like SAARC and the East Asia Summit while engaging further in the ASEM process and developing its presence in Central Asia by implementing an interregional strategy for the Central Asian region. Europe is thus increasingly reacting to the evolution of a new regional architecture in Asia. In response to China's and India's economic development and the corresponding increase of regional and global political influence, the Europeans have developed a two-tier engagement strategy toward the Asian region, which combines bilateral and multilateral policies. This approach sets the European policy vis-à-vis Asia apart from the United States'. The EU as a global actor in Asia combines bilateral cooperation with an active support of regional cooperation and integration in Asia.

From the mid-1990s onward, the EU facilitated region- and community-building processes among East Asian state actors. Via the ASEM process, the EU even actively supported the integration of China into an informal regional institution that excluded the United States. Although Washington at first firmly opposed the idea of a meeting between Europe and Asia, because it mirrored the concept of an East Asian trading bloc that had been tabled by the Malaysian prime minister Mahathir in the early 1990s, the U.S. government finally agreed to the interregional formula. For the first time the three Northeast Asian countries—China, Japan, and South Korea—and the ASEAN countries cooperated in a common institution. This development facilitated the institutionalization of the ASEAN + 3 mechanism.[57] The underlying strategy of the ASEAN countries was to engage China in an Asia-centered forum. Within this context the EU perceives East Asia as a potential community. EU relations with ASEAN and the individual ASEAN states should therefore always be seen in the context of ASEAN's role and significance for the development of a new regional system in Asia.

From the European point of view, the strategic function of the ASEAN-EU dialogue and the ASEM process vis-à-vis the ongoing development of a new regional architecture in East Asia lies in their ability to facilitate shaping the context for future policy choices in ways according to the EU's strategic interests in East Asia.[58]

Against this background, the EU's relations with China differ from its relations with India and Japan. While following its economic interests, Europe's policy toward China aims to facilitate the transformation of the Chinese political system toward a more democratic form of governance. It is a specific element of this approach that it combines bilateral cooperation with the support for regional cooperation in Asia. A parallel approach can be identified within the EU's policies toward Central Asia. While the EU follows, for example, its energy security–related interests in the region, it intends to further the transformation of the political systems through the support of regional and interregional policies.

The changing pattern of the EU-China relationship led to different assessments of the actors' underlying intentions and the future development of the interaction. While David Shambaugh once characterized the relations between the EU and China as an "emerging axis,"[59] it has been emphasized as well that the EU and China are foremost bargaining over interests because they cannot afford the opportunity costs of balancing against the United States.[60]

The China arms embargo issue symbolizes the current nature and the limits of the EU-China strategic partnership. It is strategic as the actors share the interest to further institutionalize their cooperation in order to manage the increasing interdependence between them in an increasing amount of policy fields on all the different levels of their interaction. This is an evolutionary strategy and the ongoing negotiation of a PCA can become an important milestone of this incremental approach. At the same time, EU-China relations are still a "secondary relationship,"[61] as the specifics of the Chinese political system hinder the EU to develop the relations in a way as comprehensive as Chinese interests would have it.[62] Though value-related issues do currently demarcate the limits of the scope and depth of the relations between China and the EU and its member states, the underlying logic of the Europeans' bilateral and multilateral policies toward the Asian region nevertheless aims at facilitating cooperation within the region. In that sense the EU is neither pursuing a containment strategy nor a balancing strategy with regard to the development of a new regional system in Asia. Instead Europeans are convinced that regional integration and interregional cooperation are important instruments in promoting their economic interests vis-à-vis Asia as well as their interest in a stable regional security environment in Asia.

NOTES

1. Javier Solana, "The EU's Strategic Partnership with Japan" (speech at Keio University, Tokyo, April 24, 2006), ue.eu.int/ueDocs/cms_Data/docs/pressdata/EN/discours/89298.pdf (accessed October 17, 2006), 3.

2. See Kwa Chong Guan, "The Historical Setting," in *Europe and the Asia Pacific*, ed. Hanns Maull, Gerald Segal, and Jusuf Wanandi (London: Routledge, 1998), 1–10.

3. Commission of the European Communities, *Europe and Asia: A Strategic Framework for Enhanced Partnerships*, COM(2001), 469 final (Brussels, 2001).

4. See ec.europa.eu/external_relations/asia/index.htm.

5. The EU defines the Asian region as consisting of five sub-regions, namely South Asia, Southeast Asia, Northeast Asia, Australasia, and Central Asia.

6. Paul Kennedy, "Asia, Europe and the Global Power Balance," in *Asia Changing the World*, ed. Bertelsmann Stiftung (Gütersloh: Verlag Bertelsmann Stiftung, 2007), 51–64.

7. See "Asien als strategische Herausforderung und Chance für Deutschland und Europa" [Asia as a Strategic Challenge and Opportunity for Germany and Europe] (Strategy Paper of the CDU/CSU Parliamentary Group, October 23, 2007), www.cducsu.de/Titel__Deutschlands_Blick_auf_Asien_weiten/TabID__1/SubTabID__5/InhaltTypID__4/InhaltID__7850/Inhalte.aspx (accessed November 9, 2007).

8. For a discussion of the coherence problem, see May-Britt Stumbaum, "Engaging China—United Europe? European Foreign Policy Towards China," in *European Foreign Policy in an Evolving System: The Road Towards Convergence*, ed. Nicola Casarini and Costanza Musu (London: Palgrave, 2007), 57–75.

9. According to EU statistics, the EU as a whole (i.e., the EC and the member states), accounts for nearly a third of total aid flows to Asia.

10. See Solana, "The EU's Strategic Partnership with Japan," 4.

11. Javier Solana, "Europe and Asia: A Relationship That Matters," *Hindu*, July 31, 2007, www.hinduonnet.com/thehindu/thscrip/print.pl?file=2007073154831100.htm&date=2007/07/31/&prd=th& (accessed September 3, 2007).

12. See Sebastian Bersick, "The Impact of European and Chinese Soft Power on Regional and Global Governance," in *The International Politics of EU-China Relations*, ed. David Kerr and Liu Fei (Oxford: Oxford University Press for the British Academy, 2007), 216–230.

13. Angela Merkel, speech at the Chinese Academy of Social Sciences, Beijing, August 28, 2007, www.bundesregierung.de/Content/DE/Rede/2007/08/2007-08-28-rede-merkel-chinesische-akademie.html (accessed August 29, 2007).

14. Frank-Walter Steinmeier, opening speech at the Ambassadors' Conference in the German Ministry of Foreign Affairs, Berlin, September 3, 2007, www.auswaertiges-amt.de/diplo/de/Infoservice/Presse/Reden/2007/070903-SteinmeierBoKo.html (accessed September 10, 2007).

15. Commission of the European Communities, *Europe and Asia*, ec.europa.eu/external_relations/asia/doc/com01_469_en.pdf (accessed November 20, 2005).

16. European Commission, *Regional Programming for Asia: Strategy Document, 2007–2013*, May 31, 2007, ec.europa.eu/external_relations/asia/rsp/rsp_0713_en.pdf (accessed August 15, 2007).

17. Josef Jung, "Security Cooperation in Asia: Managing Alliances and Partnerships" (speech at the Sixth IISS Asian Security Summit Shangri-La Dialogue, Singapore, June 2007), www.iiss.org/conferences/the-shangri-la-dialogue/plenary -session-speeches-2007/fifth-plenary-session—dr-franz-josef-jung/ (accessed June 17, 2007).

18. See Kay Möller, *Maritime Sicherheit und die Suche nach politischem Einfluß in Südostasien* [Maritime Security and the Search for Political Influence in Southeast Asia] (Berlin: SWP, 2006), 24–27.

19. See Günther Schucher, "The EU's Policy toward Taiwan," *Issues & Studies* 43, no. 3 (September 2007): 1–51.

20. See John Quigley, "Enhancing South-East Asia's Security: The Aceh Monitoring Mission," in *Multiregionalism and Multilateralism: Asian-European Relations in a Global Context*, ed. Sebastian Bersick, Wim Stockhof, and Paul van der Velde (Amsterdam: Amsterdam University Press, 2006), 61–82.

21. Christian Wagner, *Zurück zum Bürgerkrieg? Die internationale Vermittlung in Sri Lanka droht zu scheitern* [Back to the Civil War? The International Mediation in Sri Lanka Is Threatened to Fail] (Berlin: SWP-Aktuell, 2006),

22. Henriette Sachse, *Fragiler Staat Timor Leste* [Fragile State Timor-Leste] (Berlin: SWP-Aktuell, 2007).

23. See European Commission, *Regional Programming for Asia*.

24. I will concentrate on the relations with the People's Republic of China and not on the Republic of China, Hong Kong, or Macao. With respect to Taiwan, the EU follows a "One China Policy" and thus has no diplomatic relations with Taiwan.

25. In March 2007, German federal foreign minister Frank-Walter Steinmeier and his Cambodian colleague Hor Namhong declared that cooperation between the EU and the ASEAN represented a "cornerstone for the strategic partnership between Asia and Europe." *Joint Declaration: 16th EU-ASEAN Ministerial Meeting* (Nuremberg, March 15, 2007). Apart from the EU, individual member states have established strategic partnerships with China, for example France, Germany, and the UK.

26. Council of the European Union, *Press Release: 2771st Council Meeting*, 16291/06 (Presse 353) (Brussels: General Affairs and External Relations, December 11–12, 2006), 6, www.cortesclm.es/paginas/actualidad/europa/6/boletin134/ 2771.pdf (accessed December 2006).

27. European Commission, "The EU's China Policy," europa.eu.int/comm/ external_relations/china/intro/index.htm (accessed November 13, 2003).

28. Council of the European Union, *Press Release: 2771st Council Meeting*.

29. David Shambaugh, "China-Europe Relations Get Complicated," Brookings Northeast Asia Commentary, May 2007, www.brookings.edu/opinions/2007/ 05china_shambaugh.aspx?p=1 (accessed July 4, 2007).

30. The mandate of the PCA is confidential, but the case of the EU-Russia PCA sheds some light on the related sensitivities. The current EU-Russia Partnership and Cooperation Agreement (PCA) expired at the end of 2007. The European Parliament has repeatedly criticized the EC on its negotiations on a new PCA, and "to accord democracy, human rights and freedom of expression fundamental importance

in any future agreement, and to ensure clear mechanisms to monitor implementation." www.futurdeleurope.parlament.gv.at/sides/getDoc.do?type=CRE&reference =20061214&secondRef=ANN-01&language=RO&detail=H-2006-1007&query =QUESTION (accessed May 8, 2007).

31. Normative aspects play an important role in the EU's relations with China (as a clause on human rights within the prospected PCA indicates). An EU-China dialogue on human rights has existed since 1996, and the EC has underlined the need to increase its impact and efficiency. In September 2006 the European Parliament criticized the EU-China relationship for neglecting the question of democratic reforms, the rule of law, and the respect for human rights in the light of their trade and economic relationship. See "European Parliament Resolution on EU-China Relations," P6_TA-PROV(2006) 0346; A6-0257/2006, paragraph 4. Also, national parliaments adopt motions and resolutions that are highly critical of China. An example is when the German Bundestag condemned China's *laogai* system (reform through labor system). See "Antrag der Fraktionen CDU/CSU, SPD, FDP und BÜNDNIS 90/DIE GRÜNEN Für die Verurteilung des Systems der Laogai-Lager in China," dip.bundestag.de/btd/16/045/1604559.pdf (accessed March 10, 2007).

32. Peter Mandelson, speech in the European Parliament, Strasbourg, July 10, 2007, ec.europa.eu/commission_barroso/mandelson/speeches_articles/sppm162_en.htm (accessed July 12, 2007).

33. Mei Zhaorong, "Adjustment of the European Union's China Policy and China-EU Relations," *Foreign Affairs Journal* (Spring 2007): 65.

34. Council of the European Union, "Guidelines on the EU's Foreign and Security Policy in East Asia," 16468/07, December 14, 2007, register.consilium.europa.eu/servlet/driver?lang=EN&ssf=DATE_DOCUMENT+DESC&fc=REGAISEN&srm =25&md=400&typ=Simple&cmsid=638&ff_TITRE=East+Asia+Guidelines&ff_FT_TEXT =&ff_SOUS_COTE_MATIERE=&dd_DATE_REUNION=&rc=1&nr=3&page=Detail (accessed January 3, 2008).

35. European Commission, *Bilateral Trade Relations: India*, trade.ec.europa.eu/doclib/docs/2006/september/tradoc_113390.pdf (accessed September 18, 2007).

36. "Political Declaration on the India-EU Strategic Partnership," ec.europa.eu/external_relations/india/sum09_05/05_pol_decl_070905.pdf (accessed September 15, 2007).

37. Commission of the European Communities, "An EU-India Strategic Partnership," Commission Staff Working Document, Annex to the Communication from the Commission, COM(2004), 430 final (Brussels, 2004), ec.europa.eu/external _relations/india/news/2004_comm.pdf (accessed September 15, 2007).

38. "The India-EU Strategic Partnership Joint Action Plan," 1. ec.europa.eu/external _relations/india/sum09_05/05_jap_060905.pdf (accessed September 15, 2007).

39. Solana, "The EU's Strategic Partnership with Japan."

40. Takekazu Kawamura, "The EU and Japan as Strategic Partners" (speech by the ambassador of Japan to the European Union at the Trans European Policy Studies Association [TEPSA] International Conference, Brussels, November 27, 2006), www .eu.emb-japan.go.jp/tepsa_speech.htm (accessed July 14, 2007).

41. Figures based on EU-25, trade.ec.europa.eu/doclib/docs/2006/september/ tradoc_113403.pdf (accessed September 18, 2007).

42. Axel Berkofsky, *The EU and Japan: A Partnership in the Making*, Issue Paper 52 (Brussels: EPC, 2007), se2.isn.ch/serviceengine/FileContent?serviceID=ESDP&fileid =1877836F-3284-31AD-8879-B75076749F49&lng=en (accessed March 22, 2007).

43. Kawamura, "The EU and Japan as Strategic Partners."

44. Joint Press Statement of the 16th EU-Japan Summit, Berlin, June 5, 2007, ec.europa.eu/external_relations/japan/intro/summ_index.htm (accessed September 11, 2007).

45. European Commission, "EU—China: Closer Partners, Growing Responsibilities," October 2006, eur-lex.europa.eu/LexUriServ/site/en/com/2006/com2006 _0631en01.pdf (accessed October 16, 2006).

46. Javier Solana, "Opening Statement by EU High Representative Javier Solana at the ASEAN-EU Post Ministerial Conference, Manila, August 1, 2007," S227/07 (Brussels: European Commission, 2007).

47. The Plan of Action lists common projects in the area of political and security cooperation, for example the EU/EC's accession to the TAC once ASEAN has completed the necessary legal procedures, and of economic as well as socio-cultural cooperation. See "Plan of Action to Implement the Nuremberg Declaration on an EU-ASEAN Enhanced Partnership," www.aseansec.org/21122.pdf (accessed December 6, 2007).

48. "16th EU-ASEAN Ministerial Meeting, Joint Co-Chairmen's Statement," paragraph 2.

49. Sebastian Bersick and Paul Pasch, "Compass 2020: Germany in International Relations—Goals, Instruments, Perspectives: Southeast Asia," in *The Future of German Foreign Relations*, ed. Friedrich-Ebert-Stiftung (Berlin: Friedrich Ebert Stiftung, 2007), library.fes.de/pdf-files/iez/05001.pdf (accessed January 30, 2008).

50. See University of Helsinki Network for European Studies, "ASEM in Its Tenth Year. Looking Back, Looking Forward: An Evaluation of ASEM in Its First Decade and an Exploration of Its Future Possibilities" (Helsinki: University of Helsinki European Background Study, 2006), www.asem6.fi/news_and_documents/en_GB/ 1146144206909/ (accessed December 6, 2006).

51. For the following, see Sebastian Bersick, *Auf dem Weg in eine neue Weltordnung? Zur Politik der interregionalen Beziehungen am Beispiel des ASEM-Prozesses* [Toward a New World Order? On the Politics of Interregional Relations: The Example of the ASEM Process] (Baden-Baden: Nomos, 2004), 41–52.

52. Andrea Schmitz, "Eine politische Strategie für Zentralasien" [A Political Strategy for Central Asia], in *Aufgaben und Chancen der deutschen Ratspräsidentschaft* (Berlin: SWP, 2006), 41–44.

53. *The EU and Central Asia: Strategy for a New Partnership*, www.auswaertiges-amt .de/diplo/en/Europa/Aussenpolitik/Regionalabkommen/EU-CentralAsia-Strategy.pdf (accessed July 30, 2007).

54. "EU Outlines New Central Asia Strategy," April 24, 2007, www.euractiv.com/ en/enlargement/eu-outlines-new-central-asia-strategy/article-163327 (accessed April 24, 2007).

55. Andrea Schmitz, "Interessen, Instrumente, Einflussgrenzen. Die Europäische Union und Zentralasien" [Interests, Instruments, Spheres of Influence. The European Union and Central Asia], *Osteuropa* 57 (August/September 2007): 327–338.

56. Andrea Schmitz, "Interessen, Instrumente, Einflussgrenzen," 337.

57. For Mahathir's proposal that, according to Beeson, "paved the way for ASEAN+3," see Mark Beeson, *Regionalism and Globalization in East Asia: Politics, Security, and Economic Development* (Houndmills: Palgrave Macmillan, 2007), 228.

58. See European Institute for Asian Studies (EIAS) and Nomisma, "The European Union's Strategic Interests in East Asia," Brussels, 2005, www.eias.org/research/euasia/eustrategyexecbrief.pdf (accessed January 4, 2008).

59. David Shambaugh, "China and Europe: The Emerging Axis," *Current History*, no. 674 (September 2004): 243–248.

60. See Terry Narramore, "China and Europe: Markets, Multipolarity and Strategy," (paper presented at the 57th Political Studies Association Annual Conference "Europe and Global Politics," University of Bath, April 13–17, 2007), www.psa.ac.uk/2007/pps/Narramore.pdf (accessed May 2, 2007).

61. For this term, see Michael Yahuda, "China and Europe: The Significance of a Secondary Relationship," in *Chinese Foreign Policy. Theory and Practice*, ed. Thomas W. Robinson and David Shambaugh (New York: Oxford University Press, 1994), 266–282.

62. The normative differential between the political systems manifested itself in a diplomatic clash between Germany and China in the autumn of 2007, when a German chancellor met, for the first time on official premises, with the Dalai Lama.

IV

REGIONAL POWERS

6

China's Role in Asia

Phillip C. Saunders

After decades of exerting only modest influence in Asia, China is now a much more active and important regional actor. Economic reforms and China's subsequent integration into regional and global production networks have produced three decades of rapid economic growth that has dramatically increased China's national power. China's regional security strategy and a range of diplomatic, military, and economic assurance measures have had a significant impact in easing Asian concerns about a strong China. Several recent studies confirm that Asian views about China have generally shifted from viewing China as a threat to viewing China as an opportunity, although Japan is an exception to this trend.[1] To some degree, this reflects an accommodation to a reality that smaller Asian states are powerless to change. Nevertheless, the shift from the anti-China sentiment prevalent a decade ago is an indicator of the success of China's Asia policy. As Robert Sutter has pointed out, it is difficult to assess the degree to which Chinese influence in Asia has actually increased because China has not asked Asian states to take costly actions that are against their interests.[2]

This chapter examines China's regional strategy and the sources of Chinese influence, considers how China might use its growing power in the future, and assesses how other Asian and global powers are likely to respond to a more powerful and more influential China. It also examines competing theoretical perspectives on China's international behavior, likely implications if current trends continue, and potential developments that might alter China's regional policy. This chapter argues that China's reassurance strategy has been remarkably successful in preserving a stable regional environment and persuading its neighbors to view China as an opportunity rather than a threat. However, despite China's restrained and constructive regional behavior over the last decade, significant concerns remain about how a stronger and less constrained China might behave in the future.

CHINA'S ASIA STRATEGY

China's regional strategy derives in part from its global grand strategy.[3] The top domestic concern of Chinese leaders is maintaining political stability and ensuring the continued rule of the Chinese Communist Party (CCP). CCP leaders have tried to build new sources of political support by raising living standards through rapid economic growth and by appealing to nationalist sentiment.[4] Throughout the reform era, Chinese leaders have focused on maintaining a stable international environment that supports economic modernization. This objective requires China to avoid a hostile relationship with the United States, the dominant power in the current international system. Given the high costs of confrontation, Beijing seeks stable, cooperative relations with Washington. Yet many Chinese elites believe that the United States seeks to subvert the Chinese political system and to contain China's economic and military potential. China therefore seeks to build positive relationships with current and potential great powers to facilitate the emergence of a multipolar world order and to deny the United States the opportunity to construct a coalition to contain China and prevent its continued rise. By properly managing relations with the United States, other great powers, and developing countries, Chinese leaders hope to take advantage of the period of strategic opportunity in the first two decades of the twenty-first century to build China's comprehensive national power and improve China's international position.

This grand strategy defines the international and domestic context in which China formulates and pursues its Asia policy. Asia is the most important region of the world to China in economic, security, and political terms. It is the most important destination for Chinese exports (taking 45 percent of Chinese exports in 2004) and for Chinese investment (hosting at least $2.45 billion in Chinese foreign direct investment as of 2005).[5] Asia serves as a source of raw materials; the supplier of components, technology, and management expertise for global production networks operating in China; and increasingly as a market for finished Chinese products. Asian FDI played a critical role in fueling China's economic takeoff and export boom. Much of China's economic success can be attributed to the operations of multinational companies that import components from Asia, assemble goods using Chinese workers, and export the finished products to markets in the United States, Europe, and elsewhere. Approximately 60 percent of Chinese exports are now produced by foreign-invested enterprises, many of which are based in Asia.[6] China has become increasingly dependent on oil imported from the Middle East and on sea lanes of communication to support its trade. Much of this traffic passes through Asian waters, including through potential choke points such as the Strait of Malacca.

Geography also makes Asia critically important to China from a security perspective. China shares land borders with fourteen East Asian, South Asian, and Central Asian countries. Chinese leaders worry that neighboring countries could serve as bases for subversion or for military efforts to contain China. This is of particular concern because much of China's ethnic minority population, which Chinese leaders view as a potential separatist threat, lives in sparsely populated border regions. Chinese concerns about threats posed by "terrorism, separatism, and religious extremism" have prompted increased efforts at security cooperation with its Central Asian and South Asian neighbors. China's unresolved territorial claims are all in Asia, including claims to the Spratly Islands and the South China Sea, the Diaoyu/Senkaku Islands and parts of the East China Sea, and China's claim to Taiwan. China also worries about the possibility of encirclement and threats from conventional military forces based on its periphery. In the 1960s, the United States had significant military forces based on Taiwan, the Philippines, Japan, South Korea, and Thailand, all within striking distance of Chinese territory. Chinese strategists are highly sensitive to recent U.S. actions to improve its military power projection capability in the Pacific and the possibility that U.S. alliances in Asia might someday be turned against China.

Finally, Asia is also an important political environment. It is home to major powers such as China, Japan, India, and advanced economies such as Korea and Singapore. East Asia houses 29 percent of the world's population and produces about 19 percent of global GDP.[7] If Asia were able to act collectively, it could rival the geopolitical weight of North America and Europe. Asia has historically lacked the web of regional institutions that produced economic and security cooperation in Europe and which supported the regional integration process that led to the creation of the European Union. The political, ethnic, and cultural diversity of the region and the tendency of Asian states to jealously guard their sovereignty have impeded the creation of strong regional institutions. However, over the last decade, new regional institutions have emerged to promote regional cooperation between Asian states in the economic, security, and political domains. A robust set of non-governmental organizations and people-to-people contacts have also emerged at the societal level. Some see these processes as promoting greater regional integration, which would greatly alter the political dynamics in Asia. China has a strong stake in influencing the political evolution of the region in ways that advance Chinese interests, and in blocking developments that might work against Chinese goals.

China's preferred outcome is a stable environment in Asia that permits rapid Chinese economic growth to continue and supports a continuing increase in Chinese influence. Many Western analysts believe that China's ultimate (but unstated) goal is to eventually displace the United States as the dominant power in Asia.[8] Many Chinese analysts acknowledge that the U.S. role in supporting regional stability and protecting sea lanes of communication makes a significant contribution to regional stability and supports Chinese interests. The U.S. security alliance with Japan exerts a degree of restraint on Tokyo, although Chinese analysts believe this restraining influence has been reduced in recent years with the transformation of the alliance and the gradual lifting of legal constraints on Japanese military activities. However, the potential for U.S. power and alliances to be turned against China makes Chinese analysts uneasy at the prospect of an enduring American security role in the region. China disclaims any desire to dominate Asia, declaring that it will never seek hegemony and talking about cooperation on the basis of equality, mutual respect, and non-interference in the internal affairs of other nations. But Chinese leaders are also acutely aware of changing trends in the global and regional balance of power, which are closely followed by Chinese intelligence agencies and research institutes.

Chinese leaders are aware that rising Chinese economic and military power is viewed as a potential threat by other countries in the region.[9] This wariness partly reflects the legacy of China's earlier support for communist parties and national liberation movements in Asian countries. Beijing ended such ideologically based support by the early 1980s, but Asian countries remain wary of the possibility that China could build relationships with their ethnic Chinese citizens that undermine their sovereignty. These latent concerns were aggravated by China's aggressive efforts to pursue its territorial claims in the Spratly Islands, including its 1995 seizure and subsequent fortification of Mischief Reef, a small island in the South China Sea claimed by the Philippines. In late 1995 and March 1996, China alarmed many in the region by using military exercises (which included live ballistic missile firings in waters near Taiwan) to express its displeasure at the U.S. decision to permit Taiwan president Lee Teng-hui to visit the United States and speak at Cornell University. These actions prompted articles highlighting China's rapid economic growth, continuing military modernization, and growing nationalism and asking whether China posed a threat to the Asia-Pacific region.[10] Chinese officials and scholars attacked the "China threat theory" but also recognized the need to address the concerns of their neighbors. Yet reassurance efforts have been paralleled by continuing increases in military spending (official defense budgets have experienced double-digit real annual increases since 1999) and expanding military capabilities that are a source of concern in Asia, especially in Japan.

China's dilemma is finding a way to reconcile the rest of Asia to a dominant Chinese regional role without antagonizing the United States or destabilizing the region. This task is complicated by the Taiwan issue, given Beijing's self-defined "core interest" in preventing Taiwan independence. In the near term, China's military modernization is focused on developing capabilities that can deter Taiwan independence (which the People's Liberation Army [PLA] has defined as developing capabilities to deter and raise the costs of U.S. military intervention). Beijing has refused to rule out the use of force to resolve the Taiwan issue, although it would greatly prefer to resolve the issue peacefully. Chinese leaders have tried to compartmentalize Taiwan as an "internal affair" that has no relevance to People's Republic of China (PRC) international behavior, but most countries in Asia (and the United States) would be highly alarmed if China used force against Taiwan. China's military preparations to deal with Taiwan contingencies implicitly undercut its efforts to reassure the region that it will be responsible in how it uses its growing military power.

CHINA'S REASSURANCE CAMPAIGN

China has pursued a variety of diplomatic, economic, and military means to reassure its Asian neighbors that a stronger China will not threaten their interests. China's diplomatic efforts in Asia now rest upon a foundation of well-trained and capable diplomats who are able to convey Chinese messages effectively.[11] The content of China's diplomatic messages has also changed to have more appeal in Asia. In 1997–1998 China advanced the "New Security Concept," a reformulation of its five principles of peaceful coexistence that called for mutually beneficial cooperation on the basis of equality, mutual respect, non-interference in the internal affairs of other countries, and resolution of conflicts through dialogue.[12] This concept meshed reasonably well with the principles and preferred methods of operation of the Association of Southeast Asian Nations (ASEAN) states.[13] (The so-called ASEAN Way emphasizes decision making by consensus, respect for national sovereignty, non-interference in internal affairs, and a gradual pace to security cooperation.) Chinese pledges of non-interference and respect for sovereignty provide assurances that Beijing will not support separatist groups or intervene on behalf of ethnic Chinese outside its borders.

China has sought to reassure ASEAN states by engaging and negotiating with them on a multilateral basis, forgoing the bargaining advantages that the stronger country enjoys in bilateral negotiations. Beijing's willingness to negotiate in the "ASEAN + China" framework offered some reassurance that China would not pursue a "divide and conquer" strategy. China also launched a series of annual summits with ASEAN, began participating more actively in the ASEAN Regional Forum and its unofficial counterpart the Council for Security Cooperation in the Asia Pacific (CSCAP), and signed the "Declaration of Conduct on the South China Sea," a non-binding pledge to resolve territorial disputes peacefully. This pledge was an important confidence-building measure because four ASEAN countries claim parts of the disputed Spratly Islands but recognize they lack the power to stand up to China on their own. At the 2003 Bali Summit, China became the first non-ASEAN member to sign the Treaty of Amity and Cooperation, which codified ASEAN's preferred principles of international conduct such as non-aggression, non-interference, and peaceful resolution of disputes. Beijing also signed a strategic partnership agreement with ASEAN, giving the organization a status equal to its partnerships with other major powers.

China has also become more willing to participate substantively in regional multilateral organizations such as the Asia-Pacific Economic Cooperation (APEC) forum, ASEAN + 3 (Japan, China, Korea), the ASEAN Regional Forum, and the East Asian Summit. China had historically been reluctant to participate in multilateral forums due to fears that other countries would gang up on it and because multilateral norms and procedures could constrain its ability to pursue its interests. China's increased multilateralism is a means of channeling Chinese power in ways that make it more acceptable to its neighbors.[14] Some analysts argue that China now views multilateral and regional organizations as important political venues and has become more active in these organizations as a means of pursuing its national interests.[15] China's establishment of the Shanghai Cooperation Organisation (SCO) as a means of combating terrorism and expanding its influence in Central Asia is compatible with this view, as is China's effective use of bilateral diplomacy to influence the agenda of multilateral organizations such as ASEAN and the SCO in directions that advance Chinese interests.

China has also taken concrete measures to address Asian security concerns. One of the most important has been its efforts to resolve almost all of its outstanding land border disputes with its neighbors in the 1990s.[16] These efforts have eased concerns about potential conflicts over borders and paved the way for increased cross-border cooperation against terrorism and organized crime. In many cases, China has made territorial concessions in order to resolve these disputes (although Beijing has often sought to keep the details of these concessions secret to avoid nationalist criticism).[17] Equally important has been China's restraint in the use of its military forces. The aggressive actions that alarmed China's Asian neighbors in the mid-1990s have not been repeated in recent years.

Beijing's rhetoric claims that China's increasing military power is a force for peace that does not threaten any country. China has made some efforts to demonstrate that its military and paramilitary forces can make some useful contributions to regional and global security. These include increased participation in United Nations peacekeeping missions. As of 2006, China had 1,489 military personnel deployed on nine UN missions and in the UN Department of Peacekeeping Operations. In September 2007, Major General Zhao Jingmin became the first Chinese officer to command a UN peacekeeping mission.[18] China has also offered to increase regional cooperation on non-traditional security issues such as disaster relief, counterterrorism, and counterpiracy. Although the resources committed to these missions have been relatively modest, they provide a positive contribution to regional security and symbolize a constructive role for Chinese military power.

China has also made modest efforts to increase its transparency on military issues as a confidence-building measure. China published its first white paper on arms control and disarmament in 1995 and began publishing biannual white papers on national defense in 1998. The defense white papers provide ample assurances of China's peaceful intentions and only limited information on PLA military capabilities, but are nevertheless an important step toward greater transparency. Starting in 2002, China began to observe and then participate in bilateral and multilateral military exercises with neighboring countries as a confidence-building measure. Although most are simple search and rescue exercises, they do provide an opportunity for Asian militaries to interact with their PLA counterparts. China has also improved the quality of its participation in multilateral security dialogues at both the official and unofficial levels and established bilateral security dialogues with most major countries in Asia. Although Chinese participants remain reluctant to talk about Chinese military capabilities and often repeat official talking points, these dialogues still have some value.

In the economic realm, China has sought to persuade Asian countries that they will share in the benefits of China's rapid growth, while simultaneously advancing Chinese interests through commercial diplomacy. "Win-win" and "mutual benefit" are the watchwords of China's economic diplomacy. Chinese imports are fueling growth throughout Asia and in other regions of the world. In 2003, China became the largest export market for Japan, South Korea, and Taiwan. Demand from China is credited with helping to revive the Japanese economy from its decade-long slump. China's increasing role in world trade and expectations of future growth make it an attractive market and give Beijing leverage in dealing with trade partners. A relatively new element in China's economic diplomacy involves negotiation of regional and bilateral free trade agreements (FTAs). The China-ASEAN FTA is the most significant example, but China is currently discussing bilateral FTAs with Australia, New Zealand, Japan, South Korea, India, and others.[19] China's FTA with ASEAN includes "early har-

vest" provisions that provide additional benefits to ASEAN agricultural producers. Chinese officials also regularly use trade-facilitation agreements or
non-binding bilateral trade targets to leverage market access as a diplomatic
tool in bilateral relations.

SOURCES OF CHINESE POWER IN ASIA

Economic Power

China's rapid economic growth, and the increasing economic ties with
Asia that it has produced, is the most important source of China's increasing influence in Asia. One important pattern in China's trade relations is
that other East Asian countries are becoming more dependent on exports to
China, but China's relative dependence on East Asian markets is staying the
same. The volume of Chinese trade with East Asia has increased dramatically over the last decade, but the share of Chinese exports going to East
Asia (excluding Hong Kong) has declined from 34 percent in 1996 to 24
percent in 2006.[20] Conversely, China has become the first- or second-largest
trading partner of almost every country in the region since the turn of the
millennium (see tables 6.1 and 6.2). Despite periodic political tensions,
Japan's trade with China (not counting Hong Kong) now exceeds Japan's
trade with all ten members of ASEAN and surpassed U.S.-Japan trade levels
in 2007. ASEAN exports to China have grown rapidly in recent years, but
the China market is still only the third most important export market for
ASEAN products.

These changes in Asian dependence on the China market reflect both the
shift of export production from other East Asian economies to tap inexpensive Chinese labor and the Chinese domestic market's appetite for imports from Asia. Chinese leaders and analysts appear to believe that trade

Table 6.1. Percentage of Imports from China (China's Rank as Import Source)

	Japan	South Korea	Taiwan[a]	ASEAN 6[b]	India[c]
1986	4.7% (4)	0.0% (—)	0.28% (33)	4.0% (6)	0.55% (27)
1996	11.6% (2)	5.7% (3)	3.00% (7)	3.0% (5)	1.90% (18)
2006	20.4% (1)	15.7% (2)	12.20% (2)	11.0% (3)	9.40% (1)

Source: UN Comtrade Database.
[a]Taiwan Trade Statistics: Taiwan figures are from Taiwan's Bureau of Foreign Trade, available at cus93.trade.gov.tw/english/FSCE/FSC0011E.ASP; 1989 data (the earliest available) are used for the 1986 figure.
[b]ASEAN 6 is Singapore, Malaysia, Indonesia, Thailand, Philippines, and Brunei. ASEAN 6 data for Brunei use 1985 data and 1998 data to substitute for unavailable 1986 and 1996 data. ASEAN 6 rankings consider intra–ASEAN 6 trade with other ASEAN 6 members (e.g., ASEAN 6 exports to Singapore) as trade with other countries for ranking purposes.
[c]The 1986 India data are from the IMF Direction of Trade Statistical Yearbook 1990.

Table 6.2. Percentage of Exports to China (China's Rank as Export Market)

	Japan	South Korea	Taiwan[a]	ASEAN 6	India
1986	4.7% (4)	0.0% (—)	0.00% (—)	2.3% (12)	0.74% (28)
1996	5.3% (5)	8.8% (3)	0.54% (23)	2.9% (12)	1.8% (14)
2006	14.3% (2)	21.3% (1)	22.70% (1)	8.8% (3)	6.6% (3)

Source: UN Comtrade Database.
[a]Taiwan Trade Statistics.

dependence can generate significant political influence as groups that benefit from trade mobilize to protect their economic interests. However, these groups do not necessarily exert a dominant influence within other countries. For example, Japanese business groups have called for better Sino-Japanese relations, but this has sometimes been insufficient to outweigh other Japanese voices seeking a more assertive policy toward China.

China has also emerged as a significant source of foreign direct investment in Asia. Asia is the most important destination for Chinese FDI. Chinese statistics indicate that Chinese enterprises have invested at least $2.45 billion in East Asia as of 2005, while ASEAN statistics show $2.3 billion of Chinese FDI from 2002 to 2006. This makes a significant contribution to Southeast Asian economies, but Chinese investment only accounts for 1.3 percent of total foreign investment in ASEAN over the 2002–2006 time period, a very small percentage. China does not publish a detailed breakout of its foreign aid programs, but the poorer countries in Southeast Asia and Central Asia are significant recipients of Chinese development assistance. Much of this assistance goes to improve transportation infrastructure connecting Southeast Asian and Central Asian countries to China. This infrastructure contributes to these countries' economic development, but it also links them more closely to the Chinese economy and will produce greater trade dependence in the future.[21] China's role as a production site in regional production networks serves as an important link between Asian producers of capital goods and production inputs and developed country markets in the United States and Europe. This ties together the economic interests of Asian companies and countries in a positive-sum manner.

Military Power

Another form of Chinese power that deserves attention is China's military power. China's military, the People's Liberation Army (PLA), has historically been a large land force with a very limited ability to project and sustain power beyond China's borders. China's military power has increased significantly over the last decade, creating both newfound respect and heightened concerns in other Asian countries.[22] One analyst has described "three pillars" of PLA reform and modernization, including (1) development, procurement, and fielding of new weapons systems and capabilities; (2) institutional and systemic reforms to improve the professionalism and quality of Chinese military personnel; and (3) development of new war-fighting doctrines for employing these new capabilities.[23] China's military modernization has been supported by significant increases in defense spending, with the PLA receiving double-digit real budget increases every year since 1997. The official 2007 defense budget is approximately $45 billion, but estimates that include military-related and off-budget spending suggest that total 2007 spending may range from $85 to $135 billion.[24] This increased funding has underwritten higher salaries, expanded training and facilities, and the development and acquisition of advanced Chinese and Russian arms.

Many of the new weapons systems the PLA is acquiring appear to be focused primarily on deterring Taiwan independence and deterring or delaying possible U.S. intervention. These include development of more accurate short-range and medium-range conventional ballistic missiles, acquisition of Russian Kilo-class submarines and Sovremenny destroyers equipped with missiles designed to target U.S. aircraft carriers, and modernization of China's strategic nuclear arsenal. Chinese military strategists are exploring tactics such as attacks on U.S. military computer systems and space assets as means of deterring or delaying the arrival of U.S. military forces in the event of a Taiwan crisis. China's January 2007 test of a direct-ascent anti-satellite weapon illustrates one aspect of these efforts. To the extent that these "anti-access strategies" are actually able to hold U.S. military forces in the Western Pacific at risk, they may begin to shift regional perceptions of the military balance of power in Asia.[25]

Some of the new military capabilities China is developing will significantly expand the PLA's ability to project power within Asia. In addition to the capabilities listed above, China is also deploying tankers and air-refueling technology that will extend the range of Chinese fighters. The PLA is improving the capabilities of its airborne and amphibious forces capable of expeditionary operations and making efforts to improve its airlift and sealift capability. Chinese military officials are now openly discussing building an aircraft carrier, citing the need to contribute to humanitarian relief operations and protect China's sea lanes of communication as justification.[26] A recent study notes that the PLA already performs power projection missions to some extent by responding to crises, contributing to deterrence, and enhancing regional stability. Although lack of foreign bases constrains PLA power projection capability, the PLA is increasing its "presence deployments" through naval visits and port calls and PLA participation in joint and combined military exercises with other militaries.[27]

China's accelerated military modernization program has been accompanied by efforts to reassure its Asian neighbors that a more powerful PLA will not threaten their security. China has sought to demonstrate that its military and paramilitary forces can make useful contributions to regional and global security, including via increased participation in United Nations peacekeeping missions and humanitarian relief operations following the Indian Ocean tsunami in 2004 and the Pakistan earthquake in 2005. China has also offered to increase regional cooperation on non-traditional security issues. Although the resources committed to these missions have been relatively modest, they are intended to showcase a constructive role for Chinese military power. Chinese military officers are now discussing ways in which the PLA might contribute to regional security goals by providing "public goods" such as counterpiracy measures, humanitarian assistance and disaster relief, and by contributing to the security of sea lanes of communication. China clearly hopes that defining ways in which the Chinese military contributes to regional security will ease concerns about its military spending and improvements in its power projection capabilities.

"Soft Power"

In contrast to China's military modernization, Chinese efforts to expand its "soft power" within Asia have not raised similar concerns. The discussion below focuses on soft power in terms of China's ability to persuade others to pursue its goals and values or to emulate its behavior. One important trend is increasing contact between Chinese citizens and people in other Asian countries. Flows of tourists and students between China and other Asian countries have increased dramatically in recent years as China has loosened restrictions on overseas travel by its citizens. Chinese tourists have flocked to Asia, with about four million visiting other East Asian countries in 2004.[28] Many Chinese tourists visit Asian countries with tour groups, which do not always leave a positive impression in the countries they visit. Educational contacts between China and Asia have also increased significantly. China sent about ninety thousand students to East Asian countries in 2005 and hosted more than one hundred thousand East Asian students in 2006, with South Korea and Japan sending the most.[29] The Chinese government has supplemented these educational exchanges by supporting the establishment of "Confucius Institutes" in foreign countries to teach Chinese language and promote Chinese culture. The first Confucius Institute was established in 2004; there are now more than 210 institutes in fifty-four countries.[30] As of the end of 2007, six East Asian countries and India hosted some forty-three Confucius Institutes, with Thailand, South Korea, and Japan hosting at least ten apiece.[31]

In addition to business, tourism, and student contacts, the Chinese government actively encourages Chinese scholars and experts to participate in academic and unofficial "Track 2" policy conferences in Asia. Much of this participation occurs via Chinese government think tanks or Government-Operated Non-Governmental Organizations (GONGOs) created to interact with foreign non-government organizations. The Chinese government has sought to increase contacts between Chinese and East Asian think tanks—and to exert some degree of control over the regional agenda—by providing financial and organizational support for participation of Chinese experts and by sponsoring the establishment of the Network of East Asian Think-Tanks (NEAT) in 2003. NEAT includes members from all the ASEAN + 3 countries. The China Foreign Affairs University, which reports to the Chinese Foreign Ministry, serves as NEAT's general coordinator with responsibility for coordinating cooperation between think tanks in the ASEAN + 3 countries and coordinating Chinese domestic think tanks. NEAT's agenda is focused on increasing East Asian cooperation and promoting regional integration.[32] Chinese scholars and experts increasingly have the language skills and expertise to function effectively in these types of meetings. However, the perception that Chinese participants often deliver approved government talking points and cannot fully express their individual viewpoints probably limits their influence.

Appeals to cultural and linguistic affinities have been important in dealing with countries with significant ethnic Chinese minorities. Malaysia and Indonesia, which previously viewed their ethnic Chinese populations with suspicion, now regard them as an asset and comparative advantage in building economic relations with China. China found some sympathy in Southeast Asia for appeals to "Asian values" during its efforts to resist human rights pressure from the United States and Europe in the 1990s. Cultural and linguistic diversity in Asia is likely to limit China's ability to harness purported common "Confucian values" as a diplomatic tool. Few Asian elites are attracted to Chinese values or desire to emulate China's system of government.

In the cultural sphere, talented China artists are beginning to win regional and international recognition. Some Chinese cultural products reflect traditional Chinese culture in ways that resonate within East Asia, but many others have more limited regional appeal due to their focus on Chinese domestic concerns, their derivative nature, and language barriers. Films have arguably been China's most successful cultural exports. Some artists such as director Zhang Yimou and actress Gong Li have built international reputations based on their work in China, but the most successful Chinese actors and directors (such as Jackie Chan and Ang Lee) are actually from Hong Kong or Taiwan. A boom is under way in Chinese visual arts, but much of this work is derivative rather than setting new trends. In comparison with the work being produced in other Asian countries, Chinese cultural products are limited by the less developed Chinese market, political constraints on content, and the lack of effective intellectual property rights to ensure that innovation is appropriately compensated. Some of these constraints are likely to relax as China becomes richer, but for now other Asian countries are producing work that has more regional impact and influence. It is also worth noting that many of the most successful Chinese achieved their fame with work done outside China, including Nobel Prize–winning novelist Gao Xingjian.

Chinese companies have sought, with limited success, to build internationally recognized brand names. Haier (refrigerators) and Huawei (routers and communications products) have been most successful. However, in most cases Chinese products currently compete on the basis of price rather than quality. Nevertheless, if goods are cheap enough, Chinese products can still have a significant impact that promotes a positive image of China. For example, Chinese motorcycles that sell at about a quarter of the price of those produced in Japanese-owned factories in Thailand have become affordable for poor villagers in Laos. The resulting access to transportation has literally saved lives and has had a major improvement in the quality of life for Laotian villagers in remote areas.[33]

Many Asian elites look at China's economic success with envy and admiration. The pace of construction in China's major cities—and the number of architecturally ambitious new buildings in Beijing and Shanghai—is striking. Beijing built an impressive set of facilities and infrastructure improvements to support the 2008 Olympics. China's manned space program is regarded by some Asian elites as an important technological achievement of the Chinese system. Yet these impressive accomplishments have a darker side that is quickly evident. China's breakneck growth has been accompanied by rampant environmental degradation that has damaged China's air and water.[34] Rapid growth and construction in China's major cities has destroyed many of their most distinctive features and displaced poorer citizens to distant suburbs with limited compensation. Poor urban planning and rapid growth in the number of automobiles are making traffic a nightmare in many Chinese cities.

Some believe the Chinese approach of reforming the economy while limiting political freedom represents a new development model with considerable appeal to authoritarian leaders in developing countries.[35] China's development model actually draws heavily on orthodox development economics and benefits from special factors such as a large domestic market and large labor supply that cannot readily be replicated by most other countries.[36] Domestic problems, social inequality, environmental degradation, and periodic political clampdowns also limit China's attractiveness as a model for others to emulate. Within Asia, Vietnam has clearly been influenced by China's approach to economic development, but the country Chinese leaders have tried hardest to influence—North Korea—has proved reluctant to embrace a Chinese-style opening. A slowdown in growth or a major political incident would highlight the downsides of the Chinese model and significantly reduce China's ability to employ soft power as a diplomatic tool.

ASSESSMENT OF CHINA'S ASIA STRATEGY

China's efforts to provide reassurance of its benign intentions have had significant impact, but Asian states still have significant concerns. Some Southeast Asian states are actively encouraging the United States, Japan, and India to take a more prominent role in regional affairs to balance against Chinese influence. Asian governments have decided to treat China as an economic opportunity, but Southeast Asian businessmen regard competition from Chinese exports as a serious challenge, and Korean and Japanese businessmen worry that Chinese enterprises may quickly move up the technology ladder to compete with their exports of more advanced goods. Asian states have welcomed China's participation in multilateral organizations, but Beijing's behavior within regional forums has been mixed. In negotiations with ASEAN states over the China-ASEAN Free Trade Agreement, China let individual ASEAN states determine their own comfort level with the coverage and pace of trade liberalization commitments. The resulting agreement is a hodgepodge, but ASEAN states were pleased at Beijing's willingness to defer to their concerns. One Southeast Asian diplomat noted that China has generally been willing to adapt its proposals for regional cooperation to build consensus, deferring contentious issues or delaying proposals that are moving too fast for ASEAN sensibilities.[37]

In other areas, China's behavior has been less accommodating. Asian officials and security analysts praise Beijing's willingness to cooperate and to defer resolution of maritime territorial disputes and sovereignty issues but also note that China has been unwilling to make substantive concessions on most issues. China agreed to participate in a sub-regional organization to address Mekong River issues but has generally been unresponsive to the concerns of those in downstream countries adversely affected by Chinese dams.[38] Beijing's responsiveness to Asian concerns about food and product safety has also varied. China is quick to pull any foods that have safety issues from the Japanese market but reportedly rebuffed Indonesian efforts to apply its domestic food safety standards to Chinese imports.[39] China has pursued joint energy exploration projects with the Philippines and Vietnam in the Spratly Islands, which violate the spirit of its pledge to resolve its sovereignty claims multilaterally, and has reportedly begun to press its claims to the Spratly Islands in bilateral meetings with some ASEAN states. China's military confidence-building measures have reassured some skeptics, but others note that Beijing has provided only limited information about its military capabilities and has refused to discuss the most important security issues (such as Taiwan) in multilateral settings.

China's regional security strategy depends on increasing Chinese influence without antagonizing the United States. Chinese officials have made conscious efforts to reassure the United States that Beijing recognizes U.S. interests in Asia and has no intention of pushing the United States out of the region. Beijing has not repeated its 1997 campaign to press U.S. allies in Asia to abandon their alliances with Washington. China's cooperation on counterterrorism and critical role in efforts to persuade North Korea to abandon its nuclear weapons program have provided positive security cooperation that has helped ease U.S. concerns. Nevertheless, U.S. officials remain wary of Chinese efforts to improve its security ties with U.S. allies and have noted China's apparent preference for regional organizations such as the SCO and the East Asian Summit where the United States is not a member. U.S. officials and analysts are also paying close attention to China's military modernization efforts; China's January 2007 test of a direct-ascent anti-satellite (ASAT) weapon sparked serious debate in the United States and elsewhere about China's strategic intentions in space.[40] U.S. preoccupation with Iraq and Afghanistan has distracted attention from China's efforts to increase its influence in Asia, but these concerns have not gone away. Japanese officials share many of the same concerns about Chinese regional influence and military modernization efforts, which have become an aggravating factor in Sino-Japanese relations.

THEORETICAL PERSPECTIVES ON CHINA'S INTERNATIONAL BEHAVIOR

The preceding assessment has focused on China's efforts to increase its power and regional influence without antagonizing the United States or scaring its neighbors. China's policy has been remarkably successful to date but has not fully eased concerns about how a stronger China might behave in the future. Different theoretical lenses provide different interpretations of recent Chinese behavior and contrasting projections of how a stronger China might behave in the future.

A traditional Realist perspective would emphasize China's continuing efforts to build military capabilities and comprehensive national power in a way that increases its long-term ability to shape Asia in directions compatible with its interests. This perspective emphasizes the limitations on China's military transparency and Beijing's efforts to keep important hard security issues (such as the Taiwan issue, its rising military spending, and its nuclear modernization) out of multilateral security forums. The cooperative security approach in the new security concept may be useful in dealing with non-traditional security issues such as piracy but has limited utility in dealing with zero-sum territorial disputes or serious conflicts of interests. U.S. alliances in Asia remain important to U.S. regional interests and to the security of U.S. allies. China has not repeated its 1997–1998 diplomatic campaign against U.S. alliances in Asia but has made clear that, although it disapproves of U.S. security alliances in Asia in principle, in practice it recognizes that the alliances make some contributions to regional security. China has sought to improve bilateral relations (including bilateral security cooperation) with U.S. allies such as the Philippines and Thailand to try to ensure that U.S. alliances do not become directed against China. From a Realist perspective, China has been deferring sovereignty disputes and accepting U.S. security alliances in Asia because it lacks the power to resolve these issues in its favor. Increasing Chinese relative power may produce more aggressive behavior in the future. Realists acknowledge the importance of increasing regional economy ties but tend to see these in terms of PRC efforts to generate political leverage by making its trading partners dependent on the Chinese market. A Realist perspective highlights China's continuing reluctance to accept binding constraints on its exercise of power in Asia and is therefore suspicious about how a more powerful China might behave in the future.

A Liberal institutionalist perspective would highlight the ways in which China's membership in international organizations and the constraints of economic interdependence are likely to shape definitions of Chinese interests and constrain the ways in which Beijing chooses to pursue those interests. In general, this perspective sees China's greater engagement in the region as raising the costs of using force and increasing the incentives for China to behave in a peaceful manner when conflicts of interest arise. Common interests such as regional stability and the need for international cooperation to handle non-traditional security issues explain China's greater willingness to cooperate in regional organizations. This viewpoint sees Chinese efforts to shape international rules and norms as evidence that China will ultimately be willing to adhere to these international rules of the game. This perspective notes that China's economic growth is being achieved through greater international cooperation and participation in the global economy. As China's power rises, constraints on its international behavior and the costs of using force will also continue to rise. This perspective is therefore relatively optimistic that a more powerful China will continue to behave in a restrained manner.

A classical Liberal perspective would focus on the nature of the Chinese regime and the resulting implications for China's future behavior.

From this perspective, many of the current concerns about China's international behavior are due to the authoritarian nature of the Chinese government, which may give excessive weight to military and sovereignty concerns and produce decision-making and crisis management procedures that increase the chances for military conflict. Democracy or political liberalization in China might help address some of these factors over the long term, but the CCP's reluctance to institute genuine political reforms is a significant cause for concern about how a stronger China will behave in the future. A related approach is to consider China from the perspective of the two-level game framework developed by Robert Putnam, as David Shambaugh develops in his chapter in this volume.[41] This approach captures Beijing's efforts to balance domestic and international considerations in its foreign policy–making and can address the potential for international developments (such as the possibility of Taiwan independence or an oil shock) to generate a political crisis that threatens regime survival. This captures a significant amount of the calculative aspect of Chinese behavior but also highlights concerns that nationalism and the limited representation of business interests could limit the win set in international negotiations and produce aggressive behavior in the future. China's diplomatic practice over the last decade does not include many examples of aggressive action, but this may be because China deferred action on contentious issues such as maritime sovereignty disputes because it lacked the power to achieve its goals and was unable to compromise due to domestic constraints.

Finally, a Constructivist perspective highlights the potential for norms, culture, identity, and mutual interactions to constrain Chinese behavior in the future.[42] This viewpoint would take the stated principles underlying Chinese foreign policy more seriously as an indicator of China's genuine intentions. Some scholars view the commonalities between China's new security concept and ASEAN principles of non-interference as evidence of a growing normative convergence between China and ASEAN that might serve as the basis for a broader regional security order.[43] From this perspective, efforts by other Asian countries to engage China and China's increasing involvement in international affairs and multilateral organizations have produced significant and genuine change in Chinese foreign policy preferences that suggest a stronger China less constrained by its international environment may still behave in a restrained manner. Other Constructivist perspectives focus more on China's realpolitik strategic culture and are much less sanguine about prospects for restraint from a more powerful China.[44] Constructivist predictions depend heavily on assumptions about which elements of Chinese culture and identity matter most in explaining China's international behavior.

CONCLUSION

Different variants of international relations theory can explain some aspects of China's recent behavior, but no single theory provides a complete explanation. A persuasive model for Chinese foreign policy–making needs to integrate both international and domestic variables to explain specific Chinese foreign policy decisions. International relations theories are helpful in identifying factors that may influence how a more powerful and less constrained China might behave in the future. However, each theory identifies different factors as important, highlighting the need for analytical judgment in deciding which factors are most important and which theories are most persuasive in illuminating China's future behavior in Asia.

A useful way of thinking through future possibilities is to examine likely consequences if present trends continue as well as potential developments that could alter or reverse those trends. China's political leadership must continue to manage a host of difficult domestic challenges in order to maintain stability and support economic growth. Growth gives the central government additional resources but also aggravates problems such as pollution, inequality, and energy insecurity. China's rapid growth is increasing trade with Asia, the United States, and Europe, and providing resources that underwrite China's military modernization and help create jobs and rising living standards that contribute to social stability. If this trend continues, Chinese political influence in Asia is likely to grow. However, China will also experience increasing economic frictions with the United States and with Asian countries such as Japan and South Korea where politically important industries already complain about unfair competition with Chinese firms. The Chinese economy's demand for energy and commodity imports may also stimulate increased competition with Asian countries. If China's military modernization continues on its present path, Beijing's position with respect to Taiwan is likely strengthened considerably, but at the cost of heightened tensions with the United States, Japan, and some Southeast Asian countries as PLA capabilities increase. Efforts to reassure neighbors are likely to continue, notably through an increase in exercises with Asian militaries and increased cooperation on non-traditional security issues. A Chinese decision to acquire an aircraft carrier would be viewed as a watershed event, even if Beijing justifies the acquisition in terms of non-traditional security missions. Continued Chinese diplomatic success would likely require Beijing to pursue positive regional initiatives while exercising military restraint and deferring controversial issues to the future. A more confident China would likely continue to focus on cooperative approaches and long-term regional goals. A key question is whether China will continue to pursue a moderate course if issues such as territorial disputes or energy security force themselves onto the regional agenda.

A number of domestic and regional developments could alter the trajectory of China's Asia policy. Serious internal unrest could lead to a domestic crackdown, which would damage China's reputation within the region and heighten concerns about Chinese international behavior. A domestic economic crisis could lead China's leaders to focus on restoring growth and exporting their way out of a crisis, regardless of the negative impact on its neighbors. A regional or global economic slump could have a similar result, although the negative impact on China's relations with the region would likely be greater. Regional security problems could also produce changes in Chinese policy. A North Korean collapse or a military conflict precipitated by Pyongyang's nuclear weapons ambitions could lead to assertive Chinese actions to control the situation, which could heighten conflicts with Seoul, Tokyo, and Washington. Despite China's efforts to paint Taiwan as a "domestic issue" that is qualitatively different from its approach to international security concerns, Asian countries still view Beijing's approach to Taiwan as a litmus test for Chinese behavior. A decision to use force against Taiwan would alarm East Asian countries and could undo many of the gains made in Beijing's decade-long reassurance campaign.

Finally, heightened rivalry between China and Japan could raise bilateral tensions and potentially disrupt economic cooperation and the trend toward greater regional cooperation in the region. Both governments seek to stabilize relations, but competition for regional leadership or a security incident over resources or disputed territory in the East China Sea could alter the dynamics of the relationship in a negative direction.

During the reform era, China has sought to preserve a stable international environment that supports continued economic growth that can help maintain domestic stability, build its national wealth and power, and expand its influence. These principles have also guided China's Asia policy, which has emphasized the need to avoid a confrontation with the United States and to reassure Asian countries that a stronger China will not threaten their interests. China's policy has been remarkably successful in preserving a stable regional environment and persuading its neighbors to view China as an opportunity rather than a threat. Despite China's restrained and constructive regional behavior over the last decade, significant concerns remain about how a stronger and less constrained China might behave in the future, concerns that are especially prevalent in the United States and Japan, two of the strongest countries in the Asia-Pacific region. These uncertainties—and China's increasing role in shaping Asia's future—ensure that debate about how a stronger China will behave in the future will remain a contentious issue in both the United States and in Asia.

NOTES

1. Suisheng Zhao, ed., *Chinese Foreign Policy: Pragmatism and Strategic Behavior* (Armonk, N.Y.: M. E. Sharpe, 2004); Robert Sutter, *China's Rise in Asia: Promises and Perils* (New York: Rowman & Littlefield, 2005); Evelyn Goh, ed., *Betwixt and Between: Southeast Asian Strategic Relations with the U.S. and China* (Singapore: Institute of Defence and Strategic Studies, 2005); David Shambaugh, ed., *Power Shift: China and Asia's New Dynamics* (Berkeley: University of California Press, 2006); Michael A. Glosny, "Heading toward a Win-Win Future?: Recent Developments in China's Policy towards Southeast Asia," *Asian Security* 2, no. 1 (2006): 24–57; Bronson Percival, *The Dragon Looks South: China and Southeast Asia in the New Century* (Westport, Conn.: Praeger Security International, 2007); and Evelyn Goh and Sheldon W. Simon, eds., *China, the United States, and Southeast Asia: Contending Perspectives on Politics, Security, and Economics* (New York: Routledge, 2008).

2. Sutter, *China's Rise in Asia*, 9–10.

3. For assessments of China's grand strategy, see Michael D. Swaine and Ashley J. Tellis, *Interpreting China's Grand Strategy: Past Present and Future* (Washington, D.C.: RAND, 2000); and Avery Goldstein, *Rising to the Challenge: China's Grand Strategy and International Security* (Stanford, Calif.: Stanford University Press, 2005).

4. Erica Strecker Downs and Phillip C. Saunders, "Legitimacy and the Limits of Nationalism: China and the Diaoyu Islands," *International Security* 23, no. 3 (Winter 1998/1999): 114–146.

5. United Nations Comtrade database; MOFCOM/SAFE MOFCOM and National Statistic Bureau, "2005 Niandu Zhongguo Duiwai zhijie touzi tongji gongbao," October 2006, hzs.mofcom.gov.cn/aarticle/date/200609/20060903095437.html. For an English translation, see Open Source Center, "2005 Statistical Bulletin of China's Outward Foreign Direct Investment," CPP20070419308001.

6. David Barboza, "'Made in China' Labels Don't Tell Whole Story," *International Herald Tribune*, February 9, 2006.

7. World Bank, "Key Development Data & Statistics," available at www.worldbank.org/. East Asia percentage of global GDP is based on 2005 purchasing power parity estimates in World Bank, *2007 World Development Indicators* (Washington, D.C.: World Bank, 2007), 185.

8. Sutter, *China's Rise in Asia*; Marvin C. Ott, "Southeast Asian Security Challenges: America's Response?" *Strategic Forum*, no. 222 (October 2006), www.ndu.edu/inss/strforum/SF222/SF222.pdf (accessed January 15, 2008).

9. For accounts of how Chinese leaders and analysts came to this realization, see David Shambaugh, "China Engages Asia: Reshaping the Regional Order," *International Security* 29, no. 3 (2004–2005): 64–99; and Yong Deng, "Reputation and the Security Dilemma: China Reacts to the China Threat Theory," in *New Directions in the Study of China's Foreign Policy*, ed. Alastair Iain Johnston and Robert S. Ross (Stanford, Calif.: Stanford University Press, 2006), 186–214.

10. Michael T. Klare, "The Next Great Arms Race," *Foreign Affairs* 72, no. 3 (May/June 1993): 136–152; Denny Roy, "Hegemon on the Horizon? China's Threat to East Asian Security," *International Security* 19, no. 1 (Summer 1994): 149–168; and Richard Bernstein and Ross H. Munro, *The Coming Conflict with China* (New York: Alfred A. Knopf, 1997). For a survey of regional views and strategies, see Alas-

tair Iain Johnston and Robert S. Ross, eds., *Engaging China: The Management of an Emerging Power* (New York: Routledge, 1999).

11. Evan S. Medeiros and M. Taylor Fravel, "China's New Diplomacy," *Foreign Affairs* 82, no. 6 (2003): 22–35.

12. David M. Finkelstein, "China's New Security Concept: Reading between the Lines," *Washington Journal of Modern China* 5, no. 1 (1999): 37–50.

13. The ten ASEAN members are Brunei, Cambodia, Indonesia, Laos, Malaysia, Myanmar (Burma), the Philippines, Singapore, Thailand, and Vietnam.

14. On the role for multilateral organizations in legitimating and constraining power, see John Gerard Ruggie, ed., *Multilateralism Matters* (New York: Columbia University Press, 1993); and G. John Ikenberry, "Institutions, Strategic Restraint, and the Persistence of American Postwar Order," *International Security* 23, no. 3 (Winter 1998/1999): 43–78. On China's changing attitude and increasing participation in these institutions, see Elizabeth Economy and Michel Oksenberg, eds., *China Joins the World: Progress and Prospects* (New York: Council on Foreign Relations, 1999); Alastair Iain Johnston, "Socialization in International Institutions: The ASEAN Way and International Relations Theory," in *International Relations Theory and the Asia-Pacific*, ed. G. John Ikenberry and Michael Mastanduno (New York: Columbia University Press, 2003), 107–162; and Bates Gill, *Rising Star: China's New Security Diplomacy* (Washington, D.C.: Brookings Institution, 2007).

15. See Marc Lanteigne, *China's Engagement with International Institutions: Alternate Paths to Global Power* (New York: Routledge, 2005); and Guoguang Wu and Helen Lansdowne, eds., *China Turns to Multilateralism: Foreign Policy and Regional Security* (New York: Routledge, 2008).

16. China's border dispute with India is the one important land border dispute that remains unresolved.

17. M. Taylor Fravel, "Regime Insecurity and International Cooperation: Explaining China's Compromises in Territorial Disputes," *International Security* 30, no. 2 (Fall 2005): 46–83.

18. Information Office of the State Council of the People's Republic of China, "China's National Defense in 2006," December 2006; Xinhua, "First Chinese UN Peacekeeping Force Commander Takes Office," September 18, 2007; all available at www.xinhuanet.com.

19. "China Moves on Free Trade Negotiations," *Asia Pulse*, March 8, 2005.

20. Percentages are calculated from Chinese export statistics as reported in the UN Comtrade database.

21. John W. Garver, "Development of China's Overland Transportation Links with Central, South-west and South Asia," *China Quarterly*, no. 185 (March 2006): 1–22; Phillip C. Saunders, *China's Global Activism: Strategy, Drivers, and Tools* (Washington, D.C.: National Defense University Press, 2006), www.ndu.edu/inss/Occasional _Papers/OCP4.pdf (accessed January 15, 2008).

22. Two important recent studies of China's military are David Shambaugh, *Modernizing China's Military: Progress, Problems, and Prospects* (Berkeley: University of California Press, 2004); and Dennis J. Blasko, *The Chinese Army Today: Tradition and Transformation for the 21st Century* (New York: Routledge, 2006).

23. David M. Finkelstein, "China's National Military Strategy: An Overview of the 'Military Strategic Guidelines,'" in *Right-Sizing the People's Liberation Army: Exploring*

the Contours of China's Military, ed. Roy Kamphausen and Andrew Scobell (Carlisle, Penn.: Strategic Studies Institute, 2007), 70–72.

24. Office of the Secretary of Defense, *Military Power of the People's Republic of China, 2007*, Annual Report to Congress, 25, available at www.defenselink.mil/pubs/china.html. The higher figures are a DIA estimate of total PRC defense-related spending.

25. For an assessment of Chinese anti-access strategies and their implications, see Roger Cliff, Mark Burles, Michael S. Chase, Derek Eaton, and Kevin L. Pollpeter, *Entering the Dragon's Lair: Chinese Antiaccess Strategies and Their Implications for the United States* (Arlington, Va.: Rand Corporation, 2007).

26. Office of the Secretary of Defense, *Military Power of the People's Republic of China, 2007.*

27. Roy D. Kamphausen and Justin Liang, "PLA Power Projection: Current Realities and Emerging Trends," in *Assessing the Threat: The Chinese Military and Taiwan's Security*, ed. Michael D. Swaine, Andrew N. D. Yang, and Evan Medeiros (Washington, D.C.: Carnegie Endowment for International Peace, 2007), 111–150.

28. CLSA Special Report, *Chinese Tourists Coming, Ready or Not!* (New York: CLSA, 2005), 37.

29. Figures for 2005 outbound Chinese students are from the UNESCO Institute for Statistics, stats.uis.unesco.org/unesco/TableViewer/document.aspx?ReportId=143&IF_Language=eng; figures for 2006 East Asian students studying in China are from *China's Foreign Affairs, 2007* (Beijing: World Affairs Press, 2007), table 10.

30. Xinhua, "Confucius Institutes Welcome Sponsorship, Says Chinese Official," *People's Daily Online*, June 24, 2007, english.peopledaily.com.cn/200706/24/eng20070624_387191.html (accessed January 16, 2008).

31. Office of Chinese Language Council International, "Confucius Institutes: Asia," www.hanban.org/cn_hanban/kzxy_list.php?state1=Asia (accessed January 18, 2008).

32. Network of East Asian Think-Tanks, "About Us," www.neat.org.cn/english/gywm/index.php?topic_id=001002 (accessed January, 18, 2008).

33. Thomas Fuller, "Made in China: Cheap Products Change Lives," *New York Times*, December 27, 2007.

34. See Elizabeth C. Economy, *The River Runs Black* (Ithaca, N.Y.: Cornell University Press, 2004).

35. Joshua Cooper Ramos, *The Beijing Consensus* (London: Foreign Policy Centre, 2004), fpc.org.uk/fsblob/244.pdf (accessed January 18, 2008); Joshua Kurlantzick, "Cultural Revolution: How China Is Changing Global Diplomacy," *New Republic*, June 27, 2005, 16–21. For other views, see Minxin Pei, *China's Trapped Transition: The Limits of Developmental Autocracy* (Cambridge, Mass.: Harvard University Press, 2006); and Randall Peerenboom, *China Modernizes: Threat to the West or Model for the Rest?* (New York: Oxford University Press, 2007).

36. Chinese labor costs are beginning to rise, especially in major cities in Southeast China. Some labor-intensive production is beginning to move to countries such as Bangladesh and Vietnam that have lower labor costs.

37. Interviews with Southeast Asian diplomats, 2004–2007.

38. Alexander Liebman, "Trickle-Down Hegemony? China's 'Peaceful Rise' and Dam Building on the Mekong," *Contemporary Southeast Asia* 27, no. 2 (2005):

281–304; Richard P. Cronin, "Destructive Mekong Dams: Critical Need for Transparency," Henry L. Stimson Center, March 26, 2007, www.stimson.org/pub.cfm ?id=435; Evelyn Goh, *Developing the Mekong: Regionalism and Regional Security in China-Southeast Asia Relations,* Adelphi Paper 387 (London: IISS, 2007).

39. Interviews, Beijing, August 2007; Ariana Eunjung Cha, "Asians Say Trade Complaints Bring Out the Bully in China," *Washington Post,* September 5, 2007.

40. See for example K. K. Nair, "China's ASAT Test: Implications and Options," *Air Power* 2, no. 2 (Summer 2007): 57–74.

41. Robert Putnam, "Diplomacy and Domestic Politics: The Logic of Two-Level Games," *International Organization* 42 (1988): 427–461.

42. For an interesting application of Constructivist theory to the case of China, see Johnston, "Socialization in International Institutions," 107–162.

43. Muthiah Alagappa and Amitav Acharya express these views in their respective chapters in Muthiah Alagappa, ed., *Asian Security Order: Instrumental and Normative Features* (Stanford, Calif.: Stanford University Press, 2003).

44. On China's strategic culture, see Alastair Iain Johnston, "Cultural Realism and Strategy in Maoist China," in *The Culture of National Security: Norms and Identity in World Politics,* ed. Peter J. Katzenstein (New York: Columbia University Press, 1996), 216–270.

7

The Rise of India in Asia

Sumit Ganguly

The last decade has witnessed a dramatic transformation of India's foreign and economic policies. These changes have fundamentally enhanced India's profile in Asia and beyond. India has forged significant ties with the economically dynamic parts of Southeast Asia, signed an important free trade agreement with Singapore, become a member of the ASEAN Regional Forum (ARF), and has broadened its relationship with Japan. Through the forging of multiple bilateral and multilateral ties, it is seeking to assert itself as a significant actor in the region.

This chapter will examine the transformation of India's grand strategy in the post–Cold War era, discuss the reactions of other major powers in Asia, and assess the possibilities and limits of India's emergence as a great power. To that end, it will carefully outline sources and prospects of the transformation of India's foreign and economic policies, assess their impact on domestic capabilities and regional actors, and examine the likely reactions of other key players in Asia. The central argument of this chapter is that India aspires to be a major Asian power and is pursuing a hedging strategy against the People's Republic of China, its most likely and keenest competitor for a similar status in Asia. The chapter will also contend that while other major states in Asia are not concerned or distressed with India's rise, the PRC does view India's attempt to break free from its subcontinental status with growing concern. One of the key hurdles that confronts India on this pathway to great power status is its current inability to resolve ongoing differences with at least two of its subcontinental neighbors, Pakistan and, to a lesser degree, Bangladesh.

The chapter is organized along four levels of analysis. At the outset it deals with the transformation of the global order at the end of the Cold War and its impact on India's foreign and security policy choices. In making this argument, the chapter argues that this was a clear case of "the second image reversed"—namely, the impact of international politics on domestic political and economic arrangements.[1] It then turns to a discussion of India's relations with key Asian states. The focus then shifts to India and its dealings with its subcontinental neighbors and finally dwells upon some current features of Indian politics that can shape the future course of the country's foreign and security policy choices and thereby influence its position in Asia.

THE PRESENCE OF THE PAST

During the Cold War, as is well known, India adopted a policy of non-alignment.[2] The policy did not necessarily call for equidistance from both superpowers but instead meant that India sought not to be drawn into either superpower's ideological or strategic orbit. Despite this professed commitment to such a principle, for all practical purposes, India elided over Soviet malfeasances and was a harsh critic of the shortcomings of American foreign policy. Such a stance contributed to a frosty Indo-American relationship.[3] In turn, in the absence of long-held cultural ties, the paucity of economic interests, and lacking vital strategic interests in the region, the United States also chose to mostly ignore India. Consequently, toward the end of the Cold War, apart from cordial relations with the Soviet Union, significant portions of the Eastern Bloc, and a motley collection of poor states in Africa and Latin America, India had few viable international ties. The Third World coalition that India had sought to forge in the 1950s and 1960s had become mostly a caricature.[4]

The Cold War's end forced India's policymakers to re-examine some of the key assumptions of India's grand strategy. In the realm of foreign policy they realized that the heyday of non-alignment had long come to a close. As Inder Gujral, a former Indian prime minister, once stated, "It is a mantra that we will have to keep repeating but whom are you going to be non-aligned against?"[5] More specifically, despite this professed commitment to non-alignment, key members of India's foreign policy establishment also recognized that Russia, the principal successor state to the former Soviet Union, was unlikely (and very possibly unwilling) to play the same role of the erstwhile USSR. Namely, Russia could not be counted upon to use its veto at the United Nations Security Council on the critical Kashmir dispute with Pakistan, that it would not serve as a counterweight to a potentially revanchist People's Republic of China, and that it would no longer sell advanced weaponry at highly concessional rates. Accordingly, an unreflective reliance on Russia would ill serve India's foreign and security policy interests.

With the Soviet demise it was also apparent that the United States, for the foreseeable future, would remain as the dominant global power. This realization necessitated a fundamental re-appraisal of the Indo-U.S. relationship despite the presence of various extant bilateral differences on questions pertaining to non-proliferation, human rights, and trade issues.

Though significant segments of the policy elite came to these ineluctable conclusions, the shift in India's foreign and security policy orientations did not occur without a vigorous internal debate. Some individuals and groups within the ruling Congress Party refused to abandon their commitment to a vision of Nehruvian socialism at home and non-alignment abroad. They continued to argue that these precepts had not lost their relevance and instead should be pursued with renewed vigor.[6] They also contended that India should take the lead in forging a multipolar world order and work in concert with other powers such as the People's Republic of China (PRC), Russia, and France to balance overweening American power. A second strand of opinion, mostly associated with the right-of-center, Hindu nationalist Bharatiya Janata Party (BJP), argued for a more muscular, assertive Indian foreign policy. It also called for the abandonment of India's professed policy of nuclear abstinence, to defy the global non-proliferation regime, and overtly acquire an independent nuclear force.[7]

Kanti Bajpai, a noted Indian international relations scholar, has described India's pre–Cold War foreign and security policy strategy as "modified structuralism."[8] The key components of this strategy had involved a commitment to the maximization of India's national interests but with a resolute desire to pursue a normative world order. The pursuit of ideational goals, however, has for the most part given way to more expedient concerns at the end of the Cold War. Many of India's policy choices, especially those in the international arena, are still couched in the ideational language and rhetoric of the past. However, in practice, they increasingly reveal a more pragmatic approach designed to boost India's material well-being and national security at the cost of the pursuit of broader, normative ideals. Some manifestations of this shift toward pragmatism bear discussion.

To begin with, in 1992, India dropped its long-standing policy of treating Israel at a diplomatic arm's length and extended it full-scale diplomatic recognition.[9] India had kept its distance from Israel during much of the Cold War for two seemingly compelling reasons: first, it was concerned about the political sensitivities of its very substantial domestic Muslim minority, and second, it wanted to maintain its credentials as the standard-bearer of all Third World causes. Neither of these concerns had served India well. The Arab (and most Muslim) states had invariably sided with Pakistan in every Indo-Pakistani conflict and had rarely lost an occasion to upbraid India at the Organization of Islamic Countries (OIC) meetings for real and imagined failures to accord equal treatment to its Muslim citi-

zenry. What made the shift politically acceptable, however, was the onset
of the Madrid peace conference involving members of the Palestine Liberation Organization (PLO) and representatives of the Israeli government.
The onset of these negotiations provided the regime in New Delhi sufficient political cover to depart from its historic (and anachronistic) position on Israel.

India also dispensed with its efforts at leading a pitiful coalition of developing countries that ineffectually carped at the inequities of the global
order. Instead it has sought to forge pragmatic relationships with the United
States, the European Union, Israel, Japan, Russia, and several of the economically dynamic states of Southeast Asia.[10] Also, despite considerable international disapprobation, it blasted its way into the nuclear club in May
1998.[11] The initial reactions, especially those of the United States, the
United Kingdom, Japan, and the People's Republic of China (PRC), were
harsh and swift. Since then, most of the great powers have grudgingly accepted India as a de facto nuclear weapons state.

India was also forced to adopt a markedly different approach to economic development. Since its independence from the British Indian Empire, the country had pursued a state-led strategy of economic growth, with
an emphasis on import-substituting industrialization (ISI). India's pursuit
of a strategy of ISI and its hostility toward foreign investors had also helped
to reinforce India's international isolation. In the words of an Indian political scientist, Ramesh Thakur, India had developed a "bunker mentality"
through the twin pursuit of the policies of non-alignment and ISI.[12] This
strategy, polemical claims notwithstanding, had long outlived its utility. India's economic growth until the early 1980s had been anemic at best and
was failing to make a serious dent on rural and urban poverty. Again, the
Soviet collapse, the concomitant loss of captive markets in the Soviet Union
and the Eastern Bloc, and the discrediting of the model of state-led economic growth coupled with an unprecedented fiscal crisis in 1991 forced
India's policymakers to change course.

The fiscal crisis and the shift in economic policies virtually coincided
with two other dramatic developments in global politics: the end of the
Cold War and the dissolution of the Soviet bloc. Both these events were
fraught with significance for India. During much of the Cold War, for complex reasons, India had had close relations with the Soviet Union.[13] Suffice
to say that this relationship had largely been based upon a common distrust
of the People's Republic of China and, to a lesser degree, the United States.
The Soviets had bolstered this relationship with a highly subsidized arms
transfer arrangement and had granted India access to a substantial market
both at home and in Eastern Europe.[14]

The comfortable intellectual shibboleths that they had long relied on had
little or no utility in guiding their choices. Faced with this unprecedented

situation the Congress government of Prime Minister Narasimha Rao brought about some drastic shifts in the realm of both economic and foreign policies. Despite considerable domestic opposition from across the political spectrum, Rao and his finance minister (subsequently prime minister), an Oxford-trained economist, Manmohan Singh, dramatically cut governmental subsidies, reduced tariff rates and quotas, dispensed with parts of a regulatory maze, and sought to attract much-needed foreign investment.[15] The changes they sought to bring about were not incremental but sweeping.[16]

The fiscal crisis and the Soviet collapse left India's policymakers in a dilemma. These two external events shook the foundations of India's economic and foreign policies unlike any other prior exogenous shocks.[17] Ironically, these twin crises, which forced India to mostly abandon the lodestars of its foreign and economic policies, and thereby helped forge the components of a new grand strategy, also enabled the country to not only end its self-imposed isolation but also to start realizing its potential as a major power.

Pursuing Hard Power

In this quest for major power status, India's policymakers finally and fully embraced the principle that military power can confer considerable advantages to states in the global order. The realization had dawned earlier but thanks to the Nehruvian strand in the country's strategic culture, an element of ambivalence had long characterized the country's relationship with military power and its uses. This ambivalence was finally shed in the early 1990s as compelling external developments forced policymakers to make some critical choices to guarantee the country's long-term security. The specific circumstances that led to a drastic re-appraisal of India's security needs are discussed below.

The Soviet collapse and the concomitant loss of a tacit security guarantee, the growing military and economic clout of the PRC, and its robust nuclear and ballistic missile assistance to Pakistan prompted Indian decision makers to abandon their long-standing policy of calculated nuclear ambiguity. Contrary to widespread popular belief and much polemical commentary, the decision to cross the nuclear Rubicon did not stem from considerations of prestige, status, or the presence of a jingoistic regime in New Delhi.[18] Furthermore, key developments in the global nonproliferation arena added to India's fears.

The decision to acquire an overt nuclear weapons option emerged in the wake of the successful American-led effort to unconditionally and indefinitely extend the Nuclear Nonproliferation Treaty (NPT) and the seemingly inexorable march toward the conclusion of a Comprehensive Test Ban

Treaty (CTBT). India, an early and staunch opponent of the NPT regime, feared that it would come under concerted American and global pressure to accede to the CTBT regime, which had been designed to come into force in September 1998. The treaty's entry into force required some forty-four nations, which had ongoing nuclear power programs, to first accede to the regime.[19]

In the aftermath of the tests, the Indian nuclear weapons program has proceeded apace along with the expansion of delivery capabilities, which includes a robust missile development program. Despite some pressures from segments of India's "attentive public" to develop a substantial nuclear force, responsible Indian strategic planners, however, have made clear that the country will not adopt such a course. Given a deep-seated proclivity in India's political culture toward incremental decision making, strategic caution, and fiscal prudence, it is most unlikely that the country will embark on an open-ended a arms race with the PRC. The primary purpose of the Indian nuclear deterrent is to serve as a hedge against future Chinese nuclear blackmail and coercion. This fear has long haunted Indian strategists.[20] Accordingly, as a very able and thoughtful analyst of India's nuclear weapons program has argued, the country will remain content with the pursuit of a secure, finite deterrent that would address India's long-term security needs.[21] In the absence of a fundamental improvement in Sino-Indian relations and attempts on the part of the PRC to assuage India's legitimate security concerns, it is most unlikely that India will abandon its ongoing nuclear and ballistic missile programs.

FROM "ESTRANGED DEMOCRACIES" TO "NATURAL ALLIES"?[22]

It is perhaps no exaggeration to suggest that no bilateral relationship is more important for India than the one with the United States. Indeed the expanded role that India hopes to play in Asia depends, in considerable measure, on how it succeeds in not merely managing but strengthening this bond. The Indo-U.S. relationship, apart from a brief interlude in the early 1960s during the Kennedy administration, had been mostly frosty.[23] The United States had had few economic, strategic, or cultural links with India and could well afford to ignore it. India, initially, had kept the United States at bay because of its professed commitment to non-alignment. Subsequently, the long (albeit fitful) American military and strategic relationship with Pakistan vitiated the prospects of U.S.-Indian rapprochement. American engagement with India during much of the Cold War, especially after the mid-1960s, became almost completely derivative of its larger global concerns ranging from non-proliferation to human rights. Indeed it was not until the early 1980s, in the aftermath of the Soviet invasion and occupation of Afghanistan, that Indo-U.S. relations acquired ballast. Nevertheless, in the continuing absence of strategic ties and economic complementarities, the American preoccupation with non-proliferation and subsequently a vocal position on human rights violations in the state of Jammu and Kashmir vitiated the prospects of a viable rapprochement.

Only when India realized that the Soviet dissolution was permanent and that the principal successor state, Russia, was at best an anemic partner, did it evince an interest in forging a new relationship with the United States. Simultaneously, the United States also proved to be more forthcoming because of India's embrace, however cautious, of a market-oriented strategy of economic development.[24]

In the wake of the nuclear tests India faced a raft of sanctions from the United States and the major powers. However, through extremely deft and tenacious bilateral and multilateral diplomacy New Delhi managed to have the bulk of the sanctions lifted within two years of the tests. More importantly, it used the ensuing bilateral dialogue with the United States to fashion a vastly improved relationship.[25] The newly forged relationship transcended the second Clinton administration. Indeed, despite the advent of the Bush administration and the concomitant shift in foreign and security policy priorities, the Indo-U.S. relationship continued to thrive.[26] Even the American decision to court Pakistan in the aftermath of the September 11, 2001, attacks failed to derail the steady improvement in Indo-U.S. relations.

The bonds did not fray because, unlike in the past, they had acquired a degree of strength and robustness. Thanks to critical policy choices in both capitals, the two countries now had placed their ties on a more sound foundation. Indeed, despite profound differences on Pakistan and its role in the U.S.-led "war on terror," the Indo-U.S. bilateral relationship continued to flourish.[27] Among other matters, the Bush administration, which had far fewer qualms about India's ongoing nuclear and ballistic missile programs than its predecessor, sought to forge a wider defense and security partnership with India. To that end, it initiated the Next Steps in Strategic Partnership (NSSP), a program of defense cooperation focused on four areas: civilian nuclear technology, dual-use high technology, space research, and ballistic missile defense. The two sides also initiated a major effort to sidestep the expectations of the non-proliferation regime and worked to forge a critical bilateral accord on civilian nuclear energy cooperation.[28] Though the final elements of this agreement are yet to be consummated, the mere willingness of both sides to embark on this extremely ambitious endeavor is a sign of the growing maturity and depth of the Indo-U.S. strategic relationship.

The Indo-U.S. relationship is now largely free from the ideological cant and fervor as well as the geopolitical differences that had vitiated it during the Cold War. Instead a large degree of mutual pragmatism has come to characterize the relationship.

This newfound pragmatism has contributed to a series of bilateral military exercises, involving the respective navies, armies, and air forces. Over the past several years, Indian and American forces have held joint exercises in such disparate areas as Alaska, Ladakh, in the northern portion of the Indian-controlled state of Jammu and Kashmir, and also at the Counter Insurgency and Jungle Warfare School at Vairengte in the state of Mizoram near the Indo-Myanmar border. In 2007 a significant naval exercise, "Malabar," was held in the Bay of Bengal and involved the United States, India, Singapore, Japan, and Australia. (Four out of these five states had formed an ad hoc coalition to coordinate the provision of relief assistance in the wake of the December 2004 tsunami that had wreaked havoc across much of South and Southeast Asia.)

The growing closeness of the Indo-U.S. strategic relationship has generated a predictable domestic backlash. India's two communist parties, the Communist Party of India (CPI) and the Communist Party of India/Marxist (CPI/M), have repeatedly expressed their reservations about these defense ties and proven to be a major impediment to the consummation of the U.S.-India civilian nuclear agreement. The CPI/M, which enjoys close ties to Beijing, has been reflexively hostile toward the United States and continues to oppose any improvement in Indo-U.S. relations.

Salvaging a Relationship

Despite the dramatic improvement in Indo-U.S. relations, which the Indian political establishment deems to be critical to the pursuit of India's great power aspirations, after a significant hiatus during the Gorbachev and Yeltsin years, India has managed to resurrect elements of the former Indo-Soviet relationship with Russia. Two factors explain the persistence of the Indo-Russian relationship. At one level, a significant portion of India's arsenal is of Soviet origin. Consequently, India's military establishment still remains dependent on Moscow for spare parts and equipment. Simultaneously, given the past fickleness of the United States on arms transfers, India is loath to abandon an important source of advanced weaponry until it has found other, comparable arms suppliers.[29] Yet this relationship cannot possibly regain the status that it enjoyed in the Cold War years. Russia now has a robust arms transfer relationship with the PRC; it is besieged with a set of its own internal difficulties and views the Indo-Russian military relationship as a strictly commercial venture. This is evident from the continuing haggling over the purchase of the retrofitted aircraft carrier, the *Admiral Gorshokov*, designed to replace the aging Indian INS *Vikrant*.[30]

A small segment of India's foreign policy establishment still harbors a hope that Russia, the PRC, and India could form a loose coalition to help balance overweening American power. Even though former Russian foreign minister Yevgeny Primakov once floated this proposal, it found few serious adherents in New Delhi. Given the growing bonds in Indo-American ties and India's continuing mistrust of the PRC's interests and actions, it is most unlikely that any such coalition will emerge.

ASIAN COMPETITORS AND POTENTIAL ALLIES

Closer to home, India has attempted, with varying degrees of success, to improve relations with the People's Republic of China (PRC).[31] This relationship had been troubled since the late 1950s and had contributed to a major border war in 1962.[32] Subsequently, relations had long remained strained until 1988 when Prime Minister Rajiv Gandhi undertook an initiative to try and improve relations. Ironically, the Gandhi visit took place two years after a border clash at Sumdurong Chu in 1986 that almost contributed to yet another border war.[33] In the aftermath of Gandhi's visit a series of high-level discussions ensued to reduce tensions, to promote trade, and to expand the ambit of diplomatic cooperation. Despite these efforts, the two sides made glacial progress in their attempts to resolve the border dispute. Nevertheless, both countries found it expedient to try and limit the possibilities of inadvertent conflict along the disputed border. To that end, India reached two significant confidence-building measures (CBMs) with the PRC in 1993 and 1996.[34] Also, Sino-Indian trade expanded dramatically in the early part of the next decade, with China poised to now surpass the United States as India's largest trading partner.

Despite all these positive developments, the relationship is far from being a stable partnership.[35] At least three fundamental issues divide the two states. First, the border dispute remains unresolved, and it is highly unlikely that any swift resolution thereof is forthcoming. In November 2006, for example, the two countries had a highly publicized disagreement about the exact status of a region in India's northeast, Arunachal Pradesh. To the surprise of Indian officials, the PRC reiterated its claim to that region.[36] Second, India and China, despite an agreement to the contrary, remain locked into an inexorable competition to secure hydrocarbon resources from third parties to fuel their economic growth.[37] Such competition is simply unlikely to abate; relative gains, as scholars of international relations have long argued, matter much in global politics.[38] Finally, and perhaps most importantly, the two states have self-images as great powers in Asia and beyond. The PRC may wish to have cordial relations with India but has little or no interest in facilitating India's attempts to transcend its South Asian status. Specifically, it has expressed grave reservations about India's support for and interest in ballistic missile defenses, refused to support India's quest for a permanent seat in an expanded United Nations Security Council, and has questioned the propriety of the U.S-India civilian nuclear accord. Consequently, it is evident that despite an improvement in the *atmospherics* of this relationship, major *substantive* differences still persist. Relations between these two major Asian powers for the foreseeable future will therefore remain competitive.

It is in this context that one must examine India's growing ties to Southeast Asia. The overall transformation of India's foreign policy enabled it to repair long-neglected relations with the economically dynamic states of Southeast Asia.[39] During the Cold War India had largely shunned the Southeast Asian nations, viewing them as little more than American stooges. It had also damaged its relations with many of the key Southeast Asian states through its support for the Vietnamese invasion of Cambodia and the support of the Heng Samrin regime.

This effort to fashion a new set of relationships with Southeast Asia was part of Prime Minister Narasimha Rao's "Look East" policy designed to attract investment from and seek new markets in the region. Accordingly, in 1992, India was invited to become a sectoral dialogue partner of ASEAN. The steady opening of the Indian economy and continued diplomatic engagement enabled India to become a full dialogue partner in 1995 and a member of the ASEAN Regional Forum in 1996.

Over the past decade, the density of interactions with the ASEAN states has been dramatic and has gone well beyond the initial interest in trade, investment, and tourism. For example, in early November 2000, India proposed the creation of the Ganga-Mekong Cooperation project in Vientiane. This project is designed to enhance cooperation among India, Thailand, Vietnam, Laos, Cambodia, and Myanmar in such areas as culture, education, tourism and transport, and communications.[40] It is pertinent to underscore that two states, China and Bangladesh, were conspicuous in their absence in this new group of nations.

The steady growth of the Indian economy and its increasing openness throughout the 1990s provided increasing opportunities for cooperation with ASEAN. Accordingly, India became a summit-level partner in 2002 and at the third ASEAN-India Summit held in November 2004 in Vientiane, India and ASEAN signed the "ASEAN-India Partnership for Peace, Progress and Shared Prosperity" document. This scheme spelled out the guidelines for long-term engagement between India and ASEAN.[41]

Questions of trade and investment alone, however, were no longer the reason for the increasing density of ties between India and ASEAN after the events of September 11, 2001. Many of the ASEAN states and certainly India had coped with violent insurgent movements and various terrorist groups long before the increased focus on transnational terror that ensued in the wake of the terrorist attacks on the United States. Not surprisingly, anti-terror cooperation has also become an important strand in the Indo-ASEAN relationship.[42]

Apart from seeking to expand both trade and investment and promoting transnational cooperation against terror, there remains an unspoken element in India's quest to build a set of viable diplomatic ties with the Southeast Asian states. Though the subject of routine public denials, privately Indian policymakers concede that an important Indian strategic goal remains the desire to limit China's influence in the region. To varying degrees, various Southeast Asian states also see India as a potential balancer to growing Chinese power. Not surprisingly India has managed to quicken the growth of military-to-military contacts with a number of key Southeast Asian states.[43]

Along with this expansion of trade, diplomatic contacts, and military-to-military ties, India has also started to broaden its diplomatic contacts with Japan. Indo-Japanese relations had a mostly economic dimension during much of the Cold War as India was the recipient of Japanese economic assistance and investment. Furthermore, the Japanese had little use for India's non-alignment policies and its closeness with the Soviet Union. Sustained economic growth in India and India's more pragmatic foreign policy led to a significant change in the Indo-Japanese relationship in the 1990s. Obviously, the Indian nuclear tests of 1998 again led to a brief diplomatic rupture. However, as the other great powers, most notably the United States, grudgingly came to accept India's new status, Japan also followed suit.

Today, the Indo-Japanese relationship is taking on broader dimensions as Japan sees India's military prowess as an important asset in an uncertain strategic environment.[44] Though both parties are at pains to deny that these newfound military ties are directed at any third party, it is clear that both India and Japan share some common concerns about the possible course of China's rise and its impact on their mutual security interests.[45] Beyond this desire to pursue a hedging strategy against the PRC, the two sides have also envisaged a dramatic expansion of their bilateral ties. Following Prime Minister Manmohan Singh's visit to Japan in December 2006, the two parties spelled out a broad vision for a multifaceted relationship that would focus on, but not be limited to, cooperation in aerospace, global climate change, energy security, increased foreign direct investment, and the forging of a comprehensive economic partnership.

DISTANT NEIGHBORS:
PAKISTAN, BANGLADESH, AND SRI LANKA

There is little question that deft Indian diplomacy, the steady opening of India's economy, and a raft of internal, market-oriented reforms have done much to transform India's relations with a host of Asian states. However, it is still far from clear that India has managed to devise a set of viable strategies for dealing with its often pesky and contentious neighbors. India's problems with Pakistan, of course, hark back to the partition of the subcontinent in 1947 and are rooted in the dispute over the status of the Muslim-majority state of Jammu and Kashmir.[46] Since 1989, however, the relationship has become especially fraught with tension, thanks to the outbreak of an ethno-religious insurgency in the Indian-controlled portion of the disputed state. The roots of this insurgency can be traced to Indian domestic politics.[47] However, Pakistan's involvement in the insurgency has greatly expanded its scope and lengthened its duration.[48] As a consequence of Pakistan's support for some of the insurgent groups and their feckless actions, a series of crises have punctuated Indo-Pakistani relations over the past decade.[49] Periodic efforts to reduce tensions have mostly floundered over fundamental and seemingly irreconcilable differences over how to resolve the vexed Kashmir question. Given the unwillingness of any regime in Pakistan to reconcile itself to the status quo in Kashmir, in the end the dispute may reach a permanent stalemate. The national trajectories of India and Pakistan are markedly different, and the institutional, military, and economic gaps between the two states are likely to widen in the years ahead.[50] While Pakistan may remain utterly unreconciled to the status quo in Kashmir, its ability to coerce India into making significant concessions will steadily decline. Consequently, while political rapprochement is most unlikely, the rivalry is likely to lose much of its force.

Indeed, given India's growing presence in Central Asia (and even Afghanistan in the post-Taliban phase), Pakistan may deem it expedient to reach some accommodation with India. Despite grand hopes of using the common bonds of Islam to insinuate itself into the good graces of the former Soviet Central Asian states, Pakistan has not succeeded in gaining substantial ground. Instead, India, through concerted and deft diplomacy, has managed to steadily extend its influence in the region despite the barriers of geography through security assistance, increased trade, and diplomatic engagement.[51]

India's relations with Bangladesh, the country it helped create in 1971, remain laden with tension and distrust. Questions of sharing river waters, trade and tariff reductions, smuggling, illegal immigration from Bangladesh, the seemingly unbridled growth of Islamic militancy, and the persistence of some minor territorial disputes have long dogged Indo-Bangladeshi relations.[52] Given Bangladesh's endemic and structural problems of governance and its deep-seated fears of Indian domination, only the most sagacious Indian policies designed to assuage the real and imagined misgivings of its weak and contentious neighbor will ensure an improvement in relations. Unfortunately, few governments in New Delhi have evinced much interest in forging such a set of coherent policies that would help ameliorate the distrust that characterizes Indo-Bangladeshi relations.

Among all of India's small neighbors, India now enjoys perhaps the most cordial relationship with Sri Lanka. India's relations with Sri Lanka had plummeted in the aftermath of the ill-fated, poorly conceived, and clumsily implemented Indo–Sri Lankan Accord of 1987 and the even more disastrous Indian Peace Keeping Force episode of 1987–1989.[53] Today the government in New Delhi is keen on cooperating with the Sri Lankan regime to bolster the country's stability and to contain the Liberation Tigers of Tamil Eelam, the insurgent group that has long been fighting for the creation of a separate Tamil state in Sri Lanka.[54] Though differences still remain with Sri Lanka on questions of trade and the future of the Tamil community, the relationship today is a far cry from the troubled period of the 1980s.

THE DOMESTIC DIMENSION: STEPS FORWARD AND THE PITFALLS AHEAD

For all practical purposes, India's decision makers have broken certain "mind-forged manacles"—to borrow that evocative expression from the great English poet William Blake—and have embarked on a new grand strategy. However, a section of India's "attentive public" and some members of its political establishment, most notably those in the two communist parties, still harbor visions of resurrecting the moribund doctrine of nonalignment and strategies of state-led industrialization. Despite the turning of the global ideological tide, they maintain an unswerving commitment to the ideals of yesteryear. Consequently, these groups still constitute an important constraint on the ongoing transformation of India's foreign, security, and economic policies. India's ability to forge ahead with the substantial changes that it has managed to bring about will, in considerable part, depend on the ability of any ruling regime to limit and contain the influence of these groups.

Yet there is little question that India, while on a new and successful path of economic growth and diplomatic engagement, cannot afford to ignore some serious domestic challenges if it hopes to rise to the rank of a major power. It is unnecessary to enumerate all the domestic challenges that India confronts. However, there are some infirmities to the Indian polity that are important to underscore. Despite its professed commitment to social justice and equity, India has some of the world's worst social indicators. In 2006, for example, the United Nations Human Development Report placed India at 126 among the 177 countries surveyed. This standing is understandable given that the government of India contributes less than a quarter of the total expenditure on health care. The comparable figures for China and the United States are 36.2 percent and 44.6 percent, respectively. Similarly, there are six physicians and eight hospital beds available for every ten thousand Indian citizens. The comparable statistics are sixteen physicians and twenty-five hospital beds and twenty-three and thirty-three for China and the United States, respectively. Perhaps, in a most telling fashion, however, despite steady economic growth for well over a decade, some 26 percent of India's population still remains mired in abject, grinding, and dehumanizing poverty.[55] India's pathway to great power status consequently is still strewn with a number of important obstacles. None of them are insuperable, but they will require imaginative and efficacious policy choices if they are to be overcome.

CONCLUSION

Will India realize its long-held hopes and aspirations to emerge as a great power in Asia and beyond? The answer to that question is far from certain. The country still faces significant domestic challenges and regional constraints on the path to such a status. These hurdles are far from trivial and will require concerted efforts and sustained action on the part of any regime that comes to power in New Delhi.

Three concluding observations about the likely course of India's choices in the foreseeable future are in order. First, it is clear that despite some lingering domestic opposition, the country has now embarked upon a fundamentally new course, one that is mostly shorn of past ideological baggage both in the realms of foreign and domestic policies. The jettisoning of such ideological ballast and the concomitant policy changes have enabled the country to post high rates of economic growth, reduce rural and urban poverty, pursue defense modernization, and start a process of diplomatic engagement with the key Asian states and beyond. The degree of popular support that these policies command in India's fractious democratic polity is considerable. Consequently, barring the emergence of a vastly different political configuration in New Delhi thanks to some unexpected electoral upheaval, these policies will continue to enjoy a political consensus and will be pursued into the foreseeable future.

Second, regardless of the government in power in New Delhi, the country will not abandon its tradition of prickly independence. This drive for autonomy is deeply rooted in India's political culture and is unlikely to dissipate easily. Any major state seeking to work with India will have to take account of this deep-seated proclivity in India's decision-making apparatus.

Third, and finally, it is worth noting that despite India's dramatic rise in the past decade, few states in Asia or beyond have expressed any serious concerns about the potential dangers it may pose to the emergent Asian order. On the contrary, apart from India's subcontinental neighbors and the PRC, who have long had real and perceived grievances against India, the vast majority of Asia appears eager to engage an increasingly commercially open, diplomatically assertive, and militarily powerful India.

Three compelling reasons may be adduced to explain the lack of global and regional misgivings about India's rise. First, India, for the most part, is no longer seeking to lead a global coalition that seeks to challenge the existing international order. The hoary commitments to global disarmament, non-alignment, and Third World solidarity have, for all practical purposes, been abandoned. India may still forge ad hoc coalitions with key states such as South Africa, Brazil, and China on contentious issues such as climate change and international trade. However, these alliances will be strictly temporary, ad hoc, and confined to specific issues. They do not represent an attempt to fashion an alternative international colossus to challenge the extant great powers. Second, India has to a very large extent accepted the precepts of a neo-Liberal global order. It may seek changes in that order to suit its particular national interests, but it is downright unlikely to offer any meaningful challenge to it. Third and finally, India is a democracy. While a vigorous debate exists about the lack of war proneness among democracies, they are, however, deemed to be less threatening than autocratic or authoritarian states.[56]

What is a rising India's likely impact on the emergent Asian international order? Obviously, it is all but impossible to make firm, robust predictions about the evolution of India's foreign policy and its influence of the shape of the future Asian international order. Nevertheless, it is possible to extrapolate a few general propositions based upon existing conditions.

The discussion can be woven around three distinct issues: economic, strategic, and diplomatic. If India continues to embrace a neoliberal path of economic development, it is reasonable to expect it to become far more closely integrated with the dynamic economies of Southeast Asia. Not only should India become an important destination for investment, but it should also become a significant market for a range of goods and services from these states. On the other hand, India's continued growth will also mean that it will be in increasing competition for energy resources. This will, among other factors, without a doubt, sustain the competitive relationship with the PRC.

In the strategic arena, a more militarily powerful India will be in a position to provide certain public goods for the region. Most importantly, as a significant littoral state, it has a vital interest in maintaining the security of sea lanes athwart both its coasts. Already, in the aftermath of the terrorist attacks of September 11, 2001, units of the Indian Navy have assisted the U.S. 7th Fleet in anti-piracy and counterterrorism operations in and around the Strait of Malacca. It is entirely within reason to assume that such cooperation can easily be extended and broadened to the benefit of many Southeast Asian states.

Finally, growing Indian diplomatic engagement through the ARF could offer the states of Southeast Asia an important counterweight to an overbearing PRC. Though India's political leadership is mindful of wanting to avoid any direct confrontations with the PRC, they are nevertheless willing to work with other key Asian states, most notably Japan, to provide an element of reassurance to the smaller states of Asia, which are understandably concerned about a resurgent PRC.

NOTES

I wish to thank Devin Hagerty and Manjeet Pardesi for thoughtful comments on an earlier version of this chapter. I also wish to thank Scott Nissen for able research assistance. The usual caveats apply.

1. The argument is developed in Peter Gourevitch, "The Second Image Reversed: The International Sources of Domestic Politics," *International Organization* 32, no. 4 (Autumn 1978): 881–912. Gourevitch's innovative argument is explicitly derived from the work of Alexander Gerschenkron. Alexander Gerschenkron, *Economic Backwardness in Historical Perspective, A Book of Essays* (Cambridge, Mass.: Belknap Press of Harvard University Press, 1962).

2. The classic treatment of this subject remains A. S. Rana, *The Imperatives of Nonalignment: A Conceptual Study of India's Foreign Policy Strategy in the Nehru Period* (Delhi: Macmillan of India, 1976).

3. For a thoughtful discussion of the formative years of this relationship, see Andrew Rotter, *Comrades at Odds* (Ithaca, N.Y.: Cornell University Press, 2000).

4. For a particularly thoughtful and incisive critique, see Fouad Ajami, "The Third World Challenge: The Fate of Nonalignment," *Foreign Affairs* 59, no. 2 (Winter 1980/1981): 366–385.

5. Some Indian analysts continue to insist that non-alignment remains a viable strategy for India. According to them, non-alignment remains relevant because it enables India to pursue a policy of strategic autonomy.

6. S. D. Muni, "India and the Post–Cold War World: Opportunities and Challenges," *Asian Survey* 31, no. 9 (September 1991): 862–874.

7. Sumit Ganguly, "South Asia after the Cold War," *Washington Quarterly* 15, no. 4 (Autumn 1992): 173–184.

8. Kanti Bajpai, "India: Modified Structuralism," in *Asian Security Practice*, ed. Muthiah Alagappa (Stanford, Calif.: Stanford University Press, 1998).

9. India had long resisted granting Israel full diplomatic recognition for two reasons. First, it had wanted to win favor with the Arab world as a champion on nonalignment and Third World solidarity. Second, it was acutely concerned about the sensitivities of India's substantial Muslim minority.

10. For an important discussion of the transformation of India's foreign policy at the Cold War's end, see C. Raja Mohan, *Crossing the Rubicon* (New York: Palgrave Macmillan, 2004).

11. For a discussion of the motivations underlying the Indian nuclear tests of May 1998, see Sumit Ganguly, "India's Pathway to Pokhran II: The Sources and Prospects of India's Nuclear Weapons Program," *International Security* 23, no. 4 (Spring 1999): 148–177.

12. Ramesh Thakur, "India after Nonalignment," *Foreign Affairs* 71, no. 2 (Spring 1992): 165–182.

13. On this subject see Robert Horn, *Soviet-Indian Relations: Issues and Influence* (New York: Praeger, 1982).

14. Linda Racioppi, *Soviet Policy towards South Asia since 1970* (Cambridge: Cambridge University Press, 1994).

15. Jagdish N. Bhagwati, *India in Transition: Freeing the Economy* (Oxford: Oxford University Press, 1993).

16. Faced with a less severe economic crisis and confronted with substantial domestic opposition, Prime Minister Indira Gandhi had undertaken only piecemeal changes in India's political economy in 1966. On this issue, see Rahul Mukherji, "India's Aborted Liberalization," *Pacific Affairs* 73, no. 3 (Autumn 2000): 375–392; and David Denoon, *Devaluation under Pressure: India, Indonesia and Ghana* (Cambridge, Mass.: MIT Press, 1986).

17. The one prior exogenous shock that had contributed to a dramatic shift in India's defense policy had stemmed from the disastrous Sino-Indian border war of 1962. The grossly unprepared and utterly under-equipped Indian forces suffered a grievous defeat at the hands of the battle-hardened Chinese People's Liberation Army. In the aftermath of this war, India undertook a significant program of military modernization. For a description and analysis of the origins of the border war, see Steven Hoffman, *India and the China Crisis* (Berkeley: University of California Press, 1990); for a discussion of the impact on Indian military spending and defense policies, see Lorne J. Kavic, *India's Defense Policies, 1947–1965* (Berkeley: University of California Press, 1967).

18. The most compelling (if seriously flawed) argument that stresses considerations of prestige and status as the principal motivations underlying the Indian nuclear tests is George Perkovich, *India's Nuclear Bomb: The Impact of Global Proliferation* (Berkeley: University of California Press, 1999).

19. In the event, the Clinton administration failed to persuade a Republican-dominated Congress to ratify the CTBT because of fears of adequate verification and the possibility of cheating. For the CTBT to "enter into force," some forty-four states with ongoing nuclear power programs would have had to ratify the treaty. Obvi-

ously, the three key holdout states were India, Pakistan, and Israel. For a detailed discussion of India's concerns and the security-related motivations underlying the Indian tests, see Ganguly, "India's Pathway to Pokhran II," 148–177.

20. See for example, the extremely lucid discussion of this subject in Sisir Gupta, "The Indian Dilemma," in *A World of Nuclear Powers?* ed. Alastair Buchan (Englewood Cliffs, N.J.: Prentice-Hall, 1966).

21. See the excellent discussion in Rajesh Basrur, *Minimum Deterrence and India's Nuclear Security* (Palo Alto, Calif.: Stanford University Press, 2006).

22. The term "estranged democracies" is derived from the title of Dennis Kux, *Estranged Democracies* (Washington, D.C.: National Defense University Press, 1992); Prime Minister Atal Behari Vajpayee of India first used the term "natural allies" to describe the Indo-U.S. relationship.

23. See the two chapters on the Kennedy administration and India in Harold Gould and Sumit Ganguly, eds., *The Hope and the Reality: U.S.-Indian Relations from Roosevelt to Reagan* (Boulder, Colo.: Westview Press, 1987).

24. For a discussion of this transformation, see Sumit Ganguly, "The United States and India: The Beginning of a Beautiful Friendship?" *World Policy Journal* 20, no. 1 (Spring 2003): 37–43.

25. The negotiations and the ensuing transformation of the Indo-American relationship are discussed at length in Strobe Talbott, *Engaging India* (Washington, D.C.: Brookings Institution, 2004).

26. On this subject, see Ganguly, "The United States and India," 37–43.

27. On this subject, see the contributions in Sumit Ganguly, ed., *Indo-U.S. Defense Cooperation into the Twenty-First Century, More Than Words* (London: Routledge, 2006).

28. Jo Johnson and Edward Luce, "Welcome to the Club: A Nuclear Deal for Delhi Signals a New Strategy," *Financial Times*, August 3, 2007.

29. For a concise discussion, see Deepa Ollapally, "Indo-Russian Strategic Relations: New Choices and Constraints," *Journal of Strategic Studies* 25, no. 4 (December 2002): 135–156.

30. On this subject, see the discussion in B. M. Jain, "India and Russia: Reassessing the Time-Tested Ties," *Pacific Affairs* 76, no. 3 (Fall 2003): 375–397.

31. The post–World War II history of this complex relationship is discussed at length in John Garver, *Protracted Conflict: Sino-Indian Rivalry in the Twentieth Century* (Seattle: University of Washington Press, 2002).

32. The best analysis of the origins of the war remains Hoffman, *India and the China Crisis.*

33. For a discussion, see Sumit Ganguly, "The Sino-Indian Border Talks: A View from New Delhi," *Asian Survey* 29, no. 12 (December 1989): 1123–1135.

34. For the particulars of these two CBMs, see W. P. S. Sidhu and Jing-dong Yuan, *China and India: Cooperation or Conflict* (Boulder, Colo.: Lynne Rienner, 2003).

35. For an alternative formulation that stresses the improvement in Sino-Indian relations and potential areas of convergence, see Yong Deng, "Remolding Great Power Politics: China's Strategic Relationships with Russia, the European Union, and India," *Journal of Strategic Studies* 30, nos. 4–5 (August–October 2007): 863–903.

36. On this issue, see Seema Guha, "China Claims Arunachal Pradesh as 'Chinese Territory,'" *Daily News and Analysis* (Bombay), November 13, 2006.

37. Carola Hoyos, Jo Johnson, Richard McGregor, and Andrew Yeh, "China and India Forge Alliance on Oil," *Financial Times*, January 13, 2006.

38. For a trenchant discussion of the problem of relative gains and the concomitant difficulties of cooperation, see Joseph Grieco, Robert Powell, and Duncan Snidal, "The Relative Gains Problem for International Cooperation," *American Political Science Review* 87, no. 3 (September 1993): 727–743; on the Sino-Indian accord not to compete for petroleum resources, see Rituparna Chatterjee and Govindkrishna Seshan, "Global Oil Hunt: India, China Join Hands," December 6, 2005, www.rediff.com (accessed December 5, 2007).

39. India's neglect of ASEAN is particularly ironic given that it was one of the earliest and principal proponents of regional integration in Asia. On this subject, see Sisir Gupta, *India and Regional Integration in Asia* (New York: Asia Publishing House, 1964).

40. Faizal Yahya, "India and Southeast Asia Revisited," *Contemporary Southeast Asia* 25, no. 1 (April 2003): 79–103.

41. Zhao Gong, "India and China: Rivals or Partners in Southeast Asia?" *Contemporary Southeast Asia* 29, no. 1 (April 2007): 121–142.

42. Arabinda Acharya, "India and Southeast Asia in the Age of Terror: Building Partnerships for Peace," *Contemporary Southeast Asia* 28, no. 2 (August 2006): 297–321.

43. For an argument that suggests that China has been able to assuage some of the concerns of the Southeast Asian states, see Evelyn Goh, "Southeast Asian Perspectives on the China Challenge," *Journal of Strategic Studies* 30, nos. 4–5 (August–October 2007): 809–832.

44. Ramesh Thakur, "India's Emergence Shows Shift in Power," *Daily Yomiuri*, December 12, 2006.

45. On the security dimensions of the relationship, see C. Raja Mohan, "Japan and India: The Makings of a New Alliance?" *RSIS Commentaries*, August 27, 2007.

46. For a detailed discussion of the origins and evolution of the Indo-Pakistani dispute over Kashmir, see Sumit Ganguly, *Conflict Unending: India-Pakistan Tensions since 1947* (New York: Columbia University Press, 2001).

47. The origins of the insurgency are discussed in Sumit Ganguly, *The Crisis in Kashmir: Portents of War, Hopes of Peace* (New York: Cambridge University Press, 1997).

48. For evidence of Pakistan's involvement in the insurgency, see Daniel Byman, *Deadly Connections: States That Sponsor Terrorism* (New York: Cambridge University Press, 2005).

49. For a discussion of the crises, see Devin Hagerty and Sumit Ganguly, *Fearful Symmetry: India and Pakistan in the Shadow of Nuclear Weapons* (Seattle: University of Washington Press, 2004).

50. On this subject, see Sumit Ganguly, "Will Kashmir Stop India's Rise?" *Foreign Affairs* 85, no. 4 (July/August 2006): 45–56.

51. Stephen Blank, "India's Rising Profile in Central Asia," *Comparative Strategy* 22, no. 2 (April/May/June 2004): 139–157.

52. For a discussion of several of these issues, but especially the question of Islamic militancy in Bangladesh, see Sumit Ganguly, *The Rise of Islamist Militancy in Bangladesh*, Special Report 171 (Washington, D.C.: United States Institute of Peace, 2006), 1–12.

53. On the Indian involvement in Sri Lanka, see S. D. Muni, *The Pangs of Proximity* (New Delhi: Sage, 1993).

54. It is at least ironic to note that in the early 1980s India had trained, organized, and assisted the LTTE because of its unhappiness with certain features of Sri Lanka's foreign and domestic policies. On this matter, see Neil Devotta, *Blowback* (Palo Alto, Calif.: Stanford University Press, 2004).

55. See the discussion in Sumit Ganguly and Manjeet Pardesi, "India Rising: What Is New Delhi to Do?" *World Policy Journal* 24, no. 1 (Spring 2007): 9–18.

56. For a discussion, see Miriam Fendius Elman, ed., *Paths to Peace: Is Democracy the Answer?* (Cambridge, Mass.: MIT Press, 1997).

8

Japan in Asia

Michael Green

In his late Tokugawa-era essay, *A Discourse by Three Drunkards on Government*, Nakae Chomin imagines a master drinker leading two friends through an evening of inebriated debate about Japan's future course in Asia. One of his drinking partners is a "gentleman of Western learning" who wears European clothes and extols the virtues of democracy, individual rights, and economic development. The other wears the feudal garb of a samurai and argues for a realpolitik strategy of military expansion to supplant China and rival Britain as the dominant imperial power in Asia. In the end, the master drinker concludes that Japan must balance both courses, embracing Western learning and economic development while simultaneously expanding Japanese power in Asia. Yet this synthesis leaves the reader well aware of the unresolved tensions between these two visions of Japan's future that emerged in the period between the arrival of Commodore Perry's Black Ships and the Meiji restoration.[1]

THE SEARCH FOR STRATEGY

Few nations in history have been more racked with self-doubt about their national strategy than Japan. Fewer still have held so tenaciously to their national interests or been more acutely aware of the power relations around them. For Japan, the drivers of national strategy have essentially been the same since the time of *A Discourse by Three Drunkards on Government*: pursuing autonomy and respect in the international system based on calculation of the geopolitical strength of China (with Korea as the trigger) and accommodation to the prevailing international power structure.[2] Yet as consistent as these drivers have been throughout modern Japanese history, the tools used have varied dramatically. Indeed, Japan has reinvented itself at various periods in history to maximize its sources of national power and its relative autonomy in the context of the international system at the time. At times Japan has gone the way of the Western gentleman of learning; at other times, the way of the man of tradition.

The Meiji oligarchs at the end of the nineteenth century based their strategy on the four-character slogan *fukukoku kyohei* or "rich nation/strong arm," using Western learning to build national wealth and from that a modern army and navy. The results were astounding; from 1860 to 1938 Japan's share of global GDP only rose from 2.6 percent to 3.8 percent, yet Japan asserted itself as a contender for dominance of half the globe.[3] Japan's defeat of China in 1895 and Russia in 1905 inspired young nationalists and anti-imperialists across Asia, and Japanese strategic thinkers espoused an idealistic pan-Asianism based on Japan's own experience of *wakon/yosai* or "Japanese spirit and Western learning." That pan-Asian idealism soon gave way to a much uglier imperial order based on a traditional Asian hierarchy and dangerous brew of racial insecurity toward the West and oppressive superiority toward nations of the East. Japan also made the mistake of aligning itself with Nazi Germany in a misreading of the trends in the international power structure. The result was calamity for Japan and for Asia.

After the war Japan was forced to accommodate to a new international power structure under the American imperium and realigned its institutions to maximize Japanese power and autonomy within that new context. Under the masterful postwar prime minister Yoshida Shigeru, Japan embraced the institutions of democracy and established an alliance relationship with the United States, while ensuring that the pacifist Article Nine of the Japanese Constitution was institutionalized in domestic law and policy as a brake against entrapment in U.S. Cold War strategy. Japan pursued the minimal defense buildup necessary to retain the U.S. defense commitment while focusing on economic recovery and the pursuit of a new relationship with Asia—including communist China—based on trade.

By the end of the Cold War, many Japanese strategic thinkers began to argue that Japan's new model of economic growth had surpassed traditional capitalism and would position Japan as a dominant player in the twenty-first century, free to pursue "independent" foreign policies and shape a new Asian economic order without traditional military tools, while allied with the world's sole greatest power, but not dependent upon it. However, this vision was dashed in the 1990s as Japan was paralyzed by inaction during the Gulf War, bereft of a credible economic model after the collapse of the bubble, unable to use economic interdependence to shape China's rapidly expanding strategic and military reach, and threatened by a North Korea bent on developing nuclear weapons. After almost a decade of drift and uncertainty,

Japan began to regain its confidence with Prime Minister Koizumi Junichiro (2001–2006) and to capture international attention with a new assertiveness in international security and a relaxation of traditional postwar constraints related to Article Nine of the Constitution. But then the course of national strategy seemed uncertain again as Koizumi's successor, Abe Shinzo, stumbled politically in 2007.

Japan's search for strategy has both confounded and enriched theories of international relations. Traditional structural Realists such as Henry Kissinger and Herman Kahn have argued that it is unthinkable that Japan could develop economic power without eventually establishing commensurate military power, including nuclear weapons.[4] Constructivists like Peter Katzenstein have developed generalizable theories around the example of Japan by arguing that Japan's political culture has indeed changed as pacifism has been reinforced through postwar norms and institutions based on Article Nine of the Constitution.[5] Revisionist theories of international political economy thrived in the 1980s and early 1990s on the idea that Japan had, in fact, developed a new model of techno-nationalist economic growth and production networks in Asia.[6] Richard Samuels and Eric Heginbotham returned to Realist theories of international relations to argue that Japan's behavior was Realist, but based on a new "mercantile" Realism rather than traditional military-centered concepts of neo-Realist theory or more recent variations of economic theory.[7] I argued in *Japan's Reluctant Realism* in 2001 that Japan's strategic culture was shifting from traditional pacifism and passivity toward more pronounced balance of power behavior in response to rising external threats and the failure of traditional economic tools to enhance security.[8] In his important study of the history and revival of Japanese strategic thinking, Kenneth Pyle argued convincingly in 2007 that Japan has always been Realist and is returning to its roots in many respects as it asserts itself again in Asia.[9]

What emerges from these various studies of Japanese strategic thinking is an unmistakable trail of trial and error and exploration of tools that allow Japan to maximize its autonomy and power in light of two drivers noted earlier: calculation of the geopolitical strength of China (and Korea) and accommodation to the prevailing international power structure. Yet Japanese institutions and norms remain sticky and inflexible, confusing the search for a new strategy even as Japanese leaders attempt once again to realign their tool kit as the geopolitics of Asia enter a period of flux.

The remainder of this chapter unbundles that tool kit, assessing what has and has not worked for Japan in Asia today and what elements are most likely to characterize Japanese strategy in the years ahead. The chapter is divided into five sections. The first begins with an examination of the tools that were thought most promising until a decade ago—close relations with

China and economic leadership in bringing a new order to the region—and how failure in those areas has changed Japanese strategy and the use of these tools today. The second section examines Japan's return to the center-piece of its strategy in Asia: its alliance with the United States and the op-portunities and complications that has brought. The third section explores the Japanese balancing strategy in Asia in three areas. The fourth section ex-amines Japan's strategy for shaping regional integration and institution-building. The fifth section reviews the unfinished business of history, why it is difficult for the Japanese elite to resolve, and where it does and does not undercut Japanese influence. Finally, the chapter concludes with a review of the variables that could lead Japan in a different direction with a different tool kit than the one examined here.

CHINA

When Japan emerged from the ruins of the Second World War and prepared to re-enter the community of nations, the conservative elite advanced dif-ferent ideas about what role a newly democratized Japan would play. Some former bureaucrats from the Ministry of Commerce and Industry, like Kishi Nobusuke, wanted to align closely with the United States in the struggle against communism, even cooperating after the Korean War to turn Japan into an arsenal for Asia. Others, like Democratic Party leader Hatoyama Ichiro, wanted to establish greater independence from the United States by signing a peace treaty with Russia (still not signed to this day) and revising Japan's Constitution. Still others wanted to eschew any military buildup that might lead Japan down the road to war again. Pulling these disparate camps together into a ruling coalition fell to Yoshida Shigeru, who defined a simple strategy for Japan that brought all conservatives under one tent and assured they would dominate politics and marginalize the socialists and the communists for the next half century.

Beneath that broad conservative tent, however, were different ideas about Asia and specifically China. Yoshida established the mainstream view, which was based on a prescient assumption that communist China would eventually wean itself from the Soviet Union and grow closer to Japan based on commerce. While "anti-mainstream" conservatives contin-ued to favor the Republic of China on Taiwan, Yoshida's protégés ensured that Japan avoided any involvement in the security of Taiwan or con-frontation with Beijing as a proxy of the United States. Prime Minister Sato Eisaku agreed in a joint statement with President Nixon that Japan had an interest in the stability of the Taiwan Strait in 1969, but only because he had to do so in order to win Nixon's commitment to return Okinawa to Japanese sovereignty. There was no follow-up in defense or foreign policy strategy. Indeed, throughout that same period, Japan quietly expanded economic relations with China through the semi-official "L-T" (Liao Chengzhi and Tatsunosuke Takasaki) trade, and after Kissinger's 1972 visit to China, Japanese prime minister Tanaka Kakuei immediately normalized relations with Beijing (a full seven years before Washington did). In 1978 Japan and China signed a Treaty of Friendship that initiated Japanese yen loans, which Tokyo interpreted as aid and Beijing as compensation for Japan's war with China (amounting to over US$1 billion at their peak in the early 1990s). Japan also worked as a broker to help China and the West re-engage after the June 4, 1989, Tiananmen incident, breaking out of the West's sanctions regime set at the 1990 Houston Summit. Yoshida's predictions were uncannily accurate, and intellectuals in Japan began arguing for a more "balanced" trilateral relationship among Beijing, Washington, and Tokyo.

In the mid-1990s, however, Japan's relations with China suddenly began to change. Yoshida was right about the degree of Sino-Japanese economic interdependence, but he failed to anticipate how difficult it would be to harness that interdependence to shape Chinese behavior. The turning point came on May 15, 1995, when China tested nuclear weapons at the Lop Nor facility. Japanese diplomats warned that Sino-Japanese economic relations and yen loans could be put at risk by the tests, and Japanese political parties of all stripes were critical of Beijing. But the tests proceeded. In March 1996 China bracketed Taiwan with missiles. Japan and the United States in April of that year reaffirmed the U.S.-Japan alliance in a joint Security Declaration between Prime Minister Hashimoto Ryutaro and President Bill Clinton, and Tokyo agreed to revise its defense guidelines to plan not only for the Cold War contingencies of a direct Soviet attack on the Japanese homeland, but also for "situations in the area surrounding Japan that have a direct effect on Japan's security." Over the course of the next decade, the Sino-Japanese rivalry became an unmistakable feature of Asian international relations.

The experiences of the mid-1990s taught the Japanese public and elite how uncertain Chinese intentions were and how ill-equipped Japan was to shape Chinese behavior: economic tools were less effective than expected and China's economic growth was rising to double digits at a time when Japan was in sustained deflation and unlikely to break 2 percent growth per year under the best scenario. Specific military and diplomatic threats also grew over the next decade. Japan's Defense White Paper steadily elevated its warnings about China's military buildup, noting in 2007 that China holds a "significant number" of IRBM/MRBMs (intermediate-range ballistic missile/medium-range ballistic missiles) that could target Japan, including DF-3 and DF-21, in addition to programs to develop cruise missiles, new submarines, and a rapidly increasing inventory of fourth-generation fighters including the J-10, Su-27, and Su-30s.[10] A Chinese submarine circumnavigated Japan in 2004 and then entered Japanese territorial waters in 2005, and three Chinese destroyers aimed their deck guns at Japanese P-3C patrol planes that were sent to monitor their activities around the disputed Senkaku/Diaoyutai Islands in 2005.[11] On the diplomatic front, Chinese diplomats fanned out across Asia and Africa in 2005 to lobby against Japan's bid for a permanent UN Security Council Seat based on the "consensus" that Japan had failed to atone for its crimes from the Second World War.

Changes in Japanese domestic politics have both complicated and been propelled by these developments. The Sino-Japanese relationship during the Cold War was held in place by the mainstream factions of the Liberal Democratic Party (LDP) and particularly the faction of Prime Minister Tanaka, which dominated the party from 1972 until 1993 and sustained a largely non-ideological focus on developing the Japanese economy. The structure of Japanese politics reflected the structure of the Cold War, and with the collapse of the Soviet Union, the Japanese left quickly declined and the once mainstream Tanaka faction steadily lost ground to a younger generation of conservative politicians in both the LDP and the new opposition Democratic Party of Japan who favored the assertive and unapologetic policies of Hatoyama and Kishi. For this new generation, standing up to China has become a matter not only of national security, but also national identity.

China, too, has struggled with a Japan that it did not anticipate. The 1978 Treaty of Peace and Friendship was supposed to lock the bilateral relationship in based on the verdict of the Tokyo War Crimes Tribunal. As Chinese president Jiang Zemin said during a disastrous visit to Tokyo in October 1998, it was not a matter of accepting Japanese apologies, but for Japan to retain a contrite position forever.[12] Indeed, after the 1978 treaty, Beijing found that it could mobilize the left and center-left in Japan to oppose efforts at revising textbooks or official visits to the Yasukuni Shrine, which honors Japan's war dead (including thirteen Class A war criminals). But as President Jiang found during his visit to Tokyo in 1998, the mainstream was shifting away from China, and the more Beijing pressed for restraint on sensitive historical issues, the more the Japanese public supported a resolute prime minister who would carry forward in spite of Chinese pressures. The ability of the two governments and political systems to manage these issues hit its nadir in 2005–2006. Prime Minister Koizumi came into office in 2001 without an anti-China agenda and took an early trip to the Marco Polo Bridge where the Sino-Japanese War began in 1937 to express his regret. But he also promised the Japanese Bereaved Families Association (Izzokai) in a tearful meeting that he would go to the Yasukuni Shrine to pay respects to their lost relatives from the war. The Chinese were furious, and

President Hu Jintao tried to convince Koizumi not to go when the two met at the margins of the Bandung Summit in 2005.[13] But Koizumi promised only to do the "appropriate thing"—which meant that he eventually visited Yasukuni Shrine. Hu publicly declared that he would not have a bilateral summit with Koizumi until the Japanese prime minister promised not to visit the shrine. A majority of Japanese, even many who did not approve of the shrine visits earlier, supported Koizumi's visits.[14] When Chinese mobs attacked the car of a senior Japanese VIP after Japan defeated China in the 2005 Asia World Cup match, the Japanese public's sense of being the victim only increased.

Koizumi's final visit to Yasukuni as prime minister came on August 15, 2007, the anniversary of Japan's surrender and a highly sensitive date for all of Japan's wartime enemies and victims. Ironically, however, this opened the door for his successor, Abe Shinzo (who was more hawkish on China than Koizumi had ever been), to reach a new rapprochement by traveling to Beijing on October 9, 2007, where he was warmly received by a Chinese leadership that had grown nervous about the sudden deterioration of Sino-Japanese ties and saw in Abe a chance for a new beginning. Hu wisely chose not to press Abe publicly to stay away from Yasukuni, just as Abe wisely chose not to promise his domestic constituents that he would go.[15] Abe's successor, Fukuda Yasuo, and China's President Hu Jintao exchanged state visits in early 2008. These further improved the atmosphere between the two nations, but not the underlying sources of strategic, ideational, and military tension.

This era of "warm economics and cold politics" has defied international relations theory, and yet it characterizes the likely state of Sino-Japanese relations for some time to come. The greatest irony is that Japan's economic recovery in 2004–2006 after years of struggling with deflation required both Koizumi's reforms and a surging Chinese economy to absorb Japanese exports that eventually went to the United States after final assembly in China. Sino-Japanese trade surpassed Japan's trade with the United States in 2005, and statistics by the Japan Bank for International Cooperation indicate that Japanese executives continue to see China as their primary target for direct overseas investment.[16] Yet Japanese public opinion of China has barely improved after plummeting from the positive views held of China during the golden years of the 1980s (fig. 8.1).

The psychological, military, and diplomatic challenges posed by China's sudden rise and uncertain future are inescapable for Japan. Asia retains its hierarchical pull, and Japan and China have never been powerful at the same time the way they are today. Chinese and Japanese aspirations also collide. Both nations are motivated by a profound sense of incompleteness. China seeks territorial integrity and a return to its central role in the region, but it confronts a Japan that seeks to move beyond the postwar period and

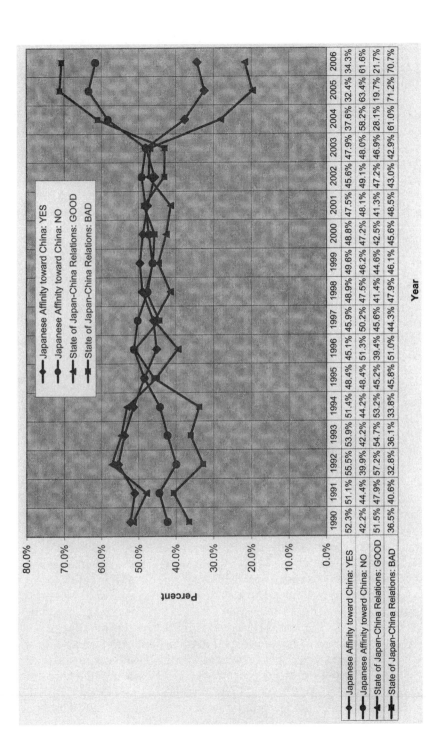

	1990	1991	1992	1993	1994	1995	1996	1997	1998	1999	2000	2001	2002	2003	2004	2005	2006
Japanese Affinity toward China: YES	52.3%	51.1%	55.5%	53.9%	51.4%	48.4%	45.1%	45.9%	48.9%	49.6%	48.8%	47.5%	45.6%	47.9%	37.6%	32.4%	34.3%
Japanese Affinity toward China: NO	42.2%	44.4%	39.9%	42.2%	44.2%	48.4%	51.3%	50.2%	47.5%	46.2%	47.2%	48.1%	49.1%	48.0%	58.2%	63.4%	61.6%
State of Japan-China Relations: GOOD	51.5%	47.9%	57.2%	54.7%	53.2%	45.2%	39.4%	45.6%	41.4%	44.6%	42.5%	41.3%	47.2%	46.9%	28.1%	19.7%	21.7%
State of Japan-China Relations: BAD	36.5%	40.6%	32.8%	36.1%	33.8%	45.8%	51.0%	44.3%	47.9%	46.1%	45.6%	48.5%	43.0%	42.9%	61.0%	71.2%	70.7%

Year

Percent

Figure 8.1. Japan's View of China.

Source: "Survey on Foreign Relations," Cabinet Office, Government of Japan.

to re-establish lost national pride. Japan's economic interdependence with China provides a stability to the two countries' bilateral relations, but not a certainty or predictability about where they will head.

THE KOREAN PENINSULA

Just behind China as the regional variable that most affects Japanese foreign policy strategy is the Korea Peninsula. Meiji oligarch Yamagata Aritomo famously referred to the Korea Peninsula as a "strategic dagger aimed at the heart of Japan." Korea was the traditional route for all things that flowed from continental Asia to Japan, including Buddhism, Chinese characters, Mongol invaders, soba noodles, and probably even sushi (though the last is still contested). It was the tension between the pro-Japan modernizers and the pro-China traditionalists in the Korean court that led Japan down the path to war with China in 1894–1895, and it was Russian expansion into Manchuria and toward Korea that led to the 1904–1905 Russo-Japanese War as Japan sought the "line of maximum advantage" to protect its interests on the peninsula. The outbreak of the Korean War in 1950 did more than any other postwar event to establish Japan's current foreign policy trajectory, including the first U.S.-Japan alliance in 1951, not to mention launching Japan's economic recovery. Throughout the Cold War, Japan was quick to dispatch emissaries to Washington to sustain U.S. support for a military presence on the Korea Peninsula, most notably in the wake of President-elect Jimmy Carter's pledge in 1976 that he would pull all U.S. troops out of South Korea.[17]

But even as Japan worked to maintain a U.S. defense commitment to South Korea, successive Japanese governments also strived to establish their own relationships on the peninsula in diplomatic and commercial terms. Diplomatic relations were established with Seoul in 1965 together with a significant Japanese aid package. North Korea proved more difficult, but as Japan emerged from the Cold War with a strong economy and a hope that bipolar tensions in the international system would contribute to a resolution of issues with Pyongyang, there was a euphoria about normalization of ties. Motivated by an estimated $600 million in annual remissions to North Koreans in Japan (much of which found its way into politicians' accounts in Tokyo) and by the chance to show independent Japanese diplomatic initiative, LDP strongman Kanemaru Shin visited North Korean leader Kim Il Sung in 1990 and emerged from a meeting with Kim Il Sung pledging to stake his political life on the goal of full normalization in a tearful press conference. Japan-DPRK (Democratic People's Republic of Korea) normalization talks have been on again and off again ever since. But the euphoria of the Kanemaru visit did not last for long.

The changing nature of the North Korean threat to Japan became apparent in 1993 when a U.S. National Intelligence Estimate (NIE) was leaked, which assessed that Pyongyang may already have the bomb, and then in 1994 when Pyongyang launched a Nodong missile over Japan (at the time the public thought it had landed in the Sea of Japan). Domestic political restructuring in Japan also had an effect. Many of the same LDP old guard leaders who had been holding together Japan-China relations were also the ones, like Kanemaru, who had been working on North Korea, backed by the Japan Socialist Party. Their demise, including the arrest of Kanemaru on corruption charges and the collapse of the socialists, left North Korea policy open to a younger and more nationalistic group of politicians. One of those politicians was Abe Shinzo, who rose to prominence as Koizumi's lieutenant and an advocate of a tougher line on North Korea. Abe's hard-line view on North Korea was popular with a public that had watched North Korea deploy two hundred Nodong missiles aimed at Japan, sell methamphetamines to Japanese kids, test a long-range Taepodong missile over Japanese airspace in 1998, and then nuclear weapons in October 2006. The most emotional issue of all was the confirmation that dozens of Japanese citizens had, in fact, been abducted by North Korean agents in the 1970s and 1980s even though the Japanese government had been denying there was proof. When Prime Minister Koizumi succeeded in winning the release of five of the abductees after a dramatic visit to Pyongyang in September 2002, the stories the returning Japanese citizens told infuriated the Japanese public even more. Today, 74 percent of Japanese express negative views toward North Korea in public opinion polls.[18]

The Japanese view of North Korea has been a critical driver of Japan's foreign policy strategy in the beginning of the twenty-first century, but many Japanese conservative elites view the North Korean threat as a useful proxy to shake the public out of its pacifist complacency and prepare for longer term competition with China without having to make difficult choices on issues such as missile defense or U.S.-Japan defense cooperation that would lead to open confrontation with Beijing.

Japan's relations with South Korea have defied that same careful strategic calculation. Relations between these two democratic allies of the United States began to improve significantly after Japanese prime minister Obuchi Keizo offered remorse and apology to South Korean president Kim Dae Jung in Tokyo in 1998 and Kim accepted the apology (something that the Chinese president had been unwilling to do a few months earlier, leading Obuchi to only express "remorse"). The U.S.-Japan-ROK Trilateral Coordination and Oversight Group (TCOG) established by U.S. special envoy for North Korea William Perry also cemented Japan-Korea ties on North Korea policy in 1999. Japan and Korea also launched negotiations on a free trade agreement (FTA) in this same period.

Given Japan's growing sense of competition with China and threat from
North Korea, one would expect Tokyo to continue courting Seoul and
maintaining an influence on the peninsula. Instead, Japan-ROK relations
unexpectedly deteriorated and Japan lost influence. The downward spiral
began in April 2004 when Shimane Prefecture passed a resolution declaring
Takeshima (Tokdo in Korean) Japanese territory, and South Korean president Roh Moo Hyun launched an anti-Japanese campaign to put the historically more pro-Japan conservatives on the defensive. Rather than focusing on its larger interests on the Korea Peninsula, the Japanese Foreign
Ministry continued pressing for international recognition of Japan's claims
to the contested territory—pouring more fuel onto the flames. Prime Minister Koizumi's visits to the Yasukuni Shrine complicated the issue further,
and then Prime Minister Abe's ill-considered comments in March 2007
seeming to justify Japan's wartime treatment of impressed sexual workers or
"comfort women" from Korea led to open competition between the two
governments as they lobbied for and against U.S. congressional legislation
condemning Japan. The Roh government's refusal to continue TCOG meetings on North Korea and attempts to list Japan as a common enemy in joint
U.S.-ROK defense planning (unsuccessful in the end) should have caused
real alarm in Tokyo, but instead the Japanese government waited and
hoped that relations would improve after Roh. With the election of a more
conservative and pro-Japanese president in Lee Myung Bok in December
2007, relations looked set for some improvement.

Japan's inability to sustain the positive trajectory with South Korea set by
Kim and Obuchi suggests that external balancing behavior against China
only goes so far. In the case of relations with South Korea, Japan's identity
politics and the domestic ideological struggle to end the "postwar regime"
trumped Realist power considerations. This occurred in spite of the fact that
the Japanese public as a whole has developed a far more positive view of
the Korean people than at any point in the two nations' history.[19] However,
the strategic result of Tokyo's preoccupation with identity and territorial
politics over realpolitik has been a weaker strategic position in Northeast
Asia.

THE U.S.-JAPAN ALLIANCE IN ASIA STRATEGY

The centerpiece of the Yoshida Doctrine was a return to Japan's hundred-
year-old tradition of accommodating to the prevailing hegemonic power, in
this case, the United States. In a broad sense, the alliance relationship has
been redefined several times since Yoshida consolidated conservative Japanese rule and Japan's postwar foreign policy trajectory around the first bilateral security treaty with Washington. In each case Japan asserted relatively

more autonomy, and the United States extracted incrementally more of a commitment to share the burden of international security. In 1960 Prime Minister Kishi negotiated a formal revision that granted the United States the right to use bases in Japan for the security of the Far East but ended the right of U.S. forces to preserve stability within Japan. In 1969 President Nixon and Prime Minister Sato agreed on the return of Okinawa to Japanese sovereignty, and Japan acknowledged the importance of Taiwan and Korea to Japan's own security (an acknowledgment that led to relatively few changes in Japanese defense policy, to the chagrin of the Nixon, Ford, and Carter administrations). In the 1977 defense guidelines and the 1982 Roles and Missions agreement, the Carter and then Reagan administrations reached an agreement that led to a more direct Japanese role in defending against the expanding Soviet military forces in the Far East, with Washington backing the Nakasone government's push for a larger Japanese role in international politics.

Yet at each stage of redefining the alliance, successive Japanese governments were careful to ensure that Article Nine of the Constitution and the ban on collective defense provided a break against "entrapment" (*makikomareru*) in any U.S. confrontation within Asia, particularly vis-à-vis China. Thus, for example, the Japanese government unilaterally determined during the Vietnam War that the "Far East" clause of the 1960 Security Treaty would allow U.S. forces to operate from Japan as far as the Philippines, an effort to prevent Japan from being drawn into the Vietnam War. Similarly, the Japanese defense buildup in the 1980s was aimed at the "exclusively defensive self-defense" of the Japanese home territories against a potential Soviet attack. This served U.S. purposes by turning the Japanese archipelago into an impenetrable phalanx to contain Soviet boomers in the Sea of Okhotsk where the U.S. Navy could attack them in the event of war in Europe, and it served Japanese purposes by keeping Japan away from any conflict with another Asian state. And, fortuitously for both, it served Chinese purposes by increasing the pressure on Moscow. Explicit arrangements to deal militarily with Japan's immediate Asian neighbors were virtually unknown.

What has been most striking about the redefinition of the alliance since the mid-1990s has been the increasingly explicit use of the "American card" for Japan's own strategic objectives in Asia. When Tokyo agreed to revise the defense guidelines with the United States in 1996 in the wake of China's missile tests against Taiwan, the revision covered "situations in the area surrounding Japan that have a direct impact on the security of Japan."[20] While Japanese foreign and defense officials did somersaults in the Diet to argue that the new guidelines had nothing to do with China or North Korea, the press soon reported that the two governments were engaged in planning for regional contingencies to complement the planning that had already been under way since the late 1980s to deal with attacks on Japan by the Soviet Union. In October 1998, the Japanese government agreed to joint research with the United States on missile defense, and by 2007 Japan was spending more on joint missile defense work with the United States than any other ally and had successfully tested an intercept off of a Kongo-class Japan Maritime Self-Defense Force (JMSDF) destroyer near Hawaii; all of this in spite of Chinese protests that eventually subsided once Beijing appreciated the Japanese would not be dissuaded.[21] Then in February 2005 as Beijing prepared to pass "anti-secession" legislation in the March National Peoples Assembly that would legislate the use of force against Taiwan to stop independence, the U.S. and Japanese governments stated explicitly that "stability in the Taiwan Strait" is a core strategic objective for the alliance.[22]

The rhetorical use of the U.S.-Japan alliance in an Asian context also shifted over this same time period. Intellectuals on the left argued for a "triangular" relationship of equal distance among Washington, Tokyo, and Beijing in the early 1990s, calling the idea *datsu-Bei, nyu-A* or "distancing from the United States and entering Asia." By the late 1990s, the more popular phrase even on the left was *Nichibei Nyu-A* or "going into Asia with the U.S.-Japan alliance." Since 1957 Japanese prime ministers opened the Diet sessions by noting that Japan's foreign policy was based on three principles: "The United Nations, the U.S.-Japan Alliance, and relations with Asia." Prime Minister Koizumi broke this trend in 2001 when he opened the Diet with a speech noting the twin pillars of Japan's foreign policy were "the U.S.-Japan alliance" and "international solidarity."[23] Koizumi played for global position and influence for Japan, assuming that Japan's leverage in Asia would flow naturally from that. Thus, his deputy chief cabinet secretary in 2003, Abe Shinzo, argued on national television that Japan's proactive role in the war against international terrorism in Afghanistan and Iraq would ensure that the United States would use its power to help Japan deal with the North Korean threat.[24]

There is no question that different Japanese governments will have relatively different stances toward China or North Korea. The shift from the hawkish Abe to the more moderate Fukuda in September 2007 presaged a new willingness to engage North Korea in diplomatic negotiations and to avoid needless provocations of China with respect to Yasukuni Shrine and other sensitive historical issues. But Fukuda and his main rival for the premiership, Aso Taro, differ little from Abe in their commitment to keeping a strong U.S.-Japan alliance to manage the complex security environment in Asia. Even the opposition Democratic Party of Japan would be unlikely to form a government based on an anti-American platform. While party leader Ozawa Ichiro blocked legislation to authorize the dispatch of JMSDF ships to assist with counterterrorism operations in the Indian Ocean and led delegations of Diet members on missions to Beijing timed to coincide with

Abe or Koizumi's visits to Washington, Ozawa's tactics were designed to embarrass the government and play on anti-Americanism that exists in Japan as it does in every country. But it is not the basis for building a ruling coalition in Japan. Ozawa's own track record in government during the 1990–1991 Gulf War was one of strengthening alliance ties with the United States, and he would have difficulty building a coalition to topple the ruling LDP if he premised it on a return to the strategy of "distancing from America to join Asia" that had some appeal before the Chinese and North Korean threats became so pronounced.

SHAPING REGIONAL INTEGRATION

Japan has always been sensitive to the international order in East Asia and has attempted to shape that order as Japanese power assets have increased. In the nineteenth century the goal was to end the unequal treaties and achieve legal parity with the Western powers, which was accomplished through bilateral treaties with Britain in 1902. Japanese intellectuals also developed a pan-Asian ideal that resonated with anti-colonial nationalists in China, Vietnam, and Korea at the beginning of the twentieth century. The perverse evolution of that pan-Asianist ideal into the Greater East Asian Co-prosperity Sphere led postwar Japanese leaders like Yoshida to be wary of ambitious schemes to shape the regional order. As Japan's economy recovered and reparations and aid began in Southeast Asia, Japanese political leaders began exploring their nation's role in the regional order again, but the U.S. push for multilateral security arrangements in the region reinforced caution and a desire for a Japanese-led regional role that was supportive of U.S. leadership but not entrapped within it. After Prime Minister Kakuei Tanaka's motorcade was stoned by protesters during a visit to Indonesia in 1974, it became clear that Japan would have to begin defining a role for itself in the regional order to move beyond memories of the war. In 1977 Prime Minister Fukuda Takeo launched the new "Fukuda Doctrine," which sought to emphasize Japan's relationship with the Association of Southeast Asian Nations (ASEAN) as a whole, including a $1.5 billion aid package and a pledge to distance from Washington and improve relations with Vietnam consistent with the wishes of Hanoi's neighbors.

The appreciation of the yen in 1985 and the resulting explosion of Japanese aid and investment in Asia intensified efforts in Tokyo to take a lead in regional integration and institution-building. While the Foreign Ministry opposed integration schemes like Malaysian prime minister Mahathir's East Asia Caucus that would exclude the United States or Gorbachev's 1985 Vladivostok proposal for a regional forum that would weaken U.S. alliances, the Ministry of International Trade and Industry (MITI) and business continued to

nurture trans-Pacific business arrangements like the Pacific Economic Cooperation Council (PECC) and the Pacific Basin Economic Council (PBEC). In
1989 the Japanese and Australian governments took the initiative in forming
the Asia-Pacific Economic Cooperation (APEC) forum in order to encourage
regional economic integration on a trans-Pacific basis that would include the
United States.

However, Japan struggled with the proper balance between an economic
integration strategy that remained open and focused on the trans-Pacific
trade relationship with Washington versus one that would allow Japan to
play a larger leadership role as the first goose in a "flying geese" strategy of
economic development in the region. Growing trade friction with Washington in the late 1980s and 1990s increased the attractiveness of Asian economic groupings that Japan could lead. In 1991 the Ministry of Finance
pushed for and funded a study at the World Bank on the "Asian Economic
Miracle" in an effort to show that Japanese and Asian capitalism was different[25] and, in the words of economist and Vice Finance Minister Sakakibara
Eisuke, had "surpassed" Western capitalism.[26] The apex of Japanese efforts
to establish alternative economic arrangements and philosophies to the so-
called Washington consensus came in the wake of the 1997 East Asian financial crisis when Sakakibara attempted to form an Asian Monetary Fund
to counter the influence of the International Monetary Fund (IMF). The
AMF scheme collapsed under pressure from Washington and concern
within Japan about accepting the moral hazard of responsibility for Asia's
weakly governed economies. But a less ambitious program for swapping
debt and exploring longer term arrangements for regional currency arrangements was established through the Chiang Mai Initiative.[27]

With the Koizumi era, the focus on building regional buttresses against
U.S. influence was steadily overshadowed by the goal of shaping the region's architecture to manage the rise of Chinese power. When ASEAN senior officials yielded to Chinese pressure to decouple a proposed East Asia
Summit from Southeast Asia and host the second meeting in Beijing, Japan
joined with Singapore and others to ensure that the summits would be
hosted by ASEAN states and that India, Australia, and New Zealand would
be invited to dilute Chinese influence and increase the voice of democracies
within the forum. As part of the strategy to move the regional architecture
to Japan's advantage rather than China's, the Japanese Foreign Ministry
pushed for what it labeled "principled multilateralism" that would enhance
democracy, governance, and the rule of law rather than Beijing's preference
for a value-neutral architecture that would retain the principle of non-interference in internal affairs.[28] In part this new emphasis on universal values was glue for the U.S.-Japan alliance and an effort by conservatives to
brand Japan as superior to China, but even the most ardent Asianists in the
Foreign Ministry were pushing for Koizumi to highlight the importance of

democracy and rule of law in Koizumi's speeches at the Bandung Asia-Africa Conference in April 2005 where no Americans were present at all.[29] This was the natural evolution of Japanese efforts to take a lead in rule-making in Asia and to ensure that Chinese norms did not undermine Japanese interests in an open, inclusive economic region reinforced by the rule of law.

Japan's efforts to lead in the creation of an East Asian Community today are multilayered and seemingly contradictory. Japan continues to work for trans-Pacific liberalization under APEC, though not with the same enthusiasm that led MITI to work with Australia to launch the forum in 1989. Meanwhile, Japan encourages the U.S. government to join the East Asia Summit and works to ensure that India, Australia, and New Zealand reinforce the theme of "principled multilateralism." Japan's strengthened ties with Australia and India have been a striking new feature of a strategy aimed at enhancing Japanese influence based not only on economic power, but also values. But Japan also still plays the "Asia" game, as the Japanese Finance Ministry has pushed other participants in the Chiang Mai Initiative to consider studying a regional currency while the Foreign Ministry has launched a new Organisation for Economic Co-operation and Development (OECD)–like arrangement for East Asia that would exclude the United States as a full member.[30] Though these efforts may seem contradictory and ill-coordinated, in fact they provide the Japanese government with a variety of forums to shape what will remain a highly fluid and uncertain process of institution-building in Asia—one that combines Japan's Asian and Western personalities.

STRENGTHS AND WEAKNESSES IN JAPAN'S DIPLOMATIC TOOL KIT

Faced with more mature economic growth rates and demographics and a rapidly rising China, Japan's leaders have diversified their diplomatic tool kit in order to sustain national power and prestige. External balancing through closer relations with the United States and now Australia and India has been complemented by a new emphasis on global norms in order to shape Asian regional integration in ways that bond the region more closely with Japan and not China. Domestic institutional reforms, including the strengthening of the prime minister's office, increasing jointness among defense forces and intelligence agencies, and the elevating of the Defense Agency to a Defense Ministry, have all enhanced the ability of the Japanese government to be more proactive on security and diplomatic affairs.

Yet Japan faces two significant drags on its potential role in the region. The first is the burden of history. It would be inaccurate to argue that Japan has not officially "apologized" for the war. Significant apologies have been issued, including Prime Minister Murayama's statement on the fiftieth anniversary of the end of the war in 1995 and Obuchi's bilateral statement with Korean President Kim Dae Jung in 1998. The problem has been that for every official apology, there has been news of right-wing politicians denying the government's interpretation of history and undercutting the original gesture. A national consensus on history will remain difficult for Japan for a host of reasons: the continued belief by many that Japan fought a war of liberation against Western imperialism; the Japanese people's ability to adopt the status of victim because of the bombings of Hiroshima and Nagasaki; the decision by the United States to retain the emperor and many leading industrialists and conservative figures in order to provide stability and help rebuild Japan; resentment of the cynical use of the history issue by politicians within Korea and China; the hypocrisy of Chinese criticism given the record of tens of millions killed during the era of Mao Zedong; the difficulty of the Korean people coming to terms with their own polarized history; and apology fatigue by the Japanese public and the desire of a generation of political figures born after the war to close the "postwar" chapter in Japan's history.

The history problem confounds Japanese foreign policy in very specific ways. Abe lost international support on the abductee issue because of his brief and ill-fated attempt as prime minister to minimize the interpretation of "coercion" of comfort women by the Japanese Imperial Army during the war. Koizumi's Yasukuni visits and the Takeshima/Tokdo territorial issue made it easier for China to enlist Roh Moo Hyun's government in opposition to Japan's UN Security Council bid. However, charges that Japan is isolated in Asia because of history are not borne out by the polling data. Polls consistently demonstrate what Gallup and Yomiuri found in 2006: large majorities (90 percent on average) of Indonesians, Vietnamese, Indians, and other Southeast Asians expressed the view that Japan plays a positive role in the region.[31] The problem is more acute in Northeast Asia, as the BBC found in polls showing Japan at the top of international opinion for its role in world affairs, except in China and South Korea where majorities (71 percent in China and 53 percent in Korea) said Japan did not play a positive role.[32] Nor would it be accurate to describe nationalism in Japan today as a dangerous return to the militarism of the 1930s and 1940s, for as Kevin Doak has revealed in his history of Japanese nationalism, the modern variant focuses more on "civic nationalism" or pride, rather than the nativism or racist views of the past.[33] Indeed, Japan's defense budget has not grown in years, in spite of the charges of renewed Japanese "militarism" popular in the media.

The second drag on Japan's world role is the unfinished business of political realignment. The old 1955 system of conservative LDP dominance and a powerful bureaucratic-business-political iron triangle began to unravel after the Cold War, but the process of political realignment has been half finished for over a decade. Though president of the LPD, Koizumi ran against the party and was wildly popular as a result. In July 2007 Abe lost control of the Upper House to the opposition party. His successor, Fukuda, could still use the ruling coalition's supermajority in the more powerful Lower House to push through legislation but is unlikely to hold that supermajority through the next Lower House election. Yet neither is the opposition Democratic Party of Japan (DPJ) likely to win a majority in the Lower House. The result is a legislative stalemate that could last for years, slowing the dramatic economic, security, and political reforms begun by Koizumi.

The Japanese people may well move toward a broader consensus on history and may empower a new generation of political leaders to break the logjam in the Diet and complete the realignment of political parties that began after the Cold War. After all, much of the world press had begun writing off Japan before Koizumi arrived dramatically on the scene. He succeeded because he spoke to what the Japanese people wanted. His more nationalistic stance was indispensable to his populist battle against the ruling establishment for economic restructuring. The next time a Koizumi emerges on the scene, he—or she—may be able to pick up the pace of economic reform and a more proactive security role while simultaneously doing what leaders like Obuchi and Fukuda did to strengthen relations with the neighborhood. There is a basis for forging just such a governing philosophy in Japan.

CONCLUSION

If Nakae Chomin's three drunkards were viewing Japan's strategic position today, they would be impressed. When they were enjoying their sake almost 150 years ago, Japan enjoyed well less than 1 percent of global GDP and even on the eve of the Second World War barely crawled to a 3.8 percent share. Today Japan is the second-largest economy in the world. While the Meiji-era leaders struggled to end unequal treaties and enjoy respect in the international system, today Japan has a leading role in all international financial institutions and within the Asia-Pacific region. Japan's alliance with the United States is in its strongest shape ever and this has enhanced rather than undermined Japan's own strategic position in Asia. This would no doubt please the master drinker and the gentleman of Western learning, though their Old World companion would likely have expressed dismay at Japan's loss of traditional values and growing identification with universal norms of democracy and rule of law, a sentiment expressed even today in best-selling books like *Kokka no Hinkaku* (The Dignity of the Nation).[34] The three drinkers might be confused by the fact of enormous Sino-Japanese economic interdependence and alarmed at China's growing military and economic power and particularly the prospect of growing Chinese influence over Korea.

The enduring strategic impulses captured in *A Discourse by Three Drunkards on Government* suggest that Japan's role in Asia will remain on its current trajectory, but much will depend on two variables: the United States and China. A catastrophic loss of U.S. hegemonic leadership—either through defeat in war in Asia or retrenchment at home—would inevitably force a reorientation of Japanese security policy in the region. Whether Japan increased internal and external balancing against China or bandwagoned with Beijing would depend on the nature and scope of Chinese and U.S. power. A collapse of regional but not global U.S. dominance would likely push Japan to balance China regionally through increased internal balancing and alignment with the United States globally. However, Chinese hegemonic power at a global level would put Japan in the position of having to consider accommodation with China as both a regional rival and leader of the international system for the first time in half a millennium. In that admittedly remote scenario, bandwagoning with China would not be out of the question, though certainly out of character for modern Japan.

Of course, the nature of the U.S. political debate about America's role in the world and also the difficulties China faces at home both suggest that either a U.S. retrenchment or a linear Chinese trajectory toward global dominance are unlikely. Japan is therefore more likely to adjust its strategy in increments depending on how these two powers conduct themselves. Generational change at home will mean that self-restraint will likely diminish as a characteristic of Japanese policy in Asia, but a more assertive security policy will still have strong structural constraints when it puts at risk Japan's beneficial security arrangement with the United States and political-economic engagement of Asia.

The Korea Peninsula has been a trigger for Japanese strategic change in the past, prompting both the Sino-Japanese and Russo-Japanese wars as the "line of maximum advantage" was recalculated. North Korea's nuclear and missile programs will continue to fuel Japanese strategic realism, but a successful multilateral framework for ending that threat could contribute to an easing of tensions with continental Asia. If Japan were somehow frozen out of such an agreement or if the United States reached an accommodation with Pyongyang that failed to eliminate the nuclear and missile threats, one would expect to see more pronounced Japanese hedging, including in the nuclear area. That scenario seems unlikely, however, since the United States will insist on addressing broader Japanese security concerns as part of any resolution, and Japan's own economic power will be indispensable for substantive reconciliation, reunification, or reconstruction of the North.

Economic interdependence within Asia, represented in the growth of intraregional trade to 50 percent of all trade, coupled with continued reliance on North American markets and global capital flows, all help to ameliorate these darker trends in the security environment around Japan. The search for an "East Asian Community" and the development of regional institutions such as APEC, the East Asia Summit, and the six-party process all help to socialize Japan and China to higher levels of cooperation. However, this institution-building process will likely remain fluid and reflect the underlying power dynamics in the region, breeding competition as often as cooperation. Ultimately, Japan's security environment and strategic trajectory will be determined by the structure of power relations, with the nature of economic interdependence and institution-building and the role of identity and nationalism as critical secondary and tertiary variables. And that is how the master drinker and his two companions would have it be.

NOTES

1. Nakae Chomin, *A Discourse by Three Drunkards on Government*, trans. Nobuko Tsukui, ed. Nobuko Tsukui and Jeffrey Hammond (New York: Weatherhill Books, 1984).

2. For a full examination of strategic roots of Japanese thinking in this early period, see Ronald P. Toby, *State and Diplomacy in Early Modern Japan: Asia in the Development of the Tokugawa Bakufu* (Stanford, Calif.: Stanford University Press, 1992); Kenneth B. Pyle, *Japan Rising: The Resurgence of Japanese Power and Purpose* (New York: Public Affairs, 2007); and Michael Auslin, *Negotiating with Imperialism: The Unequal Treaties and the Culture of Japanese Diplomacy* (Cambridge, Mass.: Harvard University Press, 2004).

3. Pyle, *Japan Rising*.

4. For an overview of this Realist perspective, see Kenneth Waltz, "Structural Realism after the Cold War," *International Security* 5, no. 21 (Summer 2000): 5–41; David Kang, "Getting Asia Wrong: The Need for New Analytical Frameworks," *International Security* 27, no. 4 (Spring 2003): 57–85; Michael J. Green, *Japan's Reluctant Realism: Foreign Policy Challenges in an Era of Uncertain Power* (London: Palgrave Press, 2001).

5. Peter Katzenstein, *Cultural Norms and National Security: Police and Military in Postwar Japan* (Ithaca, N.Y.: Cornell University Press, 1996).

6. Chalmers Johnson, Laura D'Andrea Tyson, and John Zysman, eds., *Politics and Productivity: The Real Story of Why Japan Works* (New York: Ballinger, 1989); Walter Hatch and Kozo Yamamura, *Asia in Japan's Embrace: Building a Regional Production Alliance* (Cambridge: Cambridge University Press, 1996).

7. Eric Heginbotham and Richard J. Samuels, "Mercantile Realism and Japanese Foreign Policy," in *Unipolar Politics: Realism and State Strategies after the Cold War*, ed.

Ethan B. Kapstein and Michael Mastanduno (New York: Columbia University Press, 1999), 182–217; Richard J. Samuels, *"Rich Nation, Strong Army": National Security and the Technological Transformation of Japan* (Ithaca, N.Y.: Cornell University Press, 1994).

8. Green, *Japan's Reluctant Realism*.

9. Pyle, *Japan Rising*.

10. Boueichou (Japanese Ministry of Defense), *Bouei Hakusho 2007 nendoban* [Defense of Japan, 2007], 52–53.

11. Japan Coast Guard, *Japan Coast Guard Annual Report, 2005* (Tokyo: Kokuritsu Insatsukyoku, 2006), www.kaiho.mlit.go.jp/info/books/report2005/tokushu/p018.html.

12. Recounted from media coverage and interviews with participants in Green, *Japan's Reluctant Realism*, 96–98.

13. Cabinet Office of the Prime Minister of Japan, "Speech by H.E. Mr. Junichiro Koizumi, Prime Minister of Japan" (Indonesia, April 22, 2005), www.kantei.go.jp/foreign/koizumispeech/2005/04/22speech_e.html.

14. A total of 52.3 percent of the Japanese public is opposed to the visits according to the public opinion poll done by Kyodo (www.nishinippon.co.jp/nnp/politics/20060711/20060711_003.shtml); 51 percent of the Japanese people are offended by China's "interference" in Yasukuni issue (www.yomiuri.co.jp/feature/fe6100/news/20060626it13.htm); 37 percent of the Japanese people think China is a threat to Japan (www.yomiuri.co.jp/national/news/20060704it13.htm?from=top).

15. Ministry of Foreign Affairs of the People's Republic of China, "China-Japan Joint Press Communiqué" (Beijing, October 8, 2006), www.fmprc.gov.cn/eng/wjdt/2649/t276184.htm.

16. November 30, 2007, Japan Bank for International Cooperation (JBIC), www.jbic.go.jp/autocontents/japanese/news/2007/000208/index.htm, and www.jbic.go.jp/autocontents/japanese/news/2007/000208/sokuhou.pdf.

17. The Japanese government's lobbying of the United States on U.S.-Korea alliance issues is well documented in Murata Koji, "The Origins and the Evolution of the U.S.-ROK Alliance from a Japanese Perspective" (Asia-Pacific Research Center, Stanford University, March 1997).

18. See Cabinet Office of the Prime Minister of Japan, *Gaiko ni Kansuru Yoron Chousa* [Public Survey on Diplomacy], December 3, 2007, www8.cao.go.jp/survey/index.html.

19. According to a poll conducted by the Cabinet Office of the Prime Minister of Japan in 2007, there has been an increase in recent years of the percentage of Japanese people who believe the Japan-ROK relationship has improved. See Cabinet Office of the Prime Minister of Japan, *Gaiko ni Kansuru Yoron Chousa*.

20. Ministry of Foreign Affairs, Japan, "Japan-U.S. Joint Declaration on Security: Alliance for the 21st Century" (Tokyo, April 17, 1996), www.mofa.go.jp/region/n-america/us/security/security.html; Paul S. Giarra and Akihisa Nagashima, "Managing the New U.S.-Japan Security Alliance: Enhancing Structures and Mechanisms to Address Post–Cold War Requirements," in *The U.S.-Japan Alliance: Past, Present, and Future*, ed. Patrick Cronin and Michael Green (New York: Council on Foreign Relations, 1999).

21. Hideaki Kaneda, Kazumasa Kobayashi, Hiroshi Tajima, and Hirofumi Tosaki, *Nihon no Misairu Bouei* [Japan's Missile Defense] (Tokyo: Japan Institute of International Affairs, 2006), 62.

22. U.S. Department of State, "Joint Statement of the U.S.-Japan Security Consultative Committee" (Washington, D.C., February 19, 2005), www.state.gov/r/pa/prs/ps/2005/42490.htm.

23. Ministry of Foreign Affairs of Japan, "Policy Speech by Prime Minister Junichiro Koizumi to the 153rd Session of the Diet," September 27, 2001, www.mofa.go.jp/announce/pm/koizumi/state0927.html.

24. *Nichiyo Toron* [Sunday Debate], Japan Broadcasting Corporation (NHK), August 31, 2003.

25. Edith Terry, *How Asia Got Rich: World Bank vs. Japanese Industrial Policy*, Working Paper 10 (Japan Policy Research Institute, June 1995), www.jpri.org/publications/workingpapers/wp10.html; World Bank, *The East Asian Miracle: Economic Growth and Public Policy* (New York: Oxford University Press, 1993).

26. Sakakibara Eisuke, *Shihonshugi wo Koeru Nihon no Keizai—Nihon Gata Shijo Keizai no Seiritsu to Tenkai* [A Japanese Economy That Surpasses Capitalism—Formation and Development of the Japanese Market Economy] (Tokyo: Toyo Keizai Shimposha, 1990).

27. For details see Green, *Japan's Reluctant Realism*, chapter 9.

28. See, for example, "Speech by Mr. Taro Aso, Minister for Foreign Affairs on the Occasion of the Japan Institute of International Affairs Seminar 'Arc of Freedom and Prosperity: Japan's Expanding Diplomatic Horizons,'" available at www.mofa.go.jp/announce/fm/aso/speech0611.html; and "Towards Principled Multilateralism," in *Gaiko Forum* [Forum on Foreign Affairs], no. 225 (Tokyo: Toshi Shuppan, 2007).

29. Cabinet Office of the Prime Minister of Japan, "Speech by H.E. Mr. Junichiro Koizumi."

30. "Japan, ASEAN Agree to Set Up East Asian Version of OECD in Nov.," Jiji Press, August 25, 2007.

31. *"Tonan Asia/Indo; Tainichi kankei 'yoi' kyu wari"* [90 percent in India and Southeast Asia View Relations with Japan as Positive], *Asahi Shimbun*, September 4, 2006.

32. British Broadcasting Corporation, Globescan, and the Program on International Policy Attitudes at the University of Maryland (PIPA), *BBC World Service Poll* (February 2006, March 2007), www.worldpublicopinion.org/pipa/pdf/mar07/BBC_ViewsCountries_Mar07_pr.pdf.

33. Kevin Michael Doak, *A History of Nationalism in Modern Japan: Placing the People* (Leiden and Boston: Brill, 2007); Hitoshi Tanaka, "Nationalistic Sentiments in Japan and Their Foreign Policy Implications," *East Asia Insights* (Japan Center for International Exchange) 2, no.1 (January 2007); and Thomas Berger, "The Politics of Memory in Japanese Foreign Relations," in *Japan in International Politics: The Foreign Policies of an Adaptive State*, ed. Thomas U. Berger, Mike M. Mochizuki, and Jitsuo Tsuchiyama (New York: Reiner, 2007), 179–212.

34. Masahiko Fujiwara, *The Dignity of the Nation*, trans. Giles Murray (Tokyo: IBC Publishing, 2007).

V

SUB-REGIONAL ACTORS

9

ASEAN and the New Regional Multilateralism

The Long and Bumpy Road to Community

Sheldon W. Simon

From a geopolitical perspective the Asian littoral divides into three sub-regions: *Northeast Asia* (China, Japan, the two Koreas, Taiwan, the Russian far east), *Southeast Asia* (Thailand, Burma, Cambodia, Laos, Vietnam, Philippines, Malaysia, Indonesia, Singapore, Brunei), and *South Asia* (India, Pakistan, Bangladesh, Sri Lanka). Both Northeast Asia and South Asia contain political and economic great powers. In the latter, India's economic activities and growing politico-security influence extend to all of Asia. In the former, Japan, China, South Korea, and Taiwan play significant global economic roles, while Tokyo and Beijing are also major political-security players. By contrast, Southeast Asia contains no great powers with global reach. While the region consists of several states with vibrant economies—Singapore, Malaysia, Thailand—or economic potential—Vietnam and Indonesia—in geopolitical stature, Southeast Asia pales beside its Northeast and South Asia neighbors. Yet, Southeast Asia is where most Asian regional organizations originate whose structures and procedures are determined by Southeast Asian preferences. The primary goal of this chapter is to explain how this has happened, what the implications are for Asia's future, and whether Southeast Asian states organized for the past forty years through the Association of Southeast Asian Nations (ASEAN) will be able to maintain their pivotal position in Asian affairs. For the past several decades, the Asia-Pacific region has been marked by a difficult asymmetry: disputes with the most danger for damage lie in Northeast and South Asia; however, the region's multilateral institutions designed to manage and reduce conflict have originated in Southeast Asia.

While ASEAN has maintained its organizational integrity, it has added new internal and external dimensions. The former include the incipient

ASEAN Free Trade Area (AFTA), the ASEAN Inter-parliamentary Organization, which has been particularly vocal in condemning Burma's human
rights violations, and the "Track Three" ASEAN Peoples Assembly, an NGO
that brings a variety of societal interest groups together to lobby ASEAN
governments. ASEAN-dominated organizations encompass the ASEAN Regional Forum (ARF) on security matters, ASEAN + 3 (Japan, the Republic
of Korea [ROK], China), various ASEAN + 1 dialogues with important
states, the Asia-Europe Meeting (ASEM), and most recently, regular dialogues with the Persian Gulf Cooperation Council, Africa, and Latin America. The newest and most contentious addition to the mix is the East Asia
Summit (EAS) inaugurated in December 2005. The EAS brings ASEAN + 3
countries together with India, Australia, and New Zealand—all of which
have signed ASEAN's Treaty of Amity and Cooperation (TAC) as a membership condition.

CONCEPTUALIZING ASEAN

The Asia-Pacific region has no hegemon. Instead, political, economic, and
social networks proliferate. Regional issues are addressed through collective
action. The various frameworks have diminished the strength of the absolute sovereignty norm that dominated ASEAN at the time of its 1967 creation. Over the ensuing decades, security issues have become increasingly
transnational. Money laundering, human trafficking, environmental degradation, multinational river development, migratory maritime species, terrorism, and piracy require multilateral regime building rather than ad hoc
diplomacy. In theory, at least, organizations such as ASEAN have established procedures and decision-making rules in which all governmental
stakeholders have a voice.[1]

Conceptualizing ASEAN, international relations theorists generally employ three analytical frameworks: *neo-Realism, neo-Liberalism,* and *Constructivism.*[2] Neo-Realists disdain ASEAN's role in regional security because institutions are epiphenomenal. Stability depends on the distribution of
power within the Asia-Pacific and not on an international organization of
small and medium states confined to Southeast Asia. The real locus of Asia-
Pacific power depends on relations among the major actors: the United
States, China, and Japan. Neo-Liberal theorists reject the Realists' dismissal
of ASEAN and point out that the association engages neither in balancing
or bandwagoning with the great powers but rather engages them through
multinational institutions, particularly ASEAN and its offspring (the ARF
and ASEAN + 3 [APT]).[3] By promoting economic and political cooperation
with all three great powers, ASEAN and its offspring promote what neo-Liberals call "absolute gains," meaning that collaboration provides benefits to
all through reciprocity. The distribution of those benefits—"relative gains,"

a major concern of neo-Realists—is less important to neo-Liberals than the fact that aggregate benefits increase for all from lower tariffs to maritime security patrols. Neo-Liberals were set back, however, by the 1997–1998 Asian financial crisis. Neither ASEAN, the ARF, nor the Asia-Pacific Economic Cooperation (APEC) forum were able to cope with financial distress in Indonesia, Thailand, and Malaysia. As for security, ASEAN also failed to mediate the 1999 East Timor crisis. National interests prevailed in both these challenges to neo-Liberalism. The third international relations (IR) school, *Constructivism*, emphasizes ideas, norms, and identities, arguing that the quality of interactions among states is based on whether norms are shared and how they change over time. So, Constructivists argue, ASEAN is emerging as a nascent security community as a "we feeling" develops among its members. Critics of Constructivism insist, however, that norms and cultural variables in ASEAN are too difficult to define and operationalize. Moreover, linking vague norms to actual policy outcomes in ASEAN is still based on bargaining among member states whose interests vary. Rationalists contend that Realists and neo-Liberals present more persuasive evidence for ASEAN outcomes than do Constructivists.[4]

The most useful theoretical approach to the ASEAN system may be Evelyn Goh's *enmeshment* concept. This is a process by which states are drawn into a system to gain benefits (neo-Realism and neo-Liberalism). However, through the process of interaction within the system, states' norms may also be altered.[5] Thus, beginning in the 1990s, ASEAN, led by Singapore and Thailand, has pushed for a regional security structure—the ARF—that would involve (or *enmesh*) as many great powers as possible. Nevertheless, enmeshment is not necessarily harmonious. From the American and Chinese viewpoints, there may be tension between the ARF, a security dialogue mechanism in which both are members, and the APT, which includes the People's Republic of China (PRC) but not the United States. Washington prefers that the ARF be the venue for regional security dialogue while Beijing desires to add security discussions to the APT, originally an economic dialogue group, in which the United States is not represented.

Neither ASEAN nor its offspring possess significant centralized mechanisms to enforce agreements struck by their members, monitor domestic events in member states, or anticipate emerging problems. The association's "ASEAN Way" at bottom is moral suasion—the belief (or hope) that member states will do the right thing so as not to embarrass the collectivity.[6] Clearly that hope has not been realized in Burma's case or Cambodia's. Their domestic politics constitute not only an embarrassment but have also created problems for ASEAN in dealing with Europe and the United States. On the other hand, there is an impressive example of ASEAN's ability to bind outsiders to an ASEAN norm—a point for the Constructivists. China, India, Australia, New Zealand, and Japan between 2003 and 2005 have all signed the association's Treaty of Amity and Cooperation (TAC) binding the signatories to a commitment for the peaceful resolution of regional disputes.

Peaceful resolution of interstate disputes does not translate, however, directly into multilateral security cooperation. Regional security, if truly indivisible, entails transnational involvement in states' domestic affairs whether the issue is terrorism perpetrated by Jemaah Islamiyah (JI), the regional haze emanating from Indonesian Borneo, or arms trafficking from mainland to maritime Southeast Asia. Suppressing these challenges to regional security requires some erosion of the principle of non-interference in internal affairs. Thus, to understand ASEAN requires a combination of the three major theoretical frameworks, depending on the issue being addressed.

ASEAN'S EVOLUTION

ASEAN's original *raison d'être* among its first six members (Indonesia, Malaysia, Thailand, Singapore, Philippines, Brunei) was to protect each state's sovereignty. Formed in 1967 at the Cold War's height and during America's military involvement in Indochina, the non-communist Southeast Asian states came together to hold North Vietnam, China, and the Soviet Union at bay, while permitting U.S. and British allies (Thailand, Philippines, Malaysia, Singapore) to maintain their security ties to these outside powers. Intra-ASEAN relations had another purpose. Indonesia under Sukarno (1945–1967) had been a significant source of regional trauma, opposing Malaysia and Singapore as well as the U.S. presence in the Philippines and flirting with the PRC, North Vietnam, and the USSR. After Sukarno was driven from power in the course of an abortive Indonesian communist coup, a year later the founding fathers of ASEAN saw an opportunity to integrate a new military-led Indonesia into a larger Southeast Asian political enterprise that would both provide Jakarta an opportunity for regional leadership and commit Indonesia to peaceful relations with its neighbors. From that tentative beginning, ASEAN has evolved arguably to become the best known intergovernmental organization in Asia.

As the late Michael Leifer observed,

> The Association has developed over the years into a working diplomatic community and has concurrently grown in international stature becoming in the process a factor of some significance in the calculations of both regional and extra-regional states. To that extent, despite intra-mural differences, it has been able to assume a prerogative role of a kind in an intermittent process of negotiations about establishing rules of the game.[7]

The norms purveyed by ASEAN in the final third of the twentieth century in addition to sovereignty protection included the peaceful settlement of disputes via the 1976 TAC, the avoidance of military pacts with one another, and frequent consultations to effect a common response to regional problems (if feasible).

For ASEAN's founders, non-interference in the domestic affairs of its members was the litmus test for the association; until the mid-1990s that norm was directed outward against great power intervention. With ASEAN's expansion to Indochina and Burma, however, the norm's deficiencies became apparent as human rights violations by the newest members were shielded. For Burma, Laos, and Cambodia particularly, ASEAN's socialization efforts have had little effect. Nevertheless, for the Indochinese states and Burma, joining ASEAN entailed political costs they had not anticipated. Their governments saw the association as a status quo maintenance mechanism.[8] Admittance to ASEAN had never been based on domestic political conditions. However, the harsh domestic politics practiced in Indochina and Burma were seen by ASEAN's other members to be eroding the association's international stature, especially in its relations with the United States and Europe. Still, ASEAN's TAC offered Laos and Cambodia a pledge that Vietnam would not encroach on the former's territory and that disputes would not escalate to military confrontation.

For Vietnam, adherence to ASEAN constituted diplomatic reconciliation with the association that had been branded an instrument of U.S. neo-colonialism by Hanoi during the Cold War. ASEAN's original membership wondered how Vietnam would take to ASEAN's informal process, quiet diplomacy, self-restraint, confidence building, and conflict avoidance. After all, Hanoi had entered the association with a long tradition of confrontation and intransigent demands. In fact, Vietnam has proved accommodating and eager to work within ASEAN's rules of the game.[9] While Vietnam has territorial disputes with ASEAN members, for example over the Spratly Islands with the Philippines and Malaysia, they have not interfered with overall cordial relations because ASEAN has never been a mechanism to resolve conflicting territorial claims among its members. Rather, the association restrains such conflicts. Again, the Spratlys dispute provides a good example. The Philippines and Vietnam were actively involved in negotiating an ASEAN-endorsed 2002 statement of principles on the Spratlys that pledged claimants to abjure the use of force as well as the occupation of any additional features within the Spratly Islands chain.

TERRORISM CHALLENGES THE NON-INTERFERENCE NORM

While the 1997–1998 financial crisis revealed ASEAN's inability to buttress each member's monetary system and multiple bilateral disputes between most ASEAN states have never been sent to the ASEAN High Council for resolution, terrorism as a common challenge has impacted ASEAN's non-interference norm. Because Southeast Asian radical Islamist terror groups regularly move across borders, particularly between Indonesia, Malaysia, and the Philippines but also between southern Thailand and northern Malaysia and perhaps even between Cambodia and southern Thailand, national security has come to require international cooperation. Prior to 9/11, ASEAN did not mention terrorism in either joint communiqués or chairman's statements. Insofar as terrorism was considered a regional security issue, it was associated more with separatist movements in the Philippines and Indonesia and seen, therefore, as an internal matter, requiring little cooperation among states other than as a subtype of transnational crime.[10]

After 9/11, responding to U.S. requests, ASEAN began to address terrorism as a regional concern. However, member states confronted a host of obstacles, including inconsistent legal systems as well as differing law enforcement mechanisms and security practices. To deal with terrorism as a regional issue required that ASEAN states standardize political and legal mechanisms. ASEAN's initial November 2001 Declaration on Joint Action to Counter Terrorism amounted to little more than a broad statement of support to the United States in its time of need.

The prospect of direct American involvement in ASEAN counterterrorism created new problems for the association. While U.S. aid was welcome, especially in intelligence and law enforcement training, the prospect of direct U.S. participation in regional and domestic counterterrorism would appear to involve Southeast Asian states in a war popularly perceived to be anti-Islamic. Thus, Malaysia criticized the Philippines for conducting joint military exercises aimed at eradicating the Abu Sayyaf Group believed to receive al Qaeda support.[11] Nevertheless, in May 2002, the Philippines, Indonesia, Malaysia, and later Cambodia and Thailand signed an agreement to share airline passenger lists, blacklists of known criminals, and computerized fingerprint databases as well as strengthen border controls.

The major impetus for regional counterterror collaboration came in the aftermath of the October 2002 Bali bombing perpetrated by Indonesia-based Jemaah Islamiyah, an organization with direct links to al Qaeda. Indonesia established a central counterterrorism agency with the ability to detain suspects without a trial. Subsequently, Jakarta also invited American and Australian assistance in modernizing the country's National Police, which had been hived off from the military in the post-Suharto period. Even Malaysia, more openly critical of Western involvement in its domestic affairs, agreed to host the Southeast Asian Counterterrorism Center, quietly funded by the United States. Nevertheless, while ASEAN states after 9/11 and the Bali bombings signed treaties providing for anti-terrorist and criminal suppression, these treaties did not contain extradition provisions, and it was understood that despite the treaties, which had still not been ratified by 2007, domestic laws took precedence. Intra-ASEAN differences on threat perceptions of terrorism and uneven senses of collective identity militated against counterterrorism collaboration. Sovereignty protection continued to be the prevailing ASEAN norm.

Continued terrorist bombings in the southern Philippines as well as communal violence in Indonesia and southern Thailand, however, have moved ASEAN closer to hammering out a regional anti-terrorism agreement. At its January 2007 summit in Cebu, Philippines, an ASEAN Convention on Counterterrorism was tabled. Expanding on earlier agreements, the new convention mandates cooperation on tracking movements of suspicious people and money throughout the region and for the first time urges members to agree on extradition. The pact calls upon each member state to craft legislation that will ensure intelligence sharing and the establishment of computer-compatible terrorist databases. The treaty defines terrorism in accordance with United Nations conventions and protocols. However, a unique characteristic of the document is that it draws upon the best practices related to the rehabilitation and social integration of captured terrorists back into their societies based on the experiences of Singapore, Indonesia, and Malaysia.

While the convention is undoubtedly a step toward greater anti-terrorist cooperation, there is little reason to believe that significant changes in ASEAN behavior are imminent. The association does not have a good record in taking such obligations seriously. For example, in 1993, ASEAN agreed to set up a human rights mechanism. Nothing happened until 2007 when the new ASEAN Charter under debate provided for a human rights commission. Whether it will in fact come into existence and what its powers will be remain to be seen. Of sixteen counterterrorism treaties and protocols, only the Philippines and Singapore have ratified most, while Thailand has endorsed five.[12] Human rights advocates in some ASEAN states view the new convention with suspicion, fearing it could become a further justification for the violation of civil liberties in countries experiencing domestic turmoil.[13]

BURMA AND THE NON-INTERFERENCE NORM

ASEAN's non-interference norm was based on the belief that each member's domestic affairs were no one else's concern. Thus, regime type, economic structure, and ethnic and social class compositions were not to be subjects for debate within ASEAN. However, when the domestic difficulties of one member spilled over into a neighboring state, the non-interference norm was strained. The most dramatic example of this strain has been Burma since its 1997 admission to the association. Burma has posed three serious problems for ASEAN: (1) the flight of thousands of ethnic minority Karen into northwestern Thailand fleeing Burma's military junta; (2) illegal drug trafficking from Burmese methamphetamine factories from which over a million tablets are smuggled annually into Thailand—a situation the Thai government has labeled among its greatest security threats; and (3) the brutal suppression of Burma's major opposition party, the National League for Democracy, led by Nobel-laureate Aung San Suu Kyi, who has been under house arrest for eleven years.

To cope with the Burmese junta's "un-ASEAN" behavior, Thailand has taken the lead, initially in 1998 proposing that ASEAN modify its non-interference principle by considering "flexible engagement" with fellow members who pose a problem for neighbors. This proposal was supported only by the Philippines and unsurprisingly strongly rejected by Burma. A somewhat weaker alternative called "enhanced interaction" followed, which encouraged ASEAN states to discuss their concerns but did not authorize direct interference in members' internal affairs. There the matter lay until 2003 when Thailand proposed a "road map" to reconciliation and democracy in Burma. The road map's purpose was to obtain Aung San Suu Kyi's release from house arrest—to no avail.

The most interesting condemnation of Burma came from its primary ASEAN membership sponsor, Malaysia. Prime Minister Mahathir had been the junta's ardent advocate within the association. Subsequently, he felt personally betrayed by the military regime's unyielding resistance to ASEAN's insistence on a pathway to democratization. With the Philippines, Kuala Lumpur pressed Burma to give up its projected 2006 ASEAN chairmanship, insisting that some events inside a country's borders could not be strictly described as "internal affairs."[14] At its December 2005 summit in Malaysia, ASEAN openly urged the junta to release political prisoners and expedite democratic reforms. The association also agreed to send a delegation to investigate the situation.

Nevertheless, when the junta extended Suu Kyi's house arrest for another year in May 2007, ASEAN sidestepped the issue with senior ministers simply referring to the 2005 Kuala Lumpur declaration.[15] Burma stands in stark contrast to other ASEAN members—particularly the Philippines, Indonesia, and Thailand—which have provided channels for involvement of fellow members in their internal affairs. Indonesia invited military personnel from Thailand and the Philippines to observe the peace agreement in Aceh province. Malaysia has mediated peace negotiations between the Philippine government and the Moro Islamic Liberation Front in Mindanao, and Thailand is working with Malaysia to help cope with the southern Thai Malay Muslim insurgency.[16] Of course, these latter cases differ significantly from Burma. Manila, Bangkok, and Jakarta all requested assistance from fellow ASEAN members, so arguably the non-interference norm was not breached.

Burma continues to be ASEAN's most severe test for human rights. In September 2007, a vicious crackdown by the junta to suppress peaceful demonstrations by the Buddhist *sangha* (monks) and other citizens against a sudden and precipitous 500 percent increase in fuel prices outraged world opinion and even elicited an unprecedented statement of "revulsion" from ASEAN officials. Nevertheless, the association's November summit in Singapore went no further, neither condemning Burma's rulers much less imposing any sanctions. In effect, the regime's impunity was officially ignored by ASEAN even though the new Charter adopted at the summit commits ASEAN members, including Burma, "to strengthen democracy, rule of law, . . . and promote human rights and fundamental freedoms."

WHITHER ASEAN?

Before examining other East Asian organizations spawned by ASEAN (see below), it is important to inquire about the association's future. Will it go beyond being a consultation conclave—useful as that may be—and toward a rule-making regime? Skeptics insist that ASEAN cannot be a change agent, nor was it ever intended to be a collective security regime.[17] Nevertheless, by the first decade of the new millennium, Indonesia was tolerating regional discussion of East Timor and Papua, and Burma's political travails were debated regularly in ASEAN meetings. In July 2005 at the ASEAN foreign ministers' meeting in Vientiane, an Action Agenda was proposed that included an ASEAN Charter, the basis for a rules-based regime. Such a charter would enhance ASEAN's capacity to mediate one another's internal conflicts and empower ASEAN's secretary general to provide good offices.[18] ASEAN is projecting the formation of an ASEAN Community by 2020 built on three distinct areas—economic cooperation, political and security cooperation, and socio-cultural cooperation. Its Charter has been developed by an "eminent persons group" (EPG). The Charter can be traced back to a 2003 Indonesian proposal for transforming ASEAN into a more effective East Asia entity.

At their January 2007 Summit meeting in Cebu, Philippines, ASEAN leaders approved a blueprint for the ASEAN Charter. It represented a compromise between traditional principles and new hopes. The bedrock non-interference norm is still there, but ways around it have also been planted. The Charter commits its members to democracy (for the first time), good governance, and human rights. While the EPG document does not include the word "sanctions" for non-compliance, it does provide that the ASEAN Secretariat serve as the monitoring body. Finally, the Charter sets up three ministerial councils underneath the ASEAN Council—on political-security issues, on economic issues, and on socio-cultural concerns.[19]

After three years of negotiations between ASEAN governments and the EPG, the ASEAN Charter was finally signed at the November 18–21, 2007, summit. An historic document that provides the first legal framework in the association's forty-year history, its initial aspirations were whittled away during the debates that accompanied its creation. Early drafts of the Charter provided for voting arrangements and sanctions for non-compliance for the first time in ASEAN's history. Objections from the association's authoritarian members, however, eliminated these innovations. Instead non-interference remains the dominant procedural principle. While the Charter does say that serious non-compliance may be rebuked, such decisions can only be made by ASEAN summits at which the alleged culprits, of course, have veto power. The text also promises a regional human rights body but specifies neither its purview nor procedures. Once again both are left for future summits to determine. Nor does the Charter provide a sliding scale for ASEAN's budget. Instead the equal contribution rule is retained, which means that the association Secretariat's meager funding is based on the limited means of Laos, its poorest member. Despite these gestures to national autonomy, it is still undetermined whether the Charter will be ratified by all members. The Philippines, for one, warned that its Congress would not do so unless Burma moved toward the creation of a genuine democracy.[20]

Security matters may be the area where ASEAN's future role is more promising. The association's latest counterterrorism convention was initialed at the January 2007 Summit. As with earlier declarations going back to November 2001, the latest iteration calls on members to share intelligence, training, curb terrorist financing, and rehabilitate convicted terrorists. The 2007 Convention on Counterterrorism is seen as an integral part of the putative ASEAN Security Community and closely related to the most recent ASEAN ministerial gathering of its defense ministers. ASEAN's database on terrorism and crime is also now being linked to Interpol.[21]

While these declarations promise collaboration, the one domain in which it is definitely occurring is maritime security. Indonesia, Malaysia, and Singapore's coordinated patrols, aided by Japan's provision of equipment and U.S. intelligence, have correlated to a significant reduction of piracy in the Strait of Malacca and, so far, no incidence of maritime terrorism. In fact, as the piracy/terrorism concern seems to have abated, discussions about the Strait are now focusing on maritime safety. According to the International Maritime Bureau, traffic in the Strait of Malacca will increase from 94,000 ships in 2004 to 141,000 by 2020. Under Article 43 of the 1982 UN Law of the Sea Convention, it is the responsibility of the littoral states to maintain navigational aids and prevent pollution. In recent years, the littoral states have held several Track I and Track II meetings on navigation safety and the potential impact of accidents and pollution on coastal communities. Estimates of the cost of coping with the hazards presented by increased Strait traffic could be as high as $300 million over the next decade.

Japan has long contributed financially to the Strait upkeep, and, in recent years, India, South Korea, and the United States have also pledged assistance. China, too, has offered to restore the navigational aids that were damaged in the December 2004 Indian Ocean tsunami. However, these are all voluntary contributions. The Nippon Foundation of Japan has suggested that all ships transiting the Strait contribute one U.S. cent per deadweight ton of cargo. This would generate $40 million a year toward navigational safety. Nevertheless, user states and their companies have not been forthcoming, insisting that the responsibility is solely with the littorals. In actuality, there are several stakeholders including the littorals, user states, shipping companies, and insurance agents. Safety in the Strait would be an excellent issue for ASEAN to undertake as well as other regional organizations, including the ARF and APEC.[22]

Maritime security in Southeast Asia also involves the South China Sea islands. Claimed entirely by China and Vietnam, some of the Spratlys are also occupied by the Philippines, Malaysia, Taiwan, and Brunei. Potentially rich in seabed fossil fuels as well as mineral nodules and fish, the South China Sea islands sit astride the major sea lanes from the Indian Ocean through the South China Sea and up to the Sea of Japan. ASEAN began to play a role in these disputes in 1995 when China agreed to discuss them multilaterally for the first time. These talks led to a Declaration on the Conduct of Parties in the South China Sea signed by ASEAN and the PRC in November 2002. Although not a Code of Conduct preferred by ASEAN, the Declaration provided for freedom of navigation and overflight above the South China Sea and proclaimed that territorial disputes would be resolved peacefully. The parties also agreed to exercise restraint and refrain from activities that would complicate the disputes. Nevertheless, several claimants increased their populations on the islets they occupied and enhanced their armaments.

In 2005 the Philippines, China, and Vietnam, after several years of challenging each other's oil exploration efforts, agreed to joint seismic surveys to determine the extent of hydrocarbon resources in their overlapping areas. This agreement could be the first step toward a management arrangement that addresses the increasing need for oil and gas resources. Despite this arrangement, however, China has condemned Vietnam's plan to build a pipeline from British Petroleum gas discoveries 230 miles offshore on its claimed continental shelf. On the other hand, the Philippines seemed so eager to obtain China's agreement to the joint exploration that Manila agreed to include parts of its legal continental shelf. To defuse these persistent mutual suspicions, ASEAN and China could issue another declaration containing a "without prejudice" clause that will promote joint development in the areas of overlapping claims by emphasizing that the joint activities do not impact the validity of the underlying claims to sovereignty and jurisdiction. Thus, the claimants would not give up their claims but would "freeze" them for the time necessary to determine whether there are exploitable seabed resources. If such resources are discovered, then additional negotiations would be necessary to determine an exploitation regime.[23]

With its new Charter, ASEAN surveys a future where noble aspirations will probably continue to exceed accomplishments. The aspirations suggest a desire to emulate the European Union (EU) with respect to economic integration and high-minded commitments to democracy and human rights. However, unlike the EU, no ASEAN state embodies all the essential traits of liberal democracy. Those most democratic—Indonesia, the Philippines, and Thailand (after its December 2007 transition from a military regime)— still suffer from serious rule of law deficiencies. The other seven members range from soft authoritarian (Singapore and Malaysia) to more openly one-party dictatorial (Burma, Laos, Vietnam, Cambodia, and Brunei). This range of political systems primarily concerned with regime maintenance means that ASEAN's dominant principle will continue to be sovereignty protection and noninterference. None of these domestic differences, however, should obstruct the association's ability to effect a united front toward external powers through the new ASEAN Security and Economic Committees.

ASEAN's Offspring: The ASEAN Regional Forum (ARF)

The ARF emerged in 1994 from ASEAN's post-ministerial conferences that were held after ASEAN's annual foreign ministers meeting.[24] The conferences were one-day events with Asia-Pacific great powers including the United States, China, and Japan. The subject matter was broadly political/ security. Formalization of these extra-ASEAN discussions into the ARF occurred as ASEAN realized that if the association was to remain relevant in post–Cold War Asia-Pacific security, it should ensure that its procedures would dominate Asia-Pacific security discourse and that ASEAN would be a part of all Asia-Pacific security deliberations. The ARF has achieved these goals for the association. *Realists* see the ARF as another balance of power mechanism in which most members defer to the China-U.S. relationship; *neo-Liberals* believe it is an arena for bargaining over regional security issues; and *Constructivists* insist that it is a framework for the development and practice of norms. All agree that the ARF is not meant to be a collective security arrangement.[25] Nor is the ARF designed to resolve specific regional disputes such as the Spratly Islands. Rather, as the Constructivists suggest, the ARF is aimed at bringing about long-term peace by fostering a sense of mutual trust. Whether this works depends on the quality of relationships over time among the members.

Organizationally, ARF's highest level is its annual foreign ministers meeting, always chaired by an ASEAN state. This annual meeting is supported by an annual Senior Officers Meeting (SOM) that deals with substantive issues. The SOM, in turn, is aided by a working-level venue called the Inter-sessional Support Group on Confidence-Building Measures. Confidence-building activities have remained ARF's primary focus since its inception. These groups are supplemented by gatherings of specialists on topics such as transnational crime that consist of Track II experts organized through the Councils for Security Cooperation in the Asia Pacific (CSCAP), which themselves run parallel dialogues to the ARF. CSCAP is non-governmental but also employs the ASEAN Way in its deliberations, that is, consensus and no votes.[26]

The ARF reflects ASEAN's preferred strategy of consensus diplomacy, which manages problems rather than solves them. That is why the ARF has had such difficulty moving beyond its initial stage of promoting confidence building to its proposed second stage of preventive diplomacy (PD) or to the long-postponed apex of ARF maturation: conflict resolution. Another explanation for this difficulty is that ASEAN wanted to enmesh China, the United States, and Japan as security partners who would commit to Southeast Asia's stability via confidence building by keeping an eye on each other to discourage adventurism. However, this ARF status quo orientation does not promote the kind of change inherent in preventive diplomacy and conflict resolution.

An additional ASEAN goal with respect to outside powers joining the ARF has been to extend the aims and principles of ASEAN's TAC to ARF members, meaning that all agree to resolve disputes peacefully. This refers particularly to China's South China Sea claims. For the external powers, ARF provides other benefits. Washington uses the ARF to promote dialogue between South Korea and Japan. Japan and China use the ARF as a vehicle for their enhanced Asia-Pacific diplomacy.

As for the interface between confidence-building measures (CBMs) and PD by 2000, the ARF began discussing a good offices role for the ARF chair, the creation of an Eminent Persons Group within the ARF to address future challenges, the production of an Annual Security Outlook, and voluntary background briefings by any member on regional security. Originating from a Track II advisory group, these ideas were endorsed by the ARF with the exception of a good offices role for the chair. Both China and some ASEAN states objected to this enhanced chair authority for fear that it could lead to interference in their internal affairs.[27]

The activist states within the ARF (the United States, Japan, Australia, and Canada) have promoted a PD agenda, but the ASEAN Way procedure requiring consensus has effectively blocked it. Moreover, the fact that an ASEAN state will always chair the ARF means that disputes between ASEAN and non-ASEAN members will not be deliberated before the ARF. One observer has noted that frustration with the ARF's inability to have an impact on regional security has led the United States and Japan to diminish their attention. The only ways PD will be activated in the ARF are if the non-interference principle is moderated, the ARF develops more practical PD measures, and structural reform occurs that dilutes ASEAN's dominance. None of these appear on the horizon.[28] Nevertheless, a recent innovative ARF exercise suggests there may still be hope for innovation: in January 2007, the ARF held its first simulated sea exercise in Singapore with representatives from twenty-one countries. Their task was to trace a missing ship possibly hijacked by terrorists. The key aim of the exercise was to acquaint participants with varying national protocols. While general satisfaction was expressed with the results, no plans have been made for future exercises.[29]

ASEAN Offspring: ASEAN + 3

If the ARF has been ASEAN's expansion to the Asia-Pacific and beyond for security discussions, then ASEAN + 3 (APT) is the device to link Northeast and Southeast Asia together for economic matters in the aftermath of the 1997 financial crisis. Unlike the ARF, the ASEAN ministerial conferences and the Asia-Pacific Economic Cooperation (APEC) forum, the United States is excluded while China, Japan, and the ROK were charter members. Indeed, the three Northeast Asian states have all established partnership agreements with ASEAN that link prosperity with peace. Closer East Asian cooperation in the APT emerged from the frustration and disappointment in Washington's reluctance to aid Southeast Asia during the financial crisis. Moreover, this perceived U.S. indifference toward ASEAN also made Southeast Asia aware of the danger of a unipolar world and the need to diversify economic relations. By 1998, the APT leaders agreed to hold a regular summit and a series of meetings for foreign and finance ministers. The APT's major achievement was the Chiang Mai Initiative inaugurated at the 2000 summit in Thailand. Chiang Mai was a currency swap arrangement between central banks to enable member states to protect themselves better against future speculative attacks on their currency. For ASEAN particularly, Chiang Mai was designed to offer an alternative to the Western-dominated International Monetary Fund that imposed such draconian conditions in the 1997 crisis that two governments fell (Indonesia's and Thailand's) and some ASEAN states' economies were set back for several years. In 2004, at China's initiative, the APT launched a new East Asia Summit (discussed below) that expanded the APT's purview to security issues. China, with Malaysia's endorsement, hoped the EAS would be restricted to APT members only, thus excluding the United States and other non–East Asian states.

APT has become a forum where the major powers of Northeast Asia compete for the economic leadership of Southeast Asia via a set of free trade agreements that primarily privilege the stronger Northeast Asian economies.[30] An APT unit was set up in the ASEAN Secretariat to research specific issues raised by the principals that gradually led to the creation of detailed agendas for APT meetings. Though as in all ASEAN-based organizations, decisions carried no enforcement provisions, APT through the currency swap arrangements built a significant financial reserve that could serve the practical purpose of dampening monetary crises. By early 2004, the cumulative value of these swap arrangements had risen to $36.5 billion, providing some financial psychological security that had been unavailable in 1997.[31]

ASEAN and Multilateralism's Future: The EAS

The most recent manifestation of a wider East Asia came into existence with the December 2005 inaugural East Asia Summit (EAS). While Southeast Asia had been "institutionalized" since ASEAN's creation in 1967, there was no Northeast Asian counterpart until ASEAN + 3 (China, Japan, the ROK) was put together at ASEAN's initiative in 1997. The EAS was a Malaysian proposal strongly backed by China. For Kuala Lumpur, the intention was for the EAS to develop like the APT, moving from a relatively restricted economic agenda gradually to look at "security, democracy, good government, the rule of law, every aspect of human security." Both Malaysia and China projected the EAS to be independent of the United States, an exclusively East Asian forum. Other ASEAN members plus Japan, however, fearing China's possible domination, pressed for invitations to Australia, New Zealand, and India—the result being that the EAS includes a number of America's friends and allies despite Washington's absence.[32] ASEAN also insisted that only its members could host the annual summits. Thus, comparable to the ASEAN + 3, ARF, and APT meetings, ASEAN would be in the driver's seat.

ASEAN had imposed three conditions for EAS participation: (1) adherence to the TAC, (2) dialogue partner status, and (3) "substantial" relations with ASEAN. Russia has applied to the EAS with strong support from Malaysia, China, and the Philippines despite reservations from Singapore, Indonesia, and Japan. Singapore argued that Russia's ASEAN ties were not substantial; Jakarta fears that Moscow's membership would reduce ASEAN's dominance; and Tokyo opposed because of its territorial dispute and also because it saw Russia as a Chinese ally.[33] Because of a lack of consensus, Russia was not represented at the January 2007 EAS.

U.S. reticence about the EAS is based on skepticism about the proliferation of multilateral activities in Asia and the belief that APEC and ARF should be the lead Asia-Pacific agents in economics and security. The United States often finds the Asian model of multilateralism to be inordinately concerned with consensus and, therefore, the lowest common denominator approaches to confidence building. This orientation moves the region too slowly to solve Asia's pressing political, economic, and security challenges. Washington prefers ad hoc multilateral mechanisms to deal with specific regional problems such as the Six-Party Talks on North Korea's nuclear weapons.[34] ASEAN leaders have urged the United States to sign the TAC and join the EAS. While not refusing explicitly to do so, in March 2007, the State Department stated coyly that "we are studying the various legal and policy issues related to possible U.S. accession to the treaty. The United States has not made a decision at this time on whether to sign."[35] One explanation frequently given for Washington's hesitation is concern that the TAC would limit naval movements in wartime because the treaty constitutes a non-aggression pact. However, none of America's Asian allies accept this interpretation; nor do they see their signature on the TAC as limiting their defense relationships with the United States. One other possible explanation for Washington's inaction is the administration's apprehension that the U.S. Senate will not ratify the treaty, thus worsening Washington's relations with ASEAN.

CONCLUSION

ASEAN and the ARF as cooperative security arrangements designed to enhance common interests and cope with common challenges are explicitly neither defense arrangements nor alliances. They were not formed to counter specific threats; moreover, they coexist with several of their members' separate defense arrangements with external powers, particularly the United States, but also the UK, Australia, and New Zealand through the Five Power Defence Arrangement. Although ASEAN and the ARF focus on dialogue and confidence building, they also attempt to create norms and codes of conduct as ways to avoid conflict. (These characteristics are emphasized by Constructivist theories.) Balance of power considerations operate within cooperative security regimes. For example, a major purpose in ASEAN's formation was to constrain Indonesia's hegemonic aspirations by forcing Jakarta to consider its neighbors' security needs. Nevertheless, successful cooperative security still depends on access to an external countervailing power whose own policies are compatible with the cooperative security organization's. In ASEAN's case, this is the United States. Washington's Asian military presence supports ASEAN's own goal of ensuring that no hegemon arises (China). That China and the United States are both ARF members constitutes from ASEAN's viewpoint a way of constraining China's political ambitions while keeping the United States involved in East Asian security. In recent years, however, the PRC has more effectively used the ARF and such related groups as ASEAN + 3 to promote Beijing's political and economic international agendas than has the United States, which appears from Southeast Asia's vantage point to be inordinately concerned with the Middle East and fighting radical Islamic terrorism.

ASEAN members are still suspicious of one another's policies and motives. There is a history of subversion against neighbors that led to an important institutional pledge: the Declaration of ASEAN Concord by which each member state resolved to eliminate subversive threats to neighbors. No sanctuary would be given to groups bent on overthrowing members' regimes. Nevertheless, Burmese and Laotian minority ethnic insurgents have sheltered in Thailand, and thousands of Indonesian illegal migrants have periodically strained Kuala Lumpur–Jakarta relations. Most recently, Indonesian terrorist recruits have journeyed to the southern Philippines for training in Islamic camps run by the Abu Sayyaf or radical members of the Moro Islamic Liberation Front. All of these reveal the susceptibility of several ASEAN states to domestic challenges across international boundaries. ASEAN is able to do little to counteract these intramural frictions.

The Association is more successful in *associative power balancing*. Brunei's adherence to ASEAN served to protect the tiny Borneo Sultanate from the competitive pressures of Malaysia and Indonesia. The Third Indochina Conflict illustrates ASEAN's use of extramural balancing by which the association aligned diplomatically with both China and the United States to prevent Vietnam from consolidating its hold on Cambodia. *Associative balancing* fell short when ASEAN was unable to agree on a Code of Conduct on the South China Sea to counter China's "creeping imperialism." Differences among those ASEAN members claiming some degree of sovereignty over the Spratlys blocked any consensus so that the ultimately toothless 1992 ASEAN Declaration on the South China Sea was more an effort at conflict avoidance than resolution. Vietnam, the Philippines, and China reached an agreement in 2005 completely outside ASEAN, which the other claimants (Malaysia, Brunei, Taiwan) have ignored, that provides for joint exploration of the seabed around the Spratlys while splitting the costs and future benefits. ASEAN's inability to effect a South China Sea regime may be attributed to both its intramural differences and the inability of the association to find an external countervailing power willing to contain China's hegemonic aspirations.

With the post–Cold War, the structure of East Asian politics changed. ASEAN states realized that prospects for Southeast Asia's autonomy had become obsolete. The ARF's creation in 1994 brought East Asia's two sub-regions together along with the EU, North America, Australia, and New Zealand to form the largest security discussion organization in the world. ASEAN's hope was to dominate the ARF procedurally and to impose the association's TAC as the forum's Code of Conduct, thus committing members to abjure the use of force. China and its South China Sea claims were the target. ASEAN also hoped that by including the United States, China, and Japan in the ARF, a stable distribution of power would result. The EAS whittles down the ARF's membership so that only predominantly Asian states belong, though—as in the other Asian regional organizations thus far "talk" predominates over "community."

Disappointment in the efficacy of regional bodies has meant that bilateral engagements remain the focal point of real regional security actions. A recent example is the 2007 Bali agreement between Singapore and Indonesia for a bilateral extradition treaty and defense cooperation agreement that required tough negotiations because the outcome had real effects on the signatories. Indeed, annual ASEAN summits are more significant for the bilateral deals concluded on the sidelines than any multilateral agreements at the main event. The U.S. agreement to hold a summit with ASEAN is one such sideline case in point.[36] Ironically, then, ASEAN and its offspring (ARF, ASEAN + 3, and the EAS) better serve Asian international relations as venues for smaller sideline meetings that address specific national concerns than in the larger gatherings that create rhetorical agreements with little subsequent capability or intention for implementation.

NOTES

The author wishes to thank Peter Leslie of the Arizona State University Political Science Junior Fellows Program for research assistance.

1. For a good discussion of regime creation in the Asia-Pacific, see Jim Rolfe, "A Complex of Structures: Functional Diversity, Regional Consolidation, and Community in the Asia-Pacific," *Asian Affairs: An American Review* 33, no. 4 (Winter 2007): 217–234.

2. Representative authors for these schools include Michael Leifer and Ralf Emmers for *Realism*, Shaun Narine for *neo-Liberalism*, and Amitav Acharya, Mely-Anthony Caballero, and See Seng Tan for *Constructivism*.

3. Sheldon W. Simon, "ASEAN and Its Security Offspring" (paper prepared for the Tenth Annual Security Conference of the U.S. Army War College Strategic Studies Institute, Carlisle Barracks, Pennsylvania, March 27–29, 2007).

4. An excellent discussion of these frameworks as they apply to ASEAN is found in Kai He, "Does ASEAN Matter? International Relations Theories, Institutional Realism, and ASEAN," *Asian Security* 2, no. 3 (October 2006): 189–214.

5. Evelyn Goh, "Great Powers and Southeast Asian Regional Security," *Military Technology* (January 2006): 321–323.

6. Sarah Eaton and Richard Stubbs, "Is ASEAN Powerful? Neo-Realist versus Constructivist Approaches to Power in Southeast Asia," *Pacific Review* 19, no. 2 (June 2006): 135–156.

7. Cited in Amitav Acharya, "Do Norms and Identity Matter? Community and Power in Southeast Asia's Regional Order," *Pacific Review* 18, no. 1 (March 2005): 98.

8. Ralf Emmers, "The Indochinese Enlargement of ASEAN: Security Expectations and Outcomes," *Australian Journal of International Affairs* 59, no. 1 (March 2005): 74.

9. Emmers, "The Indochinese Enlargement," 76–77.

10. Jonathon Chow, "ASEAN Counter-Terrorism Cooperation since 9/11," *Asian Survey* 45, no. 2 (March/April 2005): 304–305.

11. Chow, "ASEAN Counter-Terrorism Cooperation," 312–313.

12. Douglas Bakshian, "ASEAN Summit to Tackle Tough Issues from Terrorism to North Korea," *VOA News.com*, January 8, 2007; and Kavi Chongkittavorn, "ASEAN's Accord on Counter-terrorism a Major Step Forward," *Nation* (Bangkok), February 19, 2007.

13. "Militants Warn of Dangers of ASEAN Anti-Terror Pact," *Philstar.com* (Manila), January 11, 2007.

14. Much of this Burma discussion is taken from Ruukun Katanyuu, "Beyond Non-Interference in ASEAN: The Association's Role in Myanmar's National Reconciliation and Democratization," *Asian Survey* 46, no. 6 (November/December 2006): 825–845.

15. Estrella Torres, "ASEAN Meetings Drop Burma Issue from Agenda," *Irrawaddy*, May 23, 2007.

16. Katanyuu, "Beyond Non-Interference in ASEAN," 840.

17. See the argument by Erik Kuhonta, "Walking a Tightrope: Democracy versus Sovereignty in ASEAN's Illiberal Peace," *Pacific Review* 19, no. 3 (September 2006): 337–358.

18. Michael Vatikiotis, "Resolving Internal Conflicts in Southeast Asia: Domestic Challenges and Regional Perspectives," *Contemporary Southeast Asia* 28, no. 1 (April 2006): 42.

19. Abul Khalik interview with EPG member and former Indonesian foreign minister Ali Alatas, "ASEAN Faces 'Critical Period' in a Changing World," *Jakarta Post*, January 17, 2007.

20. A good critique of the 2007 ASEAN Summit and Charter may be found in "Fifth from the Right Is the Party Pooper," *Economist*, November 24, 2007, 43–44.

21. Rajesh M. Basrur, "The Threat of WMD Terrorism: ASEAN Needs to Respond," *RSIS Commentaries* 56 (Singapore), June 6, 2007.

22. Much of the preceding discussion is drawn from Vijay Sakhuja, "Malacca: Who's to Pay for Smooth Sailing?" *Asia Times Online*, May 16, 2007.

23. This South China Sea discussion may be found in Robert Beckman, "Joint Development in the South China Sea: Time for ASEAN and China to Promote Co-operation?" *RSIS Commentaries* 46 (Singapore), May 29, 2007; and Mark J. Valencia, "In Response to Robert Beckman," *RSIS Commentaries* 53, June 4, 2007.

24. For an essentially Realist assessment of the ARF, see Sheldon Simon, "Realism and Regionalism in Southeast Asia: The ARF and the War on Terror," in *Order and Security in Southeast Asia: Essays in Memory of Michael Leifer*, ed. Joseph Liao and Ralf Emmers (London: Routledge, 2006), 93–109.

25. Hiro Katsumata, "Establishment of the ASEAN Regional Forum," *Pacific Review* 19, no. 2 (June 2006): 182 and 194.

26. Sheldon W. Simon, "Evaluating Track II Approaches to Security Diplomacy in the Asia-Pacific: The CSCAP Experience," *Pacific Review* 15, no. 2 (2002): 176–200.

27. Takeshi Yuzawa, "The Evolution of Preventive Diplomacy in the ASEAN Regional Forum," *Asian Survey* 46, no. 5 (September/October 2006): 793–794.

28. Yuzawa, "The Evolution of Preventive Diplomacy," 802–804.

29. "ASEAN Regional Forum Holds First Simulated Sea Exercise," *Channel News Asia.com*, January 23, 2007.

30. David Martin Jones and Michael L. R. Smith, "Constructing Communities: The Curious Case of East Asian Regionalism," *Review of International Studies* 33 (2007): 181, 183.

31. Yoshimatsu Hidetaka, "Political Leadership Informality and Regional Integration in East Asia: The Evolution of ASEAN Plus Three," *European Journal of East Asian Studies* 4, no. 2 (2005): 213, 220–221.

32. Rolfe, "A Complex of Structures," 224.

33. Leszek Buszynski, "Russia and Southeast Asia: A New Relationship," *Contemporary Southeast Asia* 28, no. 2 (August 2006): 29.

34. The Stanley Foundation, *Dialogue Brief: Building an Open and Inclusive Regional Architecture for Asia* (Muscatine, Ia.: The Stanley Foundation, 2007), 5.

35. "U.S. May Sign Key ASEAN Treaty with Eye on East Asia Summit," Agence France-Presse (Hong Kong), March 22, 2007.

36. Michael Vatikiotis, "US and China Tug at ASEAN Unity," *Asia Times Online*, May 8, 2007.

10

Australia in Asia

Exploring the Conditions for Security in the Asian Century

Hugh White

Since the first European settlers landed on the Australian continent in 1788, the security of the society they founded has depended ultimately on Western strategic primacy in the East Asian littoral. For the last century, since the eclipse of Britain's global naval predominance, that primacy has been exercised by America. America's capacity to maintain strategic primacy throughout the twentieth century, as Asian powers grew into modern industrial states with modern military capabilities, has been central to Australia's sense of its security with a stable regional order in Asia since at least the visit of the Great White Fleet one hundred years ago. But the scale and pace of economic change in Asia over the last few decades, and especially in the last few years, has posed new challenges to U.S. primacy and to the regional order (that U.S. primacy has for so long maintained).

Asia's historic economic transformation has created immense economic opportunities for Australia, which have underwritten its prosperity over recent decades and raised expectations of an even richer future. But the challenges that Asian economic growth now poses to American primacy and Asian order raise big and unsettling issues for Australia. They require Australians to think deeply about what kind of new order in Asia would offer the best prospects of peace and security for Australia in the Asian Century and what their country can do to help bring such an order about. This chapter will examine these questions about Asia's new regional system from a specifically Australian viewpoint—a viewpoint that must necessarily reflect both Australia's traditional closeness to the United States, based on ties of culture, ideology, and history, and Australia's ever-deepening engagement with Asia based on ties of economics, geography, and, increasingly, demography.

In considering their approach to Asia's future, Australians have to re-examine some of their oldest and most basic strategic and political assumptions and contemplate diplomacy of a complexity that they have not had to deal with before. Consider this: for over two hundred years since the first settlement, Australia's major trading partners have been her closest allies, or, like Japan, the allies of close allies. But over the past few years China has been by far the fastest-growing market for Australia's exports, and in 2007 China overtook Japan as Australia's major trading partner.[1] China is not an ally of the United States—thus in the future, it seems, Australia's major trading partner is likely to be an active strategic competitor of its major ally. This makes Australia's international situation much more complex than ever before, and little in Australia's history has prepared it for managing this complexity. Not surprisingly, Australian policy in recent years has shown signs of confusion as it grapples with new and unfamiliar questions and issues. But a clearer pattern may now be emerging, and it is possible at least to sketch the outlines of a new Australian approach to the emerging regional order in Asia. Some of the results may be quite surprising.

Of course, these questions about the future international order in Asia are not the only topics on Australia's foreign and strategic policy agendas today, nor are they necessarily the ones that attract the most headlines. Like other countries around the world, Australia worries about a host of security concerns that seem to have little to do with traditional strategic affairs—problems like terrorism and the risks of state failure. For Australia these problems might be global, but they are not remote: for example, Australia faces major challenges in supporting the development of weak states and averting the risk of state failure on its immediate doorstep in places like East Timor and the Solomon Islands. But urgent concerns like these have not prevented concerns about Asia's future order from attracting significant attention. During the election campaign debate, Australia's new prime minister, Kevin Rudd, specifically listed the rise of China and India among the key challenges facing Australia and made no mention of the threat of terrorism. Australians today are uneasily aware of the risks inherent in their strange situation: a cosmopolitan but manifestly Western society occupying a vast, rich island continent on the margins of Asia, half in and half out of the richest, most dynamic, but arguably also the riskiest region in the world. At the dawn of what promises to be the Asian Century, both the risks and the opportunities of Australia's strange situation seem more potent than ever.

THE OLD ORDER

It helps to start by sketching how Australians have seen the existing order from which any new regional system in Asia will develop. From an Australian perspective, Asia's recent era of peace and prosperity dates from the late 1960s and early 1970s. At that time, many of the conflicts and anxieties that characterized Asia in the first two decades after the Second World War were damped down. Close to home for Australians, the risk that the erratic and adventurist Sukarno might destabilize Southeast Asia and take Indonesia into the communist camp was dispelled after 1965 when Suharto established his New Order and committed Indonesia to steady development at home and good relations with its neighbors, including Australia. The establishment of ASEAN in 1967 marked the end of post-colonial turbulence in maritime Southeast Asia and ushered in a long era of cooperation, economic growth, and social and political development. Above all, President Nixon's visit to Beijing in 1972 signaled China's acceptance of the status quo in Asia and the start of China's integration into the post-colonial Asian order. It therefore marked the end of a twenty-year period in which China posed a real threat to Australia's vision of regional peace and stability and inaugurated an unprecedented era of peace and harmony between Asia's major powers.

In retrospect, we can see that the opening to China not only provided the conditions in which America and its allies, including Australia, could withdraw from Vietnam without risking the strategic reverses that had driven our intervention in the first place. It also laid the political and strategic foundations for stable and cooperative relations between East Asia's most powerful states and thus provided the essential preconditions for China's economic transformation from the late 1970s. Since they were transformed by Nixon's diplomacy in the early 1970s, the triangle of relationships between the United States, China, and Japan, upon which peace in Asia primarily depends, has proved remarkably stable and durable. The key to this triangular set of understandings has been U.S. primacy. America's credible strategic commitment to Japan reassured Japan that it need not arm against China and reassured China that it need not fear Japan. In return both Japan and China accepted U.S. primacy. In particular, China accepted that it could achieve its ambitions domestically and internationally without contesting U.S. primacy in Asia—or, to put it another way, Beijing was willing to limit its international ambitions to conform to the reality of American power, in return for the reassurance that America provided against Japan.

Looking back over the past thirty years of peace, the emergence of this particular form of stable order in Asia after the Vietnam War has an air of inevitability. But at the time it seemed highly unlikely. As Vietnam digressed in the late 1960s, many observers expected the emergence of a new balance of power in Asia in which the United States would be forced to share power with China, Japan, the Soviet Union, and others.[2] Nixon's Guam Doctrine seemed to indicate that the United States itself expected and accepted this outcome. Australians certainly feared that the United States would play a much less active role in supporting Australian security interests than it had in the years since 1945. By the mid-1970s, however, these concerns had eased. Australians expected the United States to stay engaged in ways that would effectively stabilize Asia's major-power balance, even if Washington would no longer be so willing as before to become engaged in minor regional conflicts. In the light of this confidence, Australians put aside long-standing concerns about major-power conflict in Asia and focused their strategic attention more narrowly on their immediate neighborhood.[3]

Over the following two decades Australian strategic policy emphasized that America's role in keeping the peace between Asia's major powers was the key stabilizing factor in the Asian strategic system, and hence of Australia's own security.[4] It allowed China to abandon the economic legacy of communism and autarchy and begin its remarkable emergence as a market economy, fully integrated into the global system. Australia has been a major beneficiary, as it has become ever more deeply integrated into the Asian region. Most obviously this is true economically. Over 57 percent of Australia's total export trade is with Asia.[5] Asian trade partners occupy five of the top six positions among its leading export destinations, and they are by far the fastest-growing section of Australian exports.[6] Much of this growth in trade reflects Australia's role as a major supplier of raw materials—energy and minerals especially—to Northeast Asia's manufacturing behemoths. It would be fair to say that since the 1950s, Australia's prosperous modern society has been underwritten by its mineral and energy exports to Northeast Asia.

But Australia's engagement with Asia has not been limited to economics. Since the late 1960s Australia opened itself to immigration from Asia, and newcomers from Asia have for many years now constituted the largest source of Australia's large annual migrant intake. As a result, the country's ethnically diverse and multicultural society is taking on an increasingly Asian flavor. Travel, tourism, study, and cultural links have likewise grown; Australia, for example, is host to huge numbers of students from Asian countries. Moreover Australia has slowly built itself a place in Asia's complex regional politics. While neither projecting itself as "Asian," nor being accepted as such by its Asian neighbors, Australia has been influential in helping to build regional forums like Asia-Pacific Economic Cooperation (APEC) and the ASEAN Regional Forum (ARF) and has participated in the East Asian Summit meetings. For many years Australia has been active in prompting regional security, especially in Southeast Asia, building strong bilateral defense links, especially in maritime Southeast Asia, and actively promoting the development of regional multilateral security cooperation. By the early 1990s Australian leaders started to talk of their country seeking security "not *from* Asia, but *in and with* Asia."

Looking Ahead

Where to from here? For Australia, Asia's dynamism and the promise of an Asian century offer massive opportunities for economic growth and increasing integration into the Asian region. But at the same time, the increasing weight—economic, political, technological, and military—of Asia's major powers does raise the prospect that within a few decades the U.S. primacy that has done so much to underwrite Asia's stability and Australia's security and prosperity may wane. The American-led post-Vietnam order in Asia thus risks falling victim to its own success. Thirty years of peace between East Asia's major powers has provided the setting for unprecedented economic growth. But that growth, and the resulting revolution in power relationships that it has initiated, may now threaten to undermine the foundations of the order that made it possible.

GROWING UNEASE AND MIXED SIGNALS

Australian policymakers started to sense that China's economic growth may pose threats to the post-Vietnam regional order in the early 1990s, soon after the end of the Cold War. They identified two trends that might undermine the understandings that have been sustained between Asia's major powers.[7] First, they feared that the United States might pull back from Asia once the strategic imperatives of the Cold War were lifted. This proved to be baseless, and it eased in the mid-1990s after the Clinton administration provided a coherent and convincing rationale for sustained U.S. engagement backed by major military commitments in Asia. The second concern was that China's growing economy might eventually undermine the balance between Asia's major powers. This fear has proven to be more durable. In 1997 an official *Strategic Policy Review* published by the Australian government specifically identified China's growing power as one of the decisive dynamic elements in Australia's security environment and described how as a result Australia's strategic policy horizons would have to broaden.[8]

In the 1970s and 1980s Australia had defined an "Area of Broad Strategic Interest" limited to Southeast Asia and the Southwest Pacific.[9] The idea that Australia's strategic attention could be focused narrowly on Australia's near neighborhood reflected an assumption that major disturbances in Asia beyond this area, involving Asia's major powers, were highly unlikely because of the strength of America's stabilizing presence and the order that imposed on major-power relations in Northeast Asia. But by 1997 this view was abandoned in favor of a renewed recognition that events affecting the major-power balance in the wider Asia-Pacific were becoming more probable and that should they occur they would profoundly affect Australia's security.[10] Moreover, the 1997 *Strategic Policy Review* identified Australia's core strategic interests in the Asian major power balance. First, that Australia would not want to see Asia dominated "by any single power whose interest might be inimical to Australia's" (which was code for, "by any power other than the United States"). Second, that Australia would not want to see debilitating levels of strategic competition between the region's major powers.[11] These ideas were carried forward and refined in the Defence White Paper produced by Canberra in 2000. The 2000 White Paper recognized that Australia's security could be affected by the challenge to the regional order posed by China's rise. It was explicit in reiterating the vital role played by the United States in keeping the peace between Asia's major powers.[12] It also implied that Australia needed to place more emphasis on its ability to support the United States in conflicts with China should they occur.[13] This need significantly influenced key capability choices, including the decision to seek a fifth-generation replacement for Australia's F-18 and F-111 combat aircraft.[14]

At the same time, however, there was a growing recognition of the possibility that Australian interests in the future shape of major-power relations in Asia might diverge from those of the United States. By the late 1990s China had already become Australia's fastest-growing export market, and the government in Canberra was placing very high priority on cultivating a political relationship with Beijing that would underwrite and reinforce the burgeoning economic relationship. Over the second half of the 1990s, Beijing had made it plain that it was not disposed to criticize Australia's alliance with the United States, as long as there was no suggestion that Australia was being drawn into a U.S.-led containment strategy against China, and as long as Australia conformed strictly to the "One China Policy" on Taiwan, which Australia was happy enough to do.

On this basis, Australia-China relations have blossomed. On the other hand, the scope for divergence between U.S. and Australian views of China emerged as early as 1999, when an unofficial but highly influential meeting of Australian and American leaders in Sydney witnessed a lively debate about whether Australia would or should automatically support the United States in any conflict with China over Taiwan.[15] In these and other exchanges it became clear that for most Australians, avoiding conflict with China was a much higher priority, and supporting Taiwan a much lower priority, than for many Americans. Many Australians felt uneasy about U.S. expectations that Australia would automatically support them in a conflict over Taiwan, especially if it was caused by irresponsible actions in Taipei. So as the new century dawned, Australia had some thinking to do. Unease about the implications of China's growing power was balanced by fears that the United States might draw Australia into conflict with China over what Australians tended to see as second-order issues.

Against this background, Australian strategic policy concerning Asia in recent years has shown signs of confusion, and as a result Canberra has delivered mixed signals to allies and regional neighbors alike. The Howard government, which held office from 1996 until late 2007, often sought refuge in a kind of breezy optimism that Australia would not be faced with any hard choices. Then prime minister John Howard said in a major speech in 2004 that he "is not one of those who regards escalating strategic competition between the US and China as inevitable,"[16] and often boasted that he had managed to build close relations with Beijing while remaining a close ally of the United States. But in fact, while remaining among President Bush's staunchest allies in the "war on terror," much of Howard's diplomacy up until early 2007 showed a strong pro-China inclination.[17] This caused some mild consternation in Washington. It also raised eyebrows in Tokyo, where Australia's eagerness to build strong political links with China has been seen as something of a desertion by Canberra of old and loyal friends. Then in 2007 Howard executed something of a U-turn. His government took steps that could only be seen as a swing back to a more pro-U.S., pro-Tokyo line. Now the new Rudd government, elected in November 2007, shows signs of taking Australia back toward the more even-handed approach that characterized Howard until 2007. The resulting zigzags in Australian policy are evident especially in Australia's approach to current debates on institution-building in Asia.

BUILDING INSTITUTIONS

Like other countries in Asia, Australia often approaches questions of the future regional order in Asia via discussion of the regional institutions, especially security institutions, that might reflect or shape that order. This has not been straightforward, because Asia's existing regional security institutions appear weak and insubstantial, at least when compared with those of Europe, which is the only comparable region of powerful states. Nonetheless, no alternative approach to conceiving or building a new order in Asia has gained much momentum, so more or less by default the institutional approach has led the field, both among governments and commentators. Two themes have dominated the search for new regional security architecture in Asia. One has focused on the evolution of the U.S. alliance system in Asia. The other has been the development of new and more effective regional multilateral security forums. These alternatives are not hermetically sealed off from one another: at times the two approaches have converged and at times they have diverged, and there is clearly scope for interaction between them.

Australia has been active in many elements of these institutionally based approaches to a new Asian order since the end of the Cold War. Initially, Australia played a prominent part in the development of regional multilateral forums in the early post–Cold War years. It was among the founders of APEC and early identified the strategic and political significance of the grouping. Australia's view was always that the most important function of APEC was to bind the United States into the Western Pacific, counteracting anxieties about U.S. withdrawal after the Cold War. Likewise Australia was among the leaders of the push to establish the ASEAN Regional Forum as a way to build on the success of ASEAN (Association of Southeast Asian Nations) to create a regional forum in which security issues could be addressed and the shape of a post–Cold War strategic order in Asia negotiated.

These Australian initiatives were very much the product of the highly activist, Asia-oriented foreign policies of the Labor governments led by Bob Hawke and Paul Keating. For various reasons the more conservative Howard government, which took office in 1996, did less to promote regional security multilateralism and contribute to the creation of new forums, but it did work quite hard to win a place for Australia in some of the new forums that others have developed in recent years. Australia has been excluded from the ASEAN + 3 structure that has probably been the most important and dynamic new regional grouping to emerge over the past decade. After a major effort, it won acceptance as a participant in the East Asia Summit (EAS), which first met in Kuala Lumpur in 2005. Australia's desire to join the EAS was a significant step in the evolution of its regional diplomacy. Hitherto Australia had resisted the establishment of any regional body that excluded the United States; with the EAS, Australia was very keen to join one, suggesting that Canberra had come to accept that the trajectory of regional political evolution in the years after the East Asian economic crisis included the development of an East Asian political community that would exclude the United States but that Australia badly wanted to join. No clear policy framework underpinned this shift in interest; rather it was guided by an instinctive sense that when so many of Australia's neighbors and trading partners in regions so strategically important to Australia were meeting together, Australia would not want to be left out.

The same reactive ambivalence has characterized Australia's response to the evolution of the Six-Party Talks over North Korea, and especially the suggestions that this forum might evolve to become a standing regional security institution. Australia has always recognized the possibility that the major states engaged in Northeast Asia, where Asia's center of gravity obviously lies, might form their own security forums to manage issues between them. While appreciating the advantages to Australia of stable major-power relations that such a forum might help promote, Canberra has been uneasy at the thought of being excluded from discussions in which its interests are so clearly engaged. The result has been a clear ambivalence: keen for Northeast Asian security issues to be addressed effectively, but concerned lest it be excluded from an important forum. As the major powers are unlikely to pay much attention to Australia's views on the question one way or the other, there has never been much reason for Canberra's ambivalence on this aspect of regional security architecture to be resolved.

But on one feature of regional security architecture Australia has, until recently, been generally clear. It has resisted suggestions that the U.S. alliance structure in Asia should be modified to meet new strategic circumstances. Periodic American musings about the evolution of the San Francisco system of bilateral treaties into something more multilateral, more NATO-like, have met with responses from Canberra ranging from tepid to distinctly cool. The reason for this is simple enough. Whereas in Europe it may be credible to see alliances like NATO today primarily in post-strategic terms, as institutions for responding to non-state, sub-state, and trans-state threats and crises, in Asia they retain their primal strategic function. America's hub-and-spokes alliance structure in Asia performs, as we have seen, the primary function of stabilizing relations within the region's most problematic strategic dyad—China and Japan. It does that by a systemic ambivalence; America's role as Japan's security guarantor *both* reassures Japan *and* reassures China. That dual reassurance has been the foundation of the stable post-Vietnam order in Asia. Plans to move from the hub-and-spokes model to a regional multilateral model of alliances would threaten that mechanism if it excluded China, and it would be fanciful to presume that it wouldn't. China's inclusion would constitute an acknowledgment by China of the permanence of U.S. primacy in Asia, which seems highly unlikely. Exclusion of China would make it plain that the purpose of any "Asian NATO" would be to resist the emergence of a Chinese challenge to American primacy. That is an objective Australia has not hitherto been willing to endorse.

However, John Howard's shift in policy in 2007 suggested Australia might start feeling more positively toward a multilateralized U.S. alliance architecture in Asia. The trend started further back, in around 2001, with the establishment of a relatively modest official-level Trilateral Strategic Dialogue (TSD) between the United States, Japan, and Australia at senior officials' level. But in 2006 this dialogue was elevated to foreign minister level, with a meeting in Sydney between Condoleezza Rice, Taro Aso, and Alexander Downer.[18] Then in 2007 the dialogue was further elevated when President Bush, Prime Minister Abe, and Prime Minister Howard met in the margins of the APEC Summit in Sydney. There is no evidence that much of substance actually occurred at these meetings, but the fact that they have taken place at steadily rising levels of representation suggests that over the past two years, especially, the political symbolism if not the policy substance of the TSD has come to be valued fairly highly by the three parties.

The impression that Australia has been revising its views on a more multilateral U.S. alliance structure in Asia was then reinforced by developments in Australia's bilateral strategic relationship with Japan. Australia has for many years been cultivating low-key strategic interactions with Japan and has strongly encouraged Japan to take a more active strategic role in Asia and beyond. Australia, for example, was enthusiastic about deploying forces to support Japanese troops undertaking reconstruction work in Iraq in 2004 and 2005. However the development of this relationship took a sharper focus in early 2007 when Australia and Japan signed a bilateral Joint Declaration on Security Cooperation. In substance the Joint Declaration amounts to very little, reflecting the limits imposed on practical defense cooperation between Tokyo and Canberra imposed by distance, divergent strategic priorities, and Japanese legal and political constraints. But the way in which the agreement was presented sent a clear message that rather more was intended—at least by Australia—than the substance of the agreement itself conveyed. Australian prime minister John Howard traveled to Tokyo specifically to sign the agreement. In his press comments at the time, while acknowledging that the Joint Declaration fell well short of a full-scale security treaty, he indicated that Australia might well have been happy to sign a full-scale treaty with Japan and would be willing to consider it again in the future. And he abruptly rejected a suggestion that Australia might reach a similar agreement with China, saying that that would not be possible because China was not a democracy.[19] While doggedly denying that any of Australia's policies were directed against China, it was clear that Howard was intent on presenting an impression that Australia was building a new and qualitatively different strategic relationship with Japan, closely aligned with its U.S. alliance, and directed at supporting strategic interests shared by the democracies in Asia and not by others.

This impression was further reinforced by Australian involvement in nascent quadrilateral security interactions with the United States, Japan, and India. Whether there is any substance or momentum to the quadrilateral security construct is not yet clear, but at the least one can say that Howard's willingness for Australia to participate in the first steps through involvement in officials-level discussions was consistent with the pattern of interest outlined here in the evolution of an Asia-Pacific Alliance of democracies whose only coherent rationale could be to limit any Chinese challenge to U.S. primacy in Asia.

Howard and his conservative government having lost office, it is now hard to say whether these steps in 2007 presaged a sudden and fundamental reversal of his basic policy approach to Asia's future order. It certainly seemed that way. For a decade the Howard government had been a strong advocate of an open and inclusive approach to China. Howard's mantra had been "to focus on things that unite us not those that divide us," and he was careful to distance himself from U.S. or other policies or approaches that might be interpreted in Beijing as directed at China. He had even at times presented Australia as a kind of go-between in the U.S.-China relationship—a neutral, honest broker.[20] Then in 2007 he took a series of steps that have moved Australia quite clearly away from China and toward what might be seen as a converging U.S.-Japan consensus on the need to build a clear political and strategic alignment to meet the challenge of China's growing power. Why did this happen?

The simplest explanation would be that Howard had become more uneasy about China's growing power and the way it might be used. However, there is no clear evidence to support this view. No sharp issues of dispute have arisen between Beijing and Canberra, the trade relationship had continued to grow strongly, and China had displayed its characteristically deft diplomacy in managing the relationship so as to minimize any Australian anxieties. A more credible explanation is that the United States and Japan applied pressure to Howard to swing back a little from what they may well have seen as Canberra's excessively accommodating approach to China. On this hypothesis the evidence is mixed. Neither Tokyo nor Washington has overtly criticized Australia for being too pro-China. It is reasonable to suppose that elements of both governments have been surprised and a little disconcerted to see such a close ally and friend as Australia accommodating itself so willingly to China's aspirations for regional leadership. But the issue has hardly been at the top of the Bush administration's agenda with Australia, which has been dominated by Iraq and terrorism, and there is no evidence that Japan found ways to apply pressure on such issues to Australian governments, nor that it has tried.

So while Canberra's policy swing toward support for a multilateral alliance of democracies might have owed something to subtle, low-key diplomatic pressure from the United States and Japan, this too seems an inadequate explanation for such a sharp and significant policy shift. The missing reasons may be found in domestic politics, because the start of Howard's policy reversal coincided closely with the elevation of Kevin Rudd to the leadership of the Labor Party, still then in opposition. Rudd is a fluent Chinese speaker and served several postings in China as an Australian diplomat before entering politics. From the outset he posed a serious political challenge to John Howard, among other reasons because Howard's credentials on national security had been tarnished by Iraq and Howard's close association with the policies and personality of President Bush. It is a plausible hypothesis that Howard may have hoped to discredit Rudd by portraying him as too close to China, and in order to do that sought to relocate his own position somewhat closer to the United States. If this was Howard's plan, little came of it, because in the event there was no systematic attempt to exploit the issue politically over the course of a long and bruising election campaign. That may be because Beijing was quick to detect the trend of Howard's thinking and privately warned him not to play the "China card" against Rudd. Such a warning would carry weight: Howard's main electoral asset was the strength of Australia's economy, for which trade with China is usually given most of the credit. Beijing might have found it easy to undermine this plank of Howard's platform.

The issue remains significant, notwithstanding Howard's electoral defeat, because it provides an important example of how questions of Asia's changing regional order are affecting Australia in complex ways. But in the short term at least the election of the Rudd government is likely to quell Australia's recent enthusiasm for steps toward a regional alliance of democracies and see instead a return to the more ambivalent and cautious approach that has characterized Australian policies until Howard's U-turn in 2007. Rudd has repeatedly affirmed his support for an inclusive regional architecture in Asia that accepts and accommodates China's growing power.[21] He has expressed reservations about the bilateral Japan-Australia Joint Declaration on Security Cooperation, and his foreign minister, Stephen Smith, has indicated that Australia will not take part in further meetings of the quadripartite U.S.-Japan-India-Australia grouping. Under Rudd it seems likely then that Australia will revert to its long-standing aversion to the construction of an Asian multilateral alliance of democracies.

BACK TO BASICS

The best way to get below the complex eddies of contemporary policies and politics to gain a deeper understanding of how Australia will view the future international order in Asia is to explore the basic Australian interests engaged in the big questions that will do most to shape that order.

Australians would do well to start close to home. The simple facts of geography ensure that a primary place in Australia's strategic thinking will always be occupied by Indonesia. Australia's other close neighbors are all small, weak states incapable of posing a strategic challenge to Australia's security. Indonesia, however, is different. The fourth-largest country in the world by population, its 240 million people dwarf Australia's 20 million. No two neighboring countries in the world have so little in common: in history, culture, religion, economics, and geography, the two nations are profoundly different. Under Suharto's tough but effective New Order, relations were generally positive, and it would have seemed reasonable to expect that Indonesia's so far remarkably successful transition to democracy in the decade since Suharto fell would have drawn the two countries closer. Alas the opposite is the case; despite effective cooperation on specific bilateral and regional questions, both countries have found it hard to move the relationship forward. Tellingly, this has had little to do with tensions flowing from the "war on terror"; Indonesia as the world's largest Muslim state and Australia as one of America's closest allies have in fact generally cooperated well in counterterrorism efforts. Since the bombings in Bali 2003 that killed eighty-eight Australians, Indonesia with Australian help has mounted a relatively successful counterterrorism campaign.

The more potent source of tension has been suspicions arising after the events in East Timor in 1999, which stoked long-standing Australian perceptions of Indonesian brutality and created new Indonesian suspicions that Australia seeks to weaken Indonesia's grip on the eastern end of its sprawling archipelagic territory. These suspicions readily flare up over issues like the status of Indonesia's restive Papua province.[22]

The risk of these suspicions fueling serious conflict are somewhat constrained by the asymmetry between the two sides' military forces: Indonesia's huge army and Australia's clear predominance in air and naval forces means that in many scenarios neither side has viable military options against the other. But should Indonesia eventually achieve the reforms needed to sustain high economic growth, then it could relatively quickly start to afford air and naval forces that would challenge Australia's, and hence alter the long-term strategic calculus. This is a possibility that Australian defense planning can never afford to ignore. Moreover Indonesia remains the only country that could credibly threaten Australia with serious armed attack without there having first been major disruptions to the Asian international order.

Other threats to Australia, arising from more powerful adversaries farther away, could only arise from collapse in the stable Asian order that has been described earlier in the chapter. From Canberra, the risk and consequences of such a disruption would be determined primarily by the power relativities and political relationships between the region's major powers—the United States, China, India, and Japan. Of these, India is the least problematic of the big players from an Australian perspective. In the last decade India has clearly emerged as a major element in the Asian strategic system, and in the long term India may well turn out to be the biggest power of all, but for the next few decades at least its economic power will probably remain well behind China's and Japan's, and for that and other reasons its rise is so far not in itself disruptive to the Asian order. Indeed it would be fair to say that, so far, India's main strategic impact on the Asian regional system has been via American attempts to enlist India as a balance to China's growing power. Australia has been predictably ambivalent about this—keen to develop its own bilateral relationship with India, primarily as a trading partner, but reluctant to support a U.S. agenda to build India into a regional strategic alignment. For this reason among others, the Rudd government has decided not to follow the United States by agreeing to sell nuclear material to India.

Japan poses much trickier problems for Australia. Japan has been Australia's major trading partner for decades until recently, and Tokyo and Canberra have developed a close political relationship as well. Overall the relationship with Japan has been Australia's most successful and most significant in Asia and remains very important. But the sense of closely shared strategic interests that has underpinned this relationship has been dented by diverging perceptions of China's rise, which Japanese see as much more threatening than do Australians. In recent years, as China-Australia relations have developed strongly, a sense of competition has emerged between Tokyo and Beijing for Canberra's attention. Tokyo, for example, finally agreed to negotiate a free trade agreement (FTA) with Australia against strong domestic opposition only after China had done so, and China was quick to follow the Japan-Australia Joint Declaration on Security Cooperation with an offer of its own for high-level strategic consultations. Australia's aim in managing the relationship with Tokyo is of course to avoid having to make choices between Japan and China, but there is an increasing sense that that is exactly what Japan wants Australia to do. If so, the relationship will probably lose some luster in coming years.

That brings us to China itself. There are four points that might usefully be made here about Australian views of China's rise.

First, Australians should not assume that China's economy will continue to grow over the next few decades as strongly as it has since 1979. Any number of constraints—political, environmental, or institutional as well as economic—might slow, arrest, or even reverse China's rise. But few in Australia would be willing to bet that China will not keep growing. For three decades China has consistently shown the ability and determination to adapt and innovate to keep the economy growing notwithstanding serious constraints. In particular, any assumption that China cannot sustain strong growth without radical political reform and liberalization seems unwise. George W. Bush may believe that there is only one universally accepted model for a successful society in the twenty-first century, but most Australians would be willing to concede that the Chinese might be in the process of proving him wrong.

Second, it is clear to Australians that China's growing power is not limited to its economy alone. Its diplomatic influence has increased sharply, its military capabilities, especially at sea and in the air, are likewise growing, and massive investments in education are laying the deeper foundations of China's future strength. Third, there can be no doubt that China aims for a greater share of regional power. Even if it does liberalize politically, it seems inevitable that China will seek to escape the subordinate position it has accepted vis-à-vis the United States as its economic power approaches that of America. How soon that might happen is suggested by recent Goldman Sachs estimates that China's GDP (in market exchange rate terms) may overtake America's as soon as 2027.[23] To think that China would continue to accept U.S. primacy as the economic relativities narrow would presuppose that China can be persuaded to accept the inherent superiority of America's political system or the deeper moral foundations of its power. That seems highly improbable. Alternatively it would require one to believe that China can be contained by U.S. military power, even as the deeper economic foundations of U.S. military supremacy erode. Or it would presuppose that the United States can assemble and lead a cohesive coalition of allies that will accept U.S. leadership and will be able to impose on China collectively what the United States alone could not. That in turn would presuppose that a Chinese challenge to continued U.S. primacy would in itself be regarded by current and potential U.S. allies as an unacceptable violation of the international order, rather than a natural evolution of it in the face of changing power relativities.

Which brings us to the fourth point: that China's ambitions for a more equal role in regional affairs would not be regarded per se as unacceptable. Australians, like others in the Western Pacific, do have concerns about how China might eventually use its growing power. They are aware of the risk that China might be tempted to use military or other forms of pressure to compel compliance to China's agendas in the future. But they do not necessarily think that is likely, nor do they think that any extension of Chinese influence is necessarily illegitimate. Indeed they seem to think it would be quite reasonable for China, as its power grows, to seek a more equal position in Asia's strategic and political order than it has enjoyed for the past thirty years. Most Australians think rather well of China and seem willing to trust it to behave responsibly on the regional stage.[24] If China limits its search for greater influence to peaceful, non-coercive means, then Australians seem unlikely to object.

The key question for Australians, then, is how America responds to China's growing power and its bid for increased regional influence. Several things are clear. First, Australia's interests and inclinations strongly predispose it to support sustained U.S. primacy in Asia. The case for deep engagement is as strong today as when it was made by Joseph Nye in 1995.[25] Certainly Australians need no convincing of that. Probably no country in the world is more comfortable with U.S. power than Australia. While the policies and style of the Bush administration have been as unpopular in Australia as elsewhere, the public is easily capable of distinguishing the United States itself, and Australia's alliance with the United States, from the policies and personalities of a particular administration in Washington.

Australians remain strongly committed to the U.S. alliance and would be comfortable with the United States continuing to play the kind of stabilizing leadership role that it has sustained in recent decades.

On the other hand it appears from the policies and attitudes that have emerged over the past few years that Australia does not regard it as essential that the United States retain clear strategic primacy in Asia. It would be enough for the United States to remain engaged as a key player in Asia's new power balance, helping with others to ensure that China and Asia's other major powers do not abuse their position by attempting to dominate the Asian system through coercion. In short, Australians would be happy to see the United States remain as a—rather than the—key strategic power in Asia, in the role of offshore balancer.

Like everyone else in Asia (perhaps except Japan), Australians do not want to have to choose between the United States and China. To avoid making such a choice they are more than happy to see America retreat somewhat from its current leadership position in Asia to a more modest role, as long as the United States continues to provide a reassuring insurance policy against a Chinese bid for coercive hegemony. In particular, Australians would not be willing to surrender their hopes for a good relationship with China in order to help preserve U.S. primacy in Asia. If the price of sustaining U.S. primacy is descent into an Asian cold war in which the United States and China are locked in a systematically adversarial relationship, then for most Australians, that price is too high. Their concern is that the United States may underestimate the costs and risks of the kind of strategic competition with China that might be entailed by the determined defense of U.S. primacy. From an Australian perspective, muscular confrontation of China's growing power would be likely to destroy the international order it is trying to save.

Whether, and if so how, these attitudes can be reflected in enduring policy depends on whether the United States is willing to remain engaged in Asia on any basis less than primacy. America's foreign policy traditions provide few if any precedents, and most recent debate on U.S. policy toward China is not reassuring. America's current policy is most commonly described as "hedging" and explained as seeking to encourage China to behave well, while remaining poised to impose constraints on China if it behaves badly.[26] Of course, everything depends on what counts as behaving badly. What exactly is America aiming to hedge *against* in its policy toward China? The risk, from an Australian perspective, is that America is in fact hedging against the possibility that China does not accept U.S. primacy on U.S. terms as China's power grows. If that is the case, then the scope for Australia and the United States to drift apart in their approaches to China is quite high. Australia would far prefer to see a U.S. approach to China that hedged against the risk that China starts to use coercive means to enforce its primacy in Asia, but not against the possibility that China tries peacefully to build a greater sphere of influence in Asia and to share with America the shaping of the regional order.

In short, Australians would prefer to see the United States accept China as an equal in Asia as China's power grows. That view envisages that the United States and China evolve a concert of power in Asia in which they, and others, cooperatively shape regional affairs in the common interest. That, in turn, would require the United States to accept China as an equal. That is a big step: it implies accepting the legitimacy of China's political system, of its international interests and objectives where these may differ from, even clash with, America's, and of China's growing military power. All this seems a long way from U.S. policy today.

Something of this distance can be judged by the weight placed in U.S. discussions of China in the phrase "responsible stakeholder," proposed by Robert Zoellick a few years ago, to describe what America sees as China's legitimate future international role.[27] Of course it is fine as far as it goes, but what is striking is how little it offers to China. After all, would America not expect every country to be a "responsible stakeholder"? Australia? New Zealand? Tonga? What then does the phrase tell us about how America plans to take account of the fact that China is already no ordinary power and is likely to become within a few years the second-biggest economy in the world and, on many dimensions of national power, the second strongest? It suggests that the United States has not really come to terms with the challenge that China poses to the international order and to American primacy. It suggests that the United States is relying too heavily on its previous experience of dealing with Number Two powers. The Soviet Union it contained and eventually crushed; Japan it made a subordinate ally. To Australian eyes, neither model is likely to work with China.

Australia and the United States have enjoyed a close alliance for over fifty years, and in many ways their strategic partnership stretches back another half century before that. The alliance has worked and lasted because the two countries have consistently converged in their views of key developments in Asia over that time. Now things are changing. Different views of China threaten to create the widest breach in strategic perceptions between Canberra and Washington in a century.

NOTES

1. Australian Department of Foreign Affairs and Trade, *Monthly Summary of Trade Statistics*, www.dfat.gov.au/publications/stats-pubs/mtd/australia_trade_1207.pdf (accessed February 12, 2008).

2. See, for example, Coral Bell, *The Asian Balance of Power: A Comparison with European Precedents*, Adelphi Paper 44 (London: Institute for Strategic Studies, 1968); and Alistair Buchan, *War in Modern Society* (London: Collins, 1966).

3. Commonwealth of Australia, *Australian Defense* (Canberra: Australian Government Publishing Service, 1976), 6.

4. Commonwealth of Australia, *Defending Australia: Defense White Paper, 1994* (Canberra: Australian Government Publishing Service, 1994), 95.

5. Australian Department of Foreign Affairs and Trade, *Monthly Summary of Trade Statistics*.

6. Australian Department of Foreign Affairs and Trade, *Monthly Summary of Trade Statistics*.

7. Commonwealth of Australia, *Defending Australia*, 7–9.

8. Commonwealth of Australia, *Australia's Strategic Policy* (Canberra: Department of Defense, 1997), 9, 10, 14.

9. Commonwealth of Australia, *The Defense of Australia* (Canberra: Australian Government Publishing Service, 1987), 8.

10. Commonwealth of Australia, *Australia's Strategic Policy*, 14.

11. Commonwealth of Australia, *Australia's Strategic Policy*, 8.

12. Commonwealth of Australia, *Defense 2000: Our Future Defense Force* (Canberra: Department of Defense, 2000), 34–35.

13. Commonwealth of Australia, *Defense 2000*, 51–52.

14. Commonwealth of Australia, *Defense 2000*, 85.

15. This exchange occurred at a meeting of the Australian American Leadership Dialogue in Sydney in August 1999.

16. Hon. John Howard, "Australia in the World" (address to the Lowy Institute for International Policy, Sydney, March 31, 2005), www.pm.gov.au/news/speeches/speech1290.html.

17. Hugh White, "Australian Strategic Policy," in *Strategic Asia, 2005–06: Military Modernization in an Era of Uncertainty*, ed. Ashley Tellis and Michael Wills (Seattle: NBR, 2005), 305–331; Hugh White, "The Limits to Optimism: Australia and the Rise of China," *Australian Journal of International Affairs* 59, no. 4 (December 2005): 469–480.

18. Hugh White, "Trilateralism and Australia: Australia and the Trilateral Security Dialogue with America and Japan," in *Asia Pacific Security: US, Australia and Japan and the New Security Triangle*, ed. William Tow (New York: Routledge, 2007), 101–111.

19. Hugh White, "Welcome to Arms," *Diplomat* (April/May 2007): 72–75.

20. Howard, "Australia in the World."

21. Kevin Rudd, "The Rise of China and Strategic Implications for US-Australia Relations" (speech to the Brookings Institution, Washington, D.C., April 20, 2007).

22. Hugh White, "The New Australia-Indonesia Strategic Relationship—A Note of Caution," in *Different Societies, Shared Futures: Australia, Indonesia and the Region*, ed. John Monfries (Singapore: Institute of South East Asian Studies, 2006), 41–53.

23. Goldman Sachs, *Global Economics Weekly*, Issue 07/28, July 25, 2007.

24. Allan Gyngell, *Australia and the World: Public Opinion and Foreign Policy* (Sydney: Lowy Institute for International Policy, 2007), www.lowyinstitute.org/Publication.asp?pid=660.

25. Joseph S. Nye, "East Asian Security: The Case for Deep Engagement," *Foreign Affairs* (July/August 1995).

26. See, for example, Evan S. Medeiros, "Strategic Hedging and the Future of Asia-Pacific Security," *Washington Quarterly* 29, no. 1 (Winter 2005/2006): 145–167.

27. Deputy Secretary of State Robert B. Zoellick, "Remarks to National Committee on U.S.-China Relations" (New York, September 21, 2005).

11

Central Asia

Carving an Independent Identity among Peripheral Powers

Martha Brill Olcott

Since the disintegration of the Soviet Union, extraordinary changes have occurred in Central Asia, including the maturing of these newly independent countries into increasingly competent and confident regional actors. While extra-regional powers can and do influence developments in this region, they can no longer do so without directly engaging the governments of the region. Thus, in a literal sense, the "Great Game in Central Asia" has come to an end. Yet this has not slowed the competition for international influence in the region, with Russia, China, and the United States all trying to persuade these states to transform themselves in somewhat different ways. Following a spike after 9/11, U.S. influence has waned in Central Asia. Russia's is holding steady, while China's influence is increasing.

Less influential than the "Big Three," Iran and Turkey have also made strong efforts to influence developments in this region, especially in the early years when Turkey acted partially as a surrogate for the United States. India was courted by the Central Asians but has been relatively restrained in its engagement with these states, as have most of the principal Arab states, while Pakistan had strong interest and commercial ambitions, but not the wherewithal to pursue them.

The Central Asian states rushed to join most international organizations that would have them, including the CIS (Commonwealth of Independent States), which they joined at the Almaty (Kazakhstan) summit of December 1991. The UN admitted all of them in 1992 and each gained membership in the Organization for Security and Co-operation in Europe (OSCE) as a successor state to the USSR. They also joined ECO

(Economic Cooperation Organization),[1] OIC (Organisation of the Islamic Conference),[2] and all but Tajikistan participated in a loose grouping of Turkic states, organized by Turkey's late president Turgut Özal.[3] All but Turkmenistan joined the Collective Security Treaty Organization (CSTO),[4] organized at Russia's initiative. Likewise all but Turkmenistan are members of the Shanghai Cooperation Organisation (SCO).[5] The CSTO and SCO share many of the same goals, but the CSTO promotes real integration of the militaries of the member states while the SCO styles itself as an organization that understands modern security risks: secession, extremism, and terrorism.

All this outside interest has not really made Central Asia a safer neighborhood. The bilateral and multilateral security relationships the Central Asian states have developed do not seem sufficient protection from the risks that the region still confronts, which include social and economic pressures created by incomplete market reforms and the shocks of political transition from Soviet-era leaderships.

The continued instability in Afghanistan inflates the risk of terrorism, to which all states are vulnerable. None of the Central Asian states have problems analogous to the one Russia confronts in Chechnya or China faces in the Xinjiang Uighur Autonomous Region. All of these states believe themselves to be threatened by "extremist" groups, but often these governments employ the label "extremist" to outlaw groups that oppose the current regime but are not preaching nor seeking its armed overthrow. This battle against "extremism" diverts governments from political and economic reforms that might limit the appeal of such groups.

There is no effective regional framework for regulating shared transport links and two shared water basins (created by the Syr Dar'ya and Amu Dar'ya rivers). Competition over water is potentially a grave security concern; at various points in time the Uzbeks have threatened both the Kyrgyz and the Turkmen with military action over alleged cutoffs of supplies. Trade barriers serve to depress all of the economies to varying extents, and neither the SCO nor EurAsEC (Eurasian Economic Community)[6] has proved effective in reducing them, a goal that the Asian Development Bank has also taken upon itself in the form of the Central Asia Regional Economic Cooperation Program (CAREC).[7]

Many of these problems are "managed" on the basis of bilateral agreements, but rarely to everyone's satisfaction.[8] Border delineation is not wholly complete, and border management remains a problem. Parts of the Uzbek-Tajik border remain mined, with mine removal by the Uzbeks substantially behind schedule,[9] and there are still ethnically consolidated communities living in stranded "enclaves" that are fully located within the territory of a neighboring state.[10]

THE CENTRAL ASIAN STATES SEEK TO DEFINE
A PLACE FOR THEMSELVES

None of these problems can be solved without the direct engagement of the Central Asians. Any international actor, be it a foreign power or a multilateral organization, cannot simply take the acquiescence of any of the Central Asian states for granted. The region has become more integrated into the global economy. As tables 11.1 and 11.2 show, the volume of trade going into and out of Central Asia has increased, and the region's leaders have sought to carve out distinct international roles.

Kazakhstan has been most assertive in this regard, and founding president Nursultan Nazarbayev's claim that Kazakhstan can serve as a bridge between Europe and Asia is a defining principle of its foreign policy.[11] In less than twenty years it has developed a foreign service that now spans the globe and has included the current general secretary of the SCO, H.E. Bulat Nurgaliev;[12] the current head of EurAsEC, H.E. Tair Mansurov;[13] and long-time Kazakh foreign minister Kassymzhomart Tokaev,[14] who chairs his country's Senate.

The Kazakhs will chair the OSCE in 2010,[15] and made an unusually public diplomatic effort to get this,[16] and continued to persevere even after the United States and UK formally opposed their bid, because of their concerns that Kazakhstan's non-democratic political system made them an inappropriate choice.[17] The final deal was something of a compromise; the Kazakhs were awarded the chairmanship with a year's delay, but also with no strings attached (except that they would not change the fundamental nature of the organization).

The Emergence of Kazakhstan

Kazakhstan has also emerged as the clear leader within Central Asia. The Kazakh leader has also played the role of mentor, especially for the politically inexperienced President Gurbanguly Berdymuhammedov. Nazarbayev even participated in some of Berdymuhammedov's first negotiations with Russian president Vladimir Putin.[18]

With the strongest economy of the five Central Asian states, Kazakhstan is also playing a stronger economic role in the region, with over 20 percent of Kazakhstan's exports going to its four Central Asian neighbors.[19] The Kazakh capital is serving as an important stimulus for growth in neighboring Kyrgyzstan in particular, especially in the latter country's banking sector.[20] Kazakh investment has had more difficulty gaining a hold in Uzbekistan, given the historic rivalry between the two peoples.

The Role of Uzbekistan

Uzbekistan is the only country in the region to border every other Central Asian state, as well as Afghanistan. The Uzbeks viewed their country as the center of Central Asia but recognize that this role has been involuntarily ceded to Kazakhstan. President Nazarbayev has begun to develop some of the graciousness of a winner and has been more solicitous of the feelings of his somewhat older colleague, Islam Karimov, to the south. State visits between the Uzbek and Kazakh leaders have been exchanged in recent years, with the Kazakh leader traveling first to Uzbekistan.[21]

Tensions between Uzbekistan and Turkmenistan have also substantially dissipated since Berdymuhammedov took office. While the underlying disputes over water between the two states have not been solved, nor continued improved treatment of Turkmenistan's Uzbek minorities ensured,[22] the leaders of the two countries have had formal meetings that seem to have been quite cordial.[23] In fact, with the exception of some small and localized disturbances, there has not been any interethnic violence in Central Asia since independence.[24]

The easing of border crossings within the region is reducing the risk of interethnic conflict even further. With every passing year, the prospect of major interethnic violence grows smaller, as the states in the region demonstrate their capacity for preventing unrest in a neighboring country from sparking riots across the border. The best example of this was the ability of the Kyrgyz government to manage conflicting expectations in the handling of refugees[25] from the civil unrest in Andijon in May 2005.[26]

The international outcry over the number of civilian casualties in Andijon changed Uzbekistan's foreign policy and has had a strong impact on regional policies more generally. It led to formal sanctions on Uzbekistan by the European Union,[27] and the loss of the U.S. airbase at Karshi-Khanabad. Uzbekistan dropped out of the relatively anti-Russian GUUAM,[28] rejoined the CSTO, and signed bilateral military cooperation agreements with Russia.[29] Uzbekistan also became an ardent defender of an increased security role for the SCO.[30]

Turkmenistan in the Shadows

Turkmenistan's foreign policy has been shaped by President Saparmurad Niyazov's advocacy of "positive neutrality," a doctrine that was never clearly elaborated.[31] The Turkmen joined some international organizations, but not others (like the SCO), and did not participate formally in any military alliances. Under President Berdymukhammedov, Turkmenistan has been engaging with the international community, as "positive neutrality" is being abandoned in deed if not yet in formal fact.

THE RISE AND FALL OF U.S. INFLUENCE IN CENTRAL ASIA

One of the most striking things about Central Asia in recent years is the relative decline of U.S. influence in the region, which reached its apex in the immediate aftermath of 9/11 when basing rights were granted by Uzbekistan (Karshi-Khanabad) and Kyrgyzstan (Manas) and U.S. foreign assistance increased. High-level U.S. government attention drifted away from this problem in 2003 after the invasion of Iraq. There was some refocusing on Afghanistan a few years later, and the State Department moved all the Central Asian countries from the European bureau to the newly renamed Bureau of South and Central Asian Affairs to try and facilitate Afghan recovery as well as diminish Russia's influence in the region.

This administrative shift has led to the development of new programming for the region, some sponsored by USAID (United States Agency for International Development), and a new U.S. regional trade initiative—the Trade and Investment Framework Agreement (TIFA).[32] Many of these projects are very long term in focus, are plagued by funding problems, and even when all the pieces are in place, international aid workers are often unable to do their jobs because of persistent security risks.

This has meant that the Central Asian countries, with the exception of Tajikistan,[33] have seen relatively little benefit from the new U.S. approach, once airbase rents and supplies are excluded. Some, like Kazakhstan, have even been asked to chip in and provide development assistance to Afghanistan,[34] while states like Kyrgyzstan and Tajikistan are under pressure by Washington to support U.S. hydroelectric projects that will provide electricity to Afghanistan, rather than Russian investment projects that serve the northern market.[35] There has been an unplanned flip side to Washington's Afghan-centered policies in Central Asia, which is increasing pressure by the SCO and SCO member states for them to play a growing role, in coordination with NATO, in Afghanistan.[36]

The Central Asian states have become more suspicious of Washington's intentions since the United States began advocating President George W. Bush's "freedom agenda."[37] While the "freedom agenda" was intended to justify the ongoing human and financial costs of the war in Iraq, it coincided conveniently with the end of the political life span of two communist-era political figures. Georgia's President Eduard Shevardnadze fell from power in the "rose revolution," and then Leonid Kuchma's plans to orchestrate his own succession went awry in Ukraine's "orange revolution." Washington's heralding of these events, in which U.S. public or privately funded

NGOs played much-debated roles, left Central Asia's leaders feeling they, too, might be targeted for "regime change,"[38] especially after the ouster of Kyrgyzstan's Askar Akayev in March 2005, in the so-called tulip revolution.[39]

There is no evidence that the United States supported Akayev's ouster, which put the U.S. military presence in the region at risk, as Washington's relationship with Tashkent was deteriorating. Restrictions on U.S. foreign assistance had been introduced, and the United States was having difficulty negotiating an extension of its lease on Karshi-Khanabad.[40] Many U.S. policymakers also believed Askar Akayev's oft–publicly stated promise that he was planning to observe his constitutionally mandated requirement to leave office in late 2005, setting what Washington saw as a critical precedent for all the Central Asian states.[41]

Less than two months after Akayev's ouster there was a prison break and massive public demonstrations in Andijon, just over the border from southern Kyrgyzstan. While the Uzbek government had tolerated small demonstrations to protest the trial of a group of local businessmen tied to a fringe religious group,[42] the presence of weapons and the loss of control by local authorities triggered an altogether different and much more violent response by Uzbek authorities. The events in Andijon continue to have an impact on U.S. policy toward the region. In December 2007, the U.S. Congress debated introducing sanctions against the government in Tashkent, because of Karimov's continued refusal to offer a formal apology for what occurred. By contrast, an "international investigation" organized by Tashkent, which included mostly CIS states, found no fault with Tashkent's actions.[43]

The strikingly different reactions by the Western countries and the SCO states really highlight the value differences between the two blocs. The West was shocked by the lack of repentance by Tashkent, while the leaders of the SCO states believed that the use of force was justified.

Continued pressure from Congress suggests that the "freedom agenda" will not be abandoned. But it will also remain of secondary importance to questions of energy security, which have been a constant priority since the mid-1990s. U.S. policy emphasizes the need for multiple pipelines, but the key is that these routes bypass Russia, and also Iran.[44] Since Russia's brief cutoff of Ukrainian gas in January 2006, which led to shortages all along the line into Western Europe, the EU has been a vigorous proponent of energy diversification as well.

The shift in the EU energy agenda is also reinforced by deteriorating relations between Russia and the new EU members from the Baltic and Central European region. In this part of Europe, LNG (liquefied natural gas) is not economical. Given Iran's continued international isolation, this means that Europe needs to find a way to receive Caspian gas, under the Caspian to Baku and then on to Turkey through the BTE (Baku-Tbilisi-Erzurum) pipeline, and then onward to the proposed Nabucco pipeline,[45] which has received financing guarantees from the European Bank for Reconstruction and Development (EBRD).[46] The United States first supported an undersea Caspian gas pipeline project in the 1990s, returning to more active advocacy of it after the death of Turkmenistan president Niyazov.

With his pricing agreement with Gazprom up for renewal, President Berdymukhammedov initially seemed quite receptive to the idea of the trans-Caspian undersea pipeline, but the agreement between Turkmenistan and China for the construction of a new pipeline heading northeast across Central Asia into China, combined with the signing of a new price agreement with Russia in late 2007, effectively consigned this project once again to the back burner. The EU has already put the Nabucco project on a slower development track. While all of these states are happy to be courted by the United States, they remember quite clearly how Washington has proved a fickle friend and have no difficulty playing Russia and China, and European-dominated institutions, against the SCO.

THE FALL AND PARTIAL RISE OF RUSSIA

When the USSR broke up, Kremlin politicians assumed that Russia would be the dominant power in Central Asia, able to use the natural resources of these states to serve Russia's own economic development and to back Russian-sponsored international initiatives. In much the same spirit of the United States' nineteenth-century Monroe Doctrine, Russia's Foreign Minister Andrei Kozyrev issued the "Kozyrev Doctrine" in 1994, claiming Central Asia to be part of a Russian sphere of influence.[47] But in the early 1990s, Russia was mired in its own problems, and Boris Yeltsin's presidency was further crippled by his own ill health and divisions within the ruling elite. These reformers decided to basically evict the Central Asian and South Caucasian states from the ruble zone in late 1993, as a way to help Russia deal with runaway inflation and its debt crisis. By so doing, they lessened Russia's economic hold over these countries.[48] This decision, more than any other, helped the Central Asian states make the transition from de jure to de facto independence.

Russia applied the same policies across the region—pressing all states equally hard, for example, to grant ethnic Russians rights of dual citizenship, that local citizenship could be combined with Russian citizenship—but there were no ready mechanisms to achieve uniform influence. None of the post-Soviet states were willing to transfer sovereignty to the Commonwealth of Independent States (CIS), which left the Russians largely dependent upon bilateral arrangements to achieve their economic and geopolitical claims.

Most Central Asian leaders have complicated attitudes toward the Kremlin and its policymakers. Russia is still appealed to when leaders get in trouble. All the aspirants in Kyrgyzstan's "tulip revolution" sought Moscow's support in the run-up to the February and March parliamentary elections, and Kurmanbek Bakiyev sought the Kremlin's blessing when assuming temporary power as president, offering concessions greater than those made by Akayev, leaving Moscow with closer military ties to Bishkek than those enjoyed by NATO.[49] Similarly, Islam Karimov went to Moscow in the immediate aftermath of Andijon, reportedly offering the Russians full basing rights in the country, an offer that Moscow turned down.[50]

Russia played its largest role in Tajikistan. The presence of limited numbers of Russian troops and Russian border guards helped facilitate the transition from civil war to civil order.[51] Russia's influence began to decline after the signing of a national reconciliation agreement in 1997. From that time on, international financial institutions (IFIs) began working with the Tajik government to develop economic stabilization projects. These efforts intensified in 2002, with the opening of Afghanistan, and the departure of Russian border guards.[52] Once Russia lost the right to guard the old Soviet-era Central Asian borders, they began to place far more priority on securing their own national borders, including over three thousand miles of border with Kazakhstan.[53]

Russia has had limited success in maintaining control of Central Asia's natural resource base. The Russia-Turkmen relationship went sour in the early 1990s, and between 1997 and 1999 Turkmenistan stopped shipping gas to Russia entirely.[54] Although Russia met its export commitments to countries beyond the borders of the CIS, those in Russia and other former Soviet states experienced shortages (in some cases justified by Moscow because of unpaid bills).

Russia would have a great deal more difficulty meeting current foreign sales commitments without Turkmen gas, which is why the Kremlin has expended so much influence to trying to secure a long-term commitment from Turkmenistan that it will sell 60 bcm (billion cubic meters) of gas to Russia annually. The two countries reached agreement on a twenty-five-year purchase agreement in 2003, which shifted the gas trade to a cash basis, from the earlier part-cash part-barter arrangement.[55] But it took until November 2007 for the Turkmen and Russians to reach what appears to be a long-term pricing formula, which is based on the averaging of the sales price for gas in the three markets in which the gas is sold (Russia, the CIS, and Europe). Moreover, on December 20, 2007, Russia, Kazakhstan, and Turkmenistan signed a trilateral agreement to build a pipeline that will bypass the Caspian and ensure Russia's key role in gas transport.[56]

Overall, Moscow's most important and most durable relationship is with Kazakhstan, and the Kazakhs view Russia as their most critical one. Russia is also pleased with Nazarbayev's assumption of a leadership role in Central Asia. While not acting as a surrogate for Russia, much of Nazarbayev's agenda overlaps that of Moscow.

Under Boris Yeltsin, Russia tried to use Kazakhstan's energy debts and geographic isolation to limit its economic development. In response, the Kazakhs developed a multi-vectored foreign policy and investment strategy in order to survive. By contrast, President Putin tried a more positive approach, using the carrot more frequently than the stick, creating a series of partnerships between key industries, including in the energy sector. Putin has been a tough and sometimes underhanded negotiator. For example, at the end of a May 2007 summit between Nazarbayev and Putin, the former agreed to ship Kazakh oil through the Russian-sponsored Burgas-Aleksandropolis pipeline project, believing that he had secured Putin's approval for expanding the CPC (Caspian Pipeline Consortium) pipeline that ships Tengiz oil across Russia. However, Putin made it clear that Russia was still simply considering CPC expansion and had not yet fully committed to it.[57]

Nonetheless, one should not diminish the importance of shared values between the Kazakhs and Russians. Both want to attract foreign direct investment, but do so in a way that protects state management of the development of strategic natural resources, and while many of Putin's domestic policies have occasioned criticism in the West, they have been viewed with favor in Kazakhstan and throughout Central Asia.

CHINA'S ENTRANCE TO CENTRAL ASIA

By contrast, most of Central Asia's leaders seem to feel less competent about their ability to manage the relationship with China than they do with Russia, with whom they share historical, linguistic, or cultural experience. While they admit awe over China's extraordinary economic accomplishments, they seem concerned about China's capacity to overwhelm all of the economies in the region.[58]

Currently China does not dominate the economies of the Central Asian states. While its role in the region's energy sector is growing, its investments fall far short of those by Western super-major energy companies, who control the three largest hydrocarbon projects in the region (Kashagan, Karachaganak, and Tengiz, all in Kazakhstan). Similarly, China is unlikely to ever rival Russia as the transit route for Caspian oil or gas, the majority of which will, through existing contractual agreements, be sold on the European market.

As tables 11.1 and 11.2 illustrate, China is becoming an important trading partner for all of the Central Asian states, but not yet more important than Russia.[59] Only Kazakhstan exports more to China than it does to Russia, and

Table 11.1. Central Asian Exports (in millions of U.S. dollars)

	Kazakhstan			Kyrgyzstan			Tajikistan		
	1999	2002	2005	1999	2002	2005	1999	2002	2005
TOTAL	5,598.00	9,670.00	23,557.00	454.00	485.00	672.00	688.70	736.90	908.70
UNITED STATES	81.00	117.00	1,059.00	11.30	36.06	4.82	0.86	0.70	0.20
EUROPEAN UNION	1,606.00	1,988.00	10,284.00	190.10	31.84	18.41	263.38	314.80	496.90
RUSSIA	1,139.00	1,498.00	2,918.00	70.70	80.04	132.06	115.06	87.50	82.80
CHINA	474.00	1,024.00	2,639.00	25.30	41.26	95.05	2.62	2.20	5.70
KAZAKHSTAN	—	—	—	44.90	36.83	92.07	3.59	3.50	19.70
KYRGYZSTAN	60.00	109.00	254.00	—	—	—	3.91	3.70	3.20
TAJIKISTAN	46.00	46.00	153.00	9.50	10.19	18.73	—	—	—
TURKMENISTAN	14.00	15.00	30.00	2.80	2.41	3.78	1.30	10.00	7.60
UZBEKISTAN	66.00	101.00	230.00	46.50	27.84	24.76	180.98	72.90	66.50

(continued)

Table 11.1. (*continued*)

	Turkmenistan			Uzbekistan		
	1999	*2002*	*2005*	*1999*	*2002*	*2005*
TOTAL	1,187.10	2,815.70	5,673.90	1,962.70	1,561.70	3,448.90
UNITED STATES	9.40	48.97	132.55	25.55	74.00	88.64
EUROPEAN UNION	210.06	614.77	881.69	509.63	429.96	597.12
RUSSIA	43.50	22.95	69.91	423.22	310.56	820.00
CHINA	5.20	3.71	17.26	12.46	25.08	410.97
KAZAKHSTAN	11.50	1.88	78.48	78.82	78.66	236.42
KYRGYZSTAN	7.80	1.13	1.13	46.00	54.68	52.85
TAJIKISTAN	11.90	33.62	48.91	240.39	120.36	139.00
TURKMENISTAN	—	—	(2004) —	45.27	34.14	62.62
UZBEKISTAN	6.00	11.52	16.19	—	—	—

Table 11.2. Central Asian Imports (in millions of U.S. dollars)

	Kazakhstan			Kyrgyzstan			Tajikistan		
	1999	*2002*	*2005*	*1999*	*2002*	*2005*	*1999*	*2002*	*2005*
TOTAL	*3,687.00*	*6,584.00*	*20,235.00*	*599.70*	*586.70*	*1,102.20*	*663.00*	*720.50*	*1,330.00*
UNITED STATES	349.00	461.00	592.00	204.20	143.10	158.70	1.67	6.10	11.70
EUROPEAN UNION	1,092.00	1,799.00	4,934.00	121.80	86.79	149.83	92.08	79.70	143.00
RUSSIA	1,351.00	2,549.00	7,182.00	109.30	116.71	437.18	92.41	163.50	256.50
CHINA	83.00	313.00	4,298.00	36.80	59.12	953.12	2.56	7.60	92.80
KAZAKHSTAN	—	—	—	72.60	123.90	267.42	78.79	72.20	168.30
KYRGYZSTAN	31.00	32.00	104.00	—	—	—	7.23	5.20	20.60
TAJIKISTAN	2.00	3.00	22.00	4.00	3.48	3.52	—	—	—
TURKMENISTAN	20.00	75.00	86.00	7.80	1.73	0.90	15.19	47.10	53.80
UZBEKISTAN	87.00	87.00	260.00	50.60	60.14	58.13	264.43	132.40	152.90

(continued)

Table 11.2. (continued)

	Turkmenistan			Uzbekistan		
	1999	*2002*	*2005*	*1999*	*2002*	*2005*
TOTAL	1,478.30	2,127.90	2,709.00	2,481.20	2,075..65	3,554.60
UNITED STATES	66.30	137.33	260.92	386.65	151.91	80.85
EUROPEAN UNION	253.90	225.03	447.05	683.93	535.47	771.29
RUSSIA	167.30	360.86	246.45	264.08	498.69	946.58
CHINA	13.80	110.36	100.30	30.35	116.06	256.42
KAZAKHSTAN	19.00	26.55	32.79	73.04	111.13	253.49
KYRGYZSTAN	3.00	4.90	8.74	51.15	30.62	27.23
TAJIKISTAN	3.00	14.70	8.36	199.07	80.19	73.15
TURKMENISTAN	—	—	— (2004)	6.60	1,2674.14	17.81
UZBEKISTAN	49.80	37.55	68.88	—	—	—

that is because of the sale of oil. Only Kyrgyzstan imports more from China than it does from Russia. While official trade statistics do not reflect the considerable illegal trade between the Central Asian countries and China, its relative significance has diminished significantly in recent years.

Central Asian leaders fear that their economies could be overwhelmed by migrant farmers and small-scale entrepreneurs from China. It is hard to know how many Chinese citizens have settled in Central Asia. Kyrgyz scholars estimate that anywhere from 20,000 to 120,000 people have come there from China since independence, from all ethnic groups, including Kyrgyz, Uighurs, and Dungans, as well as Han Chinese.[60] The Kazakh government's policy of repatriating Kazakhs from China and Mongolia (Oralman) is rumored to have led to illegal Han Chinese migration under this program. There is frequent Kazakh media coverage about the risks of Chinese migration, some of which is hysterical in tone.[61] China remains more of a historical villain in Kazakh memory than Russia, as well as in Kyrgyz historic memory.

The Chinese, aware of Central Asian concerns, took something of a "go slow" approach at the outset, concentrating on reducing any direct security risks that might be posed by the independence of these states. China's short-term concerns were focused on border delineation issues and minimizing involvement by the Central Asian states in China's own ethnic minority issues.

The Central Asian states had large Uighur populations, and Uighur nationalist groups had found it easy in the confusion of the last years of Soviet-rule and first years of independence.[62] By the mid-1990s their activities had been sharply restricted, in large part because of pressure from Beijing to have these groups designated as terrorist organizations.

There are conflicting accounts of how difficult it was to delineate the Kazakh and Kyrgyz borders with China. The Tajik-Chinese border is quite small, and its delineation never became a political issue in Tajikistan. But in both Kazakhstan and Kyrgyzstan, critics of the government were very vocal about how much "ancestral land" had been turned over to Beijing's control. In the Kyrgyz case, protests by a parliamentarian (Azimbek Beknazarov) led to his arrest and a national political crisis when some of his protesting supporters were killed by police near the town of Aksy.[63] In reality, the Kazakhs and even the Kyrgyz did not lose sizable amounts of land in the border delineation process, although critical water usage issues on the Chinese side of the border remain unresolved.[64]

In recent years China has adopted a much higher profile, partly to counterbalance the U.S. military presence and Putin's success in binding these states more closely to Russia. China has been active in Kazakhstan's oil industry for over a decade, building a jointly owned 2,900-kilometer oil pipeline from Atyrau to Alashankou on the Kazakh-Chinese border. The construction of a 750-kilometer link from Kumkol to Kenkiyak will bring more Chinese-owned assets to the main pipeline in 2009.[65]

China's acquisition of oil assets has been hampered by the unwillingness of Western energy companies to partner with them. A 2003 bid by China National Offshore Oil Corporation (CNOOC) and China Petroleum and Chemical Corporation (Sinopec) to buy British Gas's share of Kazakhstan's massive offshore Kashagan deposit was blocked by the Western consortia partners. CNPC (China National Petroleum Corporation) did manage to acquire the small North Buzachi field, and then finally in 2005 CNPC purchased the assets of Petra Kazakhstan for $4 billion, giving them the assets from the Kumkol field and shared control of the Shymkent refinery.[66]

Over the last several years China has been increasing its position in Central Asia's gas market, buying up smaller and medium-sized fields, and announcing their interest in the few giant projects where exploitation rights have yet to be sold. Beijing's biggest success has been in Turkmenistan, where they contracted to buy 30 bcm of Turkmen gas annually beginning in 2009 and to develop the green field projects necessary to produce it, through a pipeline that will go through Kazakhstan and Uzbekistan, linking up gas from some smaller projects that the Chinese also control. The project has formally been launched,[67] although there are now rumors that actual construction will be delayed because the Chinese are dissatisfied with Turkmen supply guarantees.[68]

China now has a bigger role in Central Asia's security scene, although smaller than either the United States' or Russia's. Beijing has focused on bilateral initiatives and has offered substantial military assistance to Tajikistan,[69] Uzbekistan (especially in the area of telecommunications), and Kyrgyzstan. China also has been a participant in SCO joint military exercises, something of a departure for Beijing. The SCO's first-ever joint military exercises were held in the summer of 2003 and the largest, Peace Mission 2007, just before the 2007 SCO summit.[70] These exercises were intended as coordinated military exercises rather than an effort to provide a single integrated military response.

China is an important source of developmental assistance. They have lent billions of dollars to the Tajiks at 1 percent interest in recent years,[71] a far lower rate than international financial institutions offer, and have made offers of 2 percent loans to Turkmenistan.[72]

IS THE SCO THE ANSWER?

The existence of the SCO has played only a supporting role in the expansion of Chinese influence in the Central Asian region. While Beijing was instrumental in its establishment, the organization itself is still in flux, undecided about how to develop its mission, and how widely to expand its membership. While there is a lot of talk about expanding both, none of the members (large states and small alike) seem terribly enthusiastic about either, especially if one goes by off-the-record statements rather than by official accounts of the meetings.[73]

It is difficult to predict whether the SCO will move from what it largely is today, a forum for discussion of themes of common interest to its member states, and whether it will evolve into an organization invigorated by the pursuit of common goals and capable of advancing the interests of member states in the direction of achieving them. The SCO has the best chance of achieving this if it retains its current membership, expanding to include Turkmenistan and, should the situation stabilize, Afghanistan as well.

The basic lack of trust among SCO members is a major reason why the organization will have difficulty turning itself into an organization that resembles either the OSCE or NATO in the area of security relationships, or the European Union (even in its earlier incarnation as the European Community) in the area of economic cooperation. It is particularly hard to imagine that the SCO could ever develop into anything resembling NATO, an organization that has had sixty years to define a shared security mission and the shared commitment to preserve democratic systems. In many respects NATO is an old-style organization, reflecting the goals of the Cold War, but its longevity as well as nominally shared value systems have given the organization continued longevity even after the Cold War that caused its formation had ended.

The SCO is also an old-style organization, an attempt at a bloc or a counter-bloc, to help protect the encroachment of other blocs (or states) on the geopolitical and domestic interests of the members, as well as a forum for regulating shared security concerns. The latter interest helps define the former interest but does not compensate for the absence of a shared ideology among the member states or a long history of cooperation for all of the members, at least one that was purely voluntary.

All recognize that the relationships created out of their shared pasts need to be regulated, and the presence of China in the SCO provides a different kind of ballast than exists in the CIS. But the current membership of the Shanghai Cooperation Organisation is ill-equipped to function as an organization that provides an integrated security response to perceived common security risks.

To date even the CSTO (Collective Security Treaty Organization) has failed to provide an integrated security response to a concrete threat in any of the countries of that organization. They do plan regularly for such a concerted response, but have yet to test their capacity in action. Unlike the SCO, the CSTO is built on the remains of a common command and control system, that of the Red Army, and there is still a common language of command possible, at least among the officer corps.

The SCO needs to integrate the Chinese People's Liberation Army into the old Soviet command structure, something that seems problematic at best, especially given China's very limited history of participating in multilateral security organizations. So, at best, the SCO seems likely to offer a co-ordinated response to common problems, and that is a considerably less comprehensive form of joint response. Until the SCO assumes the capacity to function as a security organization that has field response capability, it is difficult to be too optimistic that it will be able to move beyond its current stage of confidence-building measures and non-traditional security cooperation, particularly in the area of counterterrorism.

The SCO might find it easier to be an organization that fosters economic cooperation between its members, serving as a force for regularizing trade and tariffs. Here too, though, it is hard to imagine that the organization will have the capacity to provide any kind of real economic integration, save under the umbrella of the WTO (World Trade Organization). But China's and Kyrgyzstan's membership in the SCO renders this function somewhat superfluous. If all members of the SCO are members of the WTO, the latter organization will likely provide a sufficient mechanism for cooperation. But if Uzbekistan (and Turkmenistan if it joins the SCO) remains outside of the WTO after Kazakhstan, Russia, and Tajikistan all join, then the SCO will be further handicapped in trying to regulate economic trade. It will, however, remain able to sponsor regional economic projects, and should China decide to use the SCO umbrella to advance Beijing's foreign assistance program, that, too, would give the organization greater vitality.

It is also highly unlikely that the SCO will develop into any sort of energy club, as Russia and China are competing for Central Asia's oil, gas, and hydroelectric power (largely in the case of transit for Russia). It does not seem that it would truly be in China's best interest to have the SCO play a major role in this area, as Beijing is successfully using bilateral relationships to advance its interests in the energy sector. To function as an energy club, the SCO would have to admit Iran, possibly Pakistan and India, and then likely consider taking in Azerbaijan and Turkey—turning the organization into something of a smaller and less effective OPEC (Organization of Petroleum Exporting Countries). However, the SCO could potentially play a highly effective role in regulating water usage and helping sponsor the development of a region-wide hydroelectric system, and in so doing the SCO would advance the cause of regional security.

The SCO has succeeded in creating an identity for itself as a forum for permitting the states of the region to discuss shared problems and possible solutions to them. But to date it has yet to create successful strategies for dealing with these problems or a strong institutional presence to advance its interest. Given the inbred competition and lack of trust between its various members it will take a lot of still undemonstrated national will by the various member states to succeed in doing this.

OUTLOOK

Whether or not the SCO succeeds does not change the fact that the dissolution of the USSR, and the ability of all five Central Asian states to weather the vicissitudes of now going on two decades of independence has an impact on European as well as Asian understandings of geopolitics and security.

Physically, virtually all of Central Asia, save the westernmost part of Kazakhstan, lies in Asia, but much like Russia, or the USSR before it, the states in this region seek to create a role for themselves in both Europe and in Asia. And being part of an unbroken landmass that spans the two, Central Asia's leaders refuse to choose between them, all of their invocations of their Asianness as a justification for their non-democratic practices notwithstanding.

Europe remains a more important trading partner for virtually all of the Central Asian states than is East Asia (including China), and trade with South Asia is still rather inconsequential, especially when the Turkmen-Iranian economic relationship is excluded. This is likely to change if, as projected, India, China and some of the other Asian economies continue their rapid economic growth. But the sale of Central Asia's oil and gas on European markets is contracted to continue for at least another quarter century, and for whatever variety of reasons, India's interest in this region has been far less than the Central Asians hoped or expected.

In terms of their basic security needs, once China is excluded, the large states of both Asia and Europe seem far away. The security horizon of most Central Asian states is what is described in this chapter—Russia, China, Afghanistan, and the former Soviet republics with which they share borders. The situation in Iran does not trouble them, for the ideological regime there has proven less directly pernicious than the fundamentalists from Saudi Arabia, the religious center for Central Asia which is Sunni, not Shia, by heritage and practice. Developments in Pakistan bother them a lot more, but they see no diplomatic leverage to manage this and hope that tighter border controls and more effective counterterrorist measures will be protection enough for them.

Moreover, while there is a lot of talk in both European and Asian capitals about the need for more effective strategies in Central Asia, which in both continents is described as of growing strategic importance, the realities on the ground in Central Asia do little to bear this out. Delegations seem to come in waves, and the promulgation of a new EU strategy seems to invariably trigger renewed interest in Tokyo and Seoul, that their economic interests must be more effectively represented in Central Asia, but this remains the periphery with regard to trade for both. Maybe this will change now that China has promised billions of dollars toward improving highways and rail links, but similar plans by the Europeans petered out when the investments were not borne out by trade projections or by projected cost savings for moving cross-continental freight in ships rather than overland. Unless the volume of trade with or through these states substantially increases, potential security problems emanating from Central Asia will get relatively little attention in most European or Asian capitals, unless there is some domestic constituency that needs to be appeased, as was the case with democracy advocates in the United States and EU after the violence in Andijon.

NOTES

1. For information about the Economic Cooperation Organization, see www
.ecosecretariat.org/.
2. For information about the Organization of the Islamic Conference, see www
.oic-oci.org/oicnew/.
3. F. Stephen Larrabee and Ian O. Lesser, *Turkish Foreign Policy in an Age of Uncertainty* (Santa Monica, Calif.: RAND Corporation, National Security Research Division, 2003), 99–126.
4. For information about the Collective Security Treaty Organization (CSTO), see www.dkb.gov.ru/; and Marcin Kaczmarski, "Russia Creates a New Security System to Replace the C.I.S." EURASIANET: Eurasia Insight, January 11, 2006, www
.eurasianet.org/departments/insight/articles/pp011106_pr.shtml.
5. Turkmenistan is the only Central Asian state that is not a member of the SCO. Uzbekistan joined the organization in 2001. Kaczmarski, "Russia Creates a New Security System to Replace the C.I.S."
6. For a description of this organization, see www.evrazes.com/, and for an unofficial translation of the description of the organization, see www.evrazes.com/files/bpage/1/e_evrazes.pdf.
7. For information about CAREC, see www.adb.org/CAREC/default.asp.
8. Zainiddin Karaev, "Water Diplomacy in Central Asia," *Middle East Review of International Affairs* 9, no. 1, article 5 (March 2005).
9. Firdavs Yakubov and Johmahmad Rajabov, *2006 Mine Action in Tajikistan* (Standing Committee Meeting on the Article 5 Implementation Progress of Tajikistan under the Ottawa Convention, April 2007), www.apminebanconvention.org/fileadmin/pdf/mbc/IWP/SC_april07/speeches-mc/Tajikistan-25April2007slides.pdf (slide 10).
10. There are three Tajik exclaves, all located in the Ferghana Valley region where Kyrgyzstan, Tajikistan, and Uzbekistan meet.

11. Nursultan Nazarbayev, "Kazakhstan's Strategy of Joining the World's 50 Most Competitive Countries," *2006 State of the Nation Address*, www.kazakhstanembassy .org.uk/cgi-bin/index/254.

12. Bulat Nurgaliev became secretary-general of the Shanghai Cooperation Organisation in 2007. He has held several diplomatic posts in the Soviet Union and Kazakhstan, including Kazakhstan's ambassador to the United States, South Korea, and Japan, and the Soviet ambassador to Pakistan and India. He began his career in the Soviet Foreign Ministry's South Asia desk.

13. Tair Mansurov has occupied high-level positions in Kazakhstan's government before becoming secretary-general of EurAsEC.

14. Kassymzhomart Tokaev served as Kazakhstan's foreign minister from 1994 to 1999 and 2003–2007. From 1999 to 2002, he was prime minister of Kazakhstan. He held numerous posts in Kazakhstan's Foreign Ministry in the 1990s.

15. "Kazakhstan Picked to Chair OSCE," BBC news, December 1, 2007, news.bbc .co.uk/2/hi/asia-pacific/7123045.stm.

16. Erkin Tukumov, "*Poleznoe OBSEnie*" [Beneficial OSCE Membership], *LITER*, December 17, 2007, www.liter.kz/print.php?lan=russian&id=151&pub=5737.

17. Bhavna Dave, "The EU and Kazakhstan: Balancing Economic Cooperation and Aiding Democratic Reforms in the Central Asian Region," *Center for European Policy Studies*, no. 127 (May 2007): 5–7.

18. Jean-Christophe Peuch, "Russia: Energy Summit Gives Putin New Trump Card," Radio Free Europe/Radio Liberty, May 16, 2007, www.rferl.org/featuresarticle/ 2007/05/2c66d7b7-9c7e-465e-a263-11a3fbab043a.html.

19. According to IMF's 2007 estimates, Kazakhstan's GDP is $95.4 billion, 364 percent larger than Turkmenistan's, which is in second place with $26.2 billion; www.imf.org/external/pubs/ft/weo/2007/02/weodata/weorept.aspx?sy=2004&ey= 2008&ssd=1&sort=country&ds=.&br=1&pr1.x=86&pr1.y=21&c=923%2C925 %2C916%2C917%2C927&s=NGDPD&grp=0&a=.

20. "Kazkommertsbank Presents Its Subsidiary in Kyrgyzstan," *KAZKOMMERTS-BANK News Release*, May 28, 2003, en.kkb.kz/Releases/show_75.shtml.

21. Marat Yermukanov, "Kazakh-Uzbek Relations Show Signs of Improvement," *Eurasia Daily Monitor*, Jamestown Foundation, March 22, 2006, www.jamestown .org/publications_details.php?volume_id=414&issue_id=3661&article_id=2370897.

22. Bernd Rechel and Martin McKee, *Human Rights and Health in Turkmenistan* (London: European Center of Health of Societies in Transition, 2005), 14.

23. State News Agency of Turkmenistan, "Islam Karimov Renders Homage to the National Sanctuaries of the Turkmen People," *Turkmenistan: The Golden Age*, October 20, 2007, www.turkmenistan.gov.tm/_en/?idr=1&id=071020a.

24. The civil war in Tajikistan did not have an interethnic character but was a competition for power among rival Tajik groups. Uzbekistan, though, did have a clear favorite in the civil war, those from Khujand province in the Ferghana Valley, whom they aided, even after formal hostilities were over. See Stephen Blank, "Russian Forces in Tajikistan: A Permanent Presence?" *Central Asia–Caucasus Institute Analyst*, June 16, 2004, www.cacianalyst.org/view_article.php?articleid=2451.

25. For more, see Elena Chadova, "Andijan Tragedy Served as Catalyst for Increased Repression in 2005," EURASIANET Civil Society, May 23, 2006, www .eurasianet.org/departments/insight/articles/eav052306.shtml.

26. On May 13, 2005, the Uzbek government lost control of parts of the densely populated city of Andijon, located near the border with Kyrgyzstan.

27. C. J. Chevers, "Europeans Set Arms Embargo to Protest Uzbeks' Crackdown," *New York Times*, October 4, 2005.

28. GUUAM (Georgia, Ukraine, Uzbekistan, Azerbaijan, and Moldova) Group was formally founded in 1996 as a political, economic, and strategic alliance designed to strengthen the independence and sovereignty of these former Soviet Union republics. Uzbekistan joined the organization in 1999 and withdrew from membership in 2005.

29. Esra Hatypodlu, "The New Great Game in the South Caucasus and Central Asia: The Interests of Global Powers and the Role of the Regional Organizations," *Turkish Review of Eurasian Studies* (Foundation of Middle East and Balkan Studies, 2006): 85–128.

30. The condemnation of a permanent U.S. military presence in Central Asia and discussions on enhancing the SCO's security role were highlights of the June 2005 SCO summit in Astana. Kabar Information Agency, "Seven Documents Signed at SCO Meeting," *KABAR Current Affairs*, July 5, 2005, en.kabar.kg/index.php?area=1&p=news&newsid=18.

31. Martha Brill Olcott, "The Maturing of the Central Asian States," *Central Asian Voices*, November 4, 2007, www.centralasianvoices.org/2007/11/the_maturing.cfm.

32. "Framework Agreement between the Government of the United States of America, the Government of the Republic of Kazakhstan, the Government of the Kyrgyz Republic, the Government of the Republic of Tajikistan, the Government of Turkmenistan, and the Government of the Republic of Uzbekistan Concerning the Development of Trade and Investment Relations," *TIFA*, June 1, 2004, www.ustr.gov/assets/Trade_Agreements/TIFA/asset_upload_file683_7722.pdf.

33. Richard E. Hoagland, "Current Status and Future of U.S.-Tajik Relations," Embassy of the United States in Tajikistan, November 30, 2005, dushanbe.usembassy.gov/sp_11302005.html.

34. Personal communication of Kazakh diplomats with author.

35. Martha Brill Olcott, "U.S. Policy in Central Asia: Balancing Priorities (Part II)" (testimony prepared for the Committee on International Relations: Hearing on the Middle East and Central Asia, April 26, 2006), www.internationalrelations.house.gov/archives/109/olc042606.pdf.

36. Leila Saralayeva, "Russia, China, Iran Warn U.S. at Summit," *Washington Post*, August 16, 2007, www.washingtonpost.com/wp-dyn/content/article/2007/08/16/AR2007081601221.html; and Roger McDermott, "Kazakhstan Notes Afghanistan's Emerging Security Agenda," *Eurasia Daily Monitor*, Jamestown Foundation, December 12, 2007, jamestown.org/edm/article.php?article_id=2372661.

37. George W. Bush, "State of the Union Address" (The White House, February 2, 2005), www.whitehouse.gov/news/releases/2005/02/20050202-11.html.

38. Gregory Gleason, "The Uzbek Expulsion of U.S. Forces and Realignment in Central Asia," *Problems of Post-Communism* 53, no. 2 (March/April 2006): 50.

39. The 2005 Kyrgyz parliamentary elections were held in February and March 2005, falling short of OSCE standards for democratic elections. The belief that the election had been rigged by the government led to widespread protests, leading to

President Askar Akayev fleeing the country on March 24. Christopher Pala, "Protests Forces Authoritarian Leader to Flee in Kyrgyzstan," *New York Times*, March 25, 2005.

40. By mid-2005, both the United States and the EU had sharply limited the kinds of direct foreign assistance that could be offered to the Uzbek government; in the European case, this meant restricting foreign aid almost exclusively to non-governmental actors. For details see Martha Brill Olcott, "Uzbekistan: A Decaying Dictatorship Withdrawn from the West," in *Worst of the Worst: Dealing with Repressive and Rogue Nations*, ed. Robert Rotberg (Washington, D.C.: Brookings Institution Press, 2007), 252.

41. According to section 2 of article 44 of the Constitution of the Kyrgyz Republic, Askar Akayev's term would have expired by December 2005.

42. Akromiya is an Islamist organization founded by Akrom Yo'ldoshev that has been designated as terrorist by the government of Uzbekistan, despite claims of its membership that they are committed to the peaceful introduction of an Islamic government.

43. "The Formation of an Independent Commission to Investigate the Events in Andijan" (Resolution of the Legislative Chamber of the Oliy Majlis [Parliament] of Uzbekistan, May 23, 2005), www.gov.uz/ru/content.scm?contentId=12831.

44. "Text of Clinton-Yeltsin News Conference," CNN.com, September 1, 1998, www.cnn.com/ALLPOLITICS/1998/09/02/lewinsky.01/transcript.html.

45. The Nabucco pipeline (approx. 3,300 kilometers), starting at the Georgian/Turkish and/or Iranian/Turkish border, respectively, leading to Baumgarten in Austria via Bulgaria, Romania, and Hungary. For more see the Nabucco Gas Pipeline Project website: www.nabucco-pipeline.com/project/project-description-pipeline route/index.html.

46. Nicklas Norling, *Gazprom's Monopoly and Nabucco's Potentials: Strategic Decisions for Europe*, Silk Road Paper (Washington, D.C.: Central Asia–Caucasus Institute and Silk Road Studies Program, 2007), 36.

47. Alexander A. Sergunin, "Russian Post-Communist Foreign Policy Thinking at the Cross-Roads: Changing Paradigms," *Journal of International Relations and Development* 3, no. 3 (September 2000).

48. Of the five Central Asian states, only Kyrgyzstan had previously chosen to leave the ruble zone before Russia called on ruble zone member states to turn over their foreign reserves to Russia and to have co-ordinate foreign investment strategies with Moscow. This was by definition unacceptable to all but Tajikistan, which was in the middle of a civil war. Martha Brill Olcott, Anders Aslund, and Sherman W. Garnett, *Getting It Wrong: Regional Cooperation and the Commonwealth of Independent States* (Washington, D.C.: Carnegie Endowment of International Peace, 2000).

49. Sergei Blagov, "Moscow Beefs Up Security Ties with Kyrgyzstan," *Eurasia Daily Monitor* (Jamestown Foundation) 3, issue 189 (October 13, 2006).

50. Personal communication with author.

51. When the Soviet Union dissolved at the end of 1991, the main military force in Tajikistan was the 201st Motorized Rifle Division, whose position and resources the Russian Federation inherited. See "Operational Group of Russian Forces in Tajikistan," Global Security.org, www.globalsecurity.org/military/world/russia/ogrv -tajikistan.htm.

52. Russian guards left the Tajik-Afghan border in July 2005.

53. "Russia-Kazakhstan Border Agreement Crucial—Diplomat," RIA Novosti, January 8, 2006, en.rian.ru/russia/20060108/42892424.html.

54. Vladimir Milov, "The Great Uncertainty: Energy Relations between Turkmenistan and Russia at the Historic Crossroads," *Carnegie Working Paper* (in press).

55. While the Turkmen often complained bitterly about this arrangement, Turkmen president Saparmurat Niyazov and his family were generally believed to have directly profited from the resale of bartered goods and to have had at least a small share of the profit generated by transshipment to Ukraine.

56. "Russia Seals Central Asian Gas Pipeline Deal," Reuters, December 20, 2007, www.reuters.com/article/email/idUSL2021770320071220?pageNumber=1&virtual BrandChannel=0.

57. Martha Brill Olcott, "The Kazakh-Russian Relationship," *Russian Analytical Digest*, no. 29 (October 16, 2007): 16.

58. This is based on personal communication with author.

59. See tables 11.1 and 11.2 on Central Asian trade figures.

60. Rafis Abazov, "Chinese in Central Asia: Loyal Citizens or Fifth Column?" *Central Asia–Caucasus Institute Analyst*, February 8, 2006, www.cacianalyst.org/?q= node/3723.

61. Marat Yermukanov, "Sino-Kazakh Pipeline Project Has Demographic, as well as Economic, Dimensions," *Eurasia Daily Monitor* (Jamestown Foundation) 2, no. 75 (April 18, 2005), www.jamestown.org/publications_details.php?volume_id=407 &issue_id=3302&article_id=2369606.

62. The Uighur population in Central Asia is estimated at four hundred thousand. Igor Rotar, "The Growing Problem of Uighur Separatism," *Eurasia Daily Monitor*, Jamestown Foundation, April 15, 2004, www.jamestown.org/edm/article .php?volume_id=395&issue_id=2935&article_id=236612.

63. Bruce Pannler, "Kyrgyzstan: Anniversary of Aksy Tragedy Marked," Radio Free Europe/Radio Liberty, March 17, 2006, www.rferl.org/featuresarticle/2006/03/ c60a075f-83b8-47d8-84df-5712689ae03c.html.

64. China, too, is an interested client for surplus electric power. Sébastien Peyrouse, *Economic Aspects of the Chinese–Central Asia Rapprochement*, Silk Road Study Paper (Washington, D.C.: Central Asia–Caucasus Institute and Silk Road Studies Program, 2007), www.silkroadstudies.org/new/docs/Silkroadpapers/2007/0709 China-Central_Asia.pdf.

65. Farkhad Sharip, "China Secures New Access to Kazakh Oil," *Eurasia Daily Monitor*, Jamestown Foundation, December 21, 2007, jamestown.org/edm/article .php?article_id=2372689.

66. For details of these transactions and a list of China's oil and gas holdings in Kazakhstan as well as the makeup of all of Kazakhstan's consortia, see Martha Brill Olcott, "KAZMUNAIGAZ: Kazakhstan's National Oil and Gas Company," in *The Changing Role of National Oil Companies in International Energy Markets*, Baker Institute Policy Report 35 (Houston, Tex.: James A. Baker III Institute for Public Policy, 2007).

67. Chemen Durdiyeva, "Berdimuhammedov Launches Turkmenistan-China Gas Pipeline Project," *Central Asia–Caucasus Institute Analyst*, September 20, 2007, www.cacianalyst.org/?q=node/4701/.

68. Personal communication with author.

69. In addition to Russia, the United States, and France, the Tajiks also receive military assistance from India. For more, see "India Looking for Energy Supplies in Central Asia," *AsiaNews.it*, September 13, 2006, www.asianews.it/index.php?l=en &art=7200&geo=4&theme=6&size=A.

70. Pan Guang, "Bishkek: SCO's Success in the Hinterland of Eurasia," *China and Eurasia Forum Quarterly by Central Asia–Caucasus Institute and Silk Road Studies Program* 5, no. 4 (2007): 3–6.

71. In 2006 China invested more than $650 million in laying two electricity transmission lines, reconstructing a highway, and digging two highway tunnels in Tajikistan. On January 15, 2007, it was also announced that Sinohydro Corporation was awarded a contract to build a large hydroelectric plant in Pendjikent district, northern Tajikistan, to be funded through a $200 million low-interest Chinese loan. "China, Tajikistan Set to Strengthen Economic Cooperation," *New Eurasia*, January 19, 2007, tajikistan.neweurasia.net/?p=155.

72. Personal communication with author.

73. For an account of the 2006 and 2007 SCO summits, respectively, see www .scosummit2006.org and www.scosummit2007.org.

12

The Korean Peninsula and Northeast Asian Stability

Scott Snyder

The Korean peninsula is at the vortex of the respective political and security interests of the great powers in Northeast Asia. The conflicting geo-strategic interests of great powers toward the Korean peninsula have inhibited the institutionalization of regional structures, to the extent that Northeast Asia has been characterized as an "anti-region."[1] Although the end of the Cold War has brought about dramatic changes in the structure of international relations in other regions, Northeast Asia has been much slower to adapt to new circumstances primarily because the structure of conflict on the peninsula between North and South Korea—at the center of Northeast Asia—remains unresolved. The security interests of the region's great powers are directly affected by the nature and orientation of the Korean peninsula, which has remained divided since the end of World War II.

The process by which the issues of peace and reunification on the Korean peninsula are resolved will inevitably influence the security interests and foreign policy options of Korea's great-power neighbors. The nature and development of regional cooperation (which has been driven in part by the ongoing North Korean nuclear crisis); the shift in economic and political strength on the peninsula in favor of Seoul as one phase in an ongoing transition to a new equilibrium on the Korean peninsula; and concerns that a resolution to the Korean standoff might inadvertently abet major power rivalry are factors that are likely to influence the relative levels of regional conflict and cooperation and will shape prospects for development of regional institutions in Northeast Asia.

This chapter will explore how the North Korean nuclear issue has been a catalyst for ad hoc multilateralism in Northeast Asia, in the process promoting the institutionalization of regional cooperation. Second, the chapter will review the security dilemmas that each of the members of the Six-Party Talks faces as they consider the implications of peace and reunification on the Korean peninsula, given the growing imbalance of power internal to the Korean peninsula in favor of Seoul. Third, the chapter will analyze the prospects for regional rivalry between China and Japan and Korean views of how such rivalry might be mitigated.

NORTH KOREAN NUCLEAR CRISIS: CATALYST FOR COOPERATIVE SECURITY DIALOGUE

The regional response to the second North Korean nuclear crisis in October 2002 initiated a new chapter in the building of multilateral cooperation to promote security and stability in Northeast Asia. The Six-Party Talks represent the latest phase in an ongoing series of efforts to expand multilateral cooperation in response to the greatest source of instability that the parties in Northeast Asia collectively face: the prospect of instability that derives from North Korea's inability to integrate itself with a broader set of collective interests in the promotion of regional stability and prosperity. Although the North Korean standoff has often been cited as the primary obstacle to the promotion of regional security cooperation in Northeast Asia, the North Korean nuclear crisis has also long been the primary catalyst for promoting multilateral cooperation among neighboring stakeholders surrounding the Korean peninsula. Despite repeated attempts since the late 1980s to formalize a regional security dialogue mechanism for the purpose of addressing security issues in Northeast Asia, the advent of the second North Korean nuclear crisis in October 2002 both highlighted the absence of such a dialogue and catalyzed the formation of the first official regional dialogue through the establishment of the Six-Party Talks.

Efforts to promote regional cooperation in Northeast Asia predate the emergence of the North Korean nuclear crisis, but the challenge of alleviating tensions on the Korean peninsula has been at the center of all of these efforts. Mikhail Gorbachev proposed expanded regional cooperation on the model of the Council for Security Cooperation in Europe at a Vladivostok speech in 1986.[2] Roh Tae Woo also put forward a proposal for a Six-Party Consultative Conference for Peace in Northeast Asia in a speech to the United Nations in 1988.[3] Former U.S. secretary of state James Baker advocated the establishment of a two plus four mechanism for dealing with Korean tensions in November 1991.[4] None of these proposals gained traction as viable mechanisms for multilateral management of Northeast Asia's security problems.

With the emergence of the first North Korean nuclear crisis and Democratic People's Republic of Korea's (DPRK) threats to withdraw from the

Nuclear Nonproliferation Treaty (NPT), the International Atomic Energy Agency (IAEA) referred the matter to the United Nations in 1993, and the UN Security Council called for dialogue among interested parties. Under the Clinton administration, the United States responded to the call and initiated a bilateral dialogue with the DPRK, much to the shock and chagrin of the Kim Young Sam administration. That dialogue eventually resulted in the Geneva Agreed Framework, but that agreement could not be implemented by the United States alone without support from its allies. The Agreed Framework called for the establishment of a multilateral consortium named the Korean Peninsula Energy Development Organization (KEDO) to implement the terms of the deal. South Korean and Japanese leaders understandably complained about "no taxation without representation," since the United States signed the agreement but asked its allies to sign the check to pay for its implementation. The fact that the bilaterally negotiated Geneva Agreed Framework required a multilateral structure to pursue its own implementation provided clear evidence that a U.S.-led bilateral approach to solving North Korea–related issues, while necessary, was by itself insufficient.

KEDO represented a practical step forward in forging multilateral cooperation to meet North Korea's energy security needs as a solution to the North Korean nuclear crisis, but as an exercise in building regional cooperation, the core membership was incomplete. The European Union joined South Korea and Japan on the board, but Russia and China remained aloof from the organization for their own reasons.[5] Another step forward in developing multilateral cooperation to solve Northeast Asian regional issues was the establishment of the Four-Party Talks (two Koreas, United States, and China), despite North Korea's initial reluctance to join. But this dialogue never really got off the ground due to North Korea's own struggle for survival during the famine. The Four-Party Talks did more to promote Chinese cooperation with the United States and South Korea than to address problems involving North Korea.

A third form of multilateral cooperation during this period involved the establishment of the Trilateral Coordination and Oversight Group (TCOG) among the United States, South Korea, and Japan. This group did much to overcome differences among allies in support of the Perry process in the late 1990s, as all parties supported cooperative efforts to engage North Korea in more active cooperation on the basis of Kim Dae Jung's sunshine policy. Suspicions about covert North Korean nuclear efforts at Keumchangri (later proved unfounded) and North Korea's Taepodong launch in 1998 catalyzed the establishment of TCOG to address differences in policy priorities among the three countries.[6]

The advent of the second North Korean nuclear crisis catalyzed a new form of regional cooperation in the form of the establishment of the Six-

Party Talks. Early in the crisis, it became apparent that the United States had no option for unilateral action through military means, and one lesson of the Agreed Framework was arguably that a U.S.-DPRK bilateral approach by itself was also likely to fail. So President Bush cast the second crisis as a "regional issue," and eventually the Six-Party Talks were established, with China taking the lead role as host and mediator for the process.[7] This time, all the regional stakeholders were represented in the forum, but the dialogue itself made little initial progress due to a combination of U.S. reluctance to engage with North Korea and North Korea's continued focus on the United States.

By early 2005, following three rounds of sporadic negotiations, many critics thought the Six-Party Talks were dead, while others asked whether the parties themselves would ever be able to agree on the conditions under which it was possible to say that all diplomatic options had been exhausted. In May 2005, Secretary of State Condoleezza Rice stopped describing the DPRK as an "outpost of tyranny" and acknowledged that the DPRK is a sovereign state. Within weeks, newly appointed assistant secretary of state Christopher Hill met bilaterally in Beijing with his counterpart, DPRK vice minister Kim Kye Gwan, to announce the resumption of Six-Party Talks after a delay of over one year, signaling a U.S. willingness to negotiate with the DPRK bilaterally in the context of the six-party process. Following intensive negotiations over the course of two sessions in July–August and September 2005, all parties agreed to a September 19 Joint Statement of Principles for addressing the North Korean nuclear crisis.

The statement itself was vague and underwhelming. The document contained few concrete measures, only pledges that the various sides would move forward on the basis of "words for words" and "actions for actions." But the Joint Statement was the first time that the regional stakeholders had identified and articulated the minimum common rhetorical objectives that through joint action and implementation might in the future bind the parties together as a "security community." The common objectives identified were (1) the denuclearization of the Korean peninsula, (2) normalization of relations among all the regional stakeholders, (3) economic development (focused on North Korea), and (4) peace on the Korean peninsula and in Northeast Asia. The rhetorical shared objectives that might constitute a Northeast Asian "security community" had been identified, but it was not yet clear that the parties were willing to take actions in pursuit of those objectives. In retrospect, the Joint Statement marked the inauguration of a rhetorical commitment to collective action in the service of these four objectives, but circumstances related to the Banco Delta Asia (BDA) issue prevented this rhetoric from being translated into action.[8]

A protracted stalemate developed in late 2005 over DPRK accounts frozen at the Macao-based Banco Delta Asia in response to U.S. Treasury concerns that the bank had facilitated North Korean money laundering. The situation was made worse by North Korean missile and nuclear tests in July and October 2006. But following the swift passage of two UN resolutions condemning the North Korean actions and imposing sanctions on the North, the Six-Party Talks resumed in December 2006. North Korea's actions had catalyzed a unified regional response that had the effect of isolating North Korea diplomatically, but the resumption of Six-Party Talks provided an avenue for the North to back down in a face-saving manner. Based on the principles agreed to in the September 2005 Joint Statement, the six parties negotiated a series of implementing measures through five working groups that focused on denuclearization, economic assistance, improvement of bilateral relations between the DPRK and Japan and the United States, respectively, and the establishment of a Northeast Asia Peace and Security mechanism. The working group on Northeast Asian peace and security was envisioned as one that would outlast the others as progress was made in resolving the North Korean nuclear crisis; eventually it would become a regular regional mechanism for the discussion of regional security.

SECURITY DILEMMAS IN NORTHEAST ASIA: ROADBLOCK TO PEACE ON THE KOREAN PENINSULA?

Despite the advancement of multilateral dialogue efforts to promote regional stability and prosperity and to overcome North Korea's continued isolation and nuclear development, those efforts are inhibited by security dilemmas that involve each of the participants to some degree. These security dilemmas constrain concerned states from pursuing more bold forms of cooperation or collective action to deal with the North Korean nuclear issue and limit the types of cooperation in which they are willing to engage to achieve these objectives.

A factor that further complicates the calculus of regional actors is that the relative balance that existed between the two Koreas on the peninsula during the most intense period of inter-Korean competition to establish respective claims to international legitimacy during the Cold War has now been replaced by a situation in which South Korea is dominant on the peninsula in every aspect, while North Korea's economic and political isolation and its pursuit of nuclear weapons for security reasons have increasingly resulted in its marginalization and isolation. To some degree, North Korea's nuclear weapons program is a last-gasp effort to compensate for the growing gap between its own power and that of South Korea.

Future political arrangements on the Korean peninsula and the shape of any future Korean reunification are much more likely to be determined in Seoul than in Pyongyang. Concerned states must consider both how their security environment will be affected by the mitigation or resolution of the North Korean nuclear issue and by the resulting security environment that would exist in the context of peace and/or reunification on the Korean peninsula. Following the achievement of peace on the Korean peninsula, some leaders may worry that their states will face a more challenging security situation in the context of a reunified Korea than currently exists. This situation exists precisely because the orientation of the Korean peninsula remains a critical security interest of major powers, especially China and Japan, which have historically viewed a friendly Korean peninsula as a critical factor affecting their own security.

North Korea

Among the six parties, North Korea's security dilemma is the most acute because it is existential. North Korea's political isolation and internal economic difficulties raise concerns about prospects for regime survival. Regime survival concerns have become a primary North Korean motivation for pursuing nuclear weapons. Unable to compete in maintaining a credible conventional military deterrent against South Korea and the United States as a result of its failing economy, North Korean leaders have sought to deter any possible attack from its enemies by pursing a nuclear development program. Although a North Korean nuclear weapons capacity might cause potential aggressors to think twice about attacking the North, North Korea's efforts have arguably enhanced its financial and political isolation, especially following its October 9, 2006, nuclear test. In response, the UN Security Council passed Resolution 1718 only five days after North Korea's nuclear test.[9] UN sanctions are set to remain in place until denuclearization occurs, offering a warning that the nuclear alternative puts North Korea's leadership at odds with the international community. To the extent that other parties are willing to undertake joint action in support of this rhetorical consensus, the six-party process relies on the latent prospect of multilateral compellance as a prod to North Korea to trade its nuclear weapons for a combination of needed economic benefits and security guarantees.

But it also depends on providing sufficient assurances that the DPRK will be confident that its security environment has improved sufficiently through a change in the U.S. "hostile policy" that the North is willing to curtail and eventually abandon its nuclear weapons program.[10] The September 19, 2005, Joint Statement among the six parties provides implicit recognition of North Korea as a full member of the Northeast Asian community, linking North Korea's denuclearization pledge to the prospect of normalized relations with both the United States and Japan, a process that would address North Korea's security dilemma by alleviating concerns about America's "hostile policy."

The February 13, 2007, implementing agreement lays out concrete initial steps, such as North Korea's shutdown and disablement of its Yongbyon facilities and American steps to remove North Korea from the terrorist list and Trading with the Enemy Act, that both sides must take toward the broader objectives of denuclearization and normalization, respectively.[11] Implementation of the agreement is a collective process, whereby each state involved in the talks will play a role in offering assurances and support to North Korea—a tangible expression of support that contributes to the survival of the North Korean regime.

More complicated, however, is that if the Joint Statement is fully implemented, North Korea's leadership may still feel an acute sense of threat if relaxation of tensions over the nuclear issue were to enable an influx of South Korean thinking and cultural norms into North Korea. Such influences might pose a direct threat to central precepts underlying the North Korean system. Thus, the alleviation of North Korea's security dilemma with the United States will only reveal the more profound dilemma that Pyongyang's leaders face in explaining to its people the success of South Korea. A second challenge is that North Korea's conception of regime survival guarantees may extend well beyond political measures to include levels of economic assistance that would both provide assurances of regime survival and eliminate motivations for internal economic reforms that are a prerequisite for the North's economic integration with its neighbors. A third complicating factor is that North Korea's political system has failed to meet minimum international governance standards necessary to assure the livelihood of its own people, posing serious political obstacles to the acceptance of any agreement with the DPRK.

The prospect of a reunified Korea offers little appeal to North Korea's leadership, which would be highly likely to lose political power in such a scenario, given the North's structural and material weakness. Given the relative strength of South Korea, any scenario would likely be shaped by preferences determined in Seoul. Even in a negotiated arrangement to promote inter-Korean reconciliation arrangements, North Korea's leadership must rely more on South Korean fears of the costs associated with the sudden collapse of the North Korean state and the residual damage that North Korea could do to South Korea's economy than on any instrument of power in inter-Korean negotiations. In the absence of any leverage of its own, North Korea continues to rely on the traditional game of playing larger powers against each other in an attempt to avoid excessive dependence on any single neighbor, attempting to leverage its economic dependency on China to catalyze South Korean economic interest in the North. North Korean leaders have even hinted to American counterparts that Pyongyang would be a valuable strategic partner in curbing China's rise.

People's Republic of China

China has historically sought to ensure that any Korean state bordering China is friendly to the PRC. For centuries, the means by which such a relationship was achieved was to ensure that the Korean peninsula was semi-dependent on China in managing its foreign affairs and that Korea remained firmly in China's cultural sphere as a tributary of China. China's security dilemma, then, is how to ensure that any future single Korean state remains friendly to—if not dependent on—China. China's overarching desire for regional stability has led the PRC to pursue policies designed to promote North Korea's survival and reform while welcoming closer economic ties with South Korea.[12]

China's primary diplomatic challenge in dealing with the North Korean nuclear issue has been the question of how to balance its interest in regional stability and the traditional view of North Korea as a "strategic buffer" against pressures from the United States to more actively play the role of a "responsible stakeholder" in the international community by taking harsh action to punish North Korea's nuclear development. China does not benefit from a nuclear North Korea to the extent that such a state triggers insecurity and is destabilizing, yet regional stability appears to remain a higher policy priority than denuclearization of the Korean peninsula. The North Korean nuclear test catalyzed a shift in Chinese security perceptions that had already been under way for some time, as the DPRK took an action that threatened regional security and negatively affected China's own national security interests. Following the test, Chinese researchers repeatedly emphasized that China's relationship with the DPRK is a "normal relationship" as opposed to the special fraternal relationship that had once existed between the two countries.[13]

The six-party process has provided China with new opportunities in its diplomacy, while also illustrating the limits of China's capacity to shape the security environment on its periphery. As host and convener of the Six-Party Talks, China for the first time played a mediating role in keeping the talks going. But the lack of progress in the talks in the initial rounds also revealed the limited tools at China's disposal to influence the United States and North Korea, respectively, to take more conciliatory positions. However, China's central role in the six-party process also guarantees that any outcome from the six-party process must conform with China's strategic interests. China's role as host of the Six-Party Talks provides implicit support to the idea of a regional security mechanism, as foreshadowed in the establishment of the Northeast Asia Peace and Security working group under the Six-Party Talks. But Chinese researchers still seem to have difficulty reconciling the existence of American alliances with the establishment of a regional security dialogue, characterizing continued adherence to the alliances as "cold-war thinking" while simultaneously acknowledging their past contributions to regional security.[14] If indeed the North Korean nuclear issue is resolved through the six-party process, it will be interesting to see whether China is willing to accept the coexistence of American alliances and multilateral Northeast Asia Peace and Security Mechanism (NEAPSM).

Recent developments have underscored Chinese anxiety to affirm its influence on the Korean peninsula. After North Korea utilized the October 2007 inter-Korean summit declaration to play on Chinese anxieties about its future role vis-à-vis the Korean peninsula by adapting language to the effect that peace might be pursued by "three or four parties," the PRC government publicly affirmed its legal and historical involvement in the negotiation of the armistice as the basis for underscoring China's indispensable role in establishing Korean peace arrangements. The opening of a U.S.-DPRK bilateral negotiating channel and U.S. chief negotiator Christopher Hill's sudden visit to Pyongyang stimulated anxieties among some Chinese analysts that an overly rapid U.S.-DPRK rapprochement might work against Chinese interests, even though the Chinese had been persistent advocates of U.S.-DPRK rapprochement.

While China continues to expand its economic influence with North Korea and to cultivate top-level interaction with Kim Jong Il, the PRC has recognized that the most important strategic decisions on the Korean peninsula will likely be made in Seoul rather than Pyongyang and has attempted to strengthen the Sino-ROK (Republic of Korea) relationship accordingly. The rapid growth of Sino-ROK economic ties has supported the improvement of the political relationship. Chinese and South Korean interests in regional stability have resulted in a convergence of their respective approaches to the North Korean nuclear issue, although historical issues, North Korean refugee issues, and South Korean fears of China's economic domination of North Korea remain points of contention.[15]

Japan

Japan faces near-term and long-term security dilemmas with respect to Japan's relations with North Korea. The near-term dilemma has intensified in the aftermath of North Korea's nuclear test and the resumption of Six-Party Talks in at least two aspects. The first aspect is related to Japan's prioritization of the abduction issue over the nuclear issue as its primary concern in dealing with North Korea. To the extent that Japanese politicians and the Japanese public continue to focus on the abduction issue as Japan's number one priority, that focus limits Japan's ability to contribute effectively to the Six-Party Talks, which are primarily focused on denuclearization. Although the abduction issue would eventually have to be dealt with as a part of the commitment on the part of the six parties to achieve normalization between Japan and the DPRK in the course of North Korea's denuclearization, Japan is not expected to participate in the implementation of the February 13, 2007, initial implementation measures because of its focus on the abduction issue. In addition, Japan-DPRK bilateral working groups held as part of the six-party process have been stalemated over the abduction issue, running the risk that the abduction issue could sidetrack the joint commitments of the six parties to the denuclearization of the Korean peninsula.

A second aspect of Japan's near-term security dilemma is related to Japanese expectations and anxieties over whether or not the United States can be depended on to defend Japan from aggression by North Korea. These anxieties are stimulated by the apparent U.S. policy about-face and decision to re-engage in Six-Party Talks after initially taking a hard-line position against North Korea's nuclear and illicit activities. To the extent that the U.S. position appears to be narrowly focused on a denuclearization-for-normalization deal, critics in Japan suggest that the United States has failed to take into account Japanese needs to see progress on the abduction issue. The 1998 North Korean Taepodong test and North Korea's 2006 missile test also remind the Japanese public that North Korean missile delivery systems pose a critical threat to Japan's security, yet missiles are not yet publicly on the U.S. diplomatic agenda or the agenda for Six-Party Talks. Six-party negotiations are a double-edged sword for Japan: to the extent that the negotiations move forward and real progress is made on denuclearization, Japan could be seen as a drag or obstacle in addressing a pressing security issue because of Japan's broader agenda; at the same time, the narrow focus on denuclearization does not fully address some of Japan's legitimate security concerns related to North Korean missile capabilities. Japan's near-term security dilemma has an impact on Japan's relationship with North Korea and its relationship with the United States and is a background factor influencing Japan-ROK relations. The September 19, 2005, Six-Party Joint Statement, however, does not envisage that Japan would be left behind; rather it envisages that Japan and the United States would both normalize relations with North Korea in exchange for North Korea's denuclearization, at which time Japan's expected economic assistance to North Korea would give Japan a major role in assisting North Korea's economic stabilization and development.

The longer-term security dilemma relates to Japanese concerns that Korean reunification might alter the status quo on the Korean peninsula in ways that might be unfavorable to Japan. To the extent that a unified Korean peninsula tilts toward China and away from Japan, such an orientation will fuel long-standing Japanese security concerns. Similar concerns would likely emerge if the deterioration of the U.S.-ROK security alliance were to result in a South Korea that would be perceived in Japan as potentially hostile or troublesome to Japan's security interests.

Russia

Russia's historical involvement in Korean peninsular affairs persists, even if its immediate capacity to influence the security situation on the peninsula is low. The opportunity to participate in the Six-Party Talks reaffirms Russia's relevance and role in Northeast Asian affairs despite its current relative lack of regional influence. Russia supports the denuclearization of the Korean peninsula and welcomes progress toward inter-Korean reconciliation and possible unification, but has relatively few diplomatic or other resources available to contribute to the process. As a result, Russia's influence on the Six-Party Talks has been marginal.

Nonetheless, Russia maintains a long-term geo-strategic interest in Korean stability. In the long term, Russian security dilemmas related to the Korean peninsula would only arise in the event that a single great power was to play a dominant role on the peninsula. Russia would welcome a unified Korea that is friendly or neutral and would oppose the continuation of a U.S. military presence in a unified Korea. But Korean reunification is unlikely to have a direct effect on Russia's vital security interests.[16]

United States

The U.S. security dilemma with respect to the situation on the Korean peninsula revolves around two primary issues. The first is the security ramifications of North Korea's nuclear program for the global proliferation regime, and especially post-9/11, as a threat to vital American security interests. American proliferation concerns are twofold. First, the United States wants to prevent transfer of fissile material to non-state actors or others who might attempt to deliver a nuclear or radiological device to the U.S. mainland. The second concern is the ramifications of North Korean proliferation for the global non-proliferation regime. In both cases, it is necessary for the Bush administration to maintain as its top priority the rollback of North Korea's nuclear program, since the costs of acceptance of the program would simply be too high to contemplate. To the extent that the non-proliferation priority is elevated above regional security concerns, it is possible that success in achieving American non-proliferation objectives may be accompanied by setbacks to American regional security interests.[17]

A secondary security dilemma that is sometimes raised for the United States is whether peace and reunification on the Korean peninsula would threaten the U.S. presence on the Korean peninsula or result in a strategic competition between the United States and China. Related to this theme is the idea that the United States needs a conflict with North Korea as a pretext for maintaining a troop presence on the Korean peninsula. However, such reasoning fails to consider that the overall trends in American global defense policy are moving in the opposite direction under the Global Posture Review. Under this strategy, the United States seeks strategic flexibility to respond to multiple potential threats and attempts to utilize advances in technology and C4I capabilities to its advantage to respond to such threats. One result is that the importance of bases focused on responding to a single fixed threat has declined.

While in the latest Quadrennial Defense Review (QDR) the Pentagon sets out as an objective to prevent the rise of a new peer competitor, this objective should not lead to the presumption that relations with China will inevitably lead to conflict. Rather, the Bush administration has clearly attempted to work together with China as a partner in addressing sources of regional stability and has actively sought China's cooperation to address the North Korean nuclear issue. Although China and the United States may have differing priorities on the Korean peninsula, China appears to be much more sensitive to the ramifications of instability on the Korean peninsula for its core national security interests than the United States is. The task for the United States is to convince China that since a nuclear North Korea is inherently destabilizing, there is no choice between regional stability and the acceptance of a nuclear North Korea. Thus far, prospects for a U.S.-China cooperative approach to North Korea's denuclearization do not appear to have been exhausted.

South Korea

South Korea is the twelfth-largest economic power in the world, while North Korea ranks near the bottom in the world in almost every development category. The tasks of reconciliation and possible reunification will impose significant burdens on South Korea as it attempts to close the socioeconomic gap between the two Koreas. In addition, future strategic orientation, economic capacity, and resources for protecting a reunified Korean peninsula within East Asia remain question marks as a factor in the broader context of Sino-Japanese relations.

South Korea's primary security dilemma lies in its simultaneous desire to pursue peace and reconciliation in inter-Korean relations and the need to see North Korea denuclearize as a task that necessarily concerns the entire region. This means that South Korea must find a way to link progress in inter-Korean reconciliation with improvements in the broader regional security environment in ways that lead to support for Seoul's position among all of South Korea's great-power neighbors. South Korean leaders must find the tools and build the capacities to manage two simultaneous tasks of promoting Korean reunification and stability while keeping in mind the security concerns and providing reassurance to its neighbors in Japan and China.

Despite the reality that Korean unification may actually be a catalyst for heightened Sino-Japanese rivalry, the task of how to achieve reunification on the peninsula absorbs so much time and energy that there is little energy left for considering how to manage the possibility of renewed Sino-Japanese rivalry. South Korean scholars have been so focused on the task of achieving inter-Korean reconciliation and eventual reunification that relatively little consideration has been given by Korean scholars to the ramifications of Korean reunification for regional stability.

A major diplomatic challenge for South Korea, then, is how to link progress in inter-Korean reconciliation with improvements in the regional security environment so as to avoid inadvertent incitement of regional rivalries. Two primary instruments draw attention among Korean analysts as a vehicle for managing such a process. First, the Roh administration has promoted Northeast Asian regional cooperation through a presidential initiative designed to lay the foundations for long-term regional security cooperation. Second, many analysts believe that the U.S.-ROK alliance remains a critical factor in maintaining regional stability that will necessarily complement efforts to expand regional security cooperation.

BEYOND THE KOREAN CONFLICT: RISING GREAT-POWER RIVALRY?

The steady progress toward establishment of a regional cooperative dialogue on how to deal with the shared problem of North Korea coexists with security dilemmas that six-party dialogue participants face as they deal with both the near-term tactics of moving forward toward denuclearization of the Korean peninsula and the long-term challenges of imagining the strategic ramifications of Korean reunification. But there are also other emerging forms of multilateral cooperation in the region driven by the motivation to hedge against China's rise. Most notably, the strengthening of the U.S.-Japan and U.S.-Australian security alliances and the signing of a new security declaration between Japan and Australia have enabled the establishment of regular trilateral security coordination dialogue among the United States, Japan, and Australia, undergirded by commonly shared democratic systems and values. In addition, the United States and Japan, respectively, have strengthened their respective relationships with India as a means by which to hedge against China's rise. However, changes in government in Japan and Australia—in combination with the inauguration of a new American president in 2009—may diminish the overt hedging character of this trilateral consultative dialogue.

One striking omission from early values-based cooperation among Asian democracies has been South Korea. Former South Korean president Roh Moo Hyun expressed concerns that a "new Cold War" in Asia would limit South Korea's diplomatic independence, flexibility, and opportunities for prosperity. The challenges for South Korean diplomacy that might be posed by renewed regional rivalry might require South Korea to maintain "relative independence from the United States."[18] However, Roh's successor, conservative pragmatist Lee Myung Bak, has welcomed closer cooperation with the United States and Japan as a priority in South Korea's foreign policy, while also seeking to maintain close ties with China based on extensive mutual economic interests.

South Korea's growing economic interdependence with China and the rise of China's political influence now requires South Korean strategists to think twice about whether China will view South Korean involvement in multilateral security arrangements as threatening. Even South Korean conservatives think twice about Chinese perceptions before being willing to return to the type of "minilateral" security cooperation signified by the Trilateral Coordination and Oversight Group of the 1990s.

CONCLUSION

The North Korean nuclear crisis has ironically proved to be a very effective catalyst for the development of regional security cooperation, culminating in the formal establishment of the Six-Party Talks as regional framework for addressing the challenge posed by North Korea's nuclear development. But each country continues to face strategic dilemmas that inhibit its willingness to fully join security cooperation at the levels necessary to fully counter North Korea's drive to become a nuclear power.

The Korean peninsula remains a strategic security concern and object of competition for influence in Northeast Asia. The division of the Korean peninsula into two separate spheres of influence, one dominated by China, the other under American domination that serves as an effective surrogate for ensuring Japan's security interests, has been a very stable and probably mutually satisfactory scenario in terms of managing China's and Japan's mutual security concerns in the Cold War context. These concerns will only be heightened in both Beijing and Tokyo if there is a change in the status quo on the Korean peninsula that has persisted since the armistice brought a halt to military conflict on the Korean peninsula. Stability between China and Japan as it relates to the Korean peninsula has come at a very high price for Koreans, who have continuously sought national reunification and restoration of a unified Korean peninsula as their highest national priority.

The de facto consolidation of power on the peninsula in the hands of Seoul, combined with North Korea's continued decline, pose internal challenges in managing any possible Korean reunification and complicate regional relations to the extent that the buffer provided by the previous rough balance between North and South is no longer sustainable. Korean reunification would likely heighten tensions and exacerbate the security dilemma between China and Japan. Both parties might compete to preserve influence on the Korean peninsula as a means to enhance their own security. Whether or not official regional security coordination mechanisms are up to the challenge of managing such a regional rivalry between great powers will be the true test of whether the institutionalization of a regional security structure can be truly effective in dispelling renewed rivalry or preventing the rise of conflicts that could jeopardize regional stability and prosperity.

NOTES

1. Paul Evans, "Constructing Multilateralism in an Anti-Region: From Six-Party Talks to a Regional Security Framework in Northeast Asia?" (paper presented at Stanford University Shorenstein Asia Pacific Research Center conference on "Crosscurrents: Regionalism and Nationalism in Northeast Asia," May 2006).

2. Andrew Mack and Pauline Kerr, "The Evolving Security Discourse in the Asia-Pacific," *Washington Quarterly* 18, no. 1 (1995): 123–140.

3. Roh Tae Woo, "Korea: A Nation Transformed," in *Selected Speeches of President Roh Tae Woo* (Seoul: Presidential Secretariat, 1990).

4. James A. Baker III, "America in Asia: Emerging Architecture for a Pacific Community," *Foreign Affairs* 70, no. 5 (Winter 1991): 1; and Don Oberdorfer, "Baker, Roh Criticize N. Korean A-Arms Effort; Future of Divided Peninsula Discussed," *Washington Post*, November 15, 1991, A36.

5. Scott Snyder, *The Korean Peninsula Energy Development Organization: Implications for Northeast Asian Regional Security Cooperation?* (Vancouver: University of British Columbia Institute for Asian Studies Working Paper Series, 2000).

6. Dennis C. Blair and John T. Hanley, "From Wheels to Webs: Reconstructing Asia Pacific Security Arrangements," *Washington Quarterly* 24, no. 1 (Winter 2001): 7.

7. "Press Conference with President George W. Bush," Federal News Service, March 6, 2003.

8. The text of the Joint Statement of the Fourth Round of Six-Party Talks may be found at www.state.gov/r/pa/prs/ps/2005/53490.htm (accessed May 22, 2007).

9. United Nations Security Council S/RES/1718 (2006), daccessdds.un.org/doc/UNDOC/GEN/N06/572/07/PDF/N0657207.pdf?OpenElement (accessed May 6, 2007).

10. Yonhap News Agency, "N. Korea Willing to Give Up Nuclear Arms if Reciprocated by US Report," November 18, 2006.

11. The text of the February 13, 2007, implementing agreement may be found at www.state.gov/r/pa/prs/ps/2007/february/80479.htm (accessed September 16, 2007).

12. See David Shambaugh, "China and the Korean Peninsula: Playing for the Long Term," *Washington Quarterly* 26, no. 2 (Spring 2003): 43–56.

13. Author interviews in Beijing, June 2007.

14. Chung Jaeho, *Between Ally and Partner: Korea-China Relations and the United States* (New York: Columbia University Press, 2006).

15. See Scott Snyder reviews of Sino-Korean relations in the quarterly e-journal *Comparative Connections* at www.csis.org/pacfor/ccejournal.html.

16. Seung-ho Joo, "Russia and the North Korean Nuclear Crisis," in *North Korea's Second Nuclear Crisis and Northeast Asian Security*, ed. Seung-ho Joo and Tae-hwan Kwak (Oxford: Ashgate, 2007), 133–150.

17. William J. Perry, "Proliferation on the Peninsula: Five North Korean Nuclear Crises," *Annals of the American Academy of Political and Social Science* 607, no. 1 (September 2006): 78–86.

18. Ki-ho Yi, "Full Text of ROK President Roh Moo-hyun's Answers to Questions in an Interview to Mark the First Anniversary of Daily Seoprise," October 21, 2005 (accessed via Open Source Center Doc #: KPP20051021053002, April 17, 2006).

VI

TRANSREGIONAL LINKAGES AND REGIONAL DYNAMICS

13

The Asian Regional Economy

Edward J. Lincoln

The Asian regional economy is the most dynamic in the world. For several decades, the region has been characterized by three important features: extreme diversity in size and affluence among the various economies, rapid economic growth, and rising intraregional linkages. Over the next several decades, the region is likely to continue growing more rapidly than most other parts of the world, and the process of intraregional economic interaction should continue to intensify. This chapter explores some of the specifics of these features.

The focus is on what is commonly termed East Asia—the countries of ASEAN (Association of Southeast Asian Nations), plus China, South Korea, Taiwan, Hong Kong, Macau, and Papua New Guinea. In addition, India is part of some of the analysis in the chapter, given India's recently increasing involvement in the Asian regional system. However, the other nations in South Asia or Central Asia are not included, mainly because they have not been engaged very much in the evolving regional economic interactions.

THE ECONOMIC LANDSCAPE

One of the striking characteristics of this region is a huge range in size and affluence among the various economies. The common measure of economic output for a country is gross domestic product (GDP), the value of all goods and services produced in a country during a specific period of time (usually measured quarterly or annually). Figure 13.1 shows the size of annual GDP in these Asian countries in 2005, with the output of each

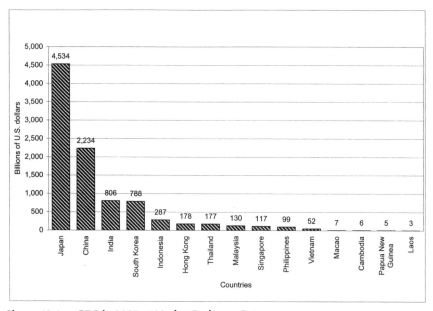

Figure 13.1.   GDP in 2005 at Market Exchange Rates.
Source: World Bank, *World Development Indicators,* online database (accessed August 12, 2007).

converted to U.S. dollars at the average exchange rate between the local currency and the U.S. dollar during the year. Market exchange rates provide an imperfect way to compare economies since these rates can sometimes make prices in a country seem unusually high or low. Nevertheless, market rates still provide a rough guide to comparing the size of countries in the region.

Japan is by far the economic giant of the region. At $4.5 trillion, Japan had an economic output 37 percent the size of the United States, making it the second-largest economy in the world (with Germany in third place). Japan represented almost 50 percent of the total output of all the Asian countries in this list. China, despite its large population, had a GDP of only $2.2 trillion, just under half the size of Japan. And the smaller economies, Macao, Cambodia, Papua New Guinea, and Laos, are only one-tenth of 1 percent the size of Japan's.

A second economic disparity in Asia is affluence. The region contains economies with high levels of economic affluence and very poor countries. The common measure that economists use is GDP divided by the total population (called GDP per capita)—showing the total amount of goods and services produced in the economy per person. While GDP per capita is a crude method of measuring affluence (since not all of the output in the country ends up as household income), it provides at least a rough means

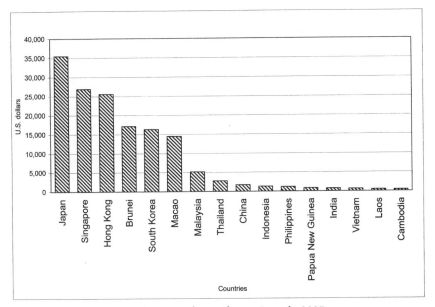

Figure 13.2.   GDP per Capita at Market Exchange Rates in 2005.
Source: World Bank, *World Development Indicators,* online database (accessed August 12, 2007).

of comparing countries. Figure 13.2 shows GDP per capita at market exchange rates for East Asian economies.

Japan began modern economic development well before most other countries in the region and by the mid-1970s was by far the most affluent economy in the region. In 2005 Japan had a GDP per capita measured at market exchange rates of $35,484, still the most affluent nation in Asia, and 85 percent the level of the United States. Japan is at roughly the same level of affluence as the major European economies. At the bottom of the distribution is Cambodia, a very poor economy with a GDP per capita of only $440, making it one of the poorest nations in the world. China's GDP per capita was $1,713, also a relatively low level, but rising rapidly over the past two decades due to the high level of economic growth.

These disparities matter when considering the possibilities for regional economic institution-building. Economies that are somewhat similar in overall size or affluence share more common economic interests. Europe exemplifies a region where the disparities among the nations that originally formed the European Union were not very large. The large disparities in Asia, on the other hand, have been an obstacle to developing institutions or region-wide economic cooperation. For example, affluent Japan (like all industrialized nations) protects its inefficient agricultural sector from imports. One particular source of friction between Japan and its Asian neighbors for many years has been Japan's policy of almost complete closure of its rice market to imports.

The final characteristic of the region is relatively high rates of economic growth. Economists argue that poor countries are capable of producing very high rates of economic growth if they can get the fundamentals for a modern market-based economy in place (along with other supporting factors such as political stability, strong education policies, and improved public health). Given the right institutional fundamentals, poor countries can accelerate growth by importing existing technology from abroad and combining it with inexpensive domestic labor. This process of "catch-up" can continue until available technology from abroad has been absorbed and growth has driven up domestic wages to levels similar to those in the advanced industrial nations. The experience of some Asian economies has provided the evidence for the possibilities for "catch-up."

The story of Asian growth begins with Japan. The process of industrialization in Japan stretches back to the 1870s, much earlier than most other economies in Asia. By the time of the Second World War, Japan had already come a long way, but lost much of its industrial facilities in a wave of destruction in the final year of the war. After the Second World War, a combination of rebuilding from wartime destruction and successful industrialization strategies resulted in the highest growth rate in the world—with an average real GDP growth rate (that is, after subtracting inflation) of almost 10 percent for the period from 1950 to 1973. This prolonged rapid growth brought Japan into the ranks of the advanced industrial nations, as noted earlier. Even after the mid-1970s, Japanese economic growth remained higher than that in the other advanced economies until the end of the 1980s.

Table 13.1 shows economic growth rates since 1980 for a number of Asian economies. Growth in Japan, the economic giant in Asia, has been quite low for much of this period. In fact, table 13.1 does not fully illustrate the problems. Japan experienced a major collapse during the 1990s in both the real estate market (with urban real estate prices falling 70 percent from an inflated high point in 1991) and stock market (with the Nikkei Index of stock prices down over 60 percent by mid-decade from its high at the end of 1989). The consequence of this collapse in asset prices, exacerbated by some mistakes in macroeconomic policy, was a decade from 1992 through 2002 when average annual growth was just under 1 percent. Growth has recovered since that time to roughly 2 percent a year. Going forward, overall growth will be further constrained by the fact that the total population (and especially the adult working-age population) began falling after 2005.

China has duplicated the high growth record of Japan over this time period, with a growth rate of almost 10 percent from 1980 to 2005. However,

Table 13.1.   Growth Rates in Asia

	1980 to 1989	*1990 to 1999*	*2000 to 2005*
Brunei	−2.4	1.4	2.8
Cambodia	NA	7.4	9.0
China	9.8	10.0	9.4
Hong Kong	7.3	3.8	5.3
India	5.9	5.7	6.5
Indonesia	6.4	4.8	4.7
Japan	3.7	1.5	1.7
South Korea	7.7	6.3	5.2
Laos	4.1	6.4	6.2
Macao	7.9	3.2	11.3
Malaysia	5.9	7.2	5.2
Myanmar	1.9	6.1	9.2
Papua New Guinea	1.4	4.9	1.1
Philippines	2.0	2.8	4.7
Singapore	7.5	7.5	5.0
Thailand	7.3	5.3	5.0
Vietnam	4.5	7.4	7.4

Source: Calculated from data in World Bank, *World Development Indicators*, online database (accessed August 20, 2007).

since China was so poor when rapid growth began, it is still far from being an affluent nation, as indicated in the earlier discussion of GDP per capita. China ought to be able to continue its high growth for several more decades, although it faces potential constraints from increasingly dysfunctional air and water pollution. In addition, China (like Japan) will experience a falling population within two more decades, due to the policy of one family, one child.

India, the other population giant in Asia, has not grown as rapidly as China. From the 1950s until the mid-1990s, India favored a development strategy called "import substitution," in which the government establishes barriers to imports and to inward investment by foreign firms in order to stimulate the growth of domestically owned firms. This strategy was not very successful, as is the case in most developing countries that have tried it. Rather than promoting domestic growth, this strategy tends to produce very inefficient domestic firms that actually impede growth beyond a certain point. Since the mid-1990s, India has lowered import barriers and encouraged investment by foreign firms. As a result, table 13.1 shows that Indian growth has accelerated from an average of 5.7 percent in the 1990s to 6.5 percent in the current decade.

Growth in the rest of the Asian economies in this table is mixed. On average, they have grown relatively fast (and faster than the averages in other parts of the developing world in Latin America, Africa, the Middle East, and

Eastern Europe), but not as fast as China. Some of these countries, and especially Thailand, Indonesia, and South Korea, were hit by a major economic crisis in 1997, sparked by a collapse in the exchange rates of their currencies (an issue considered later in this chapter). This episode is known as the Asian financial crisis. In 1998 Indonesia experienced a devastating 13 percent drop in real GDP, while the drop in Thailand was 10 percent and South Korea 7 percent. Other countries experiencing a contraction in that year included Brunei (4 percent), Japan (2 percent), Macao (5 percent), Malaysia (7 percent), Papua New Guinea (4 percent), the Philippines (1 percent), and Singapore (1 percent). All countries hit with declining GDP in that year subsequently recovered; the downturn was short-lived. However, average growth in the years from 1999 to the present has been generally somewhat lower than in the decade prior to the crisis.

Trade Flows

A principal reason people think of East Asia as an emerging cohesive region is rising trade linkages. However, much of that perception is due to the rapid rise of China as a trading partner for all other nations in the region. China's rise as a trade partner actually affects many nations in the world, including the United States and others outside Asia.

Figure 13.3 shows what has happened to the share of intraregional trade to total trade of the East Asian economies (ASEAN, Japan, China, South Korea, Hong Kong, Macao, and Taiwan). Intraregional exports of the economies within the region were around 32 percent of their global exports, while intraregional imports were 38 percent of total imports in the mid-1980s. These shares rose until the late 1990s. As of 2005, intraregional exports were 40 percent of total exports by the countries in the region, and intraregional imports were 46 percent of total imports. Although the rising intraregional trade shares leveled off after the late 1990s, the overall picture is one of a region that has become somewhat more reliant upon trade within itself (and, therefore, somewhat less reliant upon trade with the rest of the world).

The pattern of increased relative importance of trade with the region is most evident when looking at Japan. Figure 13.4 shows Japan's imports. In the twenty years since the mid-1980s, the share of Japan's imports coming from the rest of East Asia has steadily increased, from a level of 27 percent to almost 45 percent, a very sizable increase. However, all of that increase is due to imports from only one country: China. Japan's imports from East Asia other than China were no higher as a share of total imports in 2005 than they were in 1985.

The picture for Japan's exports is a bit different, as shown in figure 13.5. Once again, all of East Asia has been an increasingly important destination

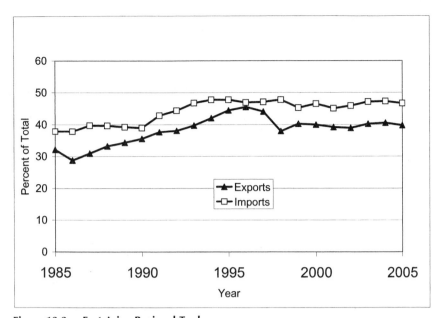

Figure 13.3. East Asian Regional Trade.
Source: International Monetary Fund, *Direction of Trade Statistics*, online database (accessed August 10, 2007).

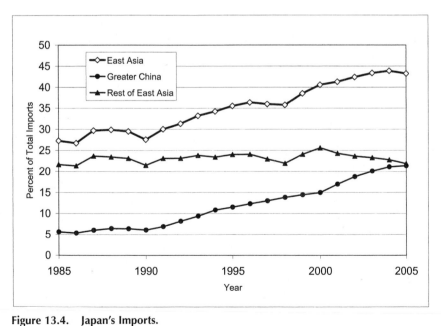

Figure 13.4. Japan's Imports.
Source: International Monetary Fund, *Direction of Trade Statistics*, online database (accessed August 10, 2007).

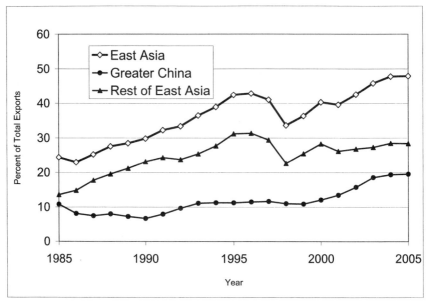

Figure 13.5.   Japan's Exports.
Source: International Monetary Fund, *Direction of Trade Statistics,* online database (accessed August 10, 2007).

for Japanese exports, rising from 25 percent of total exports in the mid-1980s to almost 50 percent by 2005. In this case, East Asia other than China absorbed a rising share of Japanese exports, rising from 15 percent to 30 percent from 1980 to 1995, but no increase has occurred since then. Instead, since 2000 all of the increase has come from China, with China expanding from 10 percent to 20 percent of all Japan's exports in only six years. These trends in Japan's trade help explain why the Japanese have been leaders in talking about the desirability of dialogue and cooperation among East Asian governments.

Figure 13.6 shows ASEAN imports. In this case, the evidence of an overall increased importance of trade with East Asia is quite modest; 50 percent of ASEAN imports were from East Asia back in 1985, rising only marginally to 55 percent by 2005. Reliance on East Asia as a source of imports is certainly high, because the ASEAN countries trade with one another and exist in a region with Japan, an economic giant that is naturally a major trading partner. But the important point is that over time there has been only a modest shift in the sourcing of ASEAN imports toward the East Asian region. Behind this general trend, though, has been an important shift away from Japan (with imports declining almost by half from 20 percent of total imports to only 12 percent over this time

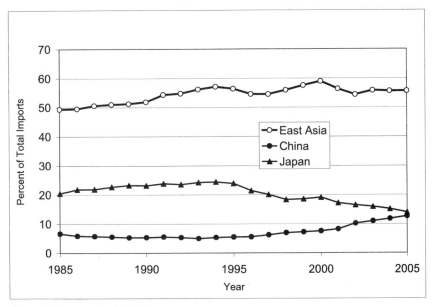

Figure 13.6.   ASEAN Imports.
Source: International Monetary Fund, *Direction of Trade Statistics,* online database (accessed August 10, 2007).

period) toward China (with imports rising from 4 percent to 12 percent of total imports).

The same picture is true of ASEAN exports, shown in figure 13.7. The share of total exports destined to the rest of East Asia was 53 percent in 1985 and 55 percent in 2005. Meanwhile, exports to China rose substantially (from 2 percent to 12 percent of total exports). The share of exports destined to Japan, on the other hand, declined (from 15 percent to 10 percent of total exports).

Finally, consider what has happened to China's trade. The definition of China here is the People's Republic of China plus Hong Kong (minus the trade between the two of them). The reason for using this definition of China is that much of Hong Kong's trade consists of transshipments to and from the PRC, so it makes no sense to treat the two of them separately. Trade between China and Hong Kong is sufficiently substantial that this adjustment lowers the share of China's intraregional trade compared to looking at the PRC alone. Figure 13.8 shows Chinese exports. The share of total exports destined to the rest of East Asia has jumped around, but with no upward trend; the share in 2005 (27 percent) was actually a bit lower than in 1985 (32 percent). Within that relatively flat trend, Japan has declined a bit as a destination while East Asia other than Japan increased slightly.

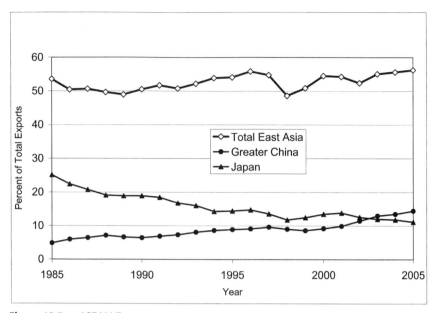

Figure 13.7.   ASEAN Exports.
Source: International Monetary Fund, *Direction of Trade Statistics,* online database (accessed August 10, 2007).

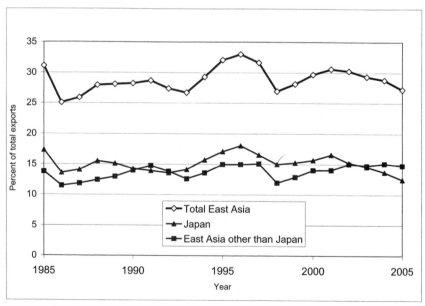

Figure 13.8.   Greater China Exports.
Source: International Monetary Fund, *Direction of Trade Statistics,* online database (accessed August 10, 2007).

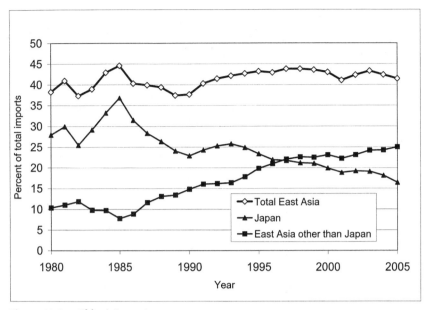

Figure 13.9. China's Imports.
Source: International Monetary Fund, *Direction of Trade Statistics,* online database (accessed August 10, 2007).

The same flat trend is true for China's imports (figure 13.9). Imports from East Asia as a whole have fluctuated in a band of 40–45 percent of total exports and were close to the same level in 2005 as in 1985. But in this case, a much sharper shift has occurred with Japan, with the share of imports sourced from Japan peaking in 1985 at 37 percent, and then falling rather steadily to only 15 percent by 2005, with East Asia other than Japan rising from 8 percent to 25 percent over the 1985–2005 period.

These trade data lead to several conclusions. First, much of what appears to be a rising East Asian bloc is due to the very rapid rise of China as a trade partner. This, however, is true for all countries that trade with China, and not just those in East Asia. The combination of very rapid economic growth and the expansion of both exports and imports as a share of GDP have resulted in this stunning growth of China as a trade partner.

Second, at the same time that China has become a more important trading partner, Japan has shrunk in relative importance. The rest of Asia is much less connected to Japan through trade today than was the case twenty years earlier. This trend is important because the initial American interest in an emerging East Asian region was driven by the notion of a region coalescing around Japan.[1] Japan's slow economic growth since the early 1990s explains why it has become a less important export destination for regional exports (relative to the more rapid growth that has sucked in more imports in China and elsewhere). A rising value for Japan's currency (the yen) against other currencies since the mid-1980s explains why Japan has declined relatively as a source for regional imports (as Japanese products have become more expensive due to the exchange rate movement).

Third, part of what is happening is the result of changing production location. The relocation of Japanese manufacturing production from high-cost Japan to lower-cost ASEAN, for example, should explain much of the decline of Japan as a relative source of China's imports since 1985. The investment by Japanese firms around the region as they sought lower-cost production bases is considered later in this chapter. As a result, *Japanese firms* are still important in explaining regional integration even though *Japan* has become less important as a trade partner.

Trade Policy

Global trade is loosely governed by the World Trade Organization (WTO), which presides over global trade negotiations in which all members agree to mutual reductions in trade barriers. A number of these negotiations have occurred in the years since 1947 when the organization was originally formed (then called the General Agreement on Tariffs and Trade). However, the WTO permits pairs or groups of its members to negotiate so-called free trade agreements among themselves (not offered to all the other members of the WTO), as long as they remove substantially all the barriers among themselves. These agreements have become quite popular around the world in the past two decades. East Asia is no exception, especially in the years since 2000.

Some of these agreements have been within the region—the ASEAN Free Trade Area, Japan-Singapore, and others. China has signed an agreement with all of ASEAN, due to come into full effect in 2010, and as of 2007 Japan was negotiating a similar agreement with ASEAN. Those agreements give the image of a region that is coming closer together as a distinctive economic bloc. Indeed, from time to time there is talk of creating a broad East Asia free trade area. Nevertheless, many of these individual agreements are between governments within the region and partners outside (South Korea–Chile, Japan-Mexico, Singapore–United States, and others). The real impact of such agreements in making the region a more cohesive whole, therefore, is still unclear.

The same lack of clarity exists for less formal discussions of economic policy. The oldest group, the Asia-Pacific Economic Cooperation (APEC) meetings, began in 1989 and includes the United States, Australia, Canada, and other governments not part of East Asia. APEC members discuss a number of broad economic issues, but the organization has worked through a principle of voluntary implementation of decisions (unlike a free trade area where the agreements are binding on the member countries). Since 1993, APEC has included an annual summit meeting (in addition to the existing ministerial and working-level meetings), often marking the one time a year that the American president travels to East Asia.

APEC has a rival in the ASEAN + 3 group (ASEAN plus Japan, China, and South Korea), a group that began meeting at the ministerial level in 1995 and added a summit meeting in 1997. In structure the two groups are quite similar—discussing a number of economic issues but reaching non-binding decisions. The two most substantial decisions emerging from this group are the Chiang Mai Initiative and the Asian Bond Fund (discussed later in this chapter), though neither development involves a membership defined entirely by membership in this group. In 2005 the ASEAN + 3 group created a new East Asian Summit meeting following immediately upon the annual ASEAN + 3 discussions that include Australia, New Zealand, and India in addition to the ASEAN + 3 members.

Whether the institutional developments that bring the region together will proceed predominantly through a broad approach that includes the United States, Australia, and others on the Pacific Rim (as in the APEC grouping) or more narrowly along an East Asian format remains unclear. And if the East Asian format dominates, will the predominant format include just the ASEAN + 3 governments or include the somewhat broader East Asian Summit participants? These remain issues to be resolved in coming years.

Direct Investment

Another reason that people viewed Japan as the pivotal force in East Asian regionalism in the 1990s was the role of Japanese manufacturing firms shifting production to other Asian locations, beginning in the mid-1980s. Particularly after the yen had risen strongly against the dollar in 1985, manufacturers were eager to relocate production to countries with lower labor costs. East Asian nations were a natural choice (since investing there involved crossing fewer time zones, easing the task of managing factories abroad). Some Japanese firms are well known for having established strong regional production networks, especially in the electronics industry.

Such developments should show up in data on foreign direct investment. These numbers measure cross-border investments where the investor has a controlling voice in the asset purchased. As a matter of statistical practice, most countries include any investment from abroad into a company that has 10 percent or more of its shares owned by a single foreign investor as a

290 *Edward J. Lincoln*

foreign direct investment, but in practice most investments involve cases where the foreign investor has a clear controlling ownership share of 50 percent to 100 percent.

Investment data for the region provide a cautious picture of regionalization based on Japan. Figure 13.10 shows foreign direct investment flows into ASEAN, comparing 1995–2000 to 2001–2005. The largest investors in ASEAN are European firms (27 percent of the total value of foreign direct investment flowing into ASEAN in the 2001–2005 period), followed by the Americans (15 percent), and trailed by Japanese firms (10 percent). The relative share of Japanese firms fell between the two time periods, having been a higher 18 percent in the 1995–2000 period. Interestingly, the creation of the ASEAN Free Trade Area ought to have led to increased intra-ASEAN investment flows, but that has not occurred. The share of intra-ASEAN investments actually declined a bit, from 15 percent in the 1995–2000 period to 11 percent in the 2001–2005 period.

Investments into South Korea and China show essentially the same results: Japanese firms are not dominant, and the relative role of Japanese firms as investors has declined over time.[2] Thus, while it is certainly true that Japanese firms have strengthened their linkages with the rest of the re-

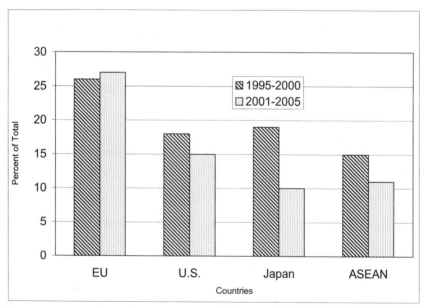

Figure 13.10. Foreign Direct Investment Flows into ASEAN.

Source: ASEAN Secretariat, "Foreign Direct Investment Statistics," www.aseansec.org/18144.htm (accessed July 31, 2007), and ASEAN Statistical Yearbook 2004, www.aseansec.org/syb2004.htm (accessed July 31, 2007).

gion through investment, so have American and European firms. East Asia is more connected to Europe and the United States in a relative sense than a decade or two before.

Financial Cooperation

Some Asian currencies and economies suffered a serious temporary blow in 1997, as previously explained. Prior to the crisis, most East Asian governments either pegged or heavily managed the exchange value of their currencies. Table 13.2 shows the International Monetary Fund's characterization of the exchange rate regimes of East Asian countries. At one end of the spectrum are independently floating rates, determined entirely (or mostly) by investors in foreign exchange markets. At the other end of the spectrum are countries with pegged rates, implying that the government is committed to maintaining a fixed rate between the domestic currency and foreign currency (most frequently the U.S. dollar). An extreme version of pegged rates is the currency board system, in which the board substitutes for the central bank, setting domestic monetary policy to be consistent with the chosen exchange rate. In between, some governments declare that their currency is allowed to float but intervene heavily in the market to influence the level of the rate.

Table 13.2.   Official Foreign Exchange Regimes

Country	1996	2006
Brunei	Currency board (Singapore dollar peg)	Currency board (Singapore dollar peg)
Cambodia	Managed float	Managed float
China	Pegged	Pegged
Hong Kong	Currency board	Currency board
India	Managed float	Managed float
Indonesia	Managed float	Managed float
South Korea	Managed float	Independent float
Japan	Independent float	Independent float
Laos	Managed float	Managed float
Malaysia	Managed float	Managed float
Myanmar	Pegged	Managed float
Papua New Guinea	Independent float	Managed float
Philippines	Independent float	Independent float
Singapore	Managed float	Managed float
Thailand	Pegged	Managed float
Vietnam	Pegged	Pegged

Source: International Monetary Fund, *Annual Report on Exchange Arrangements and Exchange Regimes* (Washington, D.C.: International Monetary Fund, 1996 and 2006 editions).
Note: A currency board is an extreme form of a pegged rate.

The danger with all pegged rates (and managed rates if they are so heavily managed as to resemble a pegged rate) is that fundamental economic conditions may become inconsistent with the existing exchange rate. Governments can defend their exchange rate by acting as participants in the foreign exchange market. In the case of a currency facing downward pressure, the government sells foreign currency from its official foreign exchange reserves (usually held in the form of U.S. dollars) in exchange for the local currency. The problem with this strategy is that central banks have finite amounts of foreign exchange reserves. Once those reserves are gone, private investors know that the government will have to abandon its effort to defend the currency. The alternative is for the government to alter macroeconomic policies to be more consistent with the exchange rate (which is what currency boards do), but governments are often reluctant to adopt such policies. The government of an economy whose currency is under pressure to fall in value would need to raise domestic interest rates and cut its fiscal deficit (raise taxes or cut government spending)—policies that would harm domestic economic growth and are, therefore, not popular.

Exactly this kind of inconsistency emerged in 1997 for several East Asian economies, affecting mostly Thailand, Indonesia, and South Korea. The crisis began in the summer with the Thai baht and quickly spread to the Indonesian rupiah. Both currencies declined sharply against the dollar once the two governments abandoned the effort to protect the exchange rate through direct intervention in the foreign exchange market. Later in 1997, South Korea faced similar pressures. By the beginning of 1998, the Thai baht had dropped 50 percent in value against the dollar, the Indonesian rupiah by 83 percent, and the South Korean won by 50 percent. Other East Asian countries experienced smaller declines.

The drop in foreign exchange rates created a problem for these countries. Domestic firms that had borrowed money abroad usually incurred loans denominated in U.S. dollars. Repaying those loans became much more difficult, since the borrowers needed to earn more in their local currencies to pay back each dollar of the loan. This problem was especially acute for firms that borrowed from abroad in dollars to finance domestic investments that generated income only in the local currency (such as building apartment buildings) rather than to finance factories producing exports (that earn foreign currency). Inability to repay loans led to widespread bankruptcies among borrowing firms in the crisis countries. This problem contributed to the short but sharp economic contraction in some East Asian countries in 1998.

The East Asian financial crisis had three main consequences. First, some governments chose to stop pegging or heavily managing their currencies. In table 13.2, the only country identified by the IMF of making a major change is South Korea, moving from a heavily managed float to an independent float. But Malaysia, Thailand, and Indonesia have permitted greater variability in their exchange rates since 1997 despite still being designated as operating managed floats. The advantage of floating rates (even if occasionally managed by the government) is that they avoid the kind of sharp break and steep decline that characterized the 1997 crisis. If foreign investors had faced a floating Thai baht, they would have been more cautious in lending to Thai borrowers (especially borrowers who would be using the funds to build businesses earning revenue in baht rather than dollars). Thus, excess borrowing from abroad based on a mistaken belief in the fixed nature of the exchange would not have occurred, and a mild depreciation of the currency rather than a sharp drop would have been the probable outcome in 1997.

The second consequence of the crisis has been for all Asian countries to increase their foreign exchange reserves in order to better protect their currencies in the future in the event that downward pressures should recur in foreign exchange markets. From $19 billion in 1996 (just before the crisis), foreign exchange reserves held by the central bank of Indonesia reached $43 billion by 2006. For Thailand, the increase was from $39 billion to $67 billion. And for South Korea, the increase was enormous, from $34 billion to $239 billion. Thus, the principal crisis countries of 1997 all had much larger foreign exchange reserves if they desired to intervene to protect their currencies from pressure to depreciate in the future.[3]

However, it is worth pointing out that the biggest holdings of foreign exchange reserves in the region had nothing to do with a desire to build protection against potential future depreciation pressures. Japan and China have very large reserves that also increased over time, due to the reluctance of either government to let their currencies appreciate as much as market pressures indicated. These two currencies have been under pressure in foreign exchange markets to appreciate (increase in value against other currencies), but the governments have entered the foreign exchange market (buying U.S. dollars) to offset the market pressure.

Japan has a floating exchange rate, but the government has attempted periodically to influence the market outcomes. The rationale of the government has been to help exports (since exporters find their products become less price competitive in global markets when the exchange rate appreciates).[4] The government has not intervened since 2004, but the result of earlier efforts, the size of Japan's official foreign exchange reserves was $900 billion by 2006. The Chinese government has been more aggressive in recent years, motivated by the same desire to help the export sector, and its foreign exchange reserves reached $1.1 trillion by 2006.[5]

This continuing large-scale intervention in foreign exchange markets to offset upward pressure on the renminbi has sparked considerable anger among import-competing businesses and politicians in other countries, and particularly in the United States. Since 2005, the Chinese government has permitted the renminbi to appreciate slowly against the dollar, but as of 2007, the currency issue remained on the American political agenda.

The third consequence of the 1997 Asian financial crisis was the initiation of a regional dialogue on financial cooperation. This dialogue has resulted in two regional policy developments—a "swap" agreement among some central banks and an Asian bond fund. Although they are both modest steps, they represent interesting steps in regional cooperation.

In May 2000, the ASEAN + 3 finance ministers' meeting reached an agreement to have their central banks create (or expand) bilateral agreements to swap foreign exchange holdings, known as the Chiang Mai Initiative (named after the Thai city where the meeting occurred). In such an arrangement, one central bank lends another holdings of another's foreign exchange reserves to another country's central bank, expanding the resources available to the borrowing government to defend its currency. The Chiang Mai Initiative provided a framework for individual central banks in East Asia to work out swap agreements with other individual central banks in the region. In general, the bilateral agreements worked out over the next several years involved central banks of Japan, South Korea, and China offering to act as lenders, and China, South Korea, Malaysia, Thailand, Philippines, Indonesia, and Singapore as borrowers.

The International Monetary Fund (IMF), the multilateral institution that oversees global financial and exchange rate issues, also lends money to governments requesting help in defending their currencies. However, IMF procedures for approving such loans can take time. One of the advantages of bilateral swap arrangements, therefore, can be speed in implementation. On the other hand, bilateral swap arrangements can undermine the central role of the IMF in dealing with international financial crises. IMF loans, for example, generally come with conditionality—requirements for the borrowing government to fix the economic problems that led to the currency crisis in the first place. Discussion of the desirability of regional cooperation originally arose out of strong dissatisfaction with the initial conditionality terms imposed by the IMF during the Asian financial crisis in the fall of 1997, conditions that were widely perceived as incorrect (a mistake later acknowledged by the IMF itself and corrected). In the fall of 1997, the Japanese government had proposed an Asian Monetary Fund, which would act as a regional substitute for the IMF, and presumably have less stringent conditionality. That proposal was not implemented—in part due to opposition from the U.S. government at the time. The Chiang Mai Initiative emerged as a lesser version of the Asian Monetary Fund.

To deflect concern by the United States or the IMF that the Chiang Mai Initiative might undermine the role of the IMF, the initial agreement called for only 10 percent of the agreed funds to become available on short notice;

the other 90 percent would become available after receiving IMF approval. In May 2005, the involved governments raised the limit from 10 percent to 20 percent, while also calling for an increase in the size of the swap amounts. The revised agreement also called for two-way agreements (principally with Japan agreeing to be potential borrower).

Table 13.3 shows the amounts of the swap arrangements as of 2007. Japan has offered the most money through these swap arrangements, for a total of $31 billion spread across agreements with seven other governments. South Korea ($13 billion) and Indonesia ($12 billion) have the largest credit lines to draw upon in these arrangements—keeping in mind that they would need to negotiate separately with each of the potential lenders before activating these loans.

The Chiang Mai Initiative was a modest step—the amounts of money are not large (in comparison to the size of daily foreign exchange transactions that occur when investors have doubts about a currency), and a limit on how much of the loans can be activated without IMF approval remains in place even though it has been relaxed somewhat. Nevertheless, the Chiang Mai Initiative is important because it represents the first time finance officials in East Asia cooperated among themselves. If nothing else, the networking among these ministries and officials occasioned by this process enhanced regional communication, something that would be important should future regional financial problems emerge.

The other regional cooperative development has been the creation of a regional bond fund—the Asian Bond Fund. This development also emerged out of the 1997 financial crisis. The theory was that if Asian governments (and local private-sector firms) could borrow long-term money from other Asian economies, then they would be less vulnerable to the behavior of (possibly fickle) Western investors. This belief led to an initial agreement in 2003 within a new regional group called the Executives' Meeting of East Asia–Pacific Central Banks (EMEAP). Although the basic concept was a topic within ASEAN + 3 discussions, this group has a different membership. The eleven members of this group are the central banks of Japan, Australia, China, Hong Kong, Indonesia, South Korea, Malaysia, New Zealand, Philippines, Singapore, and Thailand. Thus, it includes Hong Kong, Australia, and New Zealand and excludes the newer members of ASEAN.[6]

The initial Asian Bond Fund established a fund to purchase government bonds denominated in U.S. dollars by eight of the members of the AEEAP (ASEAN Environmental Education Action Plan: China, Hong Kong, Indonesia, South Korea, Malaysia, Philippines, Singapore, and Thailand). The agreement was revised in 2004 to permit purchases of bonds denominated in local currencies and those issued by quasi-governmental organizations.[7]

The Asian Bond Fund represents another modest step in regional cooperation. Involving regional central banks as buyers of bond issues by

Table 13.3. Chiang Mai Initiative Swap Arrangements

Borrower	Lender						
	Japan	China	South Korea	Indonesia	Philippines	Singapore	Thailand
Japan	—	—	—	5	0.5	1	3
China	3	—	2	—	—	—	—
South Korea	6	1	—	2	—	—	—
Indonesia	6	4	2	—	—	—	—
Malaysia	1	1	1	—	—	—	—
Philippines	6	1	3	—	—	—	—
Singapore	3	—	—	—	—	—	—
Thailand	6	2	—	—	—	—	—

Sources: Edward J. Lincoln, *East Asian Economic Regionalism* (Washington, D.C.: Brookings Institution, 2002), 221; Bank of Japan, www.boj.or.jp/en; and Bank of Korea, www.bok.or.kr/eng/index.jsp (accessed September 10, 2007).

governments and government-affiliated organizations in other regional economies creates a somewhat artificial regional bond market (if the purchases are motivated by political rather than profit considerations). True emergence of an integrated regional financial market would require a private market in which issuers in one country can issue bonds denominated in their own currencies (rather than the dollar) in the principal financial centers of the region (Tokyo, Hong Kong, and Singapore). Such a market would require further regulatory and other changes to make these centers sufficiently attractive for regional issuers to use them (rather than using New York or London).

Optimists see the modest steps of the Chiang Mai Initiative and the Asian Bond Fund as leading over a period of several decades to the kind of tight financial integration that characterizes the European Union, with its common currency.[8] A unified currency would remove currency fluctuations in the region, and presumably thereby increase the flow of trade and investment (since exporters, importers, and investors would not need to worry about losing profits through an unexpected movement in exchange rates). The chief obstacle to such a move, however, is the need for a single central bank to set a uniform monetary policy. A single regional central bank implies a willingness to cede sovereignty over domestic monetary policy to an organization that may be heavily influenced by officials from other countries. At the present time, it is unlikely that the Japanese would be willing to accept a central bank with strong Chinese involvement, or that the Chinese would want Japanese officials dominating regional monetary policy.

Aside from political leadership questions, a single monetary policy may be unworkable given the wide disparity in macroeconomic conditions across the region. Japan is a mature economy with a chronic excess of domestic savings over the desired level of domestic investment—a condition that leads to low domestic interest rates. Many of the developing countries in the region have high economic growth rates leading to strong demand for investment that often outstrips the available domestic savings—a condition that yields relatively high interest rates. Until the developing countries have undergone several more decades of rapid growth that bring them up to a level of affluence closer to Japan's, it is difficult to imagine how a single monetary policy for all would be possible.

CONCLUSION

The economic story of East Asia over the past half century has been a remarkable one. Rapid economic growth, beginning with Japan and then spreading to a number of other countries in the region, has transformed the lives of hundreds of millions of people in the region. Japan, of course, is not growing quickly now, but the main explanation lies in the fact that it is a mature, advanced industrial nation with a very high level of affluence. China has been the most remarkable growth story in recent years, although it faces challenges in the near future from both environmental problems and an eventual decline in population. India, on the other hand, appears to have shrugged off its economic sluggishness of the past as economic reforms have taken place and could become an exciting growth story of the next several decades.

Although the region includes countries that remain very poor, the region as a whole has become a model of successful economic development. Countries across the region have embraced reforms supporting market-based economic activity, as well as lowering import barriers and accepting large levels of inward foreign direct investment. Barring disruptions from military conflict or some unexpected global economic crisis, rapid growth should continue in much of the region in coming decades. Hopefully, even the poorest countries where the least reform has occurred—Laos and Cambodia—will be drawn into the circle of successful growth.

Along with rapid growth, the distinguishing feature of this region has been increasing economic interconnections and an accompanying dialogue among regional governments. This chapter has emphasized that the trade and investment interconnections should not be overestimated. Intraregional trade has increased moderately, but much of the shift is due to the very rapid rise of China as a trade partner (a rise so rapid that it has offset the decline in the relative role of Japan as a trade partner). Bilateral and subregional free trade agreements have knit together some of the members of the region, but some of these agreements also involve partners outside the region. Meanwhile, direct investment flowing into the region is expanding, but the largest investors are from outside the region (European and American firms). Finally, the intraregional financial cooperation efforts described in this chapter have been quite modest.

What should one conclude from all these developments? Regional economic ties and intergovernmental dialogue are continuing to evolve. However, the wide economic, historical, and cultural diversity in the region suggests that movement toward stronger regional agreements and institutional structures will remain slow and modest. Emergence of a strong regional institutional arrangement similar to the European Union is unlikely—at least in the next several decades. Nevertheless, East Asia is likely to continue a process of modestly increasing cooperation, and the boundaries of participation may expand, especially with India becoming more closely connected to the group of East Asian countries that formed the main part of the analysis in this chapter.

Whether the United States will be a major participant in these regional developments is unclear. Economic connections between East Asia and the

United States are strong, and the U.S. government is a leading player in APEC. Perhaps the government-level dialogue will continue to proceed on parallel tracks, with both APEC and an East Asian approach. In either approach, one of the important conclusions to draw from the developments described in this chapter is that the expanding experience with dialogue and cooperation on economic issues—all leading in the direction of encouraging expanded economic linkages—underwrites forces in favor of peaceful resolution of political or strategic problems considered in other chapters.

NOTES

1. For an example of this view, see Walter Hatch and Kozo Yamamura, *Asia in Japan's Embrace: Building a Regional Production Alliance* (Cambridge: Cambridge University Press, 1996).

2. For further detail on foreign direct investment flows in East Asia, see Edward J. Lincoln, *East Asian Economic Regionalism* (Washington, D.C.: Brookings Institution Press, 2004), 72–113.

3. Data from International Monetary Fund, *International Financial Statistics* (database accessed online, September 11, 2007).

4. For a full discussion of this policy of the Japanese government, see Taggart Murphy and Akio Mikuni, *Japan's Policy Trap: Dollars, Deflation, and the Crisis of Japanese Finance* (Washington, D.C.: Brookings Institution Press, 2002).

5. International Monetary Fund, *International Financial Statistics*, online database (accessed September 10, 2007).

6. Asian Development Bank, "EMEAP Asian Bond Fund," asianbondsonline .adb.org/regional/asean%203_asian_bond_markets_initiative/related_initiatives/ emep_asian_bond_fund.php (accessed December 8, 2007).

7. Bank of Japan, "Subscription to the Asian Bond Fund 2," www.boj.or.jp/ en/type/release/zuiji/kako03/un0412a.htm (accessed September 8, 2007).

8. For example, see C. H. Kwan, *Yen Bloc: Toward Economic Integration in Asia* (Washington, D.C.: Brookings Institution Press, 2001); or Policy Council of the Japan Forum on International Relations, *Economic Globalization and Options for Asia* (Tokyo: Japan Forum on International Relations, 2000).

14

Globalization and International Politics in Asia

Nayan Chanda

There are perhaps as many definitions of globalization as there are Hindu gods. It is thus imperative to begin with a brief outline of the definition in this chapter. In my recent book on globalization, I argued that it is a long historical process of growing connections at different levels among societies that has matured into today's interdependent world.[1] At least four distinct human motivations have created and continue to shape the interconnected world we know today: to find a safer, more prosperous, and fulfilling life as expressed in the desire to profit from trade; the urge to convert fellow human beings to one's belief; the desire to explore and enjoy the unknown; and the urge to dominate and control others. The same basic motivations drive many more actors in integrating the world: yesterday's traders are today's corporations and businesses; the ranks of religious preachers have expanded with new secular believers who now include NGOs and civil society organizations; and the desire to explore and settle that led adventurers now drives migrants and tourists. What began in the dawn of history as a leader/warrior's urge to dominate others and secure resources spawned kingdoms and empires, laying the foundation of modern states. Successors of empires have emerged as sovereign states, inheriting the role of the "warriors" or colonizers as providers of security and law.

Compared to other regions of the world, Asian countries have been shaped most of all by traders and preachers during much of the modern era. The region's openness to trade and foreign contact also gave Asia a prime position as the shaper of a globalized world. Asia's early success in manufacturing—cotton textiles and jewelry in India, silk and porcelain in China—and the lure of its products—spices, tea, pearls—have invited traders from the Mediterranean world. They traveled the Silk Road and sailed across the Arabian Sea and Indian Ocean to reach the ultimate source of luxury in Asia. Indians sipped Italian wine and the ultimate proof of wealth in the twelfth century was owning African slaves. Muslim traders from India and Arabia introduced Islam to Southeast Asia. During the Age of Exploration in the sixteenth century, those early contacts exploded into large-scale trade and the introduction of Christianity to large parts of Asia ruled by traders-turned-colonial-rulers. The Opium Wars and Commodore Perry's forcible "opening" of the Japanese "door" were only the more recent examples of traders and warriors shaping Asian history. European presence in the region also exposed Europeans to Asian philosophy and science.[2] Ironically, Taoist philosophy brought from China to France introduced the concept of laissez-faire, whereas European contact introduced Marxism-Leninism into Asia—the consequences of which are still being felt long after colonial rule has crumbled.

In the post–World War II period, traders—more than any other actors—have come to shape the Asian scene. In recent decades, trade as a percentage of the GDP has continued to grow—increasing the role of globalization in the development of the region. The word "globalization" that has become increasingly current in Asian vocabulary, however, burst into public consciousness with the storm of the 1997 Asian financial crisis—the first major traumatic event on a region-wide scale brought about by foreign connections. In the political turmoil that ensued, one regime (Indonesia) was toppled, two governments (Thailand and South Korea) had to cede place to the opposition, and in another (Malaysia) a major crisis split the ruling party. The anti-globalization movement, sputtering so far among small groups of ecologists or left-wing Asians, gained wider adherents. As Samuel Kim has noted, given the extremely trade-dependent character of East Asian countries,

> There is no exit from globalization that would not entail major economic, social and political sacrifices. The strategic choice for East Asian countries is no longer, if it ever was, between exit and engagement, it is one of constant adaptation to the logic of globalization and quickening economic, cultural and social product cycles.[3]

FINANCIAL GLOBALIZATION: ORDEAL OF FIRE

History is a continuum, and any attempt at periodization is bound to be artificial and fragmented. Still, several technological and policy developments in the field of trade and finance came together in the past two decades to make this period an intensified phase in which globalization played a critical role. The 1985 Plaza Accord forced Japan to revalue the yen and begin offshoring its production to low-cost Southeast Asia. The Big Bang financial reform in Britain (1986) was followed shortly thereafter by other European countries, and the United States opened its capital markets to the world (daily transactions in ten stock markets in the world rose from $900 million in 1992 to $1.2 billion a day in 1995). The beginning of twenty-four-hour electronic fund transfers and electronic stock trading,[4] the start of GATT's (General Agreement on Tariffs and Trade) Uruguay Round in 1986 (leading to the formation of the World Trade Organization in 1995), and the launching of Deng Xiaoping's opening of China to international trade and investment all accelerated globalization in Asia. In 1985 Deng proclaimed that the principal characteristics of the current era in international relations were "peace and development" and China needed a peaceful environment in which to pursue its economic development.[5] In 1991, faced with a financial crisis, India, too, began shedding its socialist policies and opening its door to foreign investment and trade. These were among the more important developments that boosted all the forces of globalization—most importantly that of traders, with the flow of goods and services, and adventurers, including tourists and migrants.

Booming trade and investment of the late 1980s and early 1990s, which produced Asia's economic miracle, not only resulted in the strengthening of ties among East Asian countries, but also bred new political confidence—epitomized in the claim of special "Asian values" that lay behind the region's stunning economic success. The economic boom strengthened reformers who had embraced foreign trade and investment implied by globalization. However, the 1997 financial crisis that devastated the economies of large parts of East Asia dealt a severe blow to the idea of globalization as much as it humbled the proponents of Asian values. The economic troubles, environmental degradation, terrorist threat, and rising civil society opposition that have marked the decade since the 1997 crisis offer examples of how the relationship among the states of East Asia has been affected by the actions of the other three actors of globalization, viz., preachers, adventurers, and warriors.

Beginning in the 1980s, the openness of East Asian countries allowed multinational corporations, foreign banks, financial institutions, and domestic entrepreneurs to play an increasingly dominant role in the economy. While the state formally controlled the levers of finance, they were increasingly riding the wave created by non-state actors—traders to immigrants—far from their borders. Ironically, rapid economic growth brought about by globalization raised people's living standards and conferred a degree of legitimacy on the authoritarian regimes. The patina of economic performance seemed to justify the claim that authoritarian Asian values were a recipe for stability and prosperity. With its unique approach based on dialogue, consensus, and non-interference, the Association of Southeast Asian Nations (ASEAN) was proclaimed to be leading the global order toward a "Pacific

Century." But the financial crisis that burst upon Asia with sudden fury on July 2, 1997, not only wrecked that scenario but was also a stark reminder of the lack of power held by Westphalian states before the forces released by traders and financiers around the globe.

A conjuncture of happy circumstances—from the bull run in the U.S. stock market to capital flight from post-Soviet Russia—made traders the most influential players in Asia. With its open economies, trade-friendly policies, and cheap labor, Asia drew a large part of some $938 billion in cumulative funds that was invested in 1990–1997. Awash with funds, foreign investors placed their bets on risky high-return projects and stocks. But when the first sign of trouble came from Thailand, foreign funds—much of it hot money—quickly fled the region. In 1997 alone the outflow amounted to $16 billion, or 11 percent of the GDP of the affected countries.[6] After a timid attempt to stem the tide of devaluation, currencies of the region fell like dominoes. Unlike Mexico, it was not large public-sector deficits but lack of liquidity in the private sector that humbled Asian states. Traders who had brought unprecedented prosperity were now responsible for the shipwreck.

If globalization in the shape of the outflow of foreign funds bore a major responsibility for the crisis, the recovery ironically reinforced Asia's position in an integrated world. In a dramatic display of the impotence of the nation-state, affected countries had to accept IMF bailout packages on onerous conditions that made the suffering even more acute. Any attempt to have sovereign control over national currencies by pegging them to foreign currencies was given up in favor of a float. East Asia emerged from the crisis after being forced to adopt policies and practices that had become global. The domestic price was heavy. Some twenty million people were pushed back into poverty, and several million children of jobless parents had to leave school. Globalization has always been the force behind the region's development, but the 1997 crisis can be said to have been the ordeal of fire that forced East Asia to formally and consciously join the globalized world.

Even after the ravages of the 1997 crisis, Asia was not about to recoil from globalization and retreat into isolation. The financial capital that fled in panic during the crisis returned, and within two years Asia was well on the path to recovery, thanks to FDI (foreign direct investment), resuming exports to the world market, and increasingly to China. Modular manufacturing and fragmented production systems linking different production centers in the region helped create regional "growth triangles"—such as the Johor-Riau-Singapore triangle in Southeast Asia and production hubs in Guangzhou. Closer economic integration of the region, contributing to the region's success and China's export engine, may have also been a factor in maintaining relative peace in the region. At least some Southeast

Asians believed that the "absence of war" in Southeast Asia in recent years should be attributed at least in part to the forces of globalization.[7] Trade dependence has also had a moderating effect on foreign relations. Japan's growing dependence on China as a manufacturing base and source of imports has led Japanese business interests to oppose the Japanese prime minister's visits to the Yasukuni Shrine. Taiwanese businesses, with more than a million of their employees living in China, have pressured the government to desist from provocative policies.

TRADE REDEFINES SECURITY

The drive by traders, financiers, and consumers in China to "get rich" and live better has integrated China firmly with the world economy. While it has generated a record annual growth rate of 9–10 percent, the country's security depends on forces beyond its border. China's unprecedented openness to the world economy—foreign trade accounting for 75 percent of its GDP and 70 to 80 percent of its foreign earnings invested in U.S. treasury bonds and dollar assets—has forced China to alter its Westphalian concept of territorial security. In a remarkably candid essay in 2004, Wang Zhengyi, a professor at Peking University, pointed out how China's dependence on foreign capital has led it to reconceptualize its notion of national security. Wang wrote, "Globalization and China's gradual incorporation into the world economy not only pose risks for the Chinese domestic market and its market related society . . . more important is the diminishing capacity of the state to govern Chinese economic reform and its changing society."[8]

Not only China, but the increasing global integration of all of East Asia, has left it more vulnerable to currency speculators, rapid capital flight, and market crashes than ever before. The ebb and flow of FDI has also created a more wary dynamic, both interdependent and competitive, between China and its Southeast Asian neighbors. As ASEAN countries rely on exporting similar products to the same markets as China, they have a growing fear of losing their export market and foreign investment to China. In the decade since the 1997 crisis, that fear about FDI materialized, but China has succeeded in reassuring the region by stepping up its imports from the region and by integrating its export industry closely with production of components and parts in Southeast Asia. While direct U.S. imports from non-Chinese Asian countries have dramatically declined, Chinese imports from them (mostly intermediate goods) have grown in reverse proportion—reflecting the rise of China as the regional production center for export to the United States.[9] Singapore prime minister Goh Chok Tong was blunt about the problem: "Our biggest challenge is . . . to secure a niche for ourselves as China swamps the world with her high-quality but cheaper products. . . . How does Singapore compete against 10 post-war Japans, all industrializing and exporting at the same time?"[10]

China's skillful diplomacy turned the 1997 crisis into an opportunity to win the hearts and minds of Southeast Asia. As the region reeled from the crisis and resented being lectured by the United States on the perils of crony capitalism and lack of transparency, China presented itself as a sympathetic neighbor. It kept its pledge not to engage in competitive devaluation of its currency to maintain market stability. The U.S. Treasury refused to bail out Thailand at the height of the currency crisis, while China contributed $1 billion to the stabilization fund, earning Bangkok's gratitude. Four years later China followed up its charm offensive by proposing the creation of the ASEAN-China Free Trade Area (ACFTA) in November 2002. This move not only helped China to effectively preempt the region's fear of a Chinese juggernaut crushing their export-dependent economy, but to score points against the regional rival Japan, which resisted linking a free trade area with ASEAN.

However, given the size of China's economy and its status as the world's second-biggest exporter, its trading fortune connects it to the whole world and, most importantly, to the world's biggest economy—the United States. The flip side of China's massive gain from trade and FDI flow is that its economic future, social stability, and even its security are increasingly dependent on its relations with the United States. Referring to the growing congressional anger at the Chinese trade surplus and its low renminbi, U.S. Treasury secretary Henry Paulson bluntly said, "China has become a symbol for globalization fears" in the United States. While he urged the U.S. Congress to be patient, he said it was critical "to persuade the Chinese to reform their own economy more quickly because the health of their economy affects the health of the global economy."[11] East Asia's economy has become so dependent on China that shots fired in a Sino-American trade dispute are bound to ricochet through the whole region.

Precisely because of the concern about many ricochet effects that any conflict in the region would have, globalization may have reduced the risk of open outbreak of violence. In the earliest paean for globalization (although the word did not exist then), British economist Norman Angel argued in 1910 that multiple connections among modern societies and economies had proved so beneficial that war had become an "economic impossibility."[12] As the outbreak of World War I shortly afterward proved, the optimism was premature. But the economic integration of the world has grown thousands-fold since, making the fear of massive dislocation caused by war a more plausible deterrent. It is fair to speculate that business interests in Japan and Taiwan play a calming role in nationalistic conflict with China. Even the Chinese government, despite its public posturing, cannot but be concerned about popular resentment caused by economic dislocation and hardship that a conflict with Taiwan would bring.

Globalization may have in many ways reduced state power, but in others ways it has also privileged the holders of state power and especially when private economic interests and state power have become entangled. When in January 2006 the Singapore government's investment arm, Temasek Holdings, purchased a controlling stake in Thailand's dominant phone company, Shin, owned by Prime Minister Thaksin's family, for $1.9 billion in a tax-free deal, protests broke out in Thailand against the sale of the country's communications crown jewel. Eventually the uproar set the stage for a military coup in September that removed Thaksin from power.

MIGRANTS AND TOURISTS

Uneven development in the region provided both push and pull factors for migration—both legal and illegal. The migrant workers from Asia's less developed economies served as a conduit for region-wide redistribution of the wealth generated by the global economic boom. In 1995, 1.5 million Filipinos lived abroad as permanent immigrants, and an additional 2 million were seamen or worked abroad temporarily. The ILO estimates that their remittances might amount to as high as 10 percent of the country's GNP.[13] The *Financial Times* estimates that poverty-stricken Burma, or Myanmar, earns more from the underground remittances of its workers in Thailand and Singapore than the $200 million a year it receives in foreign aid.[14]

According to a 2005 survey, some eight million Southeast Asians worked outside their own countries—mainly in Japan, Korea, Singapore, Taiwan, Hong Kong, Malaysia, and Thailand.[15] While the remittances from migrants remain a valuable source of foreign exchange and interdependence among neighbors, their treatment in host countries could equally be a source of friction. In the wake of large-scale business closures in 1997 and attempts to expel illegal migrants, tension arose among Southeast Asian neighbors who had once tolerated, even encouraged, illegal migration in times of economic boom. In particular, Malaysia deported large numbers of Indonesian workers and deployed naval patrols to block new arrivals. While new jobs are being created in labor-importing countries, the number of unemployed in labor-exporting countries is growing faster, leading to increasing concern. In January 2007 ASEAN leaders signed an agreement to aid and regulate migrant workers whose treatment could prove to be a source of tension. The smuggling of migrant Chinese workers and trafficking of women in Japan for instance, remain a potential cause for friction.

Tourism was historically driven by individuals. But with the arrival of wide-body aircraft and economic growth in the region, mass tourism has emerged as an important source of national income in many countries. Accordingly, countries with the ability to send tourist dollars have gained importance. In the late 1990s, with a swelling trade surplus causing unhappiness among its trade partners, Japan created a program that "aimed" at doubling Japanese outbound tourism. Japan hoped that the arrival of thousands of tourists would be interpreted as Japan's willingness to redistribute the economic gains from its massive trade surplus and be seen as evidence of economic fairness. The drive, however, did not last long. While Japanese golf tourism drew the ire of environmentalists, the 1997 financial crisis saw a drastic decline in tourism. After the collapse of the Japanese bubble, it was Japan's turn to develop a policy to attract foreign tourists. A rising China has since taken up the slack. Compared to only 4.5 million Chinese who traveled overseas in 1995, the figure increased to 31 million in 2005, far surpassing Japan.[16] Beijing could be seen as bestowing favor on a country by including it on its list of approved destinations.

The growth of tourism and its importance for the national budget of many countries also makes the countries vulnerable to other unpredictable outcomes of an integrated world, including environmental threats and the spread of a pandemic. The SARS crisis that hit China and Southeast Asia was a classic example of the danger inherent in the growth of mass travel on fast transports. The SARS virus emerged in South China by the end of 2002, spread to Hong Kong in early 2003, and then, thanks to busy air travel, within three months affected thirty countries worldwide, killing some eight hundred people. Flights in large parts of Asia were grounded, dealing a heavy blow to trade and tourism. It was a threat for which the Westphalian state system had no answer other than to simply batten down the hatches. As a global problem, its solution had to be found by working in close cooperation with a global institution like the World Health Organization. Deprived of tourist revenue, suffering heavy losses from business shutdowns and culling of poultry stock, regional governments were resentful of the WHO advisory on grounding flights, yet they had no option but to accept this infringement of their sovereignty. And the crisis took less of a toll than it could have without these cooperational measures.

NGOS AS THE NEW PREACHERS

The stepped-up economic development pushed by foreign investment has caused some concerns about the abuse of labor, human rights, and environmental degradation—issues that have not been a traditional priority for East Asian governments. The new preachers—non-governmental organizations and civil society community activists—have sprouted in many countries to uphold these causes and pressure governments and corporations. While eager not to discourage foreign investors, governments have often turned a blind eye to labor or environmental issues on which NGOs have campaigned and forced governments to redress grievances. To the chagrin of authoritarian governments, their advocacy of good environmental policy, transparent governance, and grassroots democracy have promoted liberal-democratic political culture and formation of civil society.

Although small NGOs concerned with local welfare and environment issues have been in existence for a while, growing trade and tourism have opened the door to linkage with international NGOs for information, coordination, and sustenance. As the NGOs have geared up to oppose policies of major international financial institutions—such as the International Monetary Fund, the World Bank, and the World Trade Organization—larger support and strategy coordination were made available from external sources. While governments have tried to control, if not altogether prevent, such international linkages (Malaysia's former prime minister Dr. Mahathir has even accused NGOs of being agents of Western neo-Liberal policy) with national NGOs, under growing public pressure, especially since the 1997 crisis, the World Bank has accepted the role of the civil society in policy-making.

Tourism that affected indigenous people's livelihoods as well as sex tourism have provoked protests by local activists and international condemnation, succeeding in bringing change in government policy.[17] Foreign investment in Southeast Asia's extractive industries and forestry has long worried environmentalists. Concern over what has been called "Japan's shadow ecology" has united activists around the region, leading to region-wide campaigns against mining, timber felling, and Japanese golf tourism.[18] Japanese environmentalist groups joined ranks in protesting Japanese corporations' role in this degradation. Since the late 1990s, however, China has replaced Japan as the largest importer of agricultural and forestry products from Southeast Asia, causing a negative environmental impact. Given the region's growing dependence on China, though, the expression of environmentalist concern has been muted. Not so in the case of Japan where acid rain has been blamed on China's coal-fired industry, causing strong public anger. The irony that some of the pollution in China could well be related to manufacturing of Japanese export goods has been conveniently ignored. Since 1997, though, the Japanese Foreign Ministry started offering a training program and grant of monitoring equipment to measure acid rain.

Some regret that the preeminence given to economic development has meant that Asian countries "have gone from resisting transnational control to offering incentives to attract foreign investors. Nationalism no longer is the glue that melds interests, and more difficult issues of class have become more central to domestic politics."[19] While rejecting the neoliberal recipe for growth through globalization, the opponents have not yet come up with an alternative that does not rely on international finance and transnational corporations and their mediating institutions.

The state's efforts to maintain its power amid globalization are challenged by the instant and constant diffusion of information and the rise of civil society activism. A case in point was a lawsuit brought by a transnational political coalition of local citizens of Aceh and North American activists and civil rights NGOs against ExxonMobil for bankrolling elements of the Indonesian armed forces, which used extreme and illegal violence to protect their gas fields and liquefied natural gas production facilities. As one author observed, foreign investors' use of local forces to protect their interest is not new in globalization, but what is new is the transnationalization of universal legal standards of justice.[20] While targeting foreign multinationals was easy, pollution caused by greedy businesses of a neighboring country has proved more difficult. In 1994 and 1997 forest fires in Indonesia caused by entrepreneurs clearing land for profitable palm oil plantations sent a thick haze all over Southeast Asia. It not only caused health problems in neighboring Singapore and Malaysia, but it also forced their airports to shut down at substantial financial losses.[21] Tempers rose and sharp editorials were written condemning Indonesia, but little else could be done.

The environmental degradation and pollution that resulted from economic development and foreign-funded projects nevertheless spawned a vigorous anti-globalization movement. Over the years, national NGOs in Thailand—the country with an established tradition of such activism—have had limited success in opposing foreign-funded projects. Kevin Hewison, who has studied the case of the Thai anti-globalization protest movement, concluded, "There is no politically sound nor a viable economic alternative proffered by the localists." Thailand's new populism, he noted, was "reactionary, romantic, anti-urban," and chauvinistic.[22] In Singapore, China, and Indonesia, NGOs supporting labor rights and human rights have been accused of being agents of "cultural imperialism" and "foreign subversion." Yet the supporters of global integration admit that emerging international civil society, concerned with human rights, the environment, and social welfare, may be a critical antidote to the negative forces of globalization. But, as the Indonesian example shows and as the Chinese government fears, it may pose a threat to the power of the state.

NEW NON-STATE ACTORS: PREACHERS OF TERROR

Islam arrived in Southeast Asia peacefully with Indian Muslim and Arab traders in the fifteenth and sixteenth centuries when the faith was mostly syncretic and moderate, adapted to the region's existing cultures. Although Indonesia made periodic attempts to institute a fundamentalist version of the faith, the country as a whole as well as Malaysia practiced a moderate, secular kind of Islam.

That, however, began changing in the early 1990s when Suharto's authoritarian regime began emphasizing the Islamic nature of the state. In 2001 Malaysian prime minister Dr. Mahathir announced the country was an Islamic state. Wider travel, foreign education, and arrival of Saudi Arabian funding for building mosques and religious schools led to a growing influence of Middle Eastern Islamic theory and practice, threatening to transform Southeast Asian Islam from an inclusive, syncretic, and pluralist religion to an exclusive Arabized form of Islam. Against such a changing background came the 9/11 terrorist attacks and the subsequent U.S. war on terror.

While a majority of Southeast Asia's peaceful, moderate Muslims were troubled by what appeared as the West's war on Islam, militant Islamic sects like Al Ma'unah (Brotherhood of Inner Power) in Northern Malaysia and Abu Sayyaf (Father of the Sword) in Southern Mindanao were emboldened in their violent anti-West campaigns. Hitherto unknown shadowy groups like Lascar Jihad and Jemaah Islamiyah (JI) with al Qaeda connections emerged in Southeast Asia to carry out terrorist attacks against Western targets and launch violent campaigns against Christians. Spates of bombings from Bali to Jakarta and the killing of Christians in Ambon were chilling reminders of the new threat. Recognition of this new global threat appearing in Asia came with five hundred U.S. Special Forces troops dispatched to the Philippines and $700 million in U.S. counterterrorism assistance granted to Indonesia.

The trader-preachers of the sixteenth century who connected Southeast Asia, where some 30 percent of world's Muslims live, with the world of Islam have now been replaced by new preachers. Aided by global travel and communication, these new preachers plot to violently supplant what they see as Western globalization with a global Islamic *ummah*.[23] Thailand's Muslim south has emerged as a hotbed for militancy where Buddhist officials, teachers, and civilians are being killed in large numbers and the government is engaged in bloody, but not-so-successful, counterinsurgency operations. With assistance and encouragement from outside, Islam in China's Xinjiang province, too, is undergoing a revival. As Dru Gladney notes, China has become more keenly aware of the importance foreign Muslim governments place on its treatment of its Muslim minorities as a factor in China's lucrative trade and military agreements. "The increased transnationalism of China's Muslims," he writes, "will be an important factor in their ethnic expression as well as in their accommodation to Chinese culture and state authority."[24]

While Christian groups in Indonesia are seeking external support in holding their ground against Islamic attacks, the faith seems to be gaining new adherents in China by leaps and bounds. According to the Center for the Study of Global Christianity, there are ten thousand conversions in China every day, and in their estimate by 2050, there will be 218 million Christians in China, 16 percent of the population—enough to make China the world's second-largest Christian nation. Given the Communist Party's attempt to retain control of various religious groups, such a growth of Christianity would be a matter of concern, especially if they get support from churches outside China.[25]

CYBERSPACE: NEW ARENA OF CONTESTATION

Over the last decade, Asia's interconnectedness has grown exponentially. The Internet, which was slow to take off in the early 1990s, accelerated dramatically during the Silicon Valley boom at the end of the twentieth century. By 2007 China boasted 137 million online users, more than a tenth of its population. China's twenty million bloggers and more than three million active writers have given China elements to build a civil society that was absent in a tightly controlled one-party state.[26] Other Asian countries have opened up this public space for discourse in addition to providing the network for businesses to expand beyond territorial borders. The Internet network enabled Asia to take full advantage of the supply chain economy and just-in-time production that revolutionized world trade in manufactured goods.

The Internet has also provided a space where citizens can let off steam, thereby diverting attention from and at least temporarily absolving the government from action. The impact of the web on domestic political stability and relations with neighbors, however, could be even more far-reaching. It was through surreptitious Internet coordination that the Falun Gong could hold their daring protest demonstration in the heart of Beijing in 1999, requiring the government to order a massive crackdown. The mistaken U.S. bombing of the Chinese embassy in Belgrade in 1999 provoked intense nationalist outrage in China. By setting up websites where the citizens could vent their anger, and thus be heard worldwide, Beijing authorities could contain the emotions from spilling over. Even then the emotion raised through the Internet boiled over into violent protests against the U.S. embassy in Beijing. The government attempt to let Chinese anger at Japanese prime minister Junichiro Koizumi's repeated visits to the Yasukuni Shrine be dissipated through online insult and vitriol did not, however, work as hoped. The Chinese government had to shut down a number of chat rooms and bulletin boards.[27]

It is ironic that closer integration of the world through technologies of the future could be used to rake the coals of ancient fires. Relations between Japan and South Korea and between China and South Korea, too, were affected by acrimony and insults hurled at each other over the Internet. Uncensored and direct criticism by nationalists on all sides not only raised public temperature, they made government efforts to pursue rational policy and solution through quiet diplomacy more difficult. Web vandalism and shrill criticism on the Internet over the somewhat esoteric subject of the origins of the Koguryo Kingdom, nearly two thousand years old, has soured relations between China and South Korea.[28]

In 2005 a so-called cyber-roots campaign against Japan's bid for a permanent seat in the UN Security Council was vigorously adopted by Chinese Internet users and managed to obtain twenty-two million signatures. Chinese nationalists have also used the Internet to call for a boycott of Japanese goods and tried to change the government's policies toward Japan. While allowing opportunity to activists to vent their anger, Beijing remains wary of the Internet as a double-edged sword. What begins as hyperventilating in cyberspace could easily spread to the street, and the target of attack could well be the government that failed to live up to the expectations created by chat-room rage.[29] The public outrage that followed a blogger's protest about "erosion of Chinese culture" from Starbucks operating inside Beijing's hallowed Forbidden City was a reminder to foreign investors about China's nationalist sensitivities.

The public space for discussion also holds the threat of upsetting the Communist Party's control. All the while encouraging the spread of the Internet as a tool of business productivity and communications, the Chinese government maintains a cyber police force estimated to be forty thousand and a security apparatus for the surveillance of the web and enforcing the government ban on dissemination of undesirable information.[30] Beijing has tracked down writers of politically sensitive e-mails and jailed them. With government efforts of employing sophisticated hardware and software for filtering and tracking the Internet output, combined with activists trying a variety of techniques to bypass controls, a veritable cat and mouse game is on. As Chinese dissident Liu Xiaobo wrote in an online essay, "The Internet provides an information channel that the Chinese dictators cannot completely censor, it allows people to speak and communicate, and it offers a platform for spontaneous civilian organization."[31]

Singapore, Thailand, and Indonesia, too, have tried with varying degree of success to control this aspect of globalization. The subversive power of the Internet was proven in Indonesia in the 1998 turmoil leading up to the fall of President Suharto. A widely circulated e-mail list titled Apakabar, providing damaging information to Indonesian elites, is credited to have countered the regime's propaganda offensive and provided ammunition to the street demonstrators.[32]

CONCLUSION

In analyzing Asia's evolving system in the light of China's rise, editor of *Power Shift* David Shambaugh posited seven possible models. They provide a useful framework to ponder the impact of globalization on international relations in the region. The seven scenarios considered are China-Dominated Hegemonic System; Major Power Rivalry model involving the United States and China; an American-centric "Hub and Spokes" model; a Concert of Powers model involving equally powerful regional countries; a U.S.-China Condominium of Power model; a region-wide Normative Community model centered on Asean, ARF (ASEAN Regional Forum), and the Shanghai Cooperation Council; and, finally, a Complex Interdependence model that rises above state structure to take into account multiple linkages brought by non-state actors (in his introductory chapter to this volume, Professor Shambaugh gives even greater attention to the importance of sub-state actors in defining international relations in Asia today). In light of the role of non-state actors surveyed in the chapter, I conclude that his last scenario offers the most accurate description of the new power equation.

From the brief survey of the non-state actors of globalization—the traders and entrepreneurs from all over the world, the religious preachers and secular activists of civil society and NGOs, and the migrants and tourists—it is clear that empowered by fast transportation and communication, these forces have been playing an increasingly important role in determining relations between states. The way the 1997 Asian financial crisis unfolded, and brought about the fall of the Suharto regime and changes of government in Thailand and South Korea, was clear evidence of the rise of a new era in which fast-paced movement of capital, instantaneous communication, and mass movement of people across territorial borders played a more decisive role in countries' relations than that played by a hegemon, a concert of regional and international powers, or even a normative community like ASEAN. As Shambaugh aptly put it, "The core actor in this [Interdependence] model is not the nation-state, but a plethora of nonstate actors and processes—many of which are difficult to measure with any precision—that operate at the societal level."[33]

In the emerging new power equation, governance no longer refers exclusively to the authority exercised by the Westphalian state. It is increasingly characterized by cooperation among states and non-state actors as they deal with non-state actors like terrorists and criminal gangs and borderless threats like pandemics and pollution. Without going as far as to claim that states have been rendered powerless, stuck as they are in the "straightjacket of globalization," one could say that relationships among states have become subject to a far more complex set of factors than the simple security concerns of the past. And in deciding what course to follow, the Asian states or any states for that matter have far less independence than they ever have had before. In order to survive and prosper in an increasingly fast and interconnected world, the states would have to abide by rules and norms that are common to all.[34] Not only international legitimacy and acceptability, but even domestic legitimacy of the governments are now determined by a larger community far removed from the territorial jurisdiction of the state.

International relations—whether in Asia or in any other region—have to be understood as part of the processes collectively called globalization. Globalization encompasses both nations and the actors, and the whole is bigger than the sum of its national parts.

NOTES

1. Nayan Chanda, *Bound Together: How Traders, Preachers, Adventurers and Warriors Shaped Globalization* (New Haven, Conn.: Yale University Press, 2007).

2. See Michael Yahuda, "The Sino-European Encounter: Historical Influences on Contemporary Relations," in *China-Europe Relations: Perceptions, Policies, and Prospects*, ed. David Shambaugh, Eberhard Sandschneider, and Zhou Hong (London: Routledge, 2007).

3. Samuel S. Kim, ed., *East Asia and Globalization* (Lanham, Md.: Rowman & Littlefield, 2000), 21.

4. Peter Conradi, "Round-the-Clock Trading Sessions Forging Links with Europe, Asia," *Toronto Star*, September 22, 1987, 7.

5. See David Shambaugh, ed., *Power Shift: China and Asia's New Dynamics* (Berkeley: University of California Press, 2005), 28.

6. Kim, *East Asia and Globalization*, 40.

7. "Globalization in Asia: Getting the Breeze without the Bugs" (report from the Conference on Globalization and Regional Security: Asian Perspectives, Honolulu, February 23–25, 1999), www.apcss.org/Publications/Report_Globalization_in_Asia.html (accessed January 24, 2008).

8. Wang Zhengyi, "Conceptualizing Economic Security and Governance—China Confronts Globalization," *Pacific Review* 17, no. 4 (2004): 523–545.

9. *Asian Development Outlook 2007* (Manila: Asian Development Bank, 2007), 66–79.

10. Quoted in Greg B. Felker, "Southeast Asian Industrialization and the Changing Global Production System," *Third World Quarterly* 24, no. 2 (2003): 255–282.

11. Anna Marie Kukec, "Paulson Says Embrace Globalization," *China Daily Herald*, September 15, 2007, www.dailyherald.com/story/?id=38463 (accessed September 15, 2007).

12. Norman Angell, *The Great Illusion: A Study of the Relation of Military Power in Nations to Their Economic and Social Advantage* (London: Heinemann, 1910), cited by Strobe Talbott, *The Great Experiment: The Story of Ancient Empires, Modern States, and the Quest for a Global Nation* (New York: Simon & Schuster, 2008), 424.

13. Annamaria Artner, "Anti-Globalization Movements: The Developments in Asia," *Contemporary Politics* 10, nos. 3–4 (September–December 2004): 243–255.

14. Amy Kazmin, "Backstreet Bankers," *Financial Times*, August 30, 2007, www .ft.com/cms/s/0/0eaab956-5725-11dc-9a3a-0000779fd2ac,dwp_uuid =05c3224e-5499-11dc-890c-0000779fd2ac.html (accessed September 15, 2007).

15. "Wandering Workers," *Economist*, January 18, 2007.

16. Howard W. French, "Next Wave of Camera-Wielding Tourists Is from China," *New York Times*, May 17, 2006.

17. Peggy Teo, "Striking a Balance for Sustainable Tourism: Implications of the Discourse on Globalization," *Journal of Sustainable Tourism* 10, no. 6 (2002): 459–474.

18. Peter J. Katzenstein and Takashi Shiraishi, eds., *Beyond Japan: The Dynamics of East Asian Regionalism* (Ithaca, N.Y.: Cornell University Press, 2006), 216.

19. William K. Tabb, "Globalization, Economic Restructuring and the Democratic Implications," in *Democracy and Civil Society in Asia*. Vol. 1: *Globalization, Democracy and Civil Society in Asia*, ed. Fahimul Quadir and Jayant Lele (London: Palgrave, 2004), 79.

20. Richard Tanter, "Law, Globalisation and the Control of Southeast Asian Military Terror: Civil Cases Are Combating Corporate Impunity," *Inside Indonesia*, www.insideindonesia.org/edit72/Politics%20Tanter.htm (accessed September 15, 2007).

21. James Shinn, ed., *Fires Across the Water: Transnational Problems in Asia* (New York: Council on Foreign Relations, 1998), 50.

22. Kevin Hewison, "Resisting Globalization: A Study of Localism in Thailand," *Pacific Review* 13, no. 2 (2000): 279–296.

23. Bryan S. Turner, "Islam, Religious Revival and the Sovereign State," *Muslim World* 97 (July 2007): 412.

24. Dru C. Gladney, "Islam in China," *The Oxford Encyclopedia of the Modern Islamic World*, ed. John L. Esposito (Oxford: Oxford University Press, 2007).

25. John L. Allen, "The Uphill Journey of Catholicism in China," *National Catholic Reporter* 6, no. 48 (August 3, 2007), ncrcafe.org/node/1252 (accessed September 12, 2007).

26. Randeep Ramesh, "China Soon to Be World's Biggest Internet User," *Guardian*, January 25, 2007, www.guardian.co.uk/china/story/0,,1998038,00.html (accessed September 14, 2007).

27. Susan Shirk, *China: Fragile Superpower* (Oxford: Oxford University Press, 2007), 93.

28. Katzenstein and Shiraishi, eds., *Beyond Japan*, 12.

29. Paul Mooney, "Internet Fans Flames of Chinese Nationalism," *YaleGlobal Online*, April 4, 2005, yaleglobal.yale.edu/display.article?id=5516 (accessed September 12, 2007).

30. Paul Mooney, "China's 'Big Mamas' in a Quandary," *YaleGlobal Online*, April 12, 2004, yaleglobal.yale.edu/display.article?id=3676 (accessed September 12, 2007).

31. Shirk, *China: Fragile Superpower*, 103.

32. Jeroen de Kloet, "Digitization and Its Asian Discontents: The Internet, Politics and Hacking in China and Indonesia," *First Monday* 7, no. 9 (September 2002), www.firstmonday.org/issues/issue7_9/kloet/index.html (accessed September 14, 2007).

33. David Shambaugh, "Introduction: The Rise of China and Asia's New Dynamics," in *Power Shift: China and Asia's New Dynamics*, ed. David Shambaugh (Berkeley: University of California Press, 2005), 16.

34. Mark Beeson, "Sovereignty under Siege: Globalization and the State in Southeast Asia," *Third World Quarterly* 24, no. 2 (2003): 357–374.

15

Security Dynamics in East Asia

Geopolitics vs. Regional Institutions

Ralph A. Cossa

The more things change, the more they remain the same! This is perhaps a counterintuitive way of describing the seemingly ever-changing security dynamics in the Asia-Pacific region. In recent years, there has been a spate of new community-building and multilateral cooperative efforts involving an ever-widening circle of players and overlapping mechanisms. There have also been real and perceived rises and declines in hard and soft power among the region's major actors, which have affected their respective roles.

China, for better or for worse, is casting a larger shadow on the region, causing its neighbors to increasingly bandwagon with, even while cautiously hedging against, Beijing. Japan, long an economic power, is now becoming more multidimensional as it strives to be a more "normal" nation. India is starting to "look east" and has been seeking a more active role in the Asia-Pacific region consistent with its great-power aspirations. ASEAN— the ten-nation Association of Southeast Asian Nations—is becoming more institutionalized as it expands its self-proclaimed role as the "driving force" behind East Asia community building. Meanwhile, the Korea Peninsula, along with China-Taiwan cross-strait tensions, remains the focus of near-term concerns, even as we ponder the long-term implications for regional security of the reunification of either or both of these societies.

At the end of the day, however, it is the old existing network of U.S. bilateral security alliances, supplemented by issue-specific "coalitions of the willing," that continues to underwrite security in the region. Even as China, Japan, India, and possibly ASEAN all rise simultaneously, this chapter argues that the role of the United States as the "outside balancer" is likely to continue to be a critical element in regional security. The combination of American soft and hard (including economic) power will continue to be a

317

primary determinant of how nations in Asia think and behave and align themselves, even as other actors and mechanisms play an ever-increasing supporting role.

This chapter will address the changing geopolitical environment and how it affects the role of the United States and its military alliances in Asia. It will look at the security challenges and dilemmas that could affect the current relative equilibrium that has allowed Asia as a whole to rise economically and politically and will examine the phenomenon of East Asia regionalism and community building as it relates to developing a post–post–Cold War (or post-9/11) security architecture for the region.

THE GEOPOLITICAL CHALLENGE AND SECURITY DILEMMAS

China is rising. Japan is rising. India is rising. Even ASEAN appears to be carving out a more influential role for itself, not as a major power per se, but due to its leading role in developing multilateral mechanisms for political, economic, and security cooperation in the region. None of these changes is, individually or collectively, either good or bad news per se. Each phenomenon could potentially be stabilizing or destabilizing, depending on how the various regional players adjust and successfully strive (or fail) to maintain regional equilibrium. The rise with the greatest current and potential long-term impact centers on China, which will draw the greatest level of attention here, with no intention of demeaning or trivializing the others.

The Rise of China

Philip Saunders's chapter in this volume chronicles China's rise, while Robert Sutter's discusses some of the implications for the United States. Sutter accurately describes Washington's "positive engagement" strategy, which seeks to reinforce the positive aspects of China's rise while also "hedging" against more negative outcomes. As discussed in David Shambaugh's introductory chapter, there are others who believe that confrontation between Washington and Beijing is inevitable, that China's rise cannot be controlled and thus must be contained.[1] There are some who suspect (and periodically accuse) Washington of already pursuing a containment strategy against China.[2] They are wrong. The United States had a policy of containment against the Soviet Union. It knows how to build and implement such a strategy. It does not begin with billions of dollars of direct foreign investment in the "enemy" to build its economy, enhance the prosperity of its people, and increase its place in the region and in the world. It does not include welcoming the "enemy" into regional economic and security forums and giving its adversary a prominent seat at its table. It does not include describing the "enemy" in the White House's 2006 *National Security Strategy* (*NSS*) as a "regional partner," further noting that "the United States will welcome the emergence of a China that is peaceful and prosperous and that cooperates with us to address common challenges and mutual interests."[3]

Is Washington hedging its bets? Is it concerned that, efforts to engage and help in the development of China notwithstanding, Beijing may decide to become more confrontational once it becomes more powerful? Of course, as the 2006 *NSS* notes, "Our strategy seeks to encourage China to make the right strategic choices for its people, while we hedge against other possibilities."[4] But no blocs have been formed against China as part of this "hedging" strategy. All the significant multilateral organizations in East Asia today have China as a central member, and America's bilateral alliances in East Asia are not directed against China or any other country, and they are not likely to be focused in this direction, unless and until Beijing takes actions that directly threaten the national security interest of the United States and its allies.

U.S. strategy toward a rising China seems based on the premise that China can, *and wants to*, play a constructive role in the emerging new world order. Ideological differences (especially as they pertain to individual freedoms) and the potential for conflict over Taiwan (more on this later) raise the possibility of conflict, as does a lack of clarity about how China itself sees its future role in the region and in the world. Does China see itself as the Germany of the first half of the twentieth century (which rose twice, each time with unhappy results)—or the Germany (or Japan) of the second half of the twentieth century, which rose responsibly to become a full partner, with considerable encouragement and assistance from the United States? A future leadership, not yet known by us or by most Chinese, will likely make that determination. U.S. policies, like those of China's neighbors, are aimed at encouraging, if not guiding or influencing, the most positive outcome, without being so naive as to recognize that, like confrontation, full cooperation is also not inevitable.

Much has been written about the "so-called China threat," to borrow Beijing's self-description, and China's impressive military expansion and modernization efforts have been well documented.[5] But the fact remains that, relative to the United States, the People's Liberation Army (PLA) is still several generations behind and the gap is not likely to close anytime soon. China's army may be the largest in Asia (or in the world, for that matter) but it is not the most capable. That moniker must go to Japan, at least in terms of self-defense capabilities—Japan does not possess offensive weapons systems.[6] Even the Pentagon, which is frequently accused of magnifying the Chinese threat, assesses that "China does not yet possess the military capability to accomplish with confidence its political objectives on the island," (i.e., successfully invade or even fully blockade Taiwan) and that "China will take until the end of this decade or later to produce a modern force capable of defeating a moderate-size adversary."[7]

The net result of China's rise has been an increased interest among China's neighbors to bandwagon with China while also hedging their bets by drawing themselves more closely to the United States. It is also not coincidental that ASEAN's growing interest in improving ties with India coincided with China's rise. Given the gradual nature of China's rise, and the clear strategy in China of conducting itself (with the exception of relations with Taiwan) in a manner that downplays the threat and focuses on bilateral and regional cooperation,[8] there is every reason to believe that regional equilibrium can be maintained despite China's rise, as long as the United States remains engaged in Asia, and no reason to believe that the United States will do otherwise, given its growing economic, political, and security interests in East Asia.

The Taiwan Imbroglio

A few words are in order regarding the main (but not only) bone of contention between the United States and China, namely Taiwan. Beijing has a one-China *principle*; Washington has a one-China *policy*. Therein lies the difference. Beijing claims that "there is only one China in the world. Both the mainland and Taiwan belong to one China. China's sovereignty and territorial integrity brook no division."[9] In Beijing's eyes, Taiwan is the last lingering battle of the Chinese civil war, a "renegade province." Reunification is the only option; peaceful reunification is much preferred, but the use of force cannot be ruled out and may be necessary if "possibilities for a peaceful reunification should be completely exhausted."[10] Washington does not preclude eventual unification, if it is the will of the people on both sides of the strait, but can foresee other alternatives as well. It has clearly announced its opposition to "unilateral changes to the status quo by either side of the Taiwan Strait," even while being careful not to clearly define what constitutes the status quo.[11]

Taiwan claims the status quo is that it is an independent, sovereign country. China claims that it is not, but seems prepared to give Taiwan "international breathing space" if Taiwan accepts the "one-China" principle. In happier times, both sides had agreed to "one China, different interpretations." This so-called 1992 Consensus allowed cross-strait dialogue for a number of years but was totally unacceptable to the Chen Shui-bian government in Taipei.[12] The one thing both sides have in common with each other and with the United States is that no side wants to see conflict across the strait. This serves no party's interests. As long as the winner of the March 2008 elections can assure Beijing that he does not seek, and will not actively pursue, de jure independence, the prospects of conflict will remain low. Washington will likely continue its policy of ambiguity or dual deterrence, aimed at persuading Taipei not to take steps that would be construed by Beijing as crossing the independence "red line," while putting China on notice that the use of force *could* induce an American military response.

One event that would dramatically change the geopolitical landscape in East Asia would be full reunification between Taiwan and the People's Republic of China (PRC), including the emplacement of PLA bases and forces on the island. While this is theoretically possible, few in the mainland forecast that this is possible in the near term—Chinese objectives are not aimed at near-term reunification but at preventing "Taiwan authorities" from precluding this as an eventual outcome—and fewer and fewer in Taiwan seem to think it possible (or desirable) at all.

As regards U.S. views, a senior American diplomat said it best off-the-record: "Any China that Taiwan would willingly and peacefully join would be a China that would not be seen as threatening to the United States."[13] Presumably, peaceful reunification requires Beijing's full embrace of democracy and ironclad assurances to the people of Taiwan regarding the preservation of their liberty, culture, and values. This is not likely to happen anytime soon.

Even if the Taiwan situation is peacefully resolved to everyone's satisfaction (and this does not necessarily or even most likely imply full reunification), there would still be political tensions between Washington and Beijing, brought about by different political systems and worldviews and the necessary adjustments required for a rising power and established power to peacefully coexist. But without the Taiwan question looming—without the prospects (however remote) of military confrontation—the remaining challenges would be much more manageable.

All American presidents since Nixon have followed a deliberate policy of engaging China and encouraging it to play a constructive role in the world. Whether or not China lives up to America's definition of what constitutes a "responsible stakeholder" remains to be seen,[14] but one cannot help but be distressed by Beijing's actions in defense of countries like Myanmar, Sudan, or Zimbabwe in the name of "non-interference." Despite these differences, Sino-U.S. relations have been and will likely remain on a generally positive track because both sides understand it is in their respective national interest to keep it that way.

The Rise of Japan

Japan is coming of age, but not without considerable growing pains. It has long been a major global economic power, but until recently had deliberately been a unidimensional power, forgoing offensive military capabilities and limiting its international involvement in large part to support of broader U.S. activities. This is changing. Japanese officials now openly discuss the potential utility of power projection forces, although Tokyo has not yet begun to pursue such weapons systems. More to the point, Tokyo is becoming more geopolitically active (and proactive). Tokyo is aggressively seeking a permanent seat on the United Nations Security Council (with Washington's backing). It has put "boots on the ground" in Iraq, albeit only after active warfare had concluded and in a non-combat role, and it is actively providing non-combat maritime support (primarily refueling services) to coalition forces working to further stabilize Afghanistan.[15]

As new generations strive to finally put the past behind them, Japan is poised to become a "normal" country, contributing to security dialogues and peacekeeping operations. Unfortunately, the history issue keeps complicating matters and the actions of the Koizumi administration (now twice-removed), especially as regards visits to Yasukuni Shrine, created considerable ill will between Japan and its East Asia neighbors, especially the Koreas and China.[16] Japan will never be able to move forward if it keeps looking backward, trying to reinvent or reinterpret the past, rather than stressing Japan's outstanding contributions to peace, stability, and prosperity over the past sixty years. Current prime minister Fukuda understands this, as did his ill-fated, short-lived predecessor, Prime Minister Abe, who began moving Sino-Japanese relations in the right direction during his October 2006 "ice-breaking" visit to China.[17]

There is a serious misperception in East Asia that Washington encourages or somehow benefits from or enjoys seeing hostile relations between Tokyo and Beijing. Nothing could be further from the truth. It is in Washington's interest to see Asia's two primary powers cooperating toward common goals of peace and prosperity. This complements Washington's "positive engagement" strategy and helps to create a Sino-Japanese economic interdependence that raises both the cost of conflict and the prospects of future cooperation.[18]

Korea Peninsula Challenges

While a still divided Korea is not "rising" in the same sense as its neighbors, few spots in Asia can have as important an impact on regional security dynamics as the Korea Peninsula. North Korea has the fourth-largest military in the world (behind China, the United States, and India and ahead of Russia)[19] and has demonstrated at least a rudimentary nuclear capability (while claiming much more).[20] South Korean forces are somewhat smaller but still rank sixth in the world and are deemed to be more capable and ready.[21] More importantly, they are complemented by roughly twenty-eight thousand U.S. Korea-based forces under the world's most integrated Combined Forces Command.[22]

It would be foolhardy to try to describe the current dynamics associated with the attempts by Washington and its Six-Party Talks interlocutors—

North and South Korea, China, Japan, and Russia—to bring about the Korea Peninsula denuclearization that all agreed to in principle on September 19, 2005.[23] The six-party process itself will be examined below, in addressing "ad hoc multilateralism." It is important to note here, however, that the December 2007 election of the more conservative Liberal Democratic Party candidate Lee Myung Bak as South Korea's new president in February 2008 increases the prospects of Washington and Seoul speaking with one voice in dealing with Pyongyang. If nothing else, this should ease some of the tensions that have existed between the two allies under the more liberal Roh Moo Hyun administration, although Pyongyang's ability to drive wedges between Washington and Seoul (or between either and the other six-party participants) should not be underestimated.[24]

Conventional wisdom is that Korea's immediate neighbors, especially Japan and China, are not eager to see Korean reunification, each for its own specific reasons.[25] Tokyo worries that a unified Korea might see Japan as its "natural enemy." Beijing worries that a unified Korea, under Seoul's rule and with the Republic of Korea (ROK)–U.S. security alliance still intact, would remove its current buffer and could place a U.S. ally (and potential future U.S. military bases) closer to its borders. If, however, the choice is between a reunified Korea Peninsula (under Seoul) or a divided peninsula with an increasingly belligerent and nuclear weapons–equipped Democratic People's Republic of Korea (DPRK), the former may be seen as a far more attractive choice, something that should give Pyongyang cause for pause.

As was the case between Tokyo and Beijing, tensions between Seoul and Tokyo are likewise disconcerting to Washington. Both alliances—the U.S.-Japan alliance and the U.S.-ROK alliance—suffer when the third leg of this important triangle is weak. Conversely, when all three cooperate—as we have seen in the past through the Trilateral Coordination and Oversight Group (TCOG)—the cause of peace and stability is well served. When a South Korean president says on the one hand that he wants to be a balancer between China and Japan and on the other declares "diplomatic war" on Tokyo, this makes it virtually impossible for the former role to be usefully played.[26]

With new leadership both in Tokyo and in Seoul, an opportunity existed in 2008 to have a fresh start. Prime Minister Fukuda has pledged not to visit Yasukuni Shrine, and incoming ROK president Lee Myung Bak has attached a high priority in restoring and rebuilding good relations between Seoul and both Tokyo and Washington, as well as with Beijing.

The Rise of India

India lies outside East Asia, but its rise has implications for the region and it has a role to play there. While India has the world's fourth-largest military force, complete with nuclear weapons and power projection forces,[27] it is neither seen, nor attempts to portray itself, as a military power in Asia. Its impact is more political and perhaps psychological; it is, after all, "the world's largest democracy" and rivals China both in size and in economic potential (although more so in the former than in the latter).

On the plus side, we see India engaging with ASEAN and its other East Asia colleagues through the ASEAN Regional Forum (ARF) and the East Asia Summit (EAS). On the negative side, it has thus far chosen not to use its limited influence over Myanmar (Burma) in a way that might promote political reform in that beleaguered nation. New Delhi also seems determined to have "strategic partnerships" with everyone.[28]

It is not too much of an exaggeration that on Monday, Wednesday, and Friday, India seems intent on cooperating with the United States and on being part of an emerging alliance of democracies, promoting multilateral cooperation (including defense cooperation) with Japan, Australia, and the United States, while on Tuesday, Thursday, and Saturday, New Delhi further enhances its strategic relations with Beijing and Moscow, aimed at preventing a unipolar world. While others may dream of playing an "India card" in the East Asia geopolitical game (recall that ASEAN brought India in as a dialogue partner and ARF member largely as a counterweight to China), New Delhi does not see itself as a "card" in anyone's deck. Nonetheless, a rising India must be factored into the geopolitical equation, and its rise, along with Japan's, gives context and perspective to China's rise.

Does Russia Still Matter?

It would be wrong to totally ignore Russia in the Asian geopolitical equation. As Russians are quick to remind, the two-headed eagle on the Russian crest points east and west; Russia is an Asian as well as a European power, even if its focus seems pointed more toward the Atlantic and its own vulnerable south than East Asia in recent years. Nonetheless, Russia is a member of the Six-Party Talks (there at Pyongyang's request), is an ASEAN dialogue partner, and participant in many of the regional multilateral organizations, including the Asia-Pacific Economic Cooperation (APEC) "gathering of economies" and the ASEAN Regional Forum. President Putin has also been knocking at the door of the East Asia Summit, but thus far, no one is answering. It also has the world's fifth-largest military, even if its Pacific-based forces are a shadow of their former selves.[29]

Russia has a long-standing "strategic partnership" with China and together with Beijing helped form the Shanghai Cooperation Organisation in 2001.[30] The SCO, which brings Russia and China together with four Central Asian states (Kazakhstan, Kyrgyzstan, Tajikistan, and Uzbekistan), is focused on promoting confidence and cooperation among its members and neighbors—India, Iran, Mongolia, Pakistan, and Turkmenistan are observers—while fighting "terrorism, splittism, and extremism" in the region and globally. While the SCO held its first military counterterrorism exercise in 2007, it is more a political, economic, and cultural than strictly security organization and should not be seen as a military alliance in the sense of NATO or any other Western definition of the term.[31]

The SCO also helps mask tensions between Moscow and Beijing over what the Russians call their "near abroad," the territory that had been an integral part of the former Soviet Union and which Moscow would like to remain in its immediate sphere of influence. The prospects of a twenty-first-century "Great Game" between Beijing and Moscow for influence in Central Asia, plus other historical avenues of mistrust and the fact that both Beijing and Moscow value good relations with Washington at least as much as they do with one another, provides limits to the utility of this strategic partnership.[32]

The Rise of ASEAN

The Association of Southeast Asian Nations was established in August 1967 to accelerate economic growth, social progress, and cultural development in the region and to promote regional peace and stability in the wake of the U.S. withdrawal from Vietnam.[33] In 2007, in marking its fortieth anniversary, it established its first formal Charter, making it a "legal entity" and bringing the ten states more closely together.[34] Even after forty years, however, it is more a political and economic than security-oriented organization. In 2003 ASEAN established an ASEAN Community comprised of three pillars—an ASEAN Security Community, an ASEAN Economic Community, and an ASEAN Socio-Cultural Community—but this is still in an embryonic state.[35]

ASEAN's real contribution to regional security is in its role as the self-proclaimed driving force behind East Asia community-building efforts and behind many of the region's key multilateral cooperative mechanisms, and especially (in terms of regional security) the ASEAN Regional Forum, which will be discussed in more detail shortly.

U.S. STRATEGY AND MILITARY ALLIANCES

Having looked at changing dynamics within the region, we turn now to America's bilateral security alliances before discussing emerging regional security arrangements. Robert Sutter's chapter has already outlined the specific alliances—with Australia, Japan, South Korea, the Philippines, and Thailand—and discussed some of the specific challenges Washington faces in sustaining these relationships. In this section, I will look at the role of alliances and American security strategy in East Asia more broadly.

During the George H. W. Bush and Clinton administrations, the Pentagon produced a series of "East Asia Strategy Reports" outlining U.S. security strategy in East Asia and the central role of Washington's East Asia alliances in underpinning this strategy. The George W. Bush administration did not continue this particular series of publications but continues to underscore that the United States "is a Pacific nation, with extensive interests throughout East and Southeast Asia."[36] The latest Bush administration *National Security Strategy* further states that "the region's stability and prosperity depend on our sustained engagement: maintaining robust partnerships supported by a forward defense posture, supporting economic integration through expanded trade and investment, and promoting democracy and human rights."[37]

Expanding upon this official description, Gerald Curtis has identified the core features of U.S. East Asia policy as "an emphasis on alliances with Japan and South Korea and deepening economic and political relations with China, support for the status quo in the Taiwan Strait, a frustrating effort to get North Korea to give up its nuclear weapons and an ambivalent attitude toward East Asian regionalism."[38] He argues that these are unlikely to change in the foreseeable future. Curtis further identifies Washington's "remarkably durable" and consistent U.S. objectives in East Asia as "preventing any country from establishing a hegemonic position, structuring a 'hub and spokes' arrangement of alliances that facilitates the deployment of American military power in the region and beyond, and encouraging economic openness through trade and capital liberalization."[39] While this author finds the references to "hub and spokes" unhelpful—all countries see themselves as the hub in describing respective foreign policies, but when used in the American context, it is usually associated with American unilateralism—Curtis is probably right when he says "there is no reason to believe that this strategy faces a major overhaul."[40]

Curtis's description coincides nicely with the views of U.S. Asia strategy and the central role played by friends and allies outlined by the current commander of the U.S. Pacific Command, Admiral Timothy Keating, in an address to a Center for Strategic and International Studies audience in Washington, D.C., in August 2007.[41] The role of alliances is further underscored by Rear Admiral (retired) Michael McDevitt's comprehensive analysis of "The *2006 Quadrennial Defense Review* and *National Security Strategy*," in which he concludes that the "continued military bases in East Asia to sustain U.S. military power overseas, along with the mutual security alliances that make them possible" constitute one of the "fundamentals" of U.S. strategy in East Asia.[42]

This is not expected to change. In their forward thinking and bipartisan prescription for American "smart power," former Bush administration deputy secretary of state Richard Armitage and former Clinton administration assistant secretary of defense Joseph Nye identify alliances, along with partnerships and multilateral institutions, as "the foundation to address global challenges."[43] They describe Washington's existing alliance network as a "force multiplier" and as one of the best guarantees against "bandwagoning" against the United States.[44] Regardless of which party comes to power in 2009, the U.S. alliance network in East Asia is likely to continue to play a central role in American East Asia security strategy; greater U.S. involvement in, and support for, regional multilateralism also appears in the cards, if Armitage and Nye's advice is heeded.

EMERGING MULTILATERAL MECHANISMS AND ASIA COMMUNITY-BUILDING EFFORTS

This final section provides a brief review of selected key institutionalized and ad hoc security-related multilateral mechanisms and how they impact regional security dynamics.

The ARF: A Useful but Limited Forum

The twenty-six-member ARF brings together foreign ministers from the ten ASEAN states plus Australia, Canada, China, the European Union, India, Japan, Mongolia, Papua New Guinea, Russia, South Korea, North Korea, New Zealand, and the United States, plus most recently Pakistan (since 2004), Timor-Leste (2005), Bangladesh (2006), and Sri Lanka (2007), for annual security-oriented discussions. While initially focused exclusively on East Asia, the introduction of more South Asian members in recent years should be ringing warning bells about the ARF's future focus and effectiveness. Broadening its membership reduces the ARF's attractiveness as a framework for East Asian or Asia-Pacific community building.

Various ARF study groups (called Inter-Sessional Support Groups or ISGs) have provided a vehicle to move multilateral security cooperation forward in areas such as preventive diplomacy, enhanced confidence building, counterproliferation, and maritime (including search and rescue) cooperation, all of which help promote greater transparency and military-to-military cooperation. Most importantly, since September 11, 2001, the ARF has helped focus regional attention on, and has served as an important vehicle for practical cooperating in, fighting terrorism and in countering the proliferation of weapons of mass destruction (WMD).[45]

Generally speaking, the ARF seems well suited to serve as the consolidating and validating instrument behind many security initiatives proposed by governments and at non-official gatherings and has become a useful vehicle in the war on terrorism. But its contribution to the regional security order remains somewhat constrained. For example, Taiwan has not been permitted to participate, and Beijing has insisted that "internal Chinese affairs" not be on the agenda, effectively blocking ARF discussion of cross-strait tensions despite their obvious broad regional implications. The Chinese have even been reluctant to address conflicting claims in the South China Sea at the ARF, insisting instead on separate talks with ASEAN or with the other claimants on an individual basis.

Few expect the ARF to solve the region's problems or even to move rapidly or proactively to undertake that mission. The agreement to "move at a pace comfortable to all participants" was aimed at tempering the desire of more Western-oriented members for immediate results in favor of the "evolutionary" approach preferred by the ASEAN states, which all too often seems to see the process as being as (or more) important as its eventual substantive products.[46] The Asian preference for "non-interference in internal affairs" also has traditionally placed some important topics essentially off-limits, although this may be changing (witness ASEAN's increased willingness to comment on Myanmar's domestic politics). Nonetheless, the evolution of the ARF from a confidence-building measures "talk shop" to a true preventive diplomacy mechanism (as called for in its 1995 Concept Paper) promises to be a long and difficult one.[47]

APEC: Cautiously Testing the Security Waters

APEC is first and foremost a "gathering of regional economies"—it is not referred to as a gathering of states or governments due to the presence in its ranks of Hong Kong and Taiwan.[48] While primarily aimed at managing the effects of growing economic interdependence, APEC has had an important political and security role as well, especially since the 1993 Seattle meeting when then U.S. president Bill Clinton invited the APEC heads of state and government to the first of what have now become regular annual Leaders' Meetings designed to elevate the importance of this economic gathering.[49] The Leaders' Meetings have become an important vehicle for fostering political relations in addition to raising the level of economic dialogue and putting pressure on the region's leaders (and especially the host state) to move the process forward.

For example, APEC 2001 provided an important venue for President Bush to explain Washington's war on terrorism to his Asian colleagues and to garner their support. In addition to the usual annual APEC Leaders' Declaration, the assembled leaders also issued an APEC Leaders' Statement on Counter-Terrorism—the first political document to be issued in APEC's thirteen-year history—which unequivocally condemned the September 11 attack and deemed it "imperative to strengthen international cooperation at all levels in combating terrorism in a comprehensive manner."[50] This was considered a real victory for President Bush and no doubt helped to increase APEC's relevance in his eyes.

The APEC Shanghai meeting also provided President Bush with his first opportunity to meet directly with Chinese president Jiang Zemin, which helped to end the downward slide in Sino-U.S. relations under way since Bush's inauguration (and especially after the collision between a U.S. reconnaissance plane and a Chinese jet fighter over the South China Sea in April 2001). The two leaders were able to put the relationship back on track, aided by China's willingness to cooperate in the battle against terrorism.[51] Security matters continue to be discussed at the APEC Leaders' Meeting, not to mention at the numerous side summits that normally accompany this gathering.

President Bush met jointly with the seven ASEAN members of APEC along the sidelines of the 2005 APEC Leaders' Meeting, in what constituted his first-ever U.S.-ASEAN Summit. Both sides expressed a desire to make this a regular event, and President Bush met with the "ASEAN Seven" again in November 2006 along the sidelines of the Hanoi APEC Leaders' Meeting and again in September 2007 in Sydney.[52]

Politics and security issues aside, APEC still is, first and foremost, aimed at promoting free trade and economic cooperation. Nonetheless, the assembled leaders also address terrorism and non-proliferation-related issues and also issue statements dealing with non-traditional security concerns, such as pandemic disease, natural disasters, and ensuring reliable supplies of energy.

As long as APEC provides a useful venue not only for the promotion of free trade but also for fighting the war on terrorism, we can expect that Washington will continue to be an active player. However, as with the ARF, it will remain more suited to talking about security problems than to actually helping to implement solutions. In addition to the usual drawbacks associated with East Asian multilateralism, APEC has the added "problem" of including Taiwan. Rather than using this venue as a vehicle for incorporating Taiwanese views and concerns into the regional security debate in a quasi-non-governmental setting, Beijing has tried to block any substantive security-oriented activities and to further isolate Taiwan from the dialogue process.

While Washington and many of its regional allies (especially Australia and Japan) attach great importance to APEC (and secondly to the ARF), many in ASEAN and others among its neighbors (especially China) seem to be placing more emphasis and value on East Asia sub-regional (as opposed to broader Asia-Pacific) institutions and community-building efforts, such as ASEAN + 3 (APT) and the East Asia Summit (EAS), which do not include the United States.

ASEAN + 3 and the East Asia Summit

While Washington focuses on ad hoc initiatives and Asia-Pacific regional-ism, the states of East Asia have continued their community-building efforts. In December 2005, Malaysia convened the first East Asia Summit. It should be noted that the EAS was not the only summit taking place in Kuala Lumpur at that time. ASEAN leaders also met among themselves, with their + 3 part-ners (China, Japan, and South Korea), and in individual ASEAN + 1 meet-ings with their Australian, New Zealand, and Indian counterparts. This was the second time that Canberra and Wellington and the third time that New Delhi participated in this conclave. Russian president Vladimir Putin also ap-peared on the ASEAN summit scene for the first time, conducting his first ASEAN + 1 dialogue.[53] He was also invited to meet with, but not to officially join, the other sixteen assembled leaders at the first annual EAS.[54] The second so-called ASEAN + 3 + 3 EAS meeting took place in January 2007 in Cebu with the sixteen core members (*sans* the Russians).[55] The same group partici-pated in the third EAS in Singapore in November 2007.[56]

Still undefined after three meetings is how the EAS (or the APT, for that matter) will interact with broader regional organizations such as APEC or the ARF. To its credit, the Chairman's Statement from the second EAS "confirmed our view that the EAS complements other existing regional mechanisms, in-cluding the ASEAN dialogue process, the ASEAN Plus Three process, the ARF, and APEC in community building efforts."[57] Details as to how these various efforts will mesh or work together are still lacking, however. The Chairman's Statement did note that in doing its work, "our officials and the ASEAN Sec-retariat will use existing mechanisms to facilitate the implementation of [pri-ority] projects," again underscoring that the EAS was not going to develop a life of its own but would remain under ASEAN and APT.

How the EAS relates to the region's other multilateral organizations and initiatives—both institutionalized (like the ARF and APEC) and ad hoc (like the Six-Party Talks and Proliferation Security Initiative)—will also be a key factor affecting Washington's attitude, as will its adoption of global norms, especially in the areas of counterterrorism and counterproliferation. Will the EAS (or APT) reinforce or dilute these efforts? Will it help regional states more effectively address growing transnational challenges . . . or pro-vide another excuse for avoiding such efforts? The answers to these ques-tions will help determine Washington's attitude toward the EAS and any subsequent East Asian Community.

Ad Hoc Multilateralism

If Washington has only limited confidence in institutionalized multilat-eral mechanisms, it is developing a clear preference for ad hoc or tailored multilateralism aimed at a specific task or objective and comprised of a "coalition of the willing." The multinational force assembled for the war in Iraq provides one example, as does the global Proliferation Security Initiative (PSI) or the regional Six-Party Talks.

Proliferation Security Initiative

The PSI was first laid out in a speech by President Bush in May 2003 and formalized at an eleven-nation meeting (involving Australia, France, Germany, Italy, Japan, the Netherlands, Poland, Portugal, Spain, the UK, and the United States) in Madrid a month later.[58] It is "a global initiative with global reach," under which coalition members have agreed "to move quickly on direct, practical measures to impede the trafficking in weapons of mass destruction (WMD), missiles, and related items."[59] As such, it is clearly "task oriented." It represents cooperation for a specific, clearly defined purpose, as opposed to dialogue for dialogue's sake or in support of more generic objectives. In September 2003, in Paris, the eleven core participants agreed on a Statement of Interdiction Principles "to establish a more coordinated and effective basis through which to impede and stop [WMD] shipments . . . consistent with national legal authorities and relevant international law and frameworks, including the UN Security Council." Over seventy nations have expressed support for these principles.[60]

Other major Asia-Pacific participants beyond the initial PSI core group include Canada, the Philippines, Russia, and Singapore. Others, like China and South Korea, claim they support the PSI's objectives but have refrained from directly participating, in part due to North Korean objections.[61] PSI participants have conducted numerous air, ground, and (mostly) sea interdiction exercises to develop and demonstrate its capability to prevent illicit trafficking in nuclear weapons and fissile material. Its most widely acknowledged success was the interception of the *BBC China* en route to Libya with a shipment of centrifuges, an action that reportedly convinced Libyan leader Mu'ammar Gadhafi to come clean about his clandestine nuclear weapons programs.[62]

PSI participants are hesitant to discuss actual interdiction operations, citing security reasons. Nonetheless, U.S. undersecretary of state for arms control and international security Robert Joseph declared that between April 2005 and April 2006, over two dozen successful interdiction operations had taken place, specifically asserting that PSI cooperation had stopped the export of controlled equipment, dual-use goods, and heavy water–related equipment to Iran during this period.[63] Joseph referred to the PSI as "an important organizing factor" in Washington's overall counterproliferation effort.

Six-Party Talks

The best example of task-oriented ad hoc multilateral cooperation in Northeast Asia is the Six-Party Talks, established by Washington to deal with the specific issue of denuclearization of the Korea Peninsula. The talks were also intended, and served, to multilateralize what many initially viewed as a bilateral U.S.-DPRK problem.

The creation of the six-party process may represent one of the Bush administration's finest diplomatic hours.[64] This initiative draws from the lessons learned during the 1993/1994 North Korea nuclear crisis, where—despite close coordination and consultation—Washington was widely perceived as unilaterally cutting a deal with Pyongyang before sticking Seoul and Tokyo with the bill. While Pyongyang argued for bilateral consultations (and a separate U.S.-DPRK non-aggression pact), Washington rightfully insisted this time that participation by Seoul and Tokyo was "essential." It also acknowledges the important role that China, and to a lesser extent Russia, must play if multilateral security guarantees are to be part of the final solution (as most would agree they are). Finally, the Bush administration recognized and tried to work around Pyongyang's strategy of trying to play all sides against one another by presenting different, conflicting messages depending on the audience.[65]

The creation of the Six-Party Talks mechanism provides a framework for broader Northeast Asia multilateral cooperation in the future. If the talks eventually succeed, most parties agree that a more formalized mechanism must evolve in order to implement the agreement, provide necessary security assurances, and monitor compliance, as well as facilitate whatever aid packages are associated with the final accord. If the talks fail, some (this author included) would argue that there will be an even greater need for some form of institutionalized cooperation in order to manage the danger posed by a nuclear weapons–equipped North Korea, if the other parties are prepared for this level of cooperation. If and how the six-party mechanism transitions into a more institutionalized Northeast Asia forum will help determine the degree of future security cooperation in this East Asia sub-region and Washington's involvement in it.

CONCLUSION

Regional security dynamics have been, are, and will likely to continue to be in a state of flux, brought about by the simultaneous rise of China and Japan within East Asia and India along its periphery and by emerging security (and economic-oriented) multilateral mechanisms that have at least a limited role to play in promoting peace and security in the region. The

United States welcomes Japan's and India's rise and is supporting, while cautiously observing, China's re-emergence in Asia and globally, hoping for and counting on the best, even as it hedges against less favorable outcomes. It also supports regional multilateral efforts such as APEC and the ARF, in which it actively participates, and has voiced no strong objection to sub-regional gatherings such as the APT and EAS which currently geographically exclude the United States. It also supports, indeed often initiates, ad hoc multilateral efforts aimed at dealing with specific challenges, such as the PSI and Six-Party Talks, focused on countering the proliferation of weapons of mass destruction.

These "coalitions of the willing" supplement the existing network of American bilateral security alliances. Together, they help ensure a continued central role for the United States in preserving peace and stability in East Asia, even as other players and institutions rise to play a more meaningful support role. Assuming that Washington continues to use its hard and soft power smartly, the United States appears destined to continue to play a leading role in East Asia security, even as it supports and urges the nations of the region to contribute more, and more effectively, to their own security.

NOTES

1. See, for example, Aaron L. Friedberg, "The Future of U.S.-China Relations: Is Conflict Inevitable?" *International Security* 30, no. 2 (Fall 2005): 7–45.

2. See, for example, "US Denies Containment Policy against China" (press release from People's Republic of China Embassy in the United States, March 17, 2005), www.chinaembassy.org/eng/xw/t240943.htm (accessed January 20, 2008).

3. *2006 National Security Strategy for the United States of America (NSS-2006)* (Washington, D.C.: The White House, 2006), 26, 46.

4. *2006 National Security Strategy*, 47.

5. For a comprehensive breakdown of the People's Liberation Army forces, see *The Military Balance 2007* (London: International Institute for Strategic Studies, 2007), 346–351. Additional details on Chinese defense expenditures are provided on 340–341.

6. For details about the Japanese Self-Defense Forces, see Hackett, ed., *The Military Balance 2007*, 354–357.

7. *Military Power of the People's Republic of China 2007* (Washington, D.C.: Office of the Secretary of Defense, 2007), 33 and 15, respectively.

8. See Robert Sutter, "Singapore Summits, Harmony, and Challenges," *Comparative Connections* 9, no. 4 (January 2008), www.csis.org/media/csis/pubs/0704qchina_seasia.pdf (accessed January 23, 2008).

9. As spelled out in Article Two of China's Anti-Secession Law, adopted at the Third Session of the 10th National People's Congress on March 14, 2005, Xinhua News Agency, March 14, 2005, www.china.org.cn/english/2005lh/122724.htm (accessed January 25, 2008).

10. Article Eight, Anti-Secession Law.

11. For a definitive statement of U.S. cross-strait policy, see Deputy Assistant Secretary of State Thomas J. Christensen, "Speech to U.S.-Taiwan Business Council Defense Industry Conference" (Annapolis, Maryland, September 11, 2007), www.us-taiwan.org/reports/2007_sept11_thomas_christensen_speech.pdf (accessed January 25, 2008).

12. A Chinese explanation of the 1992 consensus can be found at "Backgrounder: '1992 Consensus' on 'One-China' Principle," Xinhua News Agency, updated October 13, 2004, on the *China Daily* website, www.chinadaily.com.cn/english/doc/200410/13/content_382076.htm (accessed January 22, 2008).

13. The off-the-record comment was made by a senior State Department official at a Pacific Forum CSIS-hosted workshop focused on cross-strait relations in 2005, but reflects a general attitude that the United States is prepared to accept any formulation or agreement willingly accepted by both sides of the strait.

14. As originally introduced by then Deputy Secretary of State Robert Zoellick in a speech on "Whither China: From Membership to Responsibility" (to the National Committee on U.S.-China Relations, New York, September 21, 2005), www.ncuscr.org/articlesandspeeches/Zoellick.htm (accessed January 25, 2008).

15. The Afghanistan support operations were a point of contention with the reinvigorated Japanese opposition Democratic Party of Japan, which managed to temporarily halt this refueling mission, until overruled by the ruling Liberal Democratic Party. For details, see, for example, Eric Talmadge, "Japan to Resume Its Mission in Indian Ocean," *Washington Post*, January 12, 2008, A11.

16. For background on the tensions caused by Prime Minister Koizumi's visits to Yasukuni Shrine, see, for example, James Przystup, "Japan-China Relations: Looking Beyond Koizumi," and David Kang and Ji-young Lee, "Japan—Korea: *Seirei Ketsuzetsu* (Cold Politics, Warm Economics)," both in *Comparative Connections* 8, no. 1 (April 2006), www.csis.org/images/stories/pacfor/0601qjapan_china.pdf, and www.csis.org/images/stories/pacfor/0601qjapan_skorea.pdf, respectively (accessed January 25, 2008).

17. For details, see James Przystup, "Japan-China Relations: Ice Breaks at the Summit," *Comparative Connections* 8, no. 4 (January 2007), www.csis.org/media/csis/pubs/0604qjapan_china.pdf (accessed January 25, 2008).

18. For more on the impact of the Sino-Japan rivalry on U.S. national interests, please see "Sino-Japan Rivalry: A CNA, IDA, NDU/INSS, and Pacific Forum CSIS Project Report," *Issues & Insights*, no. 02-07 (March 2007), www.csis.org/media/csis/pubs/issuesinsights_v07n02.pdf (accessed January 26, 2008).

19. *The Military Balance 2007*, table 36, 406–411.

20. See *The Military Balance 2007*, 357–359, for force dispositions, and 331 for a discussion of the DPRK's nuclear weapons test and suspected capabilities.

21. *The Military Balance 2007*, 359–361.

22. See www.usfk.mil/usfk/index.html?/org/cfc.html for a description of the Combined Forces Command and the U.S. military presence in and commitment to the ROK (accessed January 25, 2008). As the ROK's military capabilities increase, the nature of the U.S.-ROK command relationship has been adjusted. Operational command of ROK forces in wartime is scheduled to shift from the United States to the

ROK in 2012. But the overall defense commitment, as outlined in the Mutual Security Treaty, remains firm and credible.

23. "Joint Statement of the Fourth Round of the Six-Party Talks, Beijing, September 19, 2005," www.state.gov/r/pa/prs/ps/2005/53490.htm (accessed January 25, 2008).

24. For this author's view on the election, please see "Lee Myung-bak Victory: Good News All Around," *PacNet* 51-07 (December 26, 2007), www.csis.org/media/csis/pubs/pac0751.pdf (accessed January 21, 2008).

25. The same feelings were held about German reunification among its European neighbors, but that appears (at least thus far) to have had a happy ending.

26. For a discussion of Roh's balancer policy, see, for example, Choe Sang-Hun, "South Korea's 'Balancer' Policy Attacked," *International Herald Tribune*, April 9, 2005, www.iht.com/articles/2005/04/08/news/seoul.php (accessed January 25, 2008).

27. *The Military Balance 2007*, 314–319.

28. For an update on India's relations with the nations of East Asia and the United States, see Satu Limaye, "India-Asia Pacific Relations: Consolidating Friendships and Nuclear Legitimacy," *Comparative Connections* 9, no. 4 (January 2008), www.csis.org/media/csis/pubs/0704qindia_asia.pdf (accessed January 20, 2008).

29. *The Military Balance 2007*, 195–205.

30. For regular updates on the Sino-Russian relationship, see Yu Bin, "China-Russia Relations: Living with Putin's Unfading Glory and Dream," *Comparative Connections* 9, no. 4 (January 2008), www.csis.org/media/csis/pubs/0704qchina_russia.pdf (accessed January 25, 2008), and earlier and future China-Russia *Comparative Connections* chapters.

31. For details, visit the SCO's website: www.sectsco.org/home.asp?Language ID=2 (accessed January 25, 2008).

32. For details on the "cracks in the facade" between China and Russia, see Charles E. Ziegler, "Putin Comes to Shove in Asia," *Far Eastern Economic Review* 171, no. 1 (January/February 2008): 20–24.

33. The five original member countries were Indonesia, Malaysia, Philippines, Singapore, and Thailand. Brunei Darussalam joined in 1984, Vietnam in 1995, Laos and Myanmar in 1997, and Cambodia in 1999. Details can be found on the ASEAN website: www.aseansec.org/home.htm (accessed January 25, 2008).

34. For contrasting views on the significance of the Charter and on ASEAN's progress to date, please see Ralph A. Cossa, "ASEAN Charter: One (Very) Small Step Forward," *PacNet* 48-07 (November 21, 2007), www.csis.org/media/csis/pubs/pac0748.pdf; and Tommy Koh, "ASEAN at 40: Perception and Reality," *PacNet* 48A-07 (November 27, 2007), www.csis.org/media/csis/pubs/pac0748a.pdf (accessed January 21, 2008).

35. See www.aseansec.org/64.htm for a detailed description of the three communities and their respective objectives and aspirations (accessed January 21, 2008).

36. *2006 National Security Strategy*, 39.

37. *2006 National Security Strategy*, 39.

38. Gerald Curtis, "The US in East Asia: Not Architecture, But Action," *Global Asia* 2, no. 2 (2007): 43.

39. Curtis, "The US in East Asia," 43.

40. Curtis, "The US in East Asia," 43.

41. For a transcript of his remarks and question and answer session, see Timothy J. Keating, "Asia-Pacific Trends: A U.S. PACOM Perspective," *Issues and Insights* 7, no. 14 (September 2007), www.csis.org/media/csis/pubs/issuesinsights_v07n14.pdf (accessed January 25, 2008).

42. Michael McDevitt, "The *2006 Quadrennial Defense Review* and *National Security Strategy*: Is There an American Strategic Vision for East Asia?" *Issues and Insights* 7, no. 1 (January 2007), www.csis.org/media/csis/pubs/issuesinsights_v07n01.pdf (accessed January 25, 2008).

43. Richard Armitage and Joseph Nye, *CSIS Commission on Smart Power* (Washington, D.C.: CSIS Press, 2007), 27. "Smart Power," as described in pages 6–7, is a skillful combination of American hard power and soft power, the latter being a phrase coined by Nye to describe the attractiveness and persuasive power of a nation's values, culture, and ideals.

44. Armitage and Nye, *CSIS Commission on Smart Power*, 32.

45. See, for example, the "Statement by the Chairman of the ASEAN Regional Forum (ARF) on the Terrorist Acts of the 11th September 2001, Bandar Seri Begawan, 4 October 2001," the "ASEAN Regional Forum Statement on Strengthening Transport Security against International Terrorism," and "ASEAN Regional Forum Statement on Non-Proliferation," issued during the July 2, 2004, Jakarta, Indonesia, ARF meeting. Such statements have become regular attachments to ARF Chairman Statements and are frequently echoed at ASEAN Summits.

46. See "Chairman's Statement: The First ASEAN Regional Forum, Bangkok, Thailand, July 25, 1994," www.aseansec.org/2105.htm (accessed September 28, 2007).

47. For more background on the ARF, see "The ASEAN Regional Forum: A Concept Paper" (Department of State, Bureau of Political-Military Affairs, Washington, D.C., July 15, 2002).

48. APEC started out as an informal dialogue group, growing from an original twelve members (Australia, Brunei, Canada, Indonesia, Japan, the Republic of Korea, Malaysia, New Zealand, the Philippines, Singapore, Thailand, and the United States) in 1989 to fifteen in 1991 (with the addition of China, Hong Kong, and "Chinese Taipei") to its current strength of twenty-one, with the addition of Mexico and Papua New Guinea (1993), Chile (1994), and Peru, Russia, and Vietnam (1997). Institutionalization began in February 1993, when the APEC Secretariat was established in Singapore. For details, see "Key APEC Milestones," APEC website, www.apec.org/apec/about_apec/history.html (accessed September 28, 2007).

49. A history of the Leaders' Meeting, and all associated documents, can be found on the APEC Secretariat website: www.apecsec.org.sg.

50. "APEC Leaders' Statement on Counter-Terrorism" (9th APEC Economic Leaders' Meeting, Shanghai, October 21, 2001), www.apec.org/apec/leaders__declarations/2001/statement_on_counter-terrorism.html (accessed September 28, 2007).

51. The Sino-U.S. interaction and cooperation can be seen in a press release made by President George W. Bush and President Jiang Zemin, "U.S., China Stand against Terrorism" (Shanghai, October 19, 2001), www.state.gov/s/ct/rls/rm/2001/5461.htm (accessed September 28, 2007).

52. There were some concerns that the 2006 ASEAN-U.S. Summit would be cancelled, due to apprehensions in Washington about President Bush meeting with Thailand's coup-installed prime minister, General Surayud Chulanont, but it went ahead as scheduled. The 2007 meeting was supposed to be a full U.S.-ASEAN Summit in Singapore after the APEC meeting, but President Bush cancelled his follow-on trip due to Iraq-related challenges, so the "ASEAN 7"—less Cambodia, Laos, and Myanmar, who are not APEC members—took place in Sydney instead (making what would otherwise have been seen as another significant step forward in U.S.-ASEAN relations appear as a consolation prize instead).

53. Chairman's Statement of the First ASEAN-Russian Federation Summit, Kuala Lumpur, December 13, 2005, www.state.gov/r/pa/prs/ps/2005/53490.htm (accessed September 28, 2007).

54. Chairman's Statement of the First East Asia Summit, Kuala Lumpur, December 14, 2005 (hereafter 2005 EAS Chairman's Statement), www.aseansec.org/18104.htm (accessed September 28, 2007).

55. The EAS was originally scheduled for December 2006 in Cebu but was postponed, ostensibly due to an incoming typhoon, although there were also press reports about concerns of a terrorist attack against the assembled leaders. The January 2007 meeting took place under heightened security.

56. For an assessment of the 2007 EAS, APT, and various other ASEAN summits, please see Ralph A. Cossa and Brad Glosserman, "Regional Overview: Tentative Multilateralism and Democracy in Action," *Comparative Connections* 9, no. 4 (January 2008), www.csis.org/media/csis/pubs/0704q_overview.pdf (accessed January 25, 2008).

57. Chairman's Statement of the Second East Asia Summit, Cebu, Philippines, January 15, 2007, www.aseansec.org/19303.htm (accessed September 28, 2007).

58. Remarks by President Bush to the People of Poland, Wawel Royal Castle, Krakow, May 31, 2003. The first PSI meeting was held on June 12, 2003, in Madrid, Spain, with representatives from all eleven core participants in attendance.

59. As described in the Chairman's Statement, Proliferation Security Initiative Second Meeting, Brisbane, Australia, July 9–10, 2003.

60. For more information on PSI, please refer to the Department of State website and, in particular, John R. Bolton, "Proliferation Security Initiative: Statement of Interdiction Principles" (remarks at the Proliferation Security Initiative Meeting, Paris, September 4, 2003), www.state.gov/t/us/rm/23801.htm (accessed September 28, 2007).

61. For a review of the PSI and East Asian attitudes toward this initiative, please see "Countering the Spread of Weapons of Mass Destruction: The Role of the Proliferation Security Initiative (A Review of the Work of the Council for Security Cooperation in the Asia Pacific International Working Group on Confidence and Security Building Measures)," Pacific Forum CSIS *Issues & Insights* 4, no. 5 (July 2004).

62. For details, see Andrew C. Winner, "The Proliferation Security Initiative: The New Face of Interdiction," *Washington Quarterly* 28, no. 2 (Spring 2005): 137.

63. Robert G. Joseph, "Broadening and Deepening Our Proliferation Security Initiative Cooperation" (speech presented at a PSI High Level Political Meeting in Warsaw, June 23, 2006). One recurring concern (accusation) is whether the PSI operates

in accordance with international law. Its Principles state that it must and, to date, there is no evidence to suggest otherwise, but suspicions persist.

64. Please note this refers to the *creation* of the multilateral process, not necessarily to its results to date, although at this writing these was cautious optimism regarding the prospects for eventual denuclearization, Pyongyang's October 2006 nuclear weapons test notwithstanding.

65. For background information on the Six-Party Talks process, see Scott Snyder, Ralph A. Cossa, and Brad Glosserman, "The Six-Party Talks: Developing a Roadmap for Future Progress," *Issues & Insights* 5, no. 8 (August 2005), available on the Pacific Forum CSIS website: www.csis.org/media/csis/pubs/issuesinsights_v05n08.pdf (accessed September 28, 2007). Read the "Regional Overview" and various Korea-related chapters of *Comparative Connections* for quarterly updates on the progress (or lack thereof) of the talks.

VII

CONCLUSION

16

Looking Ahead

A New Asian Order?

Michael Yahuda

As the preceding chapters have shown, international relations in Asia are fluid, and they have yet to settle into a clear pattern or order. By "order" I mean a situation in which there is broad agreement among the players (mainly states) about the basis for conduct among them. The agreement may be the product of a variety of sources: one state exercising hegemony, a balance of power, a concert of powers, or a security regime. It also requires, at a minimum, that there should be agreement about the norms of coexistence between the different states.[1] The United States may still be the primary power, but the use of that power is increasingly circumscribed— partly by the rise of China and the uncertainties of politics within and among the Asian states, and partly by the distraction caused by American commitments in the Middle East and in the more general war against terror. However, no other great power is able to replace the American role as the generator of Asian strategic stability or as the provider of the economic public goods, which have facilitated the remarkable economic growth of the Asian economies.

In order to peer into the future of Asian international relations, I shall first sketch out the main characteristics of the current order and the main forces that are promoting change. Unfortunately, none of the main theories of international relations by itself can successfully identify and explain the interactions between the various developments and characteristics of the current situation in Asia. Therefore I shall follow an eclectic approach to examine relations among the great powers, the significance of the lesser powers, and, finally, the uncertainties of domestic politics. I shall conclude by looking ahead to possible developments in the near future.

Much depends on which theoretical lens is used to look into the future. The three principal international relations (IR) theories—Realism, Liberalism, and Constructivism—each emphasize different elements of the regional order. A Realist sees a region that is increasingly shaped by conflict or incipient conflict centering especially upon the challenges to the United States posed by the rise of China. But Realists differ on whether that would lead to military conflict, or whether the United States would be able to accommodate China's rise and the attendant redistribution of power.[2] A Liberal view would point to the extent of cooperation between the Asian states, especially as institutionalized in regional groupings, and their deepening economic interdependence to develop a workable system of cooperative security.[3] But the Liberal approach has failed to explain why economic interdependence between the Asian states has not resulted in the elimination of the distrust between them.[4] Relations between China and Japan may be seen as a prime example of the weakness of the Liberal School. As Amitav Acharya's chapter demonstrates, a Constructivist vision would point to the significance of norms, culture, identity, and the interactions between states and societies as providing the momentum through regional institutions that are leading toward larger areas of cooperation between Asian states. Yet, other readings of Asian cultures suggest greater diversity than commonality. There is room for disagreement as to how to understand the culture of an individual country—consider, for example, the divergent interpretations of the relatively harmonious Chinese culture. Some emphasize concepts of harmony associated with Confucianism, while others see Chinese strategic culture as based on Realism.[6]

Since none of the three main theories of international relations—Realism, Liberalism, or Constructivism—are sufficient in themselves to provide an adequate explanation of the dynamics that are reshaping the current patterns of international relations in Asia, I shall use an eclectic analytical approach.

MAJOR POWER RELATIONS IN TRANSITION

The international relations of Asia are in a period of transition. The United States may still be the predominant power that provides the public goods that have facilitated the rapid economic growth of most of the Asian states, which has dramatically increased their weight in international affairs. But in part because of that, American predominance is being challenged by the rise of major powers in the region. The question of America's relative decline is much debated in Asia and in the United States itself. In particular, the evolving relations between China and the United States are raising new questions for Washington's allies and friends. As the chapter by Hugh White points out, Australia (perhaps America's most reliable ally in the Asia-Pacific) would prefer to see the United States adopt a "more modest role" that would not require Australia to side with the United States against China. At the same time, relations between the Asian great powers—China, Japan, and India—are developing their own dynamics as they simultaneously compete and cooperate with each other. The pattern that emerges from such an analysis approximates what many Chinese scholars depict as "one superpower, many powers" (*yi chao, duo qiang*).

A further feature of the emerging new Asian order is the significance of smaller and medium powers, both individually and as part of sub-regional groupings. As the chapter by Martha Brill Olcott on Central Asia illustrates, it is not only the great powers, China and Russia, who take initiatives that shape and determine the development and evolution of this sub-region, but lesser powers such as Kazakhstan can do so as well. In a different way, the states of Southeast Asia have played a significant part in shaping the conduct of international relations of their sub-region and perhaps of Asia as a whole. Through ASEAN (Association of Southeast Asian Nations) they have determined the distinctive mode of the operations of the regional institutions. Its norms of procedure by consensus and non-interference have not only facilitated China's absorption into regional multilateral institutions, but they have formed the basis for the operations of all the other regional institutions. Moreover, in the absence of trust between the regional major powers, the lesser powers like ASEAN have filled the void to address many regional problems.

Finally, it is important to consider the uncertainties caused by the unpredictable character of the domestic politics in most Asian states. Few governments can assume the durability of their political systems. The effects of rapid economic growth and the impact of globalization, which may be welcomed for their economic benefits, are also potentially destabilizing. Just as elsewhere in the world, domestic and international developments interact with each other in new and uncomfortable ways. As the chapter on Japan by Michael Green demonstrates, even such a highly developed state is still grappling with the problems of asserting an independent identity in undergoing a process of modernization whose genesis goes back to the early encounters with an imperialistic West. This is still true of most if not all of the Asian states.

American Primacy

Major power relations in Asia revolve around the United States, China, Japan, India, and occasionally Russia (sometimes Europe as a fifth power). It is true that the United States has been weakened by its wars in Iraq and Afghanistan and by the decline in its prestige, but as Robert Sutter has argued in his chapter in this volume, the United States remains "the most important power in the [Asian] region," and there is no other power or organization in the region that is "remotely able, much less willing" to provide the security guarantee and economic public goods that underpin what Sutter calls "U.S. leadership in the region." The United States also has the advantage of being the only major power that does not have territorial disputes with others in the region.

Attempts to establish some kind of counterbalance to American primacy have failed to materialize—at least to date. Russia and China, with or without India, have from time to time suggested that they may work together to counter what they regard as American hegemony, but so far to little effect.[6]

However, American primacy does not mean that the United States is able to lay down the law to others or to impose its will on others, let alone the major regional powers. The George W. Bush administration, for example, was unable to bring sufficient pressure to bear on China to revalue its currency, or even to dissuade relatively tiny Taiwan from conduct that (in the American view) threatened the island's security (even though Taiwan is totally dependent on the United States for its existence). In fact, even the Bush administration found that, despite its early rhetoric in favor of acting unilaterally, it needed to work with others in Asia in order to try and achieve its objectives, whether in the "war against terror" or in trying to persuade North Korea to abandon its nuclear program.

Even as the United States has taken steps to upgrade its alliances and to strengthen its military relations with strategic partners in the region, it is finding that its relations with its regional allies are becoming more complex and conditional. For example, the United States could not necessarily rely on the support of its allies in the event of a confrontation with China. As the chapters in this volume on Korea, Japan, and Australia indicate, America's allies do not want to be placed in a position where they have to "choose" between the United States and China.

Yet the United States remains the "indispensable" power, in soft as well as in hard power. The tsunami disaster of 2004 demonstrated that America alone had the necessary maritime resources to provide needed assistance to the affected countries. In terms of hard power, it is American military power and diplomacy that ensure that the incipient conflicts of this region do not break out into military clashes. For example, it is the American alliance with Japan that assures Japan against possible military encounters with China on the one hand, while on the other hand simultaneously reassuring China against the prospect that Japan may once again become an independent military power able to threaten China. Likewise it is the "insurance" provided by American naval power that has facilitated the engagement of China by Southeast Asian states, who as a consequence are less fearful of being embraced too tightly by China.

None of the major Asian powers is openly challenging the United States—not even China. Since the late 1990s China's diplomacy has deliberately sought to avoid open confrontations with the United States. With its main focus on domestic development, the Chinese government has cultivated cooperative relations with all its neighbors—central to that has been maintaining good working relations with the United States.[7]

There exists, however, the perception in Asia that America is in decline and that its prestige and influence have waned. This is difficult to assess. There have been other times when this has been said of American power in Asia, only to witness a reaffirmation of continuing American predominance. For example, the American withdrawal from Vietnam in 1974, and the challenge of Japan in the late 1980s until 1991, were both (incorrectly) seen at the time as heralding an American regional decline.[8] This does not mean, however, that America may not be in *relative decline*. Clearly the experience of the George W. Bush administration showed the limits of American power worldwide and of its need to pursue a policy of multilateralism rather than unilateralism. Further, there is no question that the continuing rapid growth of the Asian economies, especially those of China and to lesser extent India, is changing the balance of economic power in the region. It goes beyond the question of the relative size of respective GNPs because it affects economic relationships and how governments calculate their respective national interests. We have already seen this in the case of Australia, but the fact that China's trade with each of America's major allies and partners in Northeast Asia (Japan, South Korea, and Taiwan) began to exceed the value of their trade with the United States in the early years of the twenty-first century is not without its political consequences, especially as the trade gap continues to increase.

Not even the Chinese expect Pax Americana in Asia to end anytime soon, so as to usher in what Beijing sees as a new multipolar order. While Chinese IR analysts do claim that the turn to multipolarity is inevitable, they have yet to suggest how long it will be before that new stage is reached. Certainly they do not expect a significant change before 2020 at the earliest.

American primacy rests on several pillars, among others: the dynamism of its society, its scientific inventiveness and technological resourcefulness, the prowess of its economy, and the superior capabilities of its military. Hence the question of U.S. decline cannot be measured by simple projections of current economic trends.

More to the point is the question of whether American military force can prevail in local conflicts in Asia where the costs of victory may be too high—such as with North Korea—or where it may face insurgencies (as in Afghanistan) or where the commitment of protagonists in pursuit of what they may regard as core interests may be more intense than that of the

United States and where proximity may favor the adversary. Taiwan, for example, might be such a case.

American predominance therefore must rest on more than raw economic and military power. It requires astute diplomacy that seeks to encourage others (China especially) that it is in their interests to play by the rules of the existing order that has served them so well. America could play the role of what might be called the "offshore balancer." That would require it to pay heed to the interests and concerns of others, both great and small, even as it sought to manage relations between them.

The Asian major powers—China, Japan, India, and Russia—have not combined to balance the power of the United States for at least three reasons. First, they separately need America more than they need each other and cannot risk alienating Washington. Second, they distrust each other too much to put their trust in a strategic collaboration of this magnitude. Third, they have all benefited from the current order. Putin's Russia may be considered to be a partial exception as it was less dependent on access to the American economy and because it sees the United States as its main protagonist in its current resurgence. Thus Russia has been unhappy with America's active encouragement of the former Soviet Republics (Russia's near abroad) to democratize and to deepen links with the West. That is perhaps why Russia has been more visibly active in seeking to persuade China and India to join it in resisting "hegemonism" (i.e., the United States).

As David Shambaugh's introductory chapter notes, in practice the relationships between the major powers may be characterized as a mixture of cooperation and competition.[9] This is particularly true of China's relationships with Japan and India and to a lesser extent with Russia. China is seen as the main rising power that is increasing its political influence alongside its growing economic interactions and the rapid modernization of its armed forces. Ostensibly, other Asian states, both large and small, welcome their deepening relations with China, but as noted elsewhere in this volume, some also seek to hedge against it.

The key relationship is between China and Japan, the two greatest powers of East Asia. For the first time, the two may be said to be roughly equal independent great powers at the same time. Neither has experience of managing such a situation. Following the Western intrusion into Asia and the Meiji Restoration, Japan saw itself as superior first in military terms until its defeat in 1945, and then in economic terms from the 1960s to the early 1990s. But the bursting of the economic bubble in 1991, followed by ten years of economic stagnation, undermined Japan's economic model and its claim to provide economic leadership to the rest of Asia. At the same time, China was rising amid an explosion of anti-Japanese sentiments, boosted by official encouragement of a patriotism that made much of Japanese atrocities during the 1937–1945 war. It was against this background that

Japanese leaders began to claim that their country should adopt a more as-sertive or "normal" international role, epitomized by the desire to have a permanent seat on the United Nations Security Council, which was for-mally proposed in 2005. No country opposed the Japanese aspiration more than China. For its part, Japan has expressed misgivings about the growth of the Chinese military and its relative lack of transparency. Neither coun-try appears to have considered or taken into account what might be the le-gitimate national security interests of the other. Yet, at the same time, they are economically interdependent, as China has become Japan's leading trade partner and Japan the leading foreign investor in China.

The two appear to be facing a security dilemma as each raises objec-tions to the other's attempts to modernize its military. Not only do they criticize each other's military spending, they also raise objections to the other side's deployments of advanced weaponry. China objects to Japan's development of theater missile defense systems on the grounds that these could degrade its strategic deterrent. Japan is critical of China's missile de-ployments against Taiwan on the grounds that some of these could hit parts of Japan.

The competition between the two is evident in their diplomacy in the re-gion. Japan resisted Chinese attempts in 2005 to restrict a proposed East Asian Summit and putative community to the ASEAN ten plus the three Northeast Asian states of China, South Korea, and Japan, where it was thought Chinese influence might prevail. Instead Tokyo proposed that Aus-tralia, New Zealand, and India should also participate. In the end, the Japanese initiative, openly supported by Singapore, was accepted. Japan has also established a triangular defense relationship with Australia and the United States, and it has proposed a political partnership with the democ-racies of Australia, India, and the United States—both of which exclude China and Beijing suspects might be aimed against it. The two also compete for economic influence in Southeast Asia.

The United States, which maintains good working relations with both China and Japan, is, in effect, the guarantor of strategic stability in the com-petition between the two major powers of the region. Neither can be said to be fully confident in the role of the United States. As the chapter by Michael Green points out, Japan fears both abandonment and entrapment in that it worries that Washington could place greater emphasis upon reach-ing an understanding with China (its main challenger) about the manage-ment of security affairs in the Asia-Pacific, thereby abandoning Japan, or al-ternatively the United States could be engaged in conflict with China and trap Japan in a deteriorating relationship with its neighbor that was not in its interest. For its part, China is afraid that the U.S. alliance with Japan may not act as a constraint on the latter, but rather may lead to a strengthening of Japan so that the two could better contain China. In the absence of the development of a deeper strategic understanding between China and Japan, it falls to the United States to manage this delicate relationship.[10]

India is also engaged in competition as well as cooperation with China.[11] But the competition is less intense than between China and Japan. As the chapter by Sumit Ganguly concludes, "apart from India's subcontinental neighbors and the PRC, who have long had real and perceived grievances against India, the vast majority of Asia appears to be eager to engage an increasingly commercially open, diplomatically assertive, and militarily powerful India." However, part of the reason why a newfound Indian presence has been welcomed in Southeast Asia is that it is seen as another restraint against possible dominance by China.[12]

India's size, culture as one of the formative civilizations in world history, and its fierce tradition of pursuing an independent foreign policy all indicate that it is highly unlikely to join in a coalition designed to contain China. Despite continuing concerns about relations with China and a degree of rivalry with China within Asia, such as over influence in Myanmar, or for access to energy resources elsewhere in the world, India has been careful to avoid being seen to gang up on China. New Delhi's newfound relationship with the United States may be crucial for India's continued resurgence as an economic, political, and military power, but there is little sign of an Indian willingness to be seen as a partner in American strategic hedging against China. By the same token, India has turned down Russian attempts to direct their trilateral relationship with China into a vehicle against American "hegemony."

At the same time, India and China have been engaged in confidence-building measures between their militaries in disputed border areas and are carrying out relatively small joint military maneuvers (such as sea rescues and anti-terror exercises). Although these do not compare in scope or military significance to those conducted with the United States, as itemized in Ganguly's chapter, those with China are significant if only for symbolizing the intent to develop amicable relations. Moreover, Sino-Indian trade has picked up from a low level of $2 billion in 2000 to nearly $25 billion in 2007 with a joint target to reach $60 billion by 2010—making China India's second-largest trade partner.[13]

It is one thing, however, to improve bilateral relations and it is quite another to agree on how to accommodate their respective great power aspirations. China has refused to support India's claim to a permanent seat in the UN Security Council, and it has publicly expressed reservations about Indian interest in acquiring ballistic missile defense systems and about the civil nuclear agreement between India and the United States. For its part, India may be regarded as engaging in competitive relations with China in Southeast Asia, while its newly developing relations with Japan and the

United States also have the effect of limiting China's ability to emerge as the dominant power in Asia.

The Role of Lesser Powers

The distrust between the major powers and their attempts to hedge against each other have paradoxically both circumscribed and enlarged the space within which the small and middle-sized powers operate.

The leadership role assigned to ASEAN in the main regional associations arises less from the inherent qualities of ASEAN itself than from the failure of the major powers to agree among themselves how to handle the regional leadership issue. Clearly, it stretches credulity to accept that ASEAN states, separately or collectively, could exercise effective leadership over the major powers in the ASEAN Regional Forum (ARF), which includes all the great powers, or even the ASEAN + 3, which includes China, Japan, and South Korea. Yet ASEAN has set the terms for the way in which the regional associations conduct their affairs. As pointed out in Amitav Acharya's chapter, the ASEAN modus operandi (the "ASEAN Way") has set the norms, ideas, and even an identity that in Constructivist terms are giving a particular character to international relations in Asia. It has provided the forum, for example, for the expansion of China's diplomacy in Asia and for the operation of the Shanghai Cooperation Organisation, which China was instrumental in establishing.

The ASEAN framework provided the forum through the ARF for the induction of China into multilateralism in Asia. Rather than follow their traditional diplomacy of bilateralism in dealing with neighbors, where Chinese superiority could be used to advantage and where opportunities could be found to exploit differences between them, the Chinese found it to their advantage from 1995 onward to deal with the ASEAN countries on a multilateral basis. This was extended to negotiations on several aspects of issues concerning the South China Sea, although the Chinese have continued to argue that territorial disputes should be dealt with on a bilateral basis. China was the first external power to sign up to the ASEAN's Treaty of Amity and Cooperation, which formally sets out the terms of conduct for relations in Southeast Asia. Within the framework of the ASEAN approach, China has developed initiatives in multilateral regional diplomacy.

Asian multilateralism, which puts so much stress on process rather than the reaching of binding agreements, as distinct from Western international institutions, has not found much favor in the United States. But the United States has come under increasing pressure, especially from some of its Southeast Asian friends, to participate more in the Asian regional associations as they fear that in the absence of the United States, other major powers (notably China) will establish greater influence. While there is a tendency in the United States, and during the George W. Bush administration in particular, to dismiss these regional associations as little more than "talk shops," the regional states take them more seriously and are concerned lest the United States be marginalized by its absence, leaving them to fall under greater Chinese influence and thus reduce their room for maneuver.[14]

In Northeast Asia, as the chapter by Scott Snyder makes clear, the nuclear crisis with North Korea, and especially the prospects for its resolution, have brought to the fore new security dilemmas for all six of the parties. My concern is less to explore further the security problems of the sub-region than to draw attention to the relative freedom of maneuver the lesser powers have been able to develop in this context.

The conflicts of interest between the major powers, especially between Japan and China, but also involving the United States and to a lesser extent Russia, have contributed to allowing space for both North and South Korea to follow their own interests to a certain extent. In view of the threat to regime survival posed by continued confrontation or by exposing the country to the international economy or indeed by a full opening to the South, the North, despite its evident weaknesses, has so far been able to exploit the divisions within and between the other main parties to the talks to buy time and exploit its bargaining position. The South, which should be regarded perhaps as a medium rather than a minor power, has developed an independent approach to the problem by seeking reconciliation with the North through economic engagement, often to the chagrin of its key ally, the United States.

Similarly, as the chapter by Martha Brill Olcott on Central Asia shows, the competition between China and Russia has allowed Kazakhstan to assert a leading role in the sub-region, as perhaps befits the largest country with the most successful economy. Although the Shanghai Cooperation Organisation may suffer from some of the same defects as ASEAN as a programmatic organization, it too has been able to assert an identity of a kind. Despite the distrust between its members, in the words of Olcott, "The SCO has succeeded in creating an identity for itself as a forum for permitting the states of the region to discuss shared problems and possible solutions to them. But to date it has yet to create successful strategies for dealing with these problems."

In sum, the different security objectives and the competition between the major Asian powers have allowed space for the lesser powers in the region to hedge against the major powers and to pursue independent policies, sometimes to the annoyance of the great powers. The distrust between the major powers has also enabled the lesser powers in Southeast Asia and to a certain extent in Central Asia to develop their own regional collective identities that in turn have shaped the conduct of the great powers.

THE UNCERTAINTIES ARISING FROM DOMESTIC POLITICS

Any consideration of regional order in Asia must take account of the domestic as well as the international bases of such an order. Asia, unlike Europe, is characterized by many divisions between the character of the political systems of states and the qualities of governance, as well as by the well-known ones of geographical size, religion, levels of economic development, ethnicity, values, and so on. The Asian states are also relatively new or even in the case of old ones, such as China and Japan, totally new political systems were established in the late 1940s or early 1950s. None of them take independent statehood for granted, and few if any can be said to have well-established political systems. Their senses of vulnerability derive from these essentially domestic concerns. Most Asian governments pursue rapid economic growth and economic development not only for economic and social reasons, but also to strengthen domestic political stability and hence the security of the state as they see it.

The end of the Cold War and the growing significance of globalization have brought about a paradoxical result with regard to the interactions between the domestic and the international. The process of globalization has led to extending the reach of international influences further than ever before into the domestic societies and politics of states. At the same time, in the absence of an overarching international axis of conflict—as between the former Soviet Union and the United States—the conduct of domestic politics has been more detached from international politics.

The domestic politics of Asian states are no longer constrained as much by the external choices that were incumbent upon them as a result of the Cold War. In some cases, the end of the Cold War had profound effects on their domestic political systems. In Japan, for example, the end of what was called "the San Francisco System" brought about fundamental change in its politics. Moreover, domestic divisions and political conflicts no longer automatically attract the attentions of competing superpowers, with the attendant risk of intervention. Intervention may still take place, because of perceived threats of terrorism and the proliferation of weapons of mass destruction (WMD), or on humanitarian grounds. But unlike the Cold War period, intervention no longer takes place to alter or to uphold a balance of power between competing superpowers and their respective systems and ideologies.

Nevertheless, changes and uncertainties in domestic politics can have important consequences for the international domain. Changes of prime ministers in Japan (from Koizumi to Abe and Fukuda) had an impact on Tokyo's relations with China and the United States. Similarly, electoral changes in South Korea and Taiwan, which are largely determined by domestic issues, would have important repercussions in shaping the conduct of the major powers involved in managing the potential conflicts in their sub-regions.

Consider, also, the role of nationalism. One of the ways of consolidating statehood and mending social divisions is by encouraging nationalist sentiments. Rapid economic growth necessarily leads to rapid social change and the breakdown of traditional communities—which, in turn, provides a social basis for enhancing what one of the main writers on nationalism has called "imagined communities."[15] This nationalism builds on the remnants of anti-colonial or anti-Western nationalism to develop a new nationalism to meet contemporary needs. Although in much of Asia nationalist sentiments continue to be targeted against the United States, a good deal is targeted at Asian neighbors. The nationalism of American allies often incorporates a degree of resentment against perceived limits on their independence and on cultural identity. This has been true of South Korea, Japan, the Philippines, and even Australia, despite the continuation of basic support for maintaining the respective alliances. South Korean nationalism is directed at Japan and China, too, especially after the latter claimed in 2005 that the ancient kingdom of Koguryo had historically been a part of China, as opposed to the Koreans of both North and South who had long seen it as one of the founders of Korea. Chinese nationalism took on more of an anti-Japanese character in the 1980s, and the 1990s were bolstered by maritime territorial disputes between China and Japan. As the chapter by Sheldon Simon demonstrates, many of the Southeast Asian states not only distrust each other, but their nationalism is often directed at each other as well.

Nationalist sentiments also make it more difficult to manage the burgeoning security dilemmas discussed in Scott Snyder's chapter. This is particularly true of Sino-Japanese relations. Nationalism also accentuates the difficulties in reconciling the aspirations of each of the Asian great powers to play greater roles in international and regional affairs.

Although domestic politics may be influenced by external sources, they necessarily reflect their own social and political divisions and their dynamics are largely self-generated. But because of the greater interconnectedness of our globalizing world, domestic political developments often impact on international politics in unforeseen ways, creating new sources of uncertainty.

TOWARD A NEW ORDER IN ASIA

From an economic point of view, Asia is increasingly regarded as the most important region in the world. Indeed it is widely thought to be the next most important focal point of the world economy that may soon replace the United States as the main engine of global economic growth. The Asian economies, as the chapter by Edward Lincoln points out, are far from integrated, yet the regional production chain has made them economically interdependent. The extent to which Asia may act as a collective entity in the international economy will depend very much on politics rather than economics.

Politically, Asia is not as coherent a region as Europe. It is not characterized by common values, common institutions, or by a willingness to pool sovereignty. On the contrary, the Asian states, old and new alike, seek to protect their sovereignty and enhance their independence. They are highly diverse, and, unlike Europe, they do not share a history of interactions prior to the modern era. The Asian states do not trust each other, most have territorial disputes with their neighbors, and most are engaged in building up their respective military forces. Yet since the end of the Cold War, Asian states have established new regional institutions aimed at building mutual confidence, enhancing cooperation, and working toward the establishment of an Asian, or more strictly, an East Asian identity.

The attempt to create an Asian identity is entirely a modern enterprise. The very concept of Asia as a geographical or a cultural entity is European in origin. Asia, in the shape of Persia, was seen by the ancient Greeks as autocratic in contrast to democratic Europe as epitomized by Greece. Some two thousand years later, Karl Marx also differentiated between what he called the "Asiatic mode of production," as distinguished from European "feudalism." It was only in the late nineteenth century that nationalists, first in India and Japan, began to speak of Asia as a coherent political entity in the struggle for independence and equality. As Samuel Kim has pointed out in his chapter, the first attempt to create a self-conscious Asian regional system was the "East Asian Co-prosperity" scheme promoted by Japan from the late 1930s to its defeat in 1945.

The cohesiveness of Asia and its various sub-divisions was not widespread at this time. The concept of Southeast Asia as a regional or sub-regional entity was, in fact, the product of Anglo-American division of territorial responsibilities during the Pacific War. The first major attempt by newly independent Asian states to establish a separate alignment between the two Cold War blocs came at the Bandung Conference in 1955. Significantly, it was not confined to Asia, but included Africa as well. In any event, such solidarity as was manifested in Bandung was soon shattered by open warfare between Asian states. It was not until the end of the Cold War that a new Asian consciousness can be said to have emerged.

The Western influence on contemporary Asia is still very deep. International relations in Asia have arisen in large part out of complex processes of modernization introduced by the West. The very concept of statehood as denoting territorial integrity based on internationally recognized borders, with sovereign equality between states, now so tenaciously rooted in the region, is wholly derived from Europe.

Further, Asian international relations have been and continue to be very much a part of the worldwide international system. They, too, were subject to the bipolar division of the Cold War. In the nearly two decades since its end, their international relations are shaped to a considerable extent by the only truly global power—the United States. That is still true for the economic sphere as well. As the chapters by Robert Sutter and Edward Lincoln demonstrate, even as far as economic performance is concerned, where arguably China alone is beginning to challenge the United States, the American market, American investment, and American technology transfers still play crucial roles in the development of the Asian economies, including that of China. Moreover, it is America that continues to provide the public goods that underpin the Asian trade and security patterns. It is not possible, therefore, to identify an Asian regional order that is geographically exclusive.

Nevertheless, the United States is less dominant than it once was, and not only in the economic sphere. It faces difficult challenges in Asia and not just because of the distraction arising from its military commitments to the long, drawn out wars in Iraq and Afghanistan. Newfound problems have emerged in the handling of "hot spots" such as Taiwan and North Korea, not least because of differences with allies. More broadly, the United States is challenged by how best to manage the rise of China and the different patterns of cooperation and competition between the Asian great powers. Meanwhile Asian states have been developing regional patterns of international relations in Southeast and Central Asia largely independent of the United States.

Clearly there is no settled pattern of order in Asia. All the major powers are in processes of transition as they continue to grow and develop their economies and as they seek to play more prominent roles in international affairs. In the coming years much will depend on how successfully India, and especially China, can manage the stresses and strains of the changes brought about by rapid economic growth and whether they can carry out necessary political reforms to meet the needs of an increasingly complex economy and society. The need for domestic structural reforms and uncertainties about how best to assert a more active international and regional role are evident in Japan.

Although both India and Japan are seeking to enhance their international roles and Russia is trying to recapture something of the international and regional stature of the former Soviet Union, it is the rise of China that is contributing most to the dynamics of change in Asia and beyond. China's process of rapid economic growth began earlier than that of India, and its impact on the Asian and international economy far exceeds that of India.

Combined with deft diplomacy, China's political weight has increased and unless something drastic should occur, that influence is bound to continue to increase. China has also been rapidly modernizing its military forces, which is beginning to trouble its neighbors and is seen as a potential challenge to American ability to deter China from using force to realize its claim to Taiwan. Further, if China's other maritime territorial claims (whatever their intrinsic merits) were to be realized, China in effect would challenge the existing distribution of power in the region. China would emerge as the dominant power in Northeast Asia and by virtue of its control of the Spratly Islands, it would reach down into the heart of Southeast Asia, transforming the South China Sea into something of a Chinese lake.

Perhaps conscious of the destabilizing implications of pursuing its full nationalistic agenda, successive Chinese leaders have given their main priority to tackling pressing domestic issues. To this end, they have pursued foreign policies designed to promote a peaceful international environment within their own neighborhood. Any Chinese pursuit of a more aggressive national agenda would rapidly bring it into conflict with most of its neighbors, who would look to support from the United States. However, the priorities of the Chinese government are to focus on the demanding domestic agenda. To this end, it has cultivated cooperative relations with its neighbors and pursued what it calls "win-win" economic relationships. China's deepening enmeshment with the international economy and its key institutions has resulted in the development of an interest in the maintenance of the rules and norms of the international system, which have served its economic development so well.[16]

A resurgence of Chinese nationalism, sparked perhaps by social disorder or by a sudden change in the favorable international economic environment and/or perceived hostile policies by other powers, especially the United States, could transform China's relatively benign foreign policies into something more hostile and intransigent. The other Asian states recognize that they have to live with a China that is rising in both economic and military terms and hope to benefit from the former and to hedge against the latter. The hedging takes two forms: first, to socialize China by integrating it into the norms and processes of Asian international relations as epitomized by the various regional multilateral groupings; and, second, by relying on the countervailing power of the United States.

In the final analysis, the current order in Asia still depends on American power and Washington's willingness to continue to provide the public goods that have facilitated the rise of the Asian economies. However, America's relative economic strength is declining in the region and perhaps in the world as a whole. As China continues to rise, the United States finds that it simultaneously needs to work with China to address a range of vital issues of both regional and international significance, while also needing to hedge against it in cooperation with other Asian states. These in turn seek to maintain and develop good relations with both the United States and China and do not want to be placed in a situation where they have to "choose" between them.

The development of the New Asian order in the immediate future—say until 2015—is likely to continue to be a transitional one with marked continuities with the present. Domestic politics throughout the region will remain a source of uncertainty, though. Assuming that nothing drastic happens to derail the Chinese juggernaut, China's influence in Asia will continue to grow along present lines, balanced to a certain extent by India and Japan with whom it will continue to both cooperate and compete.[17] At the same time, the United States will continue to be the "indispensable" country even though its primacy will be challenged by the rise of China. Meanwhile, it will fall to the United States to manage the regional major power triangle involving itself, China, and Japan.

Pathways to the Future

Two scenarios suggest themselves as the likely basis for a new Asian order in the immediate future. The first is the continuation of the current order with all its stresses and strains, basically moderated by American primacy. The second would be the beginnings of a multipolar system, in which each of the great powers would have its own attributes as they competed with each other.

The first scenario of continuing American primacy would be based on its massive regional military superiority (despite its commitments elsewhere in the world). But primacy would also require an economic recovery by the United States from low growth with huge foreign indebtedness amid large budgetary and trade deficits and a weak currency. An economic recovery would be needed not so much in order to compete with the Chinese economy, but rather to reestablish confidence in its capacity to provide economic leadership. If current economic trends should continue, the impression of American economic decline will be strengthened to the point where America would no longer be the central economic player in the region. Although America might still be the ultimate guarantor of security and of the sea lanes of communication, confidence in its capacity and willingness to continue to play the role of the regional policeman would erode. At issue would be less the reality of relative economic decline (however that may be measured) and more the perception of it.

The first scenario would also call for deft American management of the rise of China and of the competitive relations between the regional powers. If Washington is to provide leadership it will also have to pay more attention to the concerns of regional states and to involve itself more in regional multilateralism.[18] Otherwise the United States will be seen to be marginalizing itself. The United States should also seek to provide active leadership to address the many dimensions of non-traditional security, using its maritime capacities and advanced technologies for the general good as it did during the tsunami disaster of 2004.

The second scenario of emerging multipolarity would follow from a deepening of America's relative economic decline and a failure to provide leadership of the kind suggested above. America's allies and friends would draw closer to Beijing, and China's influence in the region would grow. China's economic development and military capabilities would still be largely insufficient to allow it to supplant the United States as the provider of security and the public goods in the region—so that America would remain the most powerful of the major powers, but it would lose the primacy or evident preeminence that it currently enjoys. Instead, the United States would become the most powerful of a handful of major powers, each with its own particularities, strengths, and weaknesses. At issue would be whether the United States, China, Japan, India, and Russia could establish a concert of powers, perhaps along the relatively loose lines of cooperative security of the ASEAN Regional Forum. The alternative would be a shifting—and perhaps dangerous—series of coalitions in attempts to establish a balance of power.

A third possible scenario is a potential concert of powers, as envisaged in David Shambaugh's introductory chapter. With the amelioration of Sino-Japanese relations post-2007, this has become more possible.

However, the main determinant of the evolution of Asian international relations in the immediate future (up to 2015) will be the relative strength and endurance of the United States. China can be expected to continue to rise and to increase its influence, but the key question will be how the United States responds and how the other Asian states appraise that response.

NOTES

1. For further discussion of the concept, see Amitav Acharya, "Regional Institutions and Asian Security Order: Norms, Power, and Prospects for Change" in *Asian Security Order: Instrumental and Normative Features*, ed. Muthiah Alagappa (Stanford, Calif.: Stanford University Press, 2003), 210–240.

2. Zbigniew Brzezinski, for example, sees China's rise as inevitable, and although that could lead to conflict, he believes that Sino-American cooperation could prevent that, whereas John Mearsheimer believes that conflict is inevitable. See Zbigniew Brzezinski and John Mearsheimer, "Clash of the Titans," *Foreign Policy* 164 (January/February 2005).

Michael Yahuda

3. Robert O. Keohane, *After Hegemony* (Princeton, N.J.: Princeton University Press, 1984).

4. Michael Yahuda, "The Limits of Interdependence, Sino-Japanese Relations," in *New Directions in the Study of Chinese Foreign Policy*, ed. Robert S. Ross and Alastair I. Johnston (Stanford, Calif.: Stanford University Press, 2006).

5. Alastair I. Johnston, *Cultural Realism: Strategic Culture and Grand Strategy in Chinese History* (Princeton, N.J.: Princeton University Press, 1995). For an argument about the significance of justice and morality in Chinese strategic thinking, see Zhang Junbo and Yao Yunzhu, "Traditional Chinese Military Thinking: A Comparative Perspective," in *Chinese Foreign Policy: Pragmatism and Strategic Behavior*, ed. Suisheng Zhao (Armonk, N.Y.: M. E. Sharpe, 2004).

6. M. K. Bhadrakumar, "A Velvet Divorce in China," *Asia Times Online*, October 31, 2007, www.attimes.com/attimes/china/ij31Ad01.htm (accessed January 15, 2008).

7. Bates Gill, *Rising Star: China's New Security Diplomacy* (Washington, D.C.: Brookings Institution Press, 2007).

8. Perhaps the most influential of these was Paul Kennedy, *The Rise and Fall of the Great Powers* (New York: Random House, 1987). Kennedy predicted that Japan would replace the United States as the greatest global power.

9. For details and analysis see Michael Yahuda, *The Post Cold War Order in Asia and the Challenge to ASEAN* (Singapore: ISEAS, 2005).

10. For a careful analysis of Japanese views of their security dilemmas, see Richard J. Samuels, *Securing Japan* (Ithaca, N.Y.: Cornell University Press, 2007).

11. For background, see John Garver, *Protracted Conflict: Sino-Indian Rivalry in the Twentieth Century* (Seattle: University of Washington Press, 2001).

12. Ashley J. Tellis, "China and India in Asia," in *The India-China Relationship*, ed. Francine R. Frankel and Harry Harding (New York and Washington, D.C.: Columbia University Press and Woodrow Wilson Center Press, 2004), 134–177.

13. *China Daily*, December 26, 2007, www.chinadaily.com.cn/china/2007-12/26/content_6348028.htm (accessed January 9, 2008).

14. For further details and analysis, see Gill, *Rising Star*, chapters 2 and 6.

15. Benedict Anderson, *Imagined Communities*, revised and extended edition (London and New York: Verso, 1991); and Ernst Gellner, *Nations and Nationalism* (Ithaca, N.Y.: Cornell University Press, 1983).

16. See G. John Ikenberry, "The Rise of China and the Future of the West," *Foreign Affairs* 87, no. 1 (January/February 2008): 23–37.

17. See the chapters in David Shambaugh, ed., *Power Shift: China and Asia's New Dynamics* (Berkeley: University of California Press, 2005).

18. See Ralph Cossa and Akihiko Tanaka, eds., *An East Asian Community and the United States* (Washington, D.C.: Center for Strategic and International Studies, 2007).

Index

Abe administration: China relations, 12, 16, 176, 351; national strategy, 172; North Korea policy, 179; U.S. alliance, 182–83

Abe Shinzo, 186, 187, 223

Abu Sayyaf (Father of the Sword), 24, 200, 211, 310

Aceh Monitoring Mission (AMM), 108, 114

ACFTA. *See* ASEAN-China Free Trade Area (ACFTA)

Action Plan for EU-Japan Cooperation, 112

activists, role in globalization concerns, 301, 307–9

Afghanistan: border states, 237; development assistance to, 238; EDSP police force in, 108; instability, effect on terrorism, 235; Japan's support to coalition forces in, 322; SCO, role in, 238, 249; war against terrorism in, 89, 91, 108, 141, 181, 343, 354

Akayev, Askar, 238–39, 241

Alaska, 157

Almaty (Kazakhstan) summit, 234

Al Ma'unah (Brotherhood of Inner Power), 310

al Qaeda, 23–24, 200, 310

AMM. *See* Aceh Monitoring Mission (AMM)

anarchy, Realist perspective, 60, 64, 68

Andijon civil unrest, 237, 239, 241

Ang Lee, 139

anti-globalization movement, 301, 309

APEC. *See* Asia-Pacific Economic Cooperation (APEC)

APEC forum, purpose of, 184–85

APT. *See* ASEAN+3 (APT)

Arab states, 152–53, 234

ARF. *See* ASEAN Regional Forum (ARF)

Armitage, Richard, 326

Arrow War (1856–1860), 40

Arunachal Pradesh, 158

ASEAN+3 (APT): APEC compared, 289; emergence, 208–9; financial cooperation, 208, 294–97; institutionalization of, 117; NEAT membership, 138; security, impact on, 208–9, 330. *See also specific members of*

ASEAN+3+3 EAS meeting, 330

ASEAN+China, 131

ASEAN Charter, 203

ASEAN-China Free Trade Area (ACFTA), 305

About the Contributors

David Shambaugh is professor of political science and international affairs and director of the China Policy Program in the Elliott School of International Affairs at George Washington University. Since 1998 he has also been a non-resident senior fellow in the Foreign Policy Studies Program at the Brookings Institution. He is also a consultant to the U.S. government and a number of foundations and corporations. He previously served as Editor of the *China Quarterly*, was Reader in Chinese Politics at the University of London, and a fellow at the Woodrow Wilson International Center for Scholars. He serves on the editorial boards of numerous scholarly and foreign policy journals and is a member of the International Institute for Strategic Studies, National Committee on U.S.-China Relations, Council on Foreign Relations, Pacific Council on International Policy, and several other scholarly and public policy organizations. He has published widely on Chinese domestic and foreign affairs, as well as the international relations of Asia and Europe. His most recent books are *China's Communist Party: Atrophy and Adaptation* (2008), *China-Europe Relations: Perceptions, Policies and Prospects* (ed., with Eberhard Sandschneider and Zhou Hong, 2007), *China Watching: Perspectives from Europe, Japan and the United States* (ed. with Robert Ash and Seiichiro Takagi, 2007), *Power Shift: China and Asia's New Dynamics* (ed., 2005), *The Odyssey of China's Imperial Art Treasures* (with Jeannette Shambaugh Elliott, 2005), *Modernizing China's Military* (2003), and *The Modern Chinese State* (ed., 2000).

Michael Yahuda is professor emeritus in international relations at the London School of Economics and Political Science, University of London, where he taught from 1973 to 2003. He is currently a visiting scholar and adjunct professor at the Sigur Center for Asian Studies of the Elliott School of International Affairs at George Washington University. He has been a fellow at the Woodrow Wilson International Center for Scholars, the Fairbank Center for East Asian Research at Harvard, the Singapore Institute of Southeast Asian Studies, Australian National University, the University of Adelaide, and the University of Michigan. He has been an adviser to the British Foreign and Commonwealth Office and a consultant to organizations in London and Singapore. His main fields of interest are China's foreign relations and the international politics of the Asia-Pacific. He has published six books and more than two hundred articles and book chapters. His latest book, *The International Politics of the Asia-Pacific: Since 1945*, was published in 2005. He is currently preparing a book on Sino-Japanese relations and their implications for the United States.

Amitav Acharya is professor of global governance in the Department of Politics at the University of Bristol (United Kingdom), and director of its Centre for Governance and International Affairs. His books include *Constructing a Security Community in Southeast Asia* (2001), *Reassessing Security Cooperation in the Asia-Pacific* (ed., 2007), *Crafting Cooperation: Regional International Institutions in Comparative Perspective* (ed. with Alastair Iain Johnston, 2007), and *Whose Ideas Matter: Norms, Power and Institutions in Asian Regionalism* (2008). His recent journal articles have appeared in *International Organization*, *International Security*, and *World Politics*.

Sebastian Bersick is senior fellow in the Asia Research Unit at the German Institute for International and Security Affairs (SWP) in Berlin. He previously worked and lectured at the Centre for Chinese and East-Asian Studies at the Free University of Berlin, in the Department of Economics at Bremen University of Applied Sciences, and at the European Institute for Asian Studies (EIAS) in Brussels, where he was head of the Research Unit on EU-Asia Inter-Regionalism and New Regionalism in Asia. He has held consultancies for the European Commission, the European Parliament, NATO, and several NGOs. He is the coauthor of *Compass 2020: Germany in International Relations. Goals, Instruments, Perspectives: Southeast Asia* (2007), and co-editor of *Multiregionalism and Multilateralism: Asian-European Relations in a Global Context* (2006). His books on Asian-Europe relations include *Auf dem Weg in eine neue Weltordnung: Zur Politik der interregionalen Beziehungen am Beispiel des ASEM-Prozesses* [*Towards a New World Order: On the Politics of Interregional Relations; The Example of the ASEM Process*] (2004), for which he received the Ernst Reuter Prize for outstanding doctoral dissertation from the Free University of Berlin. He is also a frequent commentator in national and international media.

Nayan Chanda is the director of publications at the Yale Center for the Study of Globalization and the editor of *YaleGlobal Online*. Since 1970 he has been associated with the Hong Kong–based *Far Eastern Economic Review*, as its reporter, diplomatic correspondent, and editor. He is the author of *Brother Enemy: The War after the War* (1986) and co-author of over a dozen books on Asian politics, security, and foreign policy. His most recent book, *Bound Together: How Traders, Preachers, Adventurers, and Warriors Shaped Globalization* (2007), has been translated into Korean, Chinese, Japanese, and Italian. He is co-editor (with Strobe Talbott) of *The Age of Terror: America and the World after September 11* (2002) and co-editor (with Bruce Mazlish and Kenneth Weisbrode) of *The Paradox of a Global USA* (2007). Since 2003 he has been a non-resident senior fellow of the Brookings Institution and a member of the Advisory Council for the Brookings Center for Northeast Asian Policy Studies. He is a member of the editorial boards of *GlobalAsia* and *New Global Studies Journal*. He also writes a regular column on globalization in *BusinessWorld*. Nayan Chanda is the winner of the 2005 Shorenstein Award for Journalism, presented jointly by the Walter H. Shorenstein Forum for Asia Pacific Studies at Stanford University and the Shorenstein Center on the Press, Politics and Public Policy at Harvard University.

Ralph A. Cossa is president of the Pacific Forum CSIS in Honolulu, a non-profit foreign policy research institute affiliated with the Center for Strategic and International Studies (CSIS) in Washington, D.C. He is senior editor of the forum's quarterly electronic journal, *Comparative Connections*. Mr. Cossa is a member of the ASEAN Regional Forum (ARF) Experts and Eminent Persons Group. He is a founding member of the Steering Committee of the Council for Security Cooperation in the Asia Pacific (CSCAP). He co-chairs the CSCAP study group aimed at halting the proliferation of weapons of mass destruction in the Asia-Pacific region and also serves as Executive Director of the U.S. Member Committee (USCSCAP). He also sits on the board of the Council on U.S.-Korean Security Studies and the National Committee on U.S.-China Relations and is a member of the International Institute for Strategic Studies (London). He is a frequent contributor to regional newspapers, including the *Japan Times, Korea Times*, and *International Herald Tribune*. His most recent book is *An East Asian Community and the United States* (ed. with Akihiko Tanaka, 2007).

Sumit Ganguly holds the Rabindranath Tagore Chair in Indian Cultures and Civilizations and is professor of political science and director of research of the Center on American and Global Security at Indiana University in Bloomington. He has previously been on the faculty of James Madison College of Michigan State University, Hunter College of the City University of New York, and the University of Texas at Austin. He has also been a fellow and a guest scholar at the Woodrow Wilson International Center for Scholars in Washington, D.C., and a visiting fellow at the Center for International Security and Cooperation at Stanford University. He serves on the editorial boards of *Asian Affairs, Asian Survey, Current History,* the *Journal of Democracy,* the *Journal of Strategic Studies,* and *Security Studies.* He is the founding editor of both the *India Review* and *Asian Security* and is the author, editor, or co-editor of fifteen books on South Asia. His most recent books are *Fearful Symmetry: India-Pakistan Crises in the Shadow of Nuclear Weapons* (with Devin T. Hagerty, 2005) and *U.S.-Indian Strategic Cooperation into the 21st Century: More Than Words* (ed. with Brian Shoup and Andrew Scobell, 2006). He is a member of the Council on Foreign Relations and the International Institute for Strategic Studies. His latest book is an edited work (with Larry Diamond and Marc Plattner), *The State of India's Democracy.* He is currently working on *India since 1980.*

Michael J. Green is associate professor of international relations at the Edmund A. Walsh School of Foreign Service at Georgetown University and senior adviser and Japan chair at the Center for Strategic and International Studies in Washington, D.C. He served as special assistant to the president for national security affairs and senior director for Asian affairs on the National Security Council staff during the administration of George W. Bush, and before that as a fellow at the Council on Foreign Relations and a faculty member at the Johns Hopkins University School of Advanced International Studies. His previous publications on Japan include *Japan's Reluctant Realism* (2000) and *Arming Japan* (1995), in addition to numerous journal articles in *Foreign Affairs,* the *National Interest,* and other periodicals.

Samuel S. Kim is senior research scholar at Columbia University's Weatherhead East Asian Institute. He previously taught at The College of Foreign Affairs (Beijing, China), Princeton University, and Columbia University. He is the author or editor of twenty-two books on East Asian international relations, Chinese and Korean foreign relations, and world order studies, including *China, the United Nations, and World Order* (1979), *The War System: An Interdisciplinary Approach* (ed. with Richard A. Falk, 1980), *The Quest for a Just World Order* (1984), *North Korean Foreign Relations in the Post–Cold War Era* (ed., 1998), *Korea's Globalization* (ed., 2000), *East Asia and Globalization* (ed., 2000), *Korea's Democratization* (ed., 2003), *The International Relations of Northeast Asia* (ed., 2004), and *The Two Koreas and the Great Powers* (2006). He has published more than 160 articles in edited volumes and leading international relations journals, including the *American Journal of International Law, China Quarterly, International Organization, Journal of Chinese Law, Jour-*

nal of East Asian Studies, Journal of Peace Research, World Policy Journal, and *World Politics.*

Edward J. Lincoln is professor of economics and director of the Center for Japan-U.S. Business and Economic Studies at the Leonard N. Stern School of Business, New York University. Before joining NYU in 2006, Professor Lincoln was a senior fellow at the Council on Foreign Relations, and earlier a senior fellow at the Brookings Institution. In the mid-1990s he served as special economic adviser to Ambassador Walter Mondale at the American Embassy in Tokyo. His latest book, on the underappreciated importance of economic issues in international relations and American foreign policy, is *Winners without Losers: Why Americans Should Care More about Global Economic Policy* (2007). He is the author of eight other books and monographs, including *East Asian Economic Regionalism* (2004), *Arthritic Japan: The Slow Pace of Economic Reform* (2001), and *Troubled Times: U.S.-Japan Trade Relations in the 1990s* (1998). He has also published numerous articles and op-ed pieces on Japan, U.S.-Japan economic relations, and broader East Asian economic issues.

Martha Brill Olcott is a senior associate with the Russia and Eurasia Program at the Carnegie Endowment for International Peace in Washington, D.C. She specializes in the problems of transitions in Central Asia and the Caucasus, as well as the security challenges in the Caspian region more generally. She has followed interethnic relations in Russia and the states of the former Soviet Union for more than twenty-five years and has traveled extensively in these countries and in South Asia. In addition to her work in Washington, Olcott co-directs the Carnegie Moscow Center Program on Religion, Society, and Security in the former Soviet Union. She is professor emeritus at Colgate University, having taught political science there from 1974 to 2002. Olcott served for five years as a director of the Central Asian American Enterprise Fund. Prior to her work at the Carnegie Endowment, Olcott served as a special consultant to former secretary of state Lawrence Eagleburger. Her most recent books include *Central Asia's Second Chance* (2005), *Kazakhstan: Unfulfilled Promise* (2002), and *Getting It Wrong: Regional Cooperation and the Commonwealth of Independent States* (with Anders Aslund and Sherman W. Garnett, 1999).

Phillip C. Saunders has been a senior research fellow at the National Defense University's Institute for National Strategic Studies (INSS) since 2004. He conducts research on China and East Asian security issues. Dr. Saunders has organized and participated in a wide variety of roundtables, conferences, and seminars on Asian security issues. He previously worked at the

Monterey Institute of International Studies, where he served as Director of the East Asia Nonproliferation Program at the Center for Nonproliferation Studies from 1999 to 2004 and taught courses on Chinese politics, Chinese foreign policy, and East Asian security. He has also conducted research or consulted on East Asian security issues for Princeton University, the Council on Foreign Relations, and the National Committee on U.S.-China Relations. From 1989 to 1993, he served as an officer in the U.S. Air Force working on Asian policy issues. He has published numerous book chapters and articles on China and Asian security in journals including *International Security, China Quarterly,* the *China Journal, Survival, Asian Survey, Pacific Review, Orbis, Asia Policy,* and *Joint Forces Quarterly.* His recent monograph is *China's Global Activism: Strategy, Drivers, and Tools* (2006).

Sheldon W. Simon is professor of political science at Arizona State University and faculty affiliate of ASU's Center for Asian Research, where he has been a faculty member since 1975. Professor Simon is also senior adviser to the National Bureau of Asian Research (Seattle and Washington, D.C.) and a consultant to the U.S. Departments of State and Defense, as well as an academic associate of the National Intelligence Council and a member of the U.S. Council for Security Cooperation in the Asia Pacific. He is the author or editor of ten books and 140 scholarly articles and book chapters. His most recent books are *Religion and Conflict in South and Southeast Asia: Disrupting Violence* (ed. with Linell E. Cady, 2007) and *China, the United States, and Southeast Asia: Contending Perspectives on Politics, Security, and Economics.* Professor Simon also writes the "U.S.-Southeast Asia" chapters for the quarterly e-journal *Comparative Connections,* published by CSIS/Pacific Forum.

Scott Snyder is a senior associate in the International Relations Program of the Asia Foundation and Pacific Forum CSIS and is based in Washington, D.C. He spent four years in Seoul as Korea Representative of the Asia Foundation during 2000–2004. Previously, he has served as a program officer in the Research and Studies Program of the U.S. Institute of Peace, and as acting director of the Asia Society's Contemporary Affairs Program. His publications include *Paved with Good Intentions: The NGO Experience in North Korea* (2003, co-edited with L. Gordon Flake) and *Negotiating on the Edge: North Korean Negotiating Behavior* (1999). Snyder received his B.A. from Rice University and an M.A. from the Regional Studies–East Asia Program at Harvard University. During 2005–2006, he was a Pantech Visiting Research Fellow at Stanford University's Shorenstein Asia-Pacific Research Center (APARC). He was the recipient of an Abe Fellowship, during 1998–1999 and was a Thomas G. Watson Fellow at Yonsei University in South Korea in 1987–1988.

Robert Sutter has been visiting professor of Asian studies at the School of Foreign Service, Georgetown University, since 2001. Prior to taking this position, Sutter specialized in Asian and Pacific Affairs and U.S. foreign policy in a U.S. government career of thirty-three years involving the Congressional Research Service of the Library of Congress, the Central Intelligence Agency, the Department of State, and the Senate Foreign Relations Committee. He was, for many years, the senior specialist and director of the Foreign Affairs and National Defense Division of the Congressional Research Service. He also was the national intelligence officer for East Asia and the Pacific at the U.S. government's National Intelligence Council, and the China division director at the Department of State's Bureau of Intelligence and Research. A Ph.D. graduate in History and East Asian Languages from Harvard University, Sutter has taught part-time for over thirty years at Georgetown, George Washington, Johns Hopkins, and the University of Virginia. He has published sixteen books, over one hundred articles, and several hundred government reports dealing with contemporary East Asian and Pacific countries and their relations with the United States. His most recent book is *Chinese Foreign Relations: Power and Policy since the Cold War* (2007), and his next book, *The United States in Asia*, will be published in 2008.

Hugh White is professor of strategic studies and head of the Strategic and Defense Studies Centre at the Australian National University, and a visiting fellow at the Lowy Institute for International Policy in Sydney. He writes regularly on defense, security, and international issues for the *Australian*. His principal research interests are Australian strategic and defense policy and the regional and global security issues that most directly affect Australia. His publications include *Beyond the Defense of Australia: Rethinking the Foundations of Australian Defense Policy* (2006). He has worked on Australian strategic, defense, and foreign-policy issues for twenty-five years in a number of capacities inside and outside government. His previous positions have included director of the Australian Strategic Policy Institute (ASPI), 2000–2004; deputy secretary for strategy in the Department of Defense, 1995–2000; head of the Strategic Analysis Branch, Office of National Assessments (ONA), 1992–1993; senior adviser on international affairs to Prime Minister Bob Hawke, 1990–1991; senior adviser to Defense Minister Kim Beazley, 1984–1990; and foreign affairs and defense correspondent on the *Sydney Morning Herald*, 1983–1984. In the 1970s he studied philosophy at Melbourne and Oxford universities. In 1978 he was awarded the John Locke Prize in Mental Philosophy at Oxford University.